THE RHETORIC OF REASON

RHETORIC OF THE HUMAN SCIENCES

General Editors

John Lyne

Deirdre N. McCloskey

John S. Nelson

The Rhetoric of Reason

WRITING AND THE

ATTRACTIONS OF ARGUMENT

JAMES CROSSWHITE

THE UNIVERSITY OF WISCONSIN PRESS

The University of Wisconsin Press
114 North Murray Street
Madison, Wisconsin 53715

3 Henrietta Street
London WC2E 8LU, England

5 4 3 2 1

Printed in the United States of America

Library of Congress Cataloging-in-Publication Data
Crosswhite, James.
     The rhetoric of reason: writing and the attractions of argument / James Crosswhite.
     344 pp.   cm. — (Rhetoric of the human sciences)
     Includes bibliographical references and index.
     ISBN 0-299-14950-1 (cloth: alk. paper).
     ISBN 0-299-14954-4 (pbk.: alk. paper)
     1. Reasoning. 2. Logic. I. Title. II. Series.
   BC177.C765   1996
   168—dc20   95-44286

For my parents

Genna Roop
and
Riley Crosswhite

—did you think the demonstrable
less divine than the mythical?
—Walt Whitman

CONTENTS

ACKNOWLEDGMENTS

It is impossible to name everyone who has helped with this project, but special thanks to John Gage, Henry Johnstone, John Lyne, Marie Secor, David Bartholomae, David Kaufer, Lenore Langsdorf, Anne Laskaya, Doug Mitchell, Suzanne Clark, Bill Rossi, and Mike Bybee, who—by criticism or encouragement or both (even at the same time)—have all contributed to the completion of this work. Thanks, too, to my many friends from the Warren College Writing Program at UC, San Diego who first stirred these ideas up: Robert McDonell, Alice Green, Andrea Hattersley, Don Matson, John Herschel, Deborah Small, Bill Weeks, and many others. Thanks to you, I remain utterly convinced that the best kind of thinking and conversation can take place at the beach—but getting to the beach, like going to the woods, is no easy matter! Finally, thank you to Marsha and Hilary and Elliot and Wesley. You fill me with good reasons and more, to over-flowing.

An earlier, shorter version of Chapter 6 appeared in *Argumentation* 7.4 (1993): 385–402, as "Being Unreasonable: Perelman and the Problem of Fallacies," copyright 1993 Kluwer Academic Publishers. Parts of Chapter 5 appeared in *Philosophy and Rhetoric* 22.3 (1989): 157–73, under the title "Universality in Rhetoric: Perelman's Universal Audience," copyright 1989 Pennsylvania State University Press. Both are reprinted by permission of the publishers. The lines from Walt Whitman's *Leaves of Grass* are reprinted by permission of New York University Press.

THE RHETORIC OF REASON

INTRODUCTION

This book is an affirmation of reason by way of a reconstruction of the theory of argumentation. One of its purposes is to articulate a new defense of the teaching of written reasoning in higher education. Not surprisingly, the book defends argumentative rationality against its contemporary postmodern detractors. However, what is unusual about the approach is that this defense begins by accepting postmodern criticisms of the philosophical tradition. Thus, the reconstruction of reason draws not from logic but from rhetorical theory, and is thoroughly pragmatic. The theory the book develops is justified not by logical or metaphysical standards, but by the degree to which it accomplishes worthy social aims. In fact, the book reinterprets logic itself as a social-ethical ideal and metaphysics as a particular social-historical strategy to defend reasoning.

Thus, this book is emphatically not a handbook of argumentative techniques or a compendium of different models and schemes of argumentation. Rather, it is a sustained essay which tries to reconstruct the concept of argumentation against the background questions of whether and in what senses written reasoning is worth teaching and learning.

What is also unusual about this book is that it is addressed primarily to an audience concerned with the teaching of composition, secondarily to philosophers, teachers of critical thinking, communication theorists, and educational administrators and policymakers. College students probably think more seriously about written reasoning in their composition courses than they do in any other course. In writing courses, they are challenged to formulate, develop, clarify, defend, and revise their own ideas with a frequency and insistence that are not present in any other field of study. Writing courses provide unique and profoundly important matrices for developing the reasoning abilities of college students.

However, although this book is addressed primarily to teachers of writing, I do not suggest particular curricula for courses in written reasoning, nor do I argue for a particular kind of pedagogy or particular classroom activities. It is not that such matters are unimportant; such matters are extremely important. However, it is even more important for teachers of writing and reasoning to think for themselves about the nature and purpose of what they teach. In the absence of informed and passionate and thoughtful concern about the nature and purpose of written reasoning, a preoccupation with teaching techniques and writing exercises produces only hollow busywork.

Further, although a fair number of generalizations may be made about what good teaching is (and about what bad teaching is), I do not believe that there is any one best way to teach. My own best teachers have taught on their feet, constantly adapting themselves to the particular students with which they were faced. They were invigorated by what they taught, and they each translated that vigor in a different way. To keep faith with my experience of their teaching, I want to turn teachers of writing toward a concern with reason itself—because what reason is, and what its purposes are, are anything but settled matters. Instead, they are wellsprings of intellectual controversy, controversy which can, I hope, invigorate our teaching.

The teaching of writing in higher education is an extraordinary enterprise. From the outside, it is often understood to be a remedial effort, an attempt to salvage lost generations of students who never learned to spell and punctuate properly in school. However, from the inside it is very different. The teaching of writing is nothing less than the teaching of reasoning. To help students to learn to write is a Socratic endeavor in the best and deepest sense. It is an attempt not to transmit received knowledge, but to engage and guide students in discovering and clarifying ideas in the context of written communication. It is an attempt to draw out of students their best ideas, in their most convincing form. It is an attempt to develop and strengthen the abilities of individual people to imagine, to reason, and to judge in the medium of writing.

Thus, this book takes an implicit but uncompromising stand against the remedialization of rhetoric and of students. The essential feature of this remedialization is the severing of writing from its purposes. Writing well requires practice, but it also requires purpose. If rhetoric is concerned with anything, it is concerned with understanding communication as inevitably linked to the accomplishing of purposes. When writing is taught in isolation from its purposes, it is not taught at all, and it is not learned. One aim of this book is to clarify the purposes of written reasoning, and to recommend them to teachers of writing.

The great tradition of rhetoric understood the goal of rhetorical training not as the remedying of deficits, but as the realization of a certain kind of human potential. This book also is committed to that goal. As many of us who teach writing have learned, focusing on the most profound powers of writing as a kind of reasoning can do more to improve the grammar and style of someone's prose than an isolated focus on grammar and style can. In fact, attending to grammar and style in the context of reasoning can sometimes open up new doors for people who have been unable to comprehend the principles of grammar and style in their more abstract forms.

The difference between thinking of people as being deficient, and thinking of people as having abilities and potential that need cultivating, training, and developing is enormous, and it leads to radically different educational approaches and attitudes. One of the legacies of open admissions and mass higher education has been that, in public universities especially, there has been a strong tendency to view students as deficient and in need of remedial work—incapable, in fact, of vital intellectual experience. Where the view is not explicit, it takes the form of the low expectations that drive the undergraduate curriculum slowly along: students slumber through large lecture courses, write very little, speak very little, cram for examinations, and graduate. As the demands for educational "productivity" increase, the pressure to "handle" more and more students in this way grows enormous.

Writing programs and courses need not collaborate in this capitulation to hopelessness. Writing courses are usually the smallest classes college students take. They frequently offer the only experience most students will have of a Socratic education. This book urges a concept of argumentative reasoning as the orienting idea of writing instruction. This idea refuses remedializing ways of understanding people, and focuses instead on their abilities. It also refuses to think of writing instruction as aimed only at the mastery of a set of specific skills. Written reasoning is infinitely perfectible, and needs to be strengthened and transformed, learned anew, at each new level of intellectual endeavor, in each new domain of intellectual work. One of the most important goals of any writing curriculum is to teach students how to go on teaching themselves to write better, how to adapt their abilities to new situations.

The obstacles to placing written reasoning at the core of higher education are many. There is the perpetual and sometimes even healthy public misunderstanding of the purpose of college writing courses. This misunderstanding is shared by those professors, administrators, and journalists who are shocked, shocked, that students who have had little occasion to write for any real purpose end up writing so poorly. They imagine that writing is a kind of "basic skill" that can be taught to schoolchildren once and for all. There is also the scandalous system of staffing college writing courses with "irregular" appointees, an exploitative system that is now endemic and entrenched—a system that will not soon pass, but which militates against the serious recognition of teachers of writing as partners in the intellectual enterprise of higher

6

Introduction

education. There are also, of course, the lively and probably unavoidable political controversies that arise whenever a college's writing program puts some substance into its curriculum.

However, this book addresses itself to a different obstacle. This obstacle is the skepticism about argumentative reasoning that is fairly widespread among teachers of writing themselves. At times, this skepticism takes the form of an explicit postmodern critique of the concept of reason. At other times, it is simply a mood of aversion to reasoning and argumentation. In the absence of a passionate intellectual commitment to the teaching of written reasoning among teachers, the other obstacles make it difficult for students greatly to develop their abilities to reason convincingly in writing—at least in college. The theory of reason offered in this book is a response both to the philosophical critique of the traditional concept of reason and to the mood that prevents people from seeing argumentative reasoning for the wonder that it is. Thus, the theory is an overt effort to rouse an intellectual passion for the teaching of written reasoning.

While writing this book, I became more and more sympathetic to the arguments that opposed my own—occasionally so strongly sympathetic that I wanted to give up the project altogether. There was one objection, in particular, that kept coming back to me, and which several friends actually voiced. I would like to address it here, at the beginning. The objection was that I was talking not about actual argumentation at all, but about some nonexistent ideal. They said that what I have to say about argumentative reasoning arises not from the empirical collection, classification, and counting of actual argument-events, but rather from an ideal that I hold, one which does not and cannot really exist in the writing classroom or anywhere else. Why should anyone be persuaded by this ideal, when the reality of actual argumentation is so different? I have thought a lot about this objection, and I have come to understand how forceful it is, how bowing to it would authorize a completely different line of intellectual work, one that has its own not insignificant merits. I have been so aware of the force of this objection that I have tried to respond to the objection directly at many different points throughout the book.

However, I have also become much more content with the approach I have taken. There is a poem of Whitman's, sometimes titled "Faces." In the first part, he describes the many faces he beholds:

Sauntering the pavement or riding the country by-road, lo, such faces!
Faces of friendship, precision, caution, suavity, ideality

> The spiritual-prescient face, the always-welcome common
>   benevolent face,
>   The face of the singing of music, the grand faces of natural
>   lawyers and judges broad at the back-top,
> The faces of hunters and fishers bulged at the brows, the shaved
>   blanch'd faces of orthodox citizens,
> The pure, extravagant, yearning, questioning artist's face,
> The ugly face of some beautiful soul, the handsome detested or
>   despised face . . .
> The face withdrawn of its good and bad, a castrated face . . .
> Sauntering the pavement thus, or crossing the ceaseless ferry,
>   faces and faces and faces,
> I see them and complain not, and am content with all . . .
> Do you suppose I could be content with all if I thought them their
>   own finalè?

I take it that the use of "finale" intends both to portray faces as a kind of music and to say that faces are in the process of reaching toward a culmination, an end or purpose. This finale is not only in the future, in some redeemed world. Rather, it is visible now, for Whitman, in all the faces he sees, for the culmination is at least partly in the reaching itself. After describing several more particularly "lamentable" faces, Whitman demands: "Features of my equals would you trick me with your creas'd and cadaverous / march?" And he responds: "Well you cannot trick me. / I see your rounded never erased flow, / I see 'neath the rims of your haggard and mean disguises . . ."

Now, is Whitman seeing the faces as they actually are, or is he seeing in them some nonexistent ideal? My guess is that Whitman would refuse the distinction. "Things as they actually are" suggests an ideology of visionlessness. If faces and arguments are such that their own finale is visible in them, then one who fails to glimpse this finale has failed to see a face—or an argument—for what it is. From a pragmatic point of view, the question is, What does the angle of the finale illuminate for us, what purpose does it serve? And from the standpoint of a pragmatically oriented rhetoric of reason, the question is, What kind of life follows from giving oneself over to the claim of this angle and what kind of life comes from refusing to?

My attempt in this book is to see the finale in arguments, to see through their disguises—not to expose them for the wretched things they are, but to reveal the intrinsic hopes carried by the practice of argument. This attempt will have to be measured in pragmatic terms, and cannot fairly be prejudged by people who know that they already know what arguments really are. Thus, the question is not, Does this rhetoric of reason deal with argumentation as it actually is or does it deal with some nonexistent ideal? Rather, the question is, What does this angle on argumentation make possible for us? How well does it serve the finales in us? This is something that each of us must prove for him or herself.

The attempt I offer in this book divides into four parts. Part one, "The End of Philosophy and the Resurgence of Rhetoric," describes the philosophical situation from which a rhetoric of reason arises. Part two, "Reconstructing Argumentation," presents the main features of the new theory by offering extended accounts of claiming, questioning, and conflict. Part three, "Evaluating Arguments," addresses the problem of evaluation—of evaluating specific arguments as well as evaluating the general practice of argumentation. Part four, "Argument, Inquiry, and Education," places the reconstructed theory in its historical context, shows the relation of argumentation to inquiry and research in general, and develops the implications of the theory for the project of higher education, and especially for the teaching of writing.

Chapter 1 is in some respects the most difficult chapter. The rhetorical account of reason I present claims to be convincing against the philosophical background described in this section. Such a sketch may seem far too general to most philosophers, far too specific to most teachers of writing. However, the background is important. The book is in large measure a challenge to teachers of writing—and to theorists of argumentation—to become much more philosophical about the teaching and theory of argumentation. So, the first chapter announces the aims of the book, describes the contemporary philosophical situation by way of introductory discussions of Heidegger and Derrida, and shows the senses in which rhetorical theory is a kind of rejoinder to and fulfillment of contemporary philosophy. It follows this by reestablishing rhetoric's traditional link with education as a way of justifying the theory's concern with teaching and learning. The chapter concludes by showing the ways in which the current-traditional theory of argumentation is tied to conceptions of reason, knowledge, and mind which are no longer serviceable.

Part two begins the reconstruction of argumentation as a practice of dialogue, and shows how even apparently monological, written argumentation is implicitly dialogical. Chapter 2 focuses on the act of claiming, and gives special attention to the ethical dimensions of making claims. Chapter 3, "Questioning," analyzes the role of the questioner in argumentation, and continues Chapter 2's focus on the ethical dimensions of argumentation. Chapters 2 and 3 together portray argumentation as a specific form of the general practice of call and response.

Claims, questions, and reasons are understood not as logical ciphers but as communicative acts with complicated ethical features.

Chapter 4, "Argument and Conflict," is both the center of the book and the centerpiece of the theory. It continues the ethical interrogation into the basic features of argumentation by elaborating the many dimensions of conflict that are active in argumentative reasoning. The chapter develops in detail one of the central claims of the book: that conflict is the spirit and life of reason and argumentation. So a rhetoric of reason depends on the differences that postmodern theory describes, but with the important difference that it places conflicts in a pragmatic, ethical framework. Argumentation is an ethically powerful way of using conflict to conduct learning and inquiry, and to create change and newness.

Part three begins the difficult task of developing a specifically rhetorical way to evaluate arguments, to assess their reasonableness. Chapter 5, "Audiences and Arguments," lays out the main features of a reception theory of rationality, and offers an extended discussion of the difference between "rhetorical universality" and more traditional concepts of universality. Chapter 6 shows how a rhetorical theory of argumentation might contribute to a theory of fallacies. Chapter 7 steps back from the evaluation of arguments to attempt an evaluation of argumentation itself. Here, the theory and practice of argumentation are interrogated in order to bring their ideological leanings to light. Gender issues are used as a way to explore the general problem of reason and difference, and the challenges that theories and assertions of difference present for argumentation theory. The chapter also includes an attempt to mark off some of the limits of argumentation as a discursive practice.

Part four begins by developing the idea that argument is inquiry, and elaborates this idea against the background of the historical conflict between philosophy and science, on the one hand, and rhetoric on the other. Chapter 9 concludes the book by connecting its theoretical and historical labors to the problems of contemporary higher education, the definition of the liberal arts, and especially the teaching of written communication. This last chapter frankly acknowledges and affirms the ethical purposes of the theory, the deep ethical interests of the tradition of rhetoric, and unabashedly recommends them to educators.

PART ONE

PHILOSOPHY, RHETORIC,

AND ARGUMENTATION

1

THE END OF PHILOSOPHY

AND THE RESURGENCE

OF RHETORIC

I think that the central issue of philosophy and critical thought since the eighteenth century has been, still is, and will, I hope, remain the question, What *is this Reason that we use? What are its historical effects? What are its limits, and what are its dangers? How can we exist as rational beings, fortunately committed to practicing a rationality that is unfortunately crisscrossed by intrinsic dangers? One should remain as close to this question as possible, keeping in mind that it is extremely difficult to resolve.*
—Michel Foucault, "Space, Knowledge and Power"

The Aims of a Rhetoric of Reason

Just as people argue with one another (and themselves) for a number of reasons and thus in a number of different ways, so people study and theorize argumentation for different purposes and thus from a number of angles. My project here is to discover what a rhetorical concept of reason can bring to the theory of argumentation. Thus, the most direct purpose of this book is to make a contribution to the theory of argumentation by casting new light on its basic terms and problems and uncovering what it has left hidden. My understanding of the need for a new approach to the theory of argumentation follows from the results of post-Heideggerian (or post-Nietzschean) philosophy. In contrast to those who believe that such thought is destructive of the very concepts of reason and argument, I intend to show that contemporary philosophy (or postphilosophy) enables a profound and attractive understanding of what happens when people argue and of what it means to be reasonable. However, this understanding is not philosophical in the conventional sense, but rhetorical, and in fact includes a reliance on rhetorical theory as metaphilosophy.

Another purpose of this book is to bring the theory of argumentation into a closer relationship with the teaching of written argumentation. This effort is motivated in one way by my own two professional roles as a trained philosopher and as the director of a university-wide composition program. However, there are other reasons to bring teaching and theorizing together, reasons which follow from the collapse of traditional epistemological models of how knowledge is gained and transmitted. To put it briefly and simply, the processes of reasoning and argumentation that go on at the highest levels of theory and research are not radically different from the processes of reasoning and argumentation that go on in the composing activities of students in writing courses. In fact, as I will show, college writing courses are the inheritors of the issues raised by the development of post-Heideggerian thought. Since such courses make up the entry to and in many ways the center of the college curriculum in the United States (in many colleges, they are the only required courses), the problems of knowledge, of reason, and of argument that arise in these courses are *the* central problems of higher education in this country. This is one reason that such courses are growing increasingly controversial, to the point of attracting attention from national columnists and state legislatures.

Such a rapprochement of philosophical thinking with the idea of education places this effort in the rhetorical tradition. Advanced research in the humanities has increasingly distanced itself from the challenges of education. Many philosophers, literary theorists, and historians in universities have come to see their research as strictly unrelated to teaching. The humanities have come more and more to understand themselves on the modern model of the natural sciences. According to this model, advanced researchers produce a body of knowledge independently of any interest in communication or education, and the "transmission" of this knowledge is then placed in the hands of teachers. The specific charge given to teachers of writing is to train their students to convey this knowledge without distortion.

However, the major rhetorical theorists have always emphasized a much closer connection between their theoretical work and their mission as educators. In fact, their theories of communication and reason have been justified partly by their usefulness for helping to develop human abilities in the appropriate ways. Rhetoricians have conceived of rhetoric as an essential part of an education, and have believed that its aim is to produce a kind of ideal human being, philosophical, practical, articulate, and beneficent—in Quintilian's famous words, the "good man speaking well."

This book, too, is motivated by that ambition. However, this book also follows postmodern and pragmatic philosophy in its position that *all* reasonable discourse, including advanced research, is both rhetorical and aimed at realizing certain social aims. Thus, its conception of the scope of rhetoric is not limited to educational concerns in a way that would simply privilege them over the concerns of basic research and theory. Rather, it conceives of rhetoric as the only viable way to explain the possibility of reason itself.

Readers should be immediately warned that such goals demand that this study be interdisciplinary, and that this will create problems. One thing the rhetoric of inquiry has established is that different disciplines and professions operate with different rhetorics.[1] Different authorities are recognized by different professional groups. Different protocols and styles of reasoning hold sway in different disciplines. The special achievements of different disciplines have been enabled by specific developments in the ways they reason and conduct research. The most advanced research in any field is difficult for people outside that field to understand not simply because of a lack of background information but because the very way knowledge is produced in different fields has become specialized, obscure, and controversial. This creates insurmountable difficulties for a project like this, which will move over territory professionally claimed by philosophy, rhetoric, literary theory, communication theory, education, English composition, linguistics, and psychology. One inevitable result is to push the written reasoning in this book closer to the style of the essay, away from the styles of specialized discourses. There are both advantages and disadvantages in this.

However, there is also a difficulty about the epistemological status of the claims I will make. In view of this difficulty, I will make a claim that is a new version of a claim traditionally made by philosophers. Rhetoric is different from any other field because rhetoric is concerned with the way discursive authority operates wherever it is found. All disciplines and professions employ rhetorics as part of the way they produce knowledge, rhetorics which are thought to be especially suited for the particular purposes pursued by different intellectual enterprises. Thus, the study of rhetoric has in this sense a priority to any other kind of study. Any other kind of study will use a rhetoric to produce a particular kind of knowledge, while rhetoric is the study of this rhetoric itself. In another sense, though, this priority is illusory. After all, if rhetoric is the means by which any kind of knowledge is produced, then rhetoric is also the means by which a knowledge of rhetoric is reached. The difference between traditional claims about the priority of philosophy and my claim about the priority of rhetoric is that my claim both insists on this priority and, by insisting that it is rhetoric which has this priority and not philosophy, denies that the priority is in any sense foundational. The priority of rhetoric is something which must be earned in each case, and measured against shifting standards and realities.

In this way, rhetoric is in a position similar to that of contemporary philosophy as Jürgen Habermas understands it in "Philosophy as Stand-in and Interpreter."[2] There, Habermas recognizes that when philosophy interprets communication it is itself operating within communicative practices. It does not have a position of epistemological superiority to what it interprets, and thus is not immune from reciprocal critique. To offer an interpretation of communication is to participate in and not merely to understand communicative processes.[3] Such a position is similar to Michael Leff's explanation of why rhetoric cannot be an independent discipline.[4] Because it must be a participant in the communicative practices it attempts to interpret, it must locate itself within the rhetorics it is attempting to understand. Thus, the rhetoric of inquiry occurs as a moment within the different disciplines, or within any rhetorical community engaged in reflecting on its communicative practices, and not in a separate discipline or community.

This is the situation of rhetoric as rhetoric itself describes it, and it seems to be a formidable obstacle to anything like the more general rhetoric of reason I propose to describe in this book. However, this situation is not the obstacle it appears to be. A rhetoric of reason does not understand itself as describing the necessary a priori features of all reasoning, to which the rhetorician has some kind of privileged incontestable access. Rather, in its attempt to offer a general account of what happens when people argue, it understands itself as offering an account which is better for particular purposes, and more convincing in the context in which it is offered, than are competing accounts. That's all.

The general context in which the following account is offered is, again, the post-Heideggerian situation of contemporary philosophy, a situation I will describe in outline in just a moment. The reasons for trying to articulate a general account of what happens when people reason together, even in a situation in which all such accounts will be understood to be limited in one way or another, are found in the imperatives of education and social life. We have schools and colleges and universities, and students in these institutions will be taught to reason, and will be trained in written reasoning, in one way or another. The question is whether we will go on holding ourselves accountable to one another— as intellectuals, educators, philosophers, administrators, parents—for the way students are taught to reason, or whether we will give up holding ourselves so accountable, and let the fragmentation that philosophy has left in its wake take power over the lives of teachers and students.

The situation faced directly by education in its attempt to cultivate an intelligent citizenry is not essentially different from the situation of a country or a land faced with the need to reconcile to one another a number of different "cultures" with a number of different "rhetorics." And the need for such reconciliation is as permanent a part of the human condition as is the differentiation of human beings into different cultural groups. The central aim for a rhetoric of reason in this regard will be to show clearly what role reasoned discourse can play in such reconciliation, and what the relation is between reasoned discourse and coercion and other forms of force.

The attempt to articulate a rhetoric of reason is thus the enactment of a social hope that people will be able to reason together—even if they are from conflicting rhetorical communities. This is a far cry from the claims philosophy has traditionally made for itself. Rhetorical theory does not have access to the eternal truths of reason and communication. Rather, it has a purpose, a social purpose. It can be evaluated partly by whether or not its purpose is something desirable, partly by whether or not it really achieves its purpose. And this evaluation will be made by those it attempts to convince. As for those who are skeptical and suspicious of any attempt to give a general account such as the one I propose here, I plead for their patience. "Rhetorical universality," a kind of enabling oxymoron, is very different from totalizing conceptions of rationality. Or, at least, I hope to show so.

The Philosophical Context

The most direct effort of this work is to make a contribution to the theory of argumentation, to make argumentation new, and since the theory of argumentation we have had to do with has arisen from the philosophy we have had to do with, it seems reasonable to begin by describing a recent and notable transformation of the philosophical landscape. Specifically, I want to describe in a necessarily schematic way a few of the general consequences of Martin Heidegger's thought for some of the ways we think of knowledge and language. Both the theory of knowledge and the philosophy of language have direct implications for the senses in which rhetoric can be understood to be, once again, philosophy's successor.

The dominant problem for modern epistemology has been the difficulty in explaining knowledge as a relation between a subject and an objective world. The general ontological picture used throughout modern epistemology is some version of the Cartesian picture of a subject with ideas trying to find some way out of mere subjectivity and mere ideas and into a world that is what it is independent of the subject and its ideas. The picture itself depends on an ontology of a world of things which are in some sense innately intelligible—in themselves exactly what they are and nothing else. In this ontology, the subject is not itself merely one of these things, but does exist in the same independent way as a self-sufficient entity. The problem of language is not, in this ontology, a philosophical one. The difficulty with language is simply getting it to correspond in the proper way to the intrinsic intelligibility of entities.

Such a picture immediately generates radical skeptical challenges: how can one ever *know* that one has escaped one's internal ideas and discovered anything at all about external entities? How can one even be certain that there *is* an external world? What kind of criteria for knowledge are available to a subject lost in itself, lost in skepticism?

Descartes' general strategy, adopted by his successors, is to ask what such a subject already knows about the world, what any subject already knows. In this case, the knowledge is already built into the ontological picture. As Heidegger points out, Descartes' external world is essentially something which does not change. Real entities, of the kind that can really be known, are always what they are—and never what they are not.[5] This is a peculiarly philosophical way of pointing out something important for modern philosophy. Knowledge is essentially of two kinds. The first kind of knowledge is certain, irrefutable knowledge of things which do not change but are knowable because they are necessary and a priori. Without them, knowledge would not be possible at all. The real entities, the external world for which moderns must search, must not change with time, and must be the same for all subjects. Otherwise, they cannot really be objects of the first kind of knowledge. They cannot really assure us that we have escaped from our own minds and found the world. The second kind of knowledge is knowledge that is not certain, but which can be corrected as experience shows us new things in new ways. However, the second kind of knowledge is always built on the foundation of the first. Until we find the first kind of knowledge, there is no anchor for our ideas in the external world, no assurance that our ideas are referring to anything.

Thus, the primary form knowledge takes for Descartes is pure intellectual intuition of necessary truths—truths of the sort we seem to find in mathematics. What we *really* know about the world we know by way of mathematics. According to many intellectual historians, we have in Descartes one of the basic elements for the project of modern science:

the idea of the mathematization of the world. According to Heidegger, we also have the agenda set for all subsequent modern philosophy, which will be dominated by subjectivism.[6] And it is certainly true that the distinctions between kinds of knowledge and kinds of entities that make one kind of knowledge of one kind of entity foundational for all other kinds of knowledge of all other kinds of entities has been definitive for modern philosophy.[7]

The way of bridging the gap between subject and object through knowledge has, following Descartes, typically been conceived as Method. The projects of defining philosophical and scientific methods are projects which attempt to show both how to acquire and how to build on foundational knowledge in ways that will keep probable knowledge as close to the clarity and certainty of intellectual intuition as possible. Again, method in this tradition is thought of as essentially independent of the problems of language—and language is rarely considered a problem in itself. The problem of method is to purify language of its obscurities, to clarify it, and this is thought to be a reasonable task. The search for a *charactericas universalis* is a central theme of the modern tradition.[8]

This ontological picture has almost completely disappeared from contemporary philosophy—although, as I will try to show, it still retains a great deal of influence in higher education. It has been attacked from many angles and for many reasons, but Heidegger's systematic response to it in *Being and Time* is probably the most persuasive and influential of all the twentieth-century criticism of modern ontology. Heidegger's interrogation of modern ontology is accomplished primarily in his works on the history of philosophy—in his many published lectures, and especially in the *Nietzsche* volumes. In *Being and Time*, one of his primary objections to the Cartesian picture is that it makes use of an unexamined ontology—specifically, it assumes that the being of entities is simply present, that there is an intelligibility in the entities themselves that is unchanging and absolute for those entities for as long as they are. Heidegger wonders where the idea of such a mode of being came from, how such a mode of being ever manifested itself and came to seem self-evident. In his works on the history of philosophy, he tries out several versions of a "history of being" that narrates the coming to power of such a conception. However, in *Being and Time,* at least in relation to Descartes, he simply observes that Descartes makes an unthought use of this questionable concept of being.

He also notes that Descartes seems to know more than he admits. Descartes knows that the way he reassembles the subject and object of his ontology must resemble our *ordinary* experience of the world. That is, Descartes has a prephilosophical experience of the unity of the subject and the world which he has broken into pieces because of certain ontological prejudices which throw him into radical skepticism. His goal is to reassemble the subject and the world in a way that will both match that experience and explain how such experience is possible in terms of the ontological picture which seems so self-evident. The idea of Descartes' actual experience of the world is supposed to be suspended in radical doubt, and yet, Heidegger claims, it guides his skeptical meditations to their predetermined end.

Heidegger proposes to avoid the ontological picture of modern philosophy by *beginning* with the prephilosophical experience of the world and examining it on its own terms rather than in terms of what is usually taken to be a self-evident ontology. To do so requires new terms. In order to disempower the subject/object ontology of modernity, Heidegger calls the being that shows itself in prephilosophical experience *being-in-the-world*, a term that is intended to capture the unity of prephilosophical experience, in which the world and human beings have a mutual advent. Heidegger calls the being of human beings *Dasein. Dasein* is not a subject which must relate itself to a world, but rather has being-in-the-world as its being. Thus, Dasein is in its very being a disclosure of the world, and never exists without disclosing the world in some way or other. The world itself is that which is disclosed in being-in-the-world.

Importantly, there is no "outside" to being-in-the-world, no being or entities postulated as explanations of being-in-the-world or as guarantees of human ways of disclosing the world and interpreting the entities in it. The appearance of any such entity or way of being would itself be just another event of being-in-the-world.

Just as importantly, there is supposed to be nothing "mental" or "idealist" about being-in-the-world. Heidegger's analysis of Dasein yields in a critical respect a pragmatic view of the way beings become what they are. In general, Dasein has purposes it is always trying to accomplish, purposes which bring entities into very particular ways of being and into very particular relations to one another. Things are experienced as having some relation to Dasein's purposes—as being useful, being in the way, being capable of being made useful, or being pretty much useless. Things which have only extremely remote connections to Dasein's purposes may remain only dimly discovered. Dasein's disclosure of the world is thus a practical disclosure, connected with Dasein's pursuit of its purposes.

The rejection of the inside/outside, mind/world ontology is one way to avoid the impasses of skeptical and "realist" attacks on rhetoric. Both skepticism and "realism" depend on an absolute distinction between the world and our experience of the world in order to sustain their antirhetorical programs. Skeptics despair of our ever finding a way to get "outside" of our minds, our language, our experience, and have a direct encounter with something. "Realists" agree with skeptics that our experience distorts the appearance of entities, but they believe that the best explanation of regularities in our experience is the existence of entities whose intelligibility does not in any way depend on experience. Of course, as skeptics (and Heidegger and rhetoricians) would point out, both "existence" and the categories of intelligibility, even the idea of independence, have a human history and different human uses. For skeptics, this realization is grounds for despair. For rhetoricians, this is not the end of philosophy, but the beginning of a new metaphilosophy, a rhetoric of reason and inquiry.

There are interesting complications of Heidegger's thinking which I cannot follow up here. However, I want to be clearer about where this turn to being-in-the-world leaves us in relation to the problem of knowledge, and I also want to clarify what consequences it has for understanding the role of language in reasoning and in making knowledge. Again, my treatment here is very general, but the outline should be sufficient for showing the general matrix in which a rhetoric of reason takes shape.

Let's begin with language. The traditional concept of knowledge imagines language as a kind of medium for ideas that either accurately reflect the world or do not. Thus, propositions about the world, propositions like "the sun is the center of the solar system," are either true or false by virtue of whether they correspond to the objective world. Obviously, with the advent of the idea of being-in-the-world, we can no longer think of language in this way. So, in *Being and Time,* Heidegger thinks of language as one of the ways in which Dasein exists. He begins with the ordinary experience of prephilosophical life. He observes that entities show themselves in everyday life as being in some connection with the purposes we ordinarily pursue. Their relations to these purposes also bring them into specific relationships with one another. Although these relationships may seem to be something we *create* rather than something that belongs to the entities themselves, Heidegger would say that this "seeming" is produced by our being influenced by the traditional model of a subject on one side and objective entities on the other. Instead, it is our pursuit of our purposes which first allows entities to show themselves—and all other concepts we develop of these entities are "derivative" of (modifications of and thus dependent on) this first showing. The entire web of entities in all their relations to one another is what Heidegger means when he says "world."

However, the concept of these connections between entities as "relations" is itself dependent on the obsolete picture. After all, "relations" are what hold between independent entities. Instead, these connections among entities are called by Heidegger "references," or "significations," and they are *internal* to the being of entities. Entities are disclosed not as self-sufficient objects, but as belonging in some way or other in the world. It is to these references, says Heidegger, that words accrue. Language is the *"Ausgesprochenheit"* (literally, the "outspokenness") of being-in-the-world. So understood, language is not a thing, but is itself a disclosure of the world, an uncovering of entities, and one of the ways in which Dasein exists.[9]

Given such an understanding of language, there is no longer anything for language to "match" or "reflect" or be a "medium" for. Language is just the articulation of being-in-the-world. This creates a need to develop new interpretations of what knowledge is, of what reason and argumentation are for. Knowledge can no longer be understood to be "about" an independently intelligible set of self-sufficient beings. Language can no longer be understood to be the "transmission" or "expression" of such knowledge. And writing courses in colleges and universities can no longer depend on this model of writing as transmission or expression.

Thus, the entire framework for understanding reason and knowledge, and thus education, professional work, political life, and thinking itself has collapsed in contemporary philosophy. In its place, various kinds of relativisms and skepticisms and cynical conceptions of reason have sprung up. Much of the mistrust present in higher education is caused almost directly by the consequences of the dissolution of modern philosophy. There are those who see all attempts at reasoning as disguised attempts at gaining power for one form of life over others, and who organize their own public displays of apparent reasoning on the basis of their own preset "political" aims. Their opponents, on the other hand, continue to make fairly naive appeals to "truth" and "reason" and "objectivity" without ever clarifying how they are using these terms.

There is one more thing to add to this description of philosophy's most recent end. When Heidegger let go of the picture of a subject reaching after an object against the background assumption that real knowledge was true for all time, and thus was of some real being that was constantly present, he turned being over to time. According to the traditional picture, real truth never changes but is true "for all time." However, being-in-the-world is completely given over to historical change, and in fact, history is the way Dasein exists. Dasein exists as the constant revision of its being-in-the-world, the changing of its form of life, its language, its social organization, its philosophy, its science and technology, its understanding of being. Given this understanding of the historicity of human being, Heidegger was led from the analysis of Dasein he offered in *Being and Time* to the history of being he offered in his later work. In the end, they can't really be kept distinct. And, in the end, Heidegger will not be able to keep his own work from falling into someone else's language, someone else's history of being. In fact, I will argue in a following section that although Heidegger's philosophical work prepares the way for an understanding of rhetoric as metaphilosophy, a rhetorical metaphilosophy highlights the limitations of some of Heidegger's ideas. In addition, a rhetoric of reason brings our attention back to some pressing issues which Heidegger neglected.

The ineluctable need to address practical problems—to make choices—is the basic motive for moving from philosophy to a rhetoric of reason, and I will come to this shortly. One could, of course, move into other forms of post-Heideggerian thought, the most notable of which is certainly deconstruction. Deconstruction has taken different forms in the hands of different writers, and can be understood in some significantly divergent ways. I intend to tether most of the discussion here to a text of Derrida's, "Signature Event Context"; however, I want to begin by using "deconstruction" in a general way, in relation to what I believe are some of its most generally recognized traits.

Deconstruction and the philosophical rhetoric of reason I will propose here do share some important features. The refusal to make an absolute metaphysical distinction between signifier and signified is perhaps first among them. The corollary refusal to ground theorizing in a realm of presence that is somehow metaphysically distinct from communication and the uses of language is also shared by both deconstruction and rhetorical theory. Neither deconstruction nor philosophical rhetorical theory grounds intelligibility and reason in timeless logical ideas. Both emphasize the ways in which all meaningfulness arises in time—even the meaning of the timeless. In fact, I want to say at the outset that even though I believe that rhetoric and deconstruction diverge in significant ways, I also believe that they inhabit the same philosophical world—in fact, I think of the rhetorical theory this book will develop as a kind of response to deconstruction's overskeptical posture, a response that imagines itself in conversation with deconstruction, facing the same situation.[10]

There are some *apparent* differences between deconstruction and philosophical rhetorical theory that I believe simply do not hold up—at least, not for the rhetorical theory I will offer here. For example, rhetoric is sometimes understood to depend on the notions of agent and intention—notions deconstruction attempts to undo. However, rhetoric need not rely on these ideas in their full metaphysical force as entities that are independent of the communicative process. The theory I will elaborate attempts something like a recovery of agent and intention but only in the process of communication itself. Agents (and agencies) and intentions (in the case of argumentation, claims) take shape in specific ways in the course of reasoning, in the process of argumentation. In fact, I will try to show how arguing/reasoning is in principle a giving up of the idea that one has a metaphysically fixed identity, or that one's ideas do, in favor of a recognition of the self-transformation and learning that occur in reasoning.

However, there are some critical differences that divide deconstruction and rhetoric—differences that are profound enough to lead to important divergences of deconstruction and rhetorical theory. Most important among these differences is the fact that deconstruction, as an "unbuilding" of texts, or as a "parasitical" practice, is an exercise of suspicion. Its aim is the unraveling of supposed communication, the undermining of apparently shared judgments, the exposé of the general deferral of meaning. It is this inexhaustible and single-minded skepticism of deconstruction that decisively distinguishes it from rhetoric. Deconstruction in its strongest form is a negative hermeneutic, an endless interpretive tactic.

A central text to consider here is Derrida's "Signature Event Context," one of the more important texts in increasing the attention to Derrida's thought in the United States, and the text which embroiled its author in a famously futile exchange with John Searle. In the early part of the essay/address, Derrida maintains that the "iterability" that so obviously characterizes writing is also a characteristic of all language, even all experience, in the sense of all "making present." However, the fact that writing must always be meaningful beyond the particular situation in which it is produced, beyond the particular psychological states of any actual writers and readers, entails that meaning—however conceived—is dependent to some degree on the absence of writers and readers. Writing, to be writing, must act independently of the presence of any particular writer and reader, must have the capability to produce meaning outside of a private context. As Derrida says, a written text is a kind of "machine" that is productive on its own, long after it has passed out of the situation in which it was produced. This means, he says, that writing, in its internal transcontextuality, produces not a modification of some original presence, but actually a break in presence, the "death" of presence—and so the death of any concept of original "intention" or of some meaning-fixing "total context." Instead, meaning is constantly "deferred" because writing is constantly transcending itself, implicitly claiming that it will also be meaningful somewhere else and at some later time. Since Derrida wants to extend this analysis of writing to all intelligibility, all "making present," deconstruction, as the tracking of the constant "deferrals" of meaning in any "making intelligible," becomes a kind of endless interpretive tactic, deferring also its own incorporation into any strategy of interpretation. This practice of skeptical critique, or constant deferring, forces deconstruction and rhetoric onto separate paths. I will return to this point shortly.

Philosophical rhetorical theory would quibble with a few of the conclusions Derrida draws from the insight into iterability. The first quibble has to do with the fact that Derrida's target is a fairly limited one. He concludes that we must "break with the horizon of communication as the communication of consciousness or presences." He has in mind something like a Husserlian consciousness of ideas, which are transmitted through speech or writing or signing to someone else, in whom the ideas become objects of consciousness (fulfilled intentions in the Husserlian sense). However, rhetoric understands communication as action, and in this aligns itself with speech-act theory. From this point of view, "intention" would not be understood as a consciousness of ideas to be transmitted, but instead would be thought of as an action to be taken in relation to someone. In argumentation, to make a claim—say, that iterability is a universal feature of any way of making things intelligible— is to act on someone (perhaps oneself), to lead someone to experience the world in a particular way. To question that claim is to act on someone, too, to lead someone to see the questionableness of the claim, and perhaps then to clarify or justify it. What the "intention" is—that is, what is being claimed, and who is being claimed in the claiming—takes shape in the process of communication.

This concept of communication as action is exactly what Derrida finds appealing in Austin's *How to Do Things with Words*. However, he does not say how this concept of speech as action would rebound on his analysis of writing. Derrida believes that the fact of iterability means that writing is decisively severed from both communication (and so intention and presence) and context: "[Writing] is constituted . . . by its iterability, in the absence of whomever, and therefore ultimately in the absence of every empirically determinable 'subject' . . . All writing . . . must be able to function in the absence of every empirically determined addressee in general." These statements are followed a paragraph later by the statement that writing is "a kind of machine."

My quibble here is that Derrida exaggerates when it comes to the absence of people and the agency of writing. That is, he reifies writing as something that has agency (or being) apart from the actions of real human beings. Heidegger often speaks this way too.[11] In fact, the concept of language as agent, and the concept of human beings as relatively incapable of agency, are commonplaces in postmodern thought. And there is truth in this way of speaking. Rhetorical theory recognizes in a strong way that a *great deal* is already settled, that we have already been "claimed" by language in unfathomably deep ways, before we can ever begin to reason. However, a rhetorical view of things would also see that there is no writing without human action. Unless *someone* writes and reads, there is no writing. Unless *someone* makes a claim on someone, there is no claiming. This is true not only in the obvious sense that there could be no actual empirical text unless there were also actual empirical persons to produce and consume it. It is also true in the sense that language has the same being that human beings have—its disclosive power depends *completely* on the fact that human beings exist as a disclosure of the world. Without our sustaining the being of language in our actions, there would simply be no language. Heidegger's later homilies urge us to be good shepherds of being by maintaining being's house: language, or, our own existence. He realizes that language is sustained as language only in the actions and lives of human beings. Of course, Derrida knows this, too, but his own linguistic proclivities lead him not to admit this as often as I think he should. And so, my quibble. Writing does *not* "break with the horizon of communication" *if* we understand communication as action that "communicates a force" that in turn influences what things come to presence for us, and how. If writing were really to break from communication, it would no longer be writing, no longer be language, would not disclose. Rhetoric keeps our talk about language attuned to the fact that language subsists in action.

Another, larger quibble concerns Derrida's attack on the idea of context. He believes that it is futile to seek haven in the idea of context in the face of the constant and infinite deferral of meaning that is a feature of writing/existence. This is so because the idea of context, or horizon, is "punctured" by writing. Since it is writing's nature to be transcontextual, the attempt to stabilize meaning by reference to a particular context is impossible. Again, part of the problem here is Derrida's target. He imagines that the move to the idea of context is an epistemological/metaphysical one, an attempt to guarantee that we *know* the *real meaning* of some text. He gets in his sights two uses of the phrase "total context" in Austin's lectures, and so concludes that the meaning of "context" is "exhaustively determinable context." However, from a rhetorical point of view, the importance of context is not fundamentally epistemological but practical. Communication is action, and actions can be experienced as the actions they are only in certain contexts. These contexts need not be exhaustively determined. They need only permit the experience in question for the people in question. Further, actions constantly transform contexts, and thereby make new actions possible. This self-transformative feature of contexts does not justify a judgment that every context is therefore different from itself and so can never "anchor" any determinate meaning. That would be to see things from an epistemological point of view—and an extremely skeptical one at that. Rhetoric takes it for granted that actions do take place—that people do make claims, raise questions, give reasons, reach agreements, that people do reason. The success of these actions is, from an external point of view, always a matter of degree, always open to skeptical criticism. However, people do make choices, and do live out their consequences. They work very hard to sustain the contexts in which their actions have meaning and influence and some small measure of predictability; the ability to change one's life or situation depends on such contexts, such rhetorical habitats. Although contexts are never exhaustively determined, they are determined enough to make actions mutually comprehensible—at least, to the relative satisfaction of people who do manage to cooperate and live together.

Derrida judges iterability to entail a complete break in presence, a kind of "death." However, this, too, is an exaggeration, a kind of one-sidedness. Writing also makes possible what Gadamer calls a "fusion of horizons"—the enhancement and enlargement of understanding in an interpretive act that depends on a kind of iterability that always changes the meaning of what is written. That is, in every reading of some text, not only does language "die," it also receives new life in that it is given a new effect in a new reading. Derrida is certainly right to say that the original "meaning" is not "transmitted" and then "modified" in new readings. However, it is an exaggeration to say that we are completely cut off from the dead and the past; language itself allows horizons to merge into one another. Texts are not without practical force as they pass from group to group. We can do better or worse at interpretation, better or worse at granting texts the power that preserves certain possibilities of experience. We can widen our horizons—not by accumulating eternally self-identical ideas thought by someone in the past, but by discovering ways to let the past act on us to expand our sense of our own possibilities. Once again, the corrective here is to recognize that any experience of language is communicative, and that communication is action. Every action changes its context; every retrieval or interpretation of the disclosive force of past actions is a transformation. If one's goal is the metaphysical/epistemological goal of recovering eternally self-identical Ideas from the past, then, yes, the fact of iterability may look like death. However, if the question is how to live, if the issue is to have a better sense of what actions and choices are available, then the possibility of a fusion of horizons as a transformation of horizons is a happy find.

I have called these objections to deconstruction "quibbles" because I imagine that some of my best friends would fail to see these as real objections. In fact, they might even agree with me, and say that Derrida's analysis in "Signature Event Context" is in fact a response to metaphysical philosophies of presence or claims about a final "total context." They might say that understanding discourse as communicative action changes everything, and that Derrida would use different idioms in response to a more pragmatic rhetorical theory, idioms with which a rhetorician would be less likely to quibble. There is, in fact, some evidence in Derrida's response to Gerald Graff's questions in the afterword to *Limited Inc* that his thinking is not really so distant from the rhetorical standpoint I have begun to sketch here.

So I want to return to my earlier claim that the decisive difference between deconstruction and rhetoric lies in deconstruction's radical and persistent skepticism, its self-deployment as an infinite parasitical tactic. This feature of deconstructive thought can be seen pretty clearly in Derrida's response to Austin in "Signature Event Context." Derrida rightly points out Austin's overriding interest in focusing on communicative successes. He believes that Austin's focus on communicative success is a systematic exclusion of what is negative in speech acts, an exclusion of failure. And yet Derrida insists that the possibility of failure is an essential feature of the "structure" of speech acts. "What is a success," he asks, "when the possibility of failure constitutes its structure?" (101). Now, my ordinary response would be: "a success," not a perfect success in which there was no failure, but a success nonetheless. Derrida seems to think that such a response would miss the point—that to focus on communicative successes is somehow to deny that failure attends all success. However, I believe that I want to deny this. The possibility of experiencing success as success, of counting communicative acts as successful (to some degree or other) seems to me not only a desirable possibility to preserve but one without which it would be very difficult to go on communicating at all. I simply do not see how theorizing successful speech acts is a denial of the negative. It may appear as a neglect of the negative, a lessening of attention to the negative for the particular purpose of increasing our attention to something else. However, this is something we do all the time on a practical level when we practice some form of charity in our interpretation of one another's actions. Derrida's attack on Austin's concentration on successful speech acts seems to me a privileging of a skeptical posture. Austin shows us how speech acts succeed; Derrida objects and shows us all the ways in which they can fail, shows how failure permeates everything that might be called success and how those who conceptualize successful communication are thus naive.

This skeptical prejudice shows itself even more strongly in the attacks on the concept of the ordinary. For Austin's concept of the ordinary is indeed a concept of a context in which communication is experienced as mostly successful. Derrida finds this kind of conceptualizing to be a systematic exclusion of something essential to language—its failures and deferrals, what Austin calls "abnormalities" or "infelicities." It is at this point that I see a very strong divergence moving deconstruction and rhetoric onto separate paths. From the point of view of the rhetorical theory I will develop, the ordinary is understood not simply as a feature of a theory but as an actual historical accomplishment of real human communities—nations, neighborhoods, households. Not only is the ordinary inconceivable apart from the "negative" in communication, it is also itself an actual practical response to the negative in human life. To work to point out the ways in which this response is always a failure has its place in critique, but to point out the senses in which people do manage to achieve ordinary understandings also has its place in our attempts to know better how to live.

Derrida recognizes that he is striking an extremely skeptical posture here. He imagines the objection: "You cannot deny that there are also performatives that succeed, and they must be accounted for: sessions are opened, as Paul Ricoeur did yesterday, one says, 'I ask a question,' one bets, one challenges, boats are launched, and one even marries occasionally. Such events, it appears, have occurred. And were a single one of them to have taken place a single time, it would still have to be accounted for."[12] However, this is his response: "I will say 'perhaps.' Here we must first agree upon what the 'occurring' or the eventhood of an event consists in, when the event supposes in its allegedly present and singular intervention a statement which in itself can be only of a repetitive or citational structure, or rather, since these last words lead to confusion, of an iterable structure" (104).

My question to Derrida is: *who* must first agree? The answer is: anyone who wants to have this conversation with deconstruction. And my response is: why would anyone want to have this conversation? Why would anyone want to call into doubt whether anyone ever really gets married or whether anyone ever has really asked a question? What's the purpose? One answer might be: this is philosophy; philosophy is skeptical. It wants answers, justifications, grounding. It doesn't just assume that the obvious facts are so. It doesn't take the ordinary for granted.

But, of course, it does. Without the ordinary, there is no discourse, no communication, no philosophy or science, no deconstruction, no skepticism. Derrida knows as well as anyone how all discourse rests on a great deal that is taken for granted. He knows that deconstruction is "parasitical," dependent on some realm of the ordinary, a domain in which communication is taken to be successful. Skepticism has something to do only when there are nonskeptics willing to have conversations, nonskeptics who believe a conversation is really taking place.

However, the real question is not whether the ordinary depends on the nonordinary or the nonordinary depends on the ordinary. The real questions are: what is the purpose of skepticism? On what occasions and to what degree should we be skeptical? What are the alternatives to skepticism? When and how should we pursue them? To what purposes? The rhetorical theory I am pursuing here already has its aims: to strengthen our confidence in the possibility of nonviolent resolutions to our conflicts, to defend the possibility of social criticism, to help shape a credible account of the purpose of higher education. The rhetoric of reason begins to broach these important questions only after it has already set out in defense of the ordinary, and in quest of ways to strengthen our experience of it. This claim demands that I explain, in just a little more detail, the sense of the ordinary I have in mind here.

Let me begin with a citation from Stanley Cavell's *Must We Mean What We Say?* Cavell is discussing something very similar to the idea of iterability with which Derrida is concerned in "Signature Event Context."

> We learn and teach words in certain contexts, and then we are
> expected, and expect others, to be able to project them into
> further contexts. Nothing insures that this projection will take
> place (in particular, not the grasping of universals nor the
> grasping of books of rules), just as nothing insures that we will
> make, and understand, the same projections. That on the whole
> we do is a matter of our sharing routes of interest and feeling,
> modes of response, senses of humor and of significance and of
> fulfillment, of what is outrageous, of what is similar to what else,
> what a rebuke, what forgiveness, of when an utterance is an
> assertion, when an appeal, when an explanation—all the whirl
> of organism Wittgenstein calls "forms of life." Human speech
> and activity, sanity and community, rest upon nothing more, but
> nothing less, than this. It is a vision as simple as it is difficult,
> and as difficult as it is (and because it is) terrifying. (52)[13]

I take this to be a sketch of the ordinary—a dwelling in which people can actually get married, make promises, befriend one another, keep loyalties, ask questions, change their lives. There is no guarantor of the ordinary, no anchor. The collapse of the ordinary happens all the time, in insanity, in violence and war, in torture, in the abuse and neglect of children, in the growth of suspicion and mistrust, in betrayals of all sorts. And in the experience of skepticism. Arising as it does from the domain of the ordinary, any successful expression of skepticism amounts to a denial of something. In Derrida's case, we see the entertaining of a denial that we really do share those things Cavell sketches in the passage I have cited. Philosophy itself, in its tireless search for grounds, is also a denial of the ordinary—a demand that explanations go further than this, a denial that the attraction of the ordinary itself can be a justification.

I will discuss later the senses in which Cavell believes that this denial is at its heart a failure to *acknowledge* the other people with whom we share our lives. That is, skepticism is a dissolving of the loyalties that link us to one another. Rhetorical theory is intensely aware of how profound these loyalties must be in order for there to be reasoning and argumentation. One of the aims of this book is to strengthen our attraction to the ordinary, conceived here as a domain in which violence can be reduced, in which mutual trust and respect make possible rather extraordinary uses of the ordinary possibilities of communication.

However, it also needs to be acknowledged that skepticism not only arises from but also is part of any ordinary form of life. Sustaining the ordinary in our acknowledgment of one another, in our willingness to hand over the very intelligibility of our lives to each other, taking responsibility for this when there are no assurances—this is an overwhelming responsibility, "terrifying." And so skepticism grows from the very experience of taking such responsibility, and knowing how inadequate one is to the challenge. In addition, there are those who because of violence or hatred or extreme poverty or injustice or countless other causes are denied an ordinary life. The absence of the social conditions for successful speech acts prevents them from participating. Often this absence is produced by the organization of the ordinary. But this exclusion from the ordinary produces skepticism, too. Skepticism is the result not only of the failure to acknowledge but also of the failure to be acknowledged—and this failure is not always the result of deliberate exclusions but often of more structural features of the way we maintain our ordinary lives. The ordinary has its own victims.

Thus, the ordinary—to strengthen and maintain its ordinariness, to prevent skepticism from taking actual social and practical and violent

Part One: Philosophy, Rhetoric, and Argumentation

forms—not only must in itself be an external response to skepticism but must go on internally responding to the skepticism it inevitably produces. One way it does this is by conducting skepticism's interrogative energy into argumentation. Argumentation occurs in the domain of the ordinary, but it is animated by a negative, interrogative voice. (I will explore the activities of this voice as it energizes argumentation in Chapter 3, on questioning.) Argumentation both depends on this voice and depends on its being limited in some specific ways by the ordinary, just as the ordinary is limited in some specific ways by the demands of skepticism.

Since my motivations are to strengthen and make use of certain features of the ordinary, to reduce the prospects of violence by increasing our attraction to ordinary reasoning, rhetorical theory offers a better climate for my efforts than deconstruction, which fosters consistent and persistent suspicion of the ordinary. However, I also believe that a successful rhetorical theory must be alive to the challenges of deconstruction, and not simply contemptuous of them. I would like to think, in fact, that I share with Derrida and other adherents of deconstruction certain "routes of interest and feeling, modes of response, senses of humor and of significance and of fulfillment." In the afterword to *Limited Inc*, Derrida raises the issue of the link between deconstruction and the "yes." He reminds his critics that he speaks of "unconditional affirmation" and "unconditional appeal" in his writings on apartheid (152). Later, in the chapter on questioning, I will cite Derrida's own reservations about unconstrained questioning, reservations he develops in *Of Spirit*. At these points, I find rhetorical theory and deconstruction converging again.

Finally, and once again in *Limited Inc*, Derrida maintains that the undecidability that deconstruction exposes explains the need for choice, for decision. "It is even," he says, "its necessary condition." "A decision can only come into being in a space that exceeds the calculable program that would destroy all responsibility by transforming it into a programmable effect of determinate causes. There can be no moral or political responsibility without this trial and this passage by way of the undecidable" (116). This is rhetoric's cue. It is precisely this experience of the undecidable, in which self-evidence or certainty of any kind is impossible, that gives rise to the need to understand reason outside the expectation of certainty or formal decidability. It is as if deconstruction has provided the *absence* of ground that makes a *pragmatic rhetoric* of reason both possible and necessary. A rhetoric of reason is a theory of how, in this situation, it is possible at all to take responsibility for our choices.

After Philosophy: Rhetoric

Although the Heideggerian and Derridean versions of the end of traditional metaphysics can be experienced, from a distance, with a kind of joyful abandonment of oneself to a more playful experience of language, they also produce some rather difficult practical problems. The traditional belief in a kind of being which is outside of time, constantly present, sets a goal and measure for human knowing which is independent of particular interests, particular cultures, particular forms of life. This belief has at least three important consequences for social life. First, it offers a reasonable hope of the peaceful reconciliation of different groups with one another. Social conflicts based on disagreements about what is true or right are not intractable. Conflicting parties need not resort to violence; differences can be resolved through reason, which leads to a truth which is the same for all people in all places and at all times. Second, this belief provides an appeal to an authority beyond the authority of any actual social power. In a kind of paradox, the idea of constant presence helps to create historical time. Societies can make *progress* toward the true or right. They can go into decline as well. They can be reformed, or their historical hopes can be betrayed. Third, the idea helps to define the goals of education, especially higher education. Higher education is not simply training in the prejudices and conventions of one's own society, but is open to the influences of the reasoning and experience of all societies at all times. This openness has been understood to be a means of coming closer to the truth about what has universal constant presence. All ideas are criticizable on this basis, and as in history and politics, it is believed that the different sciences can actually progress in their knowledge about what is true for all time. The claim that higher education makes in American society is that the education it offers and the research it produces further the interests of all people, and not just the interests of particular groups, because it seeks for, and produces, universal truth.

I take it for granted that such social needs and purposes will not soon pass away. And this leads to a first-rate intellectual problem. The results of contemporary philosophical thinking seem to be at best useless and at worst destructive for the purposes of actually existing societies. Such results lead into difficult quandaries—for example, Richard Rorty's dilemma about how to prevent irony from infecting political life. On the one hand, thinkers can retreat to private spheres in which they continually revise their ultimate terms, without ever taking any one set of them perfectly seriously. They can explore being-in-the-world and its many forms of intelligibility without having finally to commit themselves to any of them. On the other hand, in the public world, they face actual suffering and cruelty, and must make decisions about saying and doing one thing rather than another—decisions that have serious consequences for other people. The need to take action and make commitments in the face of suffering deprives one of the intellectual comfort of irony.

One can get useful perspective on this problem, and return the life of the mind to the world, only by refusing philosophy's own understanding of its historical results, its "end." The collapse of the ontological picture of what truth, knowledge, and reason are is not the end of truth, knowledge, and reason themselves. Heidegger reinterpreted truth as a primordial feature of Dasein, and knowledge as a very particular way of being-in. However, he did not use these reinterpretations to contribute much to a redescription of reasoning. Neither did he successfully describe how social conflicts could be resolved by way of reasoning. Rather, Heidegger seemed to think the end of philosophy in a philosophical way as something which would somehow end history as we have known it, and take all our institutions and practices with it. Such a way of thought led him to fanatical revolutionary ideology in the 1930s and skeptical apolitical withdrawal in the 1940s and after.

The basic problem with philosophy's understanding of its own end is that it assumes that the collapse of its metaphysical understanding of the world is the collapse of the world itself. Nietzsche is perhaps the greatest perpetrator of this philosophical delusion (although Heidegger and many others have followed him in this). Nietzsche believed that the end of a "supersensible realm," a realm of constant presence, would mean the end of human beings. His word for being as constant presence was "God." The death of God was supposed to lead to an outbreak of madness, the end of history and human beings as we have known them. Nietzsche's great task was to prevent the outbreak of this madness by preparing for new human beings who could not only bear the truth in which the history of philosophy results but also create new truths which could sustain new kinds of human beings.

The delusion here is that metaphysics is the foundation of human experience and that without this foundation human experience will somehow collapse. However, there is more truth in the converse. It is human experience which produces something like metaphysics; particular forms of life and historical experience create a need for authorities to which conflicting parties can appeal. These authorities spring up among interlocutors when conflicts are resolved discursively. Concepts of timeless truth and constantly present being are philosophical interpretations of the nature of these authorities. However, the interpretations them-selves are not the authorities. These interpretations amplify and add to the power of discursive authorities, but they do not themselves gen-erate the phenomenon of interlocutors making appeals to common au-thorities that transcend the particular interests of the individual inter-locutors.

Argumentation succeeds even apart from the metaphysics which has interpreted it and reinforced its authority. It is the role of a rhetoric of reason to explain this success, to examine rhetorical authority and de-scribe how it works. Part of what it will accomplish will be to offer a new approach to metaphilosophy—a rhetorical one. For one result of the end of philosophy is that philosophy has become unable to under-stand the meaning of its end. Rhetoric can not only explain the insuffi-ciencies of philosophical accounts of philosophy but also provide new motivations to go on philosophizing—under the protection of a rheto-ric of philosophy. Such efforts are necessary if we are to respond to the continuing needs of diverse human groups to reconcile their differences peacefully, if we are to renew the possibility of genuine social criticism, and if we are to keep higher education accountable to more than paro-chial aims.

We need not only to give up the absolutes of traditional metaphysics but also to give up the absolutism that sees the absence of absolutes as grounds for madness and unreason. M. H. Abrams has pointed out that postmodern thought in general is still thinking as a kind of absolutism without absolutes. If we let go of every kind of philosophical absolut-ism, including negative absolutism, then philosophical discourse as well as reason and argumentation generally can be understood in rhetorical terms.

There have been many turns to rhetoric or communication theory as means of developing a new metaphilosophy.[14] In fact, much of contem-porary metaphilosophy is now incorporated by rhetoricians as part of the history of rhetoric.[15] However, I believe that the single most impor-tant event in contemporary rhetorical theory understood as a response and alternative to metaphysics took place in 1958 with the publication of Chaim Perelman and Lucie Olbrechts-Tyteca's *La nouvelle rhétorique: Traité de l'argumentation*. The writers of this still insufficiently understood five-hundred-plus-page treatise are clear about their ambitions: Their work, they say, "constitutes *a break with a concept of reason and reasoning due to Descartes* which has set its mark on Western philosophy for the last three centuries" (1).

This break has three important features which are determinative for any attempt to follow through on a rhetoric of reason. First, Perelman and Olbrechts-Tyteca completely abandon the idea that our reasoning is an attempt to correspond to or give access to something which has constant presence. The measure of reasoning is not some timeless logical standard located in the essential nature of constantly present things. And self-evidence is not the chief characteristic of reason and real knowledge. Rather the aim of argumentation is to gain the adherence of other people; all argumentation develops in terms of an audience. The merit of an argument can be determined by knowing the quality of the audience which would assent to it. Thus, a rhetoric of reason calls for a reception theory of rationality.

Second, since the aim of argumentation is the adherence of an audience to some claim made upon it, and since such adherence is a matter of degree, argumentation must be understood as succeeding or failing to varying degrees as well as with various audiences. This means that the expectation of bivalence in the evaluation of claims is set aside. Reason does not demand a "true" or "false" judgment on claims or a "valid" or "invalid" judgment on arguments. The need to take action, and thus the need for choice, sometimes forces bivalence—that is, demands a yes or no to the claims of arguments—but this should not be confused with the demands of reason. Arguments can be better or worse, and their claims can be more or less compelling.

Third, reason is a practice which has an essentially ethical motivation. The framework for argumentation is made up of ethical elements, and involves specifically ethical commitments. And many particular argumentative strategies are imbued with certain ethical appeals. According to Perelman, the central guiding principle of argumentation is the idea of justice, which is at the heart of the very concepts of reason and argumentation. Justice is typically thought to be a way of deciding how different claims can be reconciled in relation to the distribution of goods, the protection of rights and liberties, and so on. However, Perelman's insight is to see the idea in a much broader way. To put it in terms Perelman did not use: people make conflicting claims on each other's being-in-the-world in the largest sense. Each of us is a disclosure of the world, an uncovering of entities; however, each of these disclosures is in some respects different from all the others. And yet these disclosures make claims on each other. These claims often need to be reconciled with the idea of justice: that beings of the same kind be treated in the same way. Argumentation is the attempt to reconcile the claims of different disclosures of the world in a way that is fair and just.

The most immediate application of this idea is that argumentation is the renunciation of violence and is the practice of respect for others' disclosures of what is. The task a rhetoric of reason takes on is in large part explaining how reasoning can have effect (have "force"), while forgoing violence and furthering respect. The larger task is to determine whether a rhetoric of reason following from such perspectives can meet the real social needs that much contemporary philosophy has neglected.

Teaching after Philosophy

The teaching of written reasoning has suffered from the absence of a rhetoric of reason. The project of teaching writing in higher education has absorbed the consequences of the breakup of philosophy, and has accepted the fragmentation of reason as a basic fact. And this has delivered to teachers of written reasoning a first-class practical problem. Which rhetoric do students need to learn? Which should they be taught? Some of the discussion surrounding this question has taken place as a discussion of the importance of the concept of discourse communities in thinking about the teaching of writing.[16] Discourse communities are taken to differ in relation to the purposes for which people communicate and the conventions different groups develop in order to realize those purposes.[17] To misunderstand the purposes or to violate the conventions usually makes a participant a less than persuasive member of a discourse community. It turns out that discourse is very different in different communities and different situations, and it is different precisely along the lines of what will be taken to be convincing communication, and thus, from a rhetorical point of view, successful reasoning. Private discourse is different from public discourse; interethnic discourse is different from intra-ethnic discourse; academic discourse is different from everyday discourse. Not only what is arguable and inarguable, but also what counts as evidence is different in different communities. One of the major rifts in the teaching of writing has been along the question of whether teachers should teach specifically academic discourse to college students or whether they should, supposing they knew how, strengthen their students' abilities to write well in a discourse community of their own choosing.

However, even among those who decide for academic discourse, the question of what rhetoric to teach is still a troubling one. For what is most significant about academic discourse is the strongly specialized writing conventions of the different disciplines and professions. Anyone who has thought about developing a college composition curriculum that would serve to initiate students into "the academic discourse community" has had to face the fact that what is often rhetorically and linguistically most interesting about engineering, business, law, medicine, history, chemistry, computer science, and English is not what they have in common but those respects in which they differ.

Many educational administrators and many educators are unaware not only of the philosophical events that have put the teaching of written reasoning in a new light, but also of the growing amount of research into disciplinary communication that shows how quite ordinary writing tasks are "committed" in one way or another to the special purposes of different disciplines. To take a single example, teaching students to document their sources is an essential part of teaching written reasoning in colleges and universities. However, the different styles of documentation not only vary from year to year and from discipline to discipline but also embody particular ideas about what knowledge is and how it is transmitted, ideas which also vary from year to year and from discipline to discipline.[18] Thus, in an effort to avoid making philosophical commitments which would narrow the markets for their books, publishers of writing handbooks typically include more than one section on proper documentation style, each section explaining the style of a different faction of higher education. The contents of such chapters change fairly frequently, as most writing teachers know. However, this is only one example. When one considers how the concept of what counts as evidence varies from field to field, how the degree of authority possessed by different theories and researchers is different in different disciplines, how even the styles of reasoning shift from field to field, one begins to see how difficult it is to situate the teaching of written reasoning within the "general education" requirements of a college or university.[19]

It is partly in response to this fact that writing-across-the-curriculum programs have been developed in colleges and universities across the United States. Many of these programs are sophisticated and thoughtful responses to contemporary research in rhetoric. They seem to me an essential feature of any undergraduate curriculum that would claim to give a serious place to writing. However, fragmenting the teaching of writing along disciplinary faults does not solve the problem of having to decide what to teach in English composition or in critical thinking classrooms or in the general education curriculum. The most serious problem of the undergraduate curriculum is not designing courses which teach discipline-specific writing conventions. The most serious problem is cultivating students' *general* abilities to communicate in writing—their abilities to reason, to draw from very different specialized sources, to adapt to different audiences, to understand and respond reasonably to all the various and quickly changing communicative situations they will deal with in their lives. In the most skeptical and desperate institutional settings, writing across the curriculum can become an excuse for abandoning altogether the goal of developing courses which can lay claim to being an essential part of a general or liberal education.

In the absence of a theoretical account of a general rhetoric, some writing teachers have also concluded that since there is no deciding the question of what to teach on any rational grounds the only solution is a de facto one: teachers should teach whatever they desire to teach without having to justify it. They will decide on very different rhetorics, but there is nothing to be said or done about this, except for them to announce to their students that they are in fact teaching the rhetoric of some specific discourse community because they happen to favor the purposes of that community. Students are told that they should not be alarmed because all teaching of writing favors the purposes of some group or other, and at least teachers who announce their biases are not disguising that fact. So one group of students studies and writes belletristic essays and another studies and writes personal journals. Still another group studies folk stories, or writes fables, or samples the rhetorics of various academic disciplines. Still another reads the diaries of nineteenth-century pioneer women or a number of different "discourse types" from a multicultural anthology. The variations are endless.

There is something very important about the diversity of voices such a de facto solution includes in the writing curriculum. However, the incoherence of purpose in such a solution also devalues those voices, and isolates them from the central issues of both scholarship and public life. It devalues them because the amplification of such voices is taken to be a result of the idiosyncratic predilections of a teacher, and not an essential feature of written reasoning itself. It isolates them when their study is enacted in the absence of an understanding of the traditions from which these voices take their difference. However, I want to say at once that there are *some* virtues in such isolation (although not enough) and that dominant traditions themselves are both constituted by internal differences and identified by differences from nondominant traditions.

The field of composition needs a purpose, one on which a consensus (or a "disciplined dissensus," in George Dillon's words) can be reached, and which nonetheless takes for a fact the plurality of rhetorics and the ultimate general undecidability of their conflicts. I believe that the teaching of written argumentation can fulfill such a role, not only for

the teaching of writing but also for the teaching of critical thinking—
but only when argumentation is understood theoretically in such a
manner that the recognition of the fact of difference is a starting point
and ending point. Whether the theory of argumentation I am offering
here can actually fulfill such a role can be determined only once the
theory is set forth.

Thus, the goal of this work is to provide the outlines of a theory of argumentation which will both have its own intrinsic merit as a theory of
rationality and be able to fill the role of an informing theoretical matrix
for those whose task it is to teach written reasoning. Such a theory will
offer a new interpretation of higher education's claim to be independent of parochial aims, as well as offer new ways of understanding the
claims of social criticism. Most important, it will also show how we actually do transform social conflict into the nonviolent discovery of new
kinds of thought and action, and even new forms of life.

Argument: The Traditional Theory and Its Problems

The usual view of argument is that it is monological
and disembodied. Arguments exist in themselves somehow and are
valid or invalid quite apart from who is offering them and to whom and
about what and on what occasion and why. What make arguments
valid are formal relations among their parts. Thus, in themselves arguments have nothing to do with dialogue or audience or social-historical
conflict—they may be used for social purposes, but what they *are* does
not depend on such uses and purposes.

Further, argumentation has traditionally been thought to be univocal
and explicit. In pursuit of univocality, logicians have devised formal
languages which facilitate argumentation that is unhindered by the ambiguities of natural languages. Arguments are understood to be explicit
in that the premises and rules and propositions which have the appropriate formal relations to one another are all that is needed to make an
argument go through. There are no background assumptions or skills
or cultural know-how needed to make arguments work. Rather, in
order to argue well, one must take a detached view; one must separate
oneself from one's interests, one's particular culture, one's ordinary beliefs. Above all, one must not let emotions or feelings or desires inter-
fere with the process of reasoning.

In fact, it has often been thought that arguments can be constructed and evaluated in a single, isolated mind, a kind of Cartesian mind—a mind from which emotions, gender, experience, and opinions have all been banished. Such a mind is an unsocialized mind, free from the limitations of culture, politics, and commitment. It would be misleading to say that this mind is the mind of an individual, since individuals are *different* from one another, their differences made possible by the ways societies enable individuation. By contrast, this mind is a universal rational mind, and its world is a world of ideas and their formal relations. This mind is the performer of arguments, and its rational acts are generated solely by formal rules. This mind is in all of us, and the way to argue logically, the way to reason well, is to overcome all the bodily, historical, social, and cultural styles of thought which are obstacles to reasoning, and to activate what is universal in us.

The metaphysical support for this traditional philosophical understanding of argumentation has come under serious criticism in the last century. From Nietzsche to Heidegger and his successors and from William James to Richard Rorty, the idea that reason subsists in a mind that is independent of the different purposes people pursue has been exposed as just one more way some people pursue their particular purposes. However now, after this series of exposés, the traditional concept of reason is no longer persuasive enough, for enough people, to serve the purposes it once did.

The exposé of the way the idea of reason has been used to further very partisan purposes has been made possible in part by a critique of the ideas of explicitness and univocality. The general challenge of this critique is to claim that we can never make our ideas fully explicit because there is a background that is always brought into play whenever we speak or write or sign, and this background makes our experience what it is. Behind particular utterances stand deep skills and competences that help us to recognize which questions are decidable and which are not, which are worth discussing and with whom, what is relevant and what is not. We could never "neutralize" this background by making it completely explicit, and examining it, because it would already be put into play as the background of any such attempt.

Thus, along with whatever we assert, we both make assumptions and affirm the appropriateness of the competences that guide us. For this reason, our utterances are never univocal. We never simply assert a proposition. We affirm competences, and expand the domain of our competences; we project and promote a form of life which results from the history of our language and the purposes of the groups which shape our discursive practices.

We sometimes become aware of this background when communication breaks down, when our utterances are no longer taken the way we expect them to be taken, or when the utterances of others make no sense to us. Ron and Suzanne Scollon studied such breakdowns in the communication between Native Athabaskans and English-speaking residents of Alaska. There was evidence of a problem with interethnic communication in Alaskan courts in that Athabaskans were receiving longer sentences than whites received for similar crimes. The Scollons discovered an intriguing set of mutually conflicting interpretations of the discursive practices of each group, which they believed was a factor in the breakdown in the courts. For example, the Athabaskans complained that English speakers talked too much, always talked first, talked to strangers or people they didn't know, bragged about themselves, asked too many questions, talked only about what they were interested in, and weren't careful when they talked about things or people. On the other hand, English speakers complained that Athabaskans were too quiet, never started a conversation, wanted to talk only to close acquaintances, played down their own abilities, avoided direct questions, talked off the topic, asked questions in unusual places, never said anything about themselves, were too indirect and inexplicit, and just didn't make sense. In addition, English speakers believed that Athabaskans refused to plan, while Athabaskans said that English speakers thought they could predict the future and were always talking about what was going to happen later (36).

Importantly, the Scollons emphasize that the background competences for understanding one another in these terms are not simply beliefs; they *lead* to certain beliefs when different cultures encounter one another, but they are deeper than explicit beliefs. Athabaskans may believe that English speakers talk too much, but they do not *believe* that they themselves speak indirectly and inexplicitly. To describe Athabaskan discourse practices as "beliefs" is to talk about Athabaskans in a way they would not talk about themselves and to miss something important about the "background." The Scollons are very clear on this:

> Discourse patterns are very closely tied up with a person's personality and culture . . . If we suggest change we have to be very aware that we are not only suggesting change in discourse patterns. We are suggesting change in a person's identity. If someone says that an English speaker should be less talkative, less self-assertive, less interested in the future, he is saying at the same time that he should become a different person. He is saying that he should identify less with his own culture and more with another. If someone says an Athabaskan should talk more about plans, should speak out more on his own opinions, or not be so

indirect, he is saying that he should stop being so Athabaskan. He is saying he should change in personal identity and cultural identity (37).

The Scollons here make the Heideggerian point that certain deep competences are better understood as ontological features of human beings than as beliefs or any kind of relation between a subject and an object.

This places substantial obstacles in the way of the traditional theory of argumentation. What is being forwarded in argumentation is often not explicit. Arguments forward not only propositions but a whole host of cultural competences and skills. The capacity for reason lies not in an independent rational mind but at least partly in the deep competences people have to be members of social groups that disclose the world and interpret things in a shared way. The theory of argumentation requires a reconstruction that stops seeing these facts as obstacles and instead uses these facts to explain better what reasoning and argument really are.

Recognizing that arguments promote ways of being and seeing that are not made explicit in those arguments not only makes the traditional theory of argumentation vulnerable to criticism but also makes the practice of argumentation itself vulnerable in a new way. In everyday life, to "argue" or "have an argument" suggests something negative, aggressive, a kind of breakdown in the preferred modes of communication. This is also the classical idea of argument as eristic. To have an argument is something like having a fight, and in such arguments the aim is to defeat another person. Thus, students often have a natural resistance to argumentation—they see it as aggressive and somewhat hostile because they see "rational" argumentation or "scholarly" argument as continuous with the attempts at discursive domination that are so familiar in everyday life. In the past, using the traditional model of argumentation, it was possible to distinguish in a fairly strict fashion the "arguing" that goes on when people are trying to dominate one another from the arguing that goes on in scholarly inquiry or deliberative rhetoric. Hostile arguing, the story went, is full of emotion, is concerned not with truth but with victory, is full of unclarified ambiguities, makes unexamined assumptions based on cultural prejudices or irrational commitments—in short, is not a rational movement from proposition to proposition generated by rules of logic.

Obviously, distinguishing between the two senses of "argument" by appealing to the old metaphysical dualism—no matter how disguised or modified—will no longer do. Thus, a number of recent writers have criticized argumentation itself as a form of discourse which is obsolete and ought to be retired. They claim that it is in actuality a kind of discourse which is aggressive and domineering. Its pretensions to be otherwise make it not only undesirable but dangerous. Even when an arguer does not intend to dominate or act aggressively, domination and aggression happen anyway because a background is always promoted and furthered—independently of an arguer's intentions and against the appearances that argument puts up. The background being furthered may consist of communicative competences specific to a particular culture, as in the discursive conflicts between English speakers and Athabaskans, or it may consist of a competence for particular speech roles that are gendered within a culture, but it promotes itself at the expense of certain groups and in the disguise of rationality.[20]

Any reconstruction of the theory of argumentation must recognize these facts. Thus, I have devoted Chapter 7 to a discussion of "argument and ideology," and I will try to be as specific as possible there about what kind of ideology the practice of argumentation carries with it. Simply reconstructing the theory of argumentation cannot directly change what happens when people argue. However, a reconstructed theory can change our interpretation of what happens when we argue, and our attitude toward it, as well as our sense of what modifications are possible and desirable in our practices.

My main purpose here is to reconstruct the theory of argumentation as a way of bringing to light those features of argumentation that enable us to live together better than we otherwise would. At the same time, I have made an effort to uncover and set aside lingering resentments at the discovery that we are not as autonomous as some of us once thought we were, and I have tried to preserve a deep respect for our differences from one another, differences that the practice of argument seems sometimes to obscure. It goes without saying, I hope, that a reconstructed defense of argumentation, and of the teaching of argumentation, will be a much weaker kind of defense than the traditional one.

A reconstruction is a reconstruction and not a demolition. Thus, it must consider in a serious way the motivations for the traditional theory of argumentation. Again, a major motivation for constructing the traditional conception of argument is a desire to find some way of settling otherwise intractable conflicts and disagreements. The idea is that if we could put aside our strong feelings, our particular opinions, our gender, our nationality and ethnic identities, then we could dispassionately reason our way to agreements, for we would be subordinating ourselves to a universal reason, one that was the same for all of us. Although the metaphysics of a residual independent "rational mind" today lies in ruin, the concept of reason that accompanied it, and especially the theory of argumentation that belonged to it, have not been as quick to self-destruct. There is a very powerful reason for this. The social needs which argumentation meets have not vanished. The most obvious of these needs is the need to resolve social conflicts nonviolently. The traditional concepts of reason and argument depended on the assumption that there was something we all had in common, that it was possible to settle our differences peacefully provided only that we were willing to reason. This is an attractive idea, and the motivations for using it are not just wrong or naive, even if many of its uses have been oppressive, and even if the idea itself is no longer as persuasive among intellectuals as it once was.

In addition, there are the other needs I mentioned earlier. The possibility of meaningful social criticism depends on an account of reasoning that can make social criticism understandable as more than simply the complaints of one self-seeking group against another. And continued public support for higher education depends partly on an account of research and scholarship that explains the knowledge that is produced and transmitted in colleges and universities as something that has a claim on all of us, regardless of which faction of society we belong to.

The motivations for the traditional theory grew more complex as the results of argumentative rationality became more diverse. Although theories of argumentation and rationality were developed primarily in societies which used argumentation to settle social conflicts, argumentative rationality proved capable of establishing itself as a means of reasoning about and inquiring into matters which had only the most tenuous connection to actual social conflicts, or at least, had a connection to social conflicts of only the most subtle sort. Scientific inquiry is carried out in argumentation. Theoretical conflicts are decided by way of argumentation. Interpretation is a kind of argument. Argumentative rationality enables inquiry into what is not known. A reconstructed theory of argumentation must also account for this strong historical connection between argumentation and inquiry and knowledge.

I have chosen to attempt to reconstruct the theory of argumentation rather than simply to criticize it because I believe that our present historical circumstances, as well as our cultural mood, put us in need of an affirmative way to understand our agreements rather than in need of one more suspicious theory that shows us that our affirmations are naive. We have recently come once more to deeper understandings of how profound the differences are among human groups; we have not reached as deep an understanding of what we can do to avoid violence when such differences become conflicts which are just as profound. Again, I realize that the practice of argumentation carries with it an ideology, and I will try to be explicit about the ideological features of argument. I realize, too, that many people suspect that argument is a form of coercion or discursive violence, and so I will try to be very precise about the relation between violence and argument; in fact, this relation makes up a central part of the theory I offer. I know, too, that many people believe that the practice of argument reinforces traditional philosophical illusions about truth, meaning, and univocality. I can only say that I understand such suspicions. However, I take them to be part of the motivation to theorize argumentation anew and not reasons to attack the practice of argument.[21]

The reconstruction of argumentation is also important because of its connection to what can be understood as the problem of solipsism. In its social form, the problem of solipsism is the problem of how we can sustain an openness to people who are seriously different from us in ways that cannot be made explicit—either because making them explicit would require nonexistent commensurate discourses or because these differences are matters of deep background competences. It is often thought that argumentative discourse suppresses or obscures such differences, and if one thinks in terms of the traditional theory this is certainly right. However, argumentation is also capable of being understood as an event in which differences are recognized and used to make unanticipated discoveries. A reconstructed theory of argumentation should explain both how argumentation encloses discourse and occludes differences and how it articulates differences and uses them to disclose the world in new ways. That is, a reconstructed theory should show both how argumentation is complicit in solipsistic tendencies and how it resists them.

As I have said, there is an important difference between the traditional theory of reason and argumentation and the actual practices of reasoning and arguing that go on in all of our lives. The traditional theory was a way to explain and strengthen the practices of argumentation which developed historically without the help of a metaphysics of reason or a philosophy of logic. The traditional theory has certainly had an influence on the historical development of the practice of argument, and has exercised and continues to exercise a very strong (and often deleterious) influence on the way people are taught to reason and argue in schools. However, many of the realities and successes of argumentation are no more dependent on metaphysical theories of reason and argument than the origin of argumentation was. Actual reasoning is informed by theories, but rarely the full-blown metaphysical theories of the philosophical tradition. What we need is a way to understand what the realities and successes of argumentation are and how they might have continuing importance for our own historical projects.

In what follows, I am going to deny that argument is what it traditionally has been thought to be, and I am going to offer a very different account of what argument is. I am going to do so in a way that explains its actual successes and its continuing importance not in terms of the power of the illusions created by the ideas of "mind" and "reason" and "truth," but rather in terms of its having accomplished some of what it set out to accomplish, i.e., in terms of the quite remarkable forms of sociality argumentation has made possible. These forms include the peaceful resolution of conflicts, meaningful social criticism, higher education, and even self-transformation. Argumentation is the practice of a very tenuous hope that people can settle their conflicts nonviolently, that they can act differently from the way they otherwise would because they can open themselves to the dialogues that arguments are. In the process of developing this ability, a great deal more is accomplished, for this dialogue which is argumentation is finally indistinguishable from learning itself, indistinguishable from the practice of inquiry.

PART TWO

RECONSTRUCTING

ARGUMENTATION

2 CLAIMING

Argument as Dialogue

The traditional concept of argument is well represented in logic textbooks. Here is a typical example: "An argument is any group of propositions of which one is claimed to follow from the others, which are regarded as providing evidence for the truth of that one."[1] The essential ideas are clear enough: arguments are sets of *propositions*; these propositions have a logical relation to one another that constitutes them as an argument; the aim of argumentation is truth. Propositions and the relations between them are what they are independently of human beings and their actions. Logic-based theories of argumentation and formalizing and schematizing accounts of argument, as well as the teaching they influence, all share these essential assumptions. Implicitly, they assume the existence of a mind which grasps propositions univocally, intuits the natural force of logical relations, and is motivated solely by a pure interest in working through these formal relations. According to the traditional concept, argumentative reasoning is a monological, monovocal movement from proposition to proposition. The standard model grows out of a metaphysical and epistemological tradition that is incapable of meaningful dialogue with Heideggerian conceptions of historicity or Derridean accounts of the transcontextual instability of writing and experience.

Against this account of argument, I propose that any argument is, *internally*, a communicative process, a process of question and answer, challenge and reply, affirmation and negation—all of which are subclasses of the general category of call and response, an essentially social action. This is as true for individualized argumentative reasoning as it is for written argumentation. What follows from this is that this process can take place only in a social-historical context; argument is not intelligible outside this context.

Before launching into a detailed discussion of the parts of the theory, I want to offer a short outline discussion of the general ideas, so that the particulars will make more sense and their place in the whole will be more readily grasped.

Consider arguments in which a claim and support for the claim are offered explicitly. Let's call these "ordinary arguments." The first thing to notice about an ordinary argument is that it is a matter not of abstract propositions but of speech acts. A proposition must be asserted to get into an argument; it must be understood as a claim. Argumentation is a way of justifying one's making of a particular claim. The second thing to notice is that support for a claim doesn't just emerge from nowhere; it is elicited by another speech act, one that is implicit in ordinary arguments. Specifically, a justification of a claim is a response to some calling of the claim into question. That is, in between the two explicit speech acts in ordinary arguments lies an implicit one: usually a request for clarification or justification. Thus, the process of argument is a process of speech actions. Argumentation has to do with asserting and challenging, assenting and dissenting—in general, with making claims, challenging them, modifying and defending them.

If argumentation is engaging in speech acts, then one can always ask, Who's speaking? And even if the answer is not immediately forthcoming, one can quickly see that argumentation is a conflict between *speakers* engaging in speech acts—whatever the status of these speakers and their identity. This conflict is in a very straightforward sense a social conflict between someone making a claim and someone else who will not readily accept it. Claims, questions about claims, objections, modifications of claims, counterclaims—these are offered by people, and by social groups. If no one offered claims and made challenges to them, there would be no argumentation, no reason.

This is true even for the arguing we do with ourselves, and for the arguing we do in writing. The very form of it is conversational. We think of a claim's being made. We change roles and demand a justification. We reason argumentatively by giving voice to imaginary interlocutors who engage in an imaginary conversation with one another. Since we ordinarily take this ability to change roles for granted, it's hard to imagine what it would be like without it. Argumentation couldn't take place because a claim wouldn't raise a question for itself. If I make a claim to myself, who is there to oppose me? If I am the audience for my own assertions, why is a justification necessary? In order for individualized argumentative reasoning to be possible, there must be an imaginary splitting of the one who is making the claim into roles. But our acquaintance with these roles comes from social experience, from the experience of conversation and the experience of being challenged and witnessing challenges. These roles are not innate. They are social roles.

The voices and actions of other people are the sources of the questions, objections, and counterclaims that are offered imaginatively in our inward reasonings, and which find their way into our writing. Lev Vygotsky refers to this kind of inner conversation as verbal thought, inner speech of a special sort. It is not identical with thought as such, which has, he believes, a different, a biological root. Individualized argumentative reasoning, whether inward or written, is developed out of the actual discursive conflict to which we are witnesses and in which we are participants. To quote Vygotsky, who doesn't speak explicitly of argument: "Verbal thought is not an innate, natural form of behavior but is determined by a historical-cultural process that has specific properties that cannot be found in the natural forms of thought and speech" (51). After observing "egocentric" speech in children—a kind of individualized conversation—Vygotsky concluded that inner speech is internalized conversation.

This is especially true of argumentative reasoning.[2] Since argument is in itself a communicative process, constituted by speech acts, it cannot be understood except in terms of a complex background of social agreements. On the simplest level, when confronted with an ordinary argument, one must be able to make explicit the implicit speech acts which connect a claim to whatever grounds are given for its support, or to whatever clarifications or modifications are offered. If the motivation for the challenge cannot be understood, then the argument itself cannot be understood as an argument, because one cannot know the extent to which the reply is a satisfactory response to the challenge. Thus, to understand an argument as an argument is to have the ability to imagine someone's inhabiting the role of the challenger. This means, in some cases, imagining people very different from ourselves, and forms of life different from our own.

At a more complicated level, any argumentative conversation depends on a fairly extensive network of shared competences and agreements—for example, an understanding of what speech acts are appropriate in the argumentation, a shared understanding of how to engage in them, agreements about what will not be challenged in the argumentation—that is, shared knowledge, values, beliefs, and abilities that are taken for granted, as well as some conception of what kinds of challenges are relevant. Argumentation is possible only on the basis of deep agreements of many sorts; unless one shares these understandings with the participants in an argument, or recognizes that they are operating, one cannot experience an argument as an argument.

There are three distinct roles in any argument. Although one person can fill all these roles, and although each single role may be divided among several people, the roles themselves may be thought of as distinct. First, there is the role of the one who makes a claim and offers reasons in its support. Let's call the one who fills this role the "claimant." Next, there is the one who questions the claim, or asks for it to be clarified, or challenges it in some way. Let's call this the respondent. Finally, since arguments are always more or less persuasive *for someone*, there must be a role for those who judge the argumentation. Let's call this the audience. In the chapters which follow, I consider in detail these roles and the actions which belong to them in an effort to reconstruct argument as an actual practice. In this chapter, I will explore the pragmatic-dialectical features of claims.

What Is a Claim?

Most treatments of argumentation take claims for granted, or treat them in logical terms as propositions. At best, they may discuss methods for coming up with claims, or ways of classifying them; rarely do they ask what a claim is in the context of someone's actually making a claim. If a theory of argumentation does include a treatment of claiming, it typically falls into immediate psychologizing—the objectification of the claimant according to, say, schemes of intellectual maturity.[3] However, if we treat argumentation from a pragmatic, rhetorical point of view, we take claims seriously as actions that have motives, and that may have roots deep in the kind of beings we are.

All attempts at reasoning, and thus logic and psychology themselves, depend on claiming. A pragmatic rhetoric of reason, as an instance of reasoning, depends on claiming as well. However, it does not, like logic, objectify claims as propositions or, like psychology, objectify claiming as the behavior of an objectified subject. Instead, it conceives of propositions as reified, context-stripped abstractions from claims, and claiming as an activity in which selves come to be, an activity in which agents take shape.

I said in Chapter 1 that rhetoric has a priority to other intellectual enterprises but that this priority is not foundational. In this case, too, a pragmatic-rhetorical approach to claiming offers an account which is better than other accounts in that it is better for particular purposes than competing accounts and more convincing in the context in which it is offered. Once again, one of my purposes here is frankly epideictic. I want to describe argumentation in a way that leads people to want to teach and practice written reasoning more and better than they do now, and this for the purposes of both increasing our capacities for resolving conflicts peacefully and strengthening our abilities to use conflicts to inquire and create.

Consider arguments in which a claim and support for the claim are offered explicitly. Let's call these "ordinary arguments." Once again, the first thing to notice about an ordinary argument is that it is a matter not of abstract propositions but of speech acts. A proposition must be *asserted* to get into an argument; it must become a *claim*. However, even to put it this way is misleading for it defers to a metaphysics of propositions that a pragmatic rhetoric of reason would reject. According to this metaphysics, propositions precede claims. Propositions are independent entities that can be made explicit, or expressed, in different modalities by incorporating them into speech acts. However, from a rhetorical-pragmatic angle, the opposite is the case. Propositions are epiphenomenal, dependent on speech acts—maybe sometimes silent, inward speech acts, but speech acts nonetheless. Proposition-talk is often very useful in the work of interpreting speech acts, of elaborating on them, and it gives us a way of talking and thinking about the similarities among them, but propositions are epiphenomenal and dependent on speech acts through and through. Strictly speaking, a proof as a series of propositions doesn't assert anything to anyone, and the system of rules by which the propositions are connected makes no claim about how human beings do or should reason. Only in the philosophy of logic, which proceeds by way of argumentation, are claims about proofs made and arguments about logic itself set forth.

However, even in proofs we imagine the premises being asserted, and this is the case even if the premises are known to be false. We imagine the assertion of false premises in order to see where such assertions lead. We give reasons (rules) for inferences because we imagine that we must justify our inferences before an audience of logicians. The entire practice of creating proofs occurs only in a rhetorical situation. Thus, distinguishing between propositions and claims is a matter of degree and audience. The audience that judges when a proposition is pure enough, sufficiently uncontaminated by ambiguity and rhetorical-pragmatic-linguistic messiness, is a specialized, highly universalized audience. I will investigate this audience in more detail in Chapter 5, in the section on rhetoric and logic. I want to make it clear that this argument should in no sense be taken as an "attack" on logic. Logic and mathematics and the sciences informed by them are astonishing achievements enabled by our capacity to imagine ourselves as universal audiences—and so to become more than we would otherwise be. I can hardly imagine doing without this practice.

However, arguments are kindled by claims. "Claim" comes from the Latin *clamare*, which means to call or to cry out. There is something already social about a claim: someone makes a claim about something to *someone*; someone calls out to *someone else*. When one asserts something in this way, there is the expectation that someone else can hear the call, that someone else will understand the claim *as a claim*. To be able to understand a claim as a claim, an assertion as an assertion and not as an exclamation or a command or a plea, requires a complicated background of common understanding.

Although propositions are sometimes thought to have a timeless existence, speech acts such as assertions can come into being only in the social-historical time of communication. Most obviously, people who make claims to each other must have a common language and a way of communicating with one another—for example, by writing, speaking, signing. However, they must also share a pragmatic understanding of what counts as an assertion and the occasions on which the making of claims and offering of arguments are appropriate. Further, and very importantly, when one makes a claim to someone, one enters into a very complicated ethical relationship with that person, and this requires a common background understanding of the ethical realities of a society and the ethical realities of communication. For example, if a claim is an invitation to a certain kind of response, then making a claim is implicitly recognizing the qualifications of the person who will make the response. To make a claim is to some degree to subordinate oneself to other people and the responses they make. These actions help to constitute an ethical-rhetorical community, a community of people who have the requisite mutual regard for one another. Making a claim in the context of argumentation entails making a judgment about the people with whom to enter into this relationship.

Making a claim to some degree subordinates one to other people because assertions made in the context of an argument are social actions which in principle make one vulnerable to criticism. To call out in an assertive way is always at the same time to call up the possibility of challenges to one's assertion. Remaining silent, singing a song, giving a command, or telling a story do not invite criticism in the same way that an assertion does. Experiencing an argumentative claim as a claim does not come automatically; the experience is possible and likely only in certain cultural settings, where a background familiarity with claiming is common.

It is critical to recognize from the start that not everything that is important can or should be made the material of a public assertion or a claim. Many cultures preserve domains of privacy and secrecy where matters of the highest importance are kept literally sacred in the practice of silence. Some things may not be told without changing one's relation to them. The reason for this is pretty clear. There are some things which are simply not up for public scrutiny and deliberation, some events which are not public matters, some actions whose meanings change dramatically when publicized. There are still ways to "call out" about such matters, to make indirect claims, without using assertions and arguments. Songs and stories and art and dance and many other communicative actions allow us to do this.

Let me also point out right away that many utterances which may look like assertions really aren't. If a commander says to his troops that the war is going well and that success is just around the corner, he may not be making an assertion at all. Rather, he may be saying: don't argue with me about the success of this war (a command or threat, not an assertion), or: keep morale high! let's fight on! (a command, an encouragement, or something else). Whether something that looks like an assertion really is an assertion depends not on the form of the proposition but on the social relations and mutual understandings of the speakers and listeners. It is important to recognize this because some of the critics of argumentation focus on arguments which are not arguments at all but rather exchanges of threats and demands. They rightly object to this kind of communication as being an exercise of power whose purpose is to dominate and cow and silence other people. Part of what a theory of argumentation must do is to explain the relation of this kind of communication to argumentation.

Jürgen Habermas and Validity Claims

Assertions open assertors to criticism in several different ways. I would like to develop this idea in detail by using Jürgen Habermas' concept of validity claims. Habermas believes that speech acts cannot be understood as such unless they are understood to be making implicit validity claims. He emphasizes four different kinds of validity claim—sincerity, truth, rightness, and intelligibility—and stresses their distinctness as a way of distinguishing different kinds of speech acts: expressions, statements, evaluations.[4] I will treat these in order.

The principal aim of expressive speech acts is to bring to light the feelings and beliefs of the speaker or writer. If someone says, "I feel afraid whenever anyone speaks loudly," we ordinarily assume that the speaker is being sincere, honest, truthful. That is, there is an implicit validity claim about sincerity. If we doubt the speaker's sincerity, then communication does not proceed according to ordinary assumptions, and may break down altogether. To redeem a validity claim about sincerity requires examining the life of the speaker, and showing that the feeling or belief that has been expressed is consistent with the speaker's actual life, with other things the speaker has said and done, felt and believed. Thus,

Part Two: Reconstructing Argumentation

the argumentation, the critical thinking, and the inquiry that go on in relation to expressive discourse focus on the speaker or writer.

Of course, not all apparently expressive communication is meant to be sincere, even if it is meant to sound sincere. Sometimes we have good reasons to conceal our thoughts from one another, even in situations in which there is social pressure to reveal them. In such situations, argumentation about sincerity would be a struggle to keep one's insincerity concealed or to unmask a speaker's attempts at concealment. This kind of communication is oriented not toward reaching mutual understanding and agreement but toward using communication and one's interlocutors to achieve other aims. Many of Socrates' conversations with the Sophists, conversations which often sound like philosophical arguments, are really probings into the sincerity of a Sophist, attempts to bring to light the fact that the Sophist does not say what he truly believes.[5]

However, Habermas is interested in communication that is motivated by an honest attempt to reach a shared understanding. Usually, if there is a challenge to an implicit validity claim of this sort, it is because speakers are to some degree deceived about their own feelings and beliefs, or at least are not as reasonable and informed about them as most other people expect them to be. In these cases, Habermas takes the argumentation about validity claims to be "therapeutic" discourse because it is aimed at overcoming self-deception or ignorance of self and clarifying a person's thoughts, beliefs, actions, and utterances. The knowledge which is gained in this kind of argumentation is, for the speaker, self-knowledge.

A second kind of communication has to do with the world of things, and Habermas calls this kind of communication cognitive-instrumental. He thinks of statements like "There are wombats in Australia," and "The car will handle better if the wheels are balanced," as statements belonging to this category. The validity claim implicit in these statements is, most generally, truth, less generally, efficacy. The idea is that every speech act of this kind is what it is by its making an implicit claim about the truth of the assertion. Validity claims of this sort are redeemed in what Habermas calls "theoretical discourse." In theoretical discourse, we argue about the truth of statements.

A third kind of validity claim is a claim about the rightness of certain norms of actions. Habermas takes it to be a feature of rational people that when they act they implicitly claim that their actions are defensible. Speech acts which recommend or evaluate actions in a practical/moral way raise validity claims about the rightness of the norms involved in much the same way. These claims about rightness are redeemed in what Habermas calls "practical discourse."

Habermas takes evaluative statements regarding art, music, and literature to be much like moral/practical statements about actions. They implicitly claim that the standards to which they are appealing are the right ones. The kind of argumentation which sets out to redeem such claims is called by Habermas "aesthetic criticism."

Finally, Habermas recognizes that we also make implicit validity claims about the intelligibility of what we say. He says that this validity claim is redeemed in "explicative discourse." He doesn't make this validity claim a logical feature of a class of speech acts; he emphasizes rather that all utterances make this claim. However, we might imagine that this validity claim is most controversial in poetic communication— and I mean by "poetic" the saying of something new, whether it is a new scientific theory or a new kind of meaning which requires a new kind of sentence. In these cases, the major controversy may focus on the new uses of language involved, and the disputed claim will be the claim that the language is in fact comprehensible to the people to whom it is made.

The most important feature of Habermas' account is that it uncovers a strong logical connection between claims and invitations to criticism. The connection is both strong and specific. One cannot understand a claim as a claim unless one understands the implicit invitation to criticism that makes the claim what it is. And one cannot understand the kind of communication involved in a claim unless one understands the specific kind of challenge being invited.

This is a critical issue for the theory of argumentation. Assertions are calls for response; they contain in themselves very specific invitations for questions and challenges. A claim made in the context of argumentation is not a monological asocial proposition but an event in a dialogue, a call for response. A claim is an assertion which contains an implicit plan of its own criticism. This is worlds away from the idea of a claim as a proposition.

As I mentioned before, our challenges to assertions thematize one validity claim over others because of the kind of speech act we take the assertion to be. However, it is easy to see that all the validity claims Habermas mentions can be implicit in a single utterance. If I say, "Annie Dillard is a better nature writer than Barry Lopez," I could be challenged to redeem any of the validity claims discussed so far. For example, implicit in the statement is an assumption that the two authors really are nature writers. This assumption invites challenges to its truth. Someone could object, say, that Annie Dillard is not a nature writer at all, that I am mistaken. If the truth of the assumption is not contested, the intelligibility of the claim could still be challenged. It could be objected that "nature writer" is so vague that it's impossible to tell what I'm claiming. Or one could ask whether I meant the description in some slightly derogatory sense, akin to the way some people might describe some man as a "nature boy." One could also challenge the appropriateness, the rightness, of the utterance itself—that is, one could take it not as a locution but as an action. For example, if we had been discussing why the United States imprisons a greater percentage of its citizens than any other nation does, and I suddenly said, "Annie Dillard is a better nature writer than Barry Lopez," then the appropriateness of my making the utterance at that time and place could be challenged. The ordinary norm of such conversations is that remarks must be somehow relevant to the subject being discussed, and I could be challenged to show this.

However, the most obvious challenge would be the one that is most specifically invited by the claim itself. That is, ordinarily someone would be more likely to elicit from me the standard to which I am appealing and then to challenge that standard. If we then argued about the standard, we would be engaging in what Habermas calls "aesthetic criticism," arguing about what makes one nature writer better than another.

Again, the important point is that we understand claims as speech acts which are intrinsically calls for response and question, and not as asocial, monological propositions suspended in some timeless intellectual ether. The theory of argumentation I am developing depends strongly on such a conception. However, one should not underestimate the consequences of adopting this view of claims. I believe that one consequence is that one must abandon completely any hope of evaluating arguments by logical standards. The traditional concept of an argument as a series of propositions with certain formal relations to one another makes it possible to evaluate those relations against formal rules. However, claims and questions and responses to questions must be measured in a different way. I take up the problems of evaluating argumentation in Chapters 6 and 7. However, with this discussion of claiming, the theory has already taken a decisive step away from logical models of argumentation. Specifically, not only is a claim not a proposition, but it is not essentially the assertion of a proposition either. Instead, a claim is an action we take, an attempt to influence someone in some way. *A claim is essentially a claim on someone—not a claim that something.* A claim *that something* is an attempt to act on generalized or idealized others.

I should say very clearly here that although I accept Habermas' account of the validity claims implicit in speech acts, I reject his deployment of the distinctions among different kinds of discourse as a mark of rationality. According to Habermas, the distinction between nature and culture and the corresponding distinction between the validity claims of truth and rightness are constitutive of rationality (and of modernity). "Mythical" interpretations of the world fail to make these distinctions. Natural events are often interpreted in the language of kinship relations, or natural accidents are understood to result from violations of cultural codes. In mythical discourse, it is impossible to know whether an implicit claim is being made about truth or about rightness, since mythical discourse does not make such a distinction very neatly.

Making rationality the privileged possession of modern societies will be of little help in reconstructing the theory of argumentation. I think it can fairly easily be seen that Habermas' conception of rationality begs some important questions. For example, imagine a man, a father, in a mythically oriented society. His daughter has been killed by a tree which fell during a windstorm. He asks: why did the tree fall on my daughter? A modern would reply: because the tree was old and the wind was high. The father could reply in return: no, you do not understand my question. Why did the tree fall on *my* daughter? At this point the modern falls silent (or recommends a therapist or a lawyer). Habermas believes that such a question arises out of a failure to distinguish between the natural and social worlds. The father is asking something like: what is the meaning of the tree's having fallen on my daughter? Where is the justice in it? How can it be fair? To ask in this way is to try to understand the natural world in categories that are appropriate only to the social world.

However, in a mythically oriented society there may be answers to such questions. Nature may be comprehensible in terms which are not available to us moderns. A discourse which explains such deaths, or enables the father to make sense of an otherwise senseless event, may be a feature of such a society.

It is very difficult to see why we would want to call a society of this sort "irrational," or to deny that the reasoning which goes on in such discourses is argumentation. Is it "irrational" for a society to develop discourses which enable its members to make sense of their lives in ways that modern societies cannot? There is one way in which it could be argued that such societies are *more* rational than modern societies. For if Habermas is right in his locating of a distinction between mythical and modern societies, then modern society is marked by a *contraction* in the sphere of what is questionable, what can be reasoned about. The father in the example can ask a meaningful question about his daughter's death and expect answers—maybe conflicting answers, but answers that are claims that permit reasoning. A modern father cannot ask such a question meaningfully. If he uttered such a question, it would be taken as an expression of his grief, and not as an invitation to reason seriously with him about his loss. If we measure a society's rationality by whether it has a contracted or an expansive domain for reasoning, then mythically oriented societies may have the edge.

Again, however, what is most important about Habermas' account is not the way he deploys the idea of validity claims for the purposes of a theory of rationality, but the way in which he has identified the intrinsically dialogical and self-critical shape of claims. There are other ways to respond to claims beside the ways provided by the intrinsic features of claims themselves. I will treat some of these other kinds of response when I discuss the actions of the respondent, as well as in my discussion of audience.

Claims as Invitations

Although claims are calls for response, they are not *in the first place* calls for criticism. They are above all invitations to share a particular way of making sense of something. If someone says, "There's deep purple starting to show in the eastern sky," she probably does not imagine that this will become a claim in an argument. (Although, of course, it could. Someone could reply, "But it's only 3 A.M.!" She could respond, "But morning comes early at this latitude," and so on.) Rather, she is probably inviting her companions to share a perception, to recognize the dawn—in general, to take part with her in revealing the world in a specific way. Most assertions are of this sort. If someone says, "I'm tired," he is not usually asking people to question his sincerity. He is entreating them to think of him and to act toward him as one would toward a tired man. If someone says, "Before that development along the river, it never flooded in this town," she is probably asking her neighbors to understand a flood as a result of human actions and social policies and not just as a natural event.

Assertions are typically one of the ways we achieve social solidarity in our understanding of the world. They are means of sharing very specific and explicit understandings, and they usually go unquestioned. They go unquestioned not because they are unquestionable but because of the really quite remarkable deference we pay to each other in daily life. In general, in everyday life the sharing of understandings with others is taken to be an obvious good. If someone says, "Look at how red this apple is!" we look. We look not because we have independent reasons for believing we should look to see how red the apple really is, but because we were invited to share a revealing of something, invited to notice something with someone. Ordinarily, this invitation is enough. We argue when simple invitations and entreaties are not enough—when the conflict between one way of noticing things and another way is too strong and overrides the usual deference we pay to one another.

Cultures differ in respect to how often and how easy it is to make claims on one other, to invite others to share experiences. In *The Winged Serpent* Margaret Astrov points out that Native American cultures typically held a very different attitude toward silence and speech from what most Europeans and Americans hold today. They were nowhere near as energetic in pressing their invitations to share experiences. This aligns well with the Scollons' observations of the differences between Athabaskan- and English-speaking Alaskans. It also aligns well with a cultural practice among some tribal peoples which is rare among Euro-Americans: doing things alone together. Since certain ritual practices are marked by silence—sometimes for extended periods—participants are effectively alone together; they are side by side, but they make no claims on each other's experience, and the experience itself may be taken to be sacred and so appropriately preserved in silence. Such practices do not require and are perhaps incompatible with the complicated social coordination found in societies dominated by routines in which communication is more frequent and specific.

This kind of cultural difference does not call into question argumentation's ability to resolve conflicts fairly. It does point out that the social practice of making claims differs from culture to culture. Specifically, how often claims may be made, who may make claims and to whom and about what—these things differ. However, that there is a claimant's role in argumentative discourse does not seem to carry with it a strong cultural prejudice. It is hard to imagine a society whose members did not make claims on one another at all; I myself cannot easily imagine a *society* without the practice of making claims.

Finally, some claims to which responses are made are implicit in actions, and only later made explicit—sometimes in challenges to the implicit claims. In these instances, whether someone is making a claim, and to whom, and about what, can be very controversial. When Thoreau went to Walden Pond his neighbors interpreted his action as a kind of claim, a communication with an embedded assertion. Thoreau writes at the beginning of *Walden* that the book is a response, an answer to those who have challenged his action with questions. When he says in the second chapter of the book, "I went to the woods because I wished to live deliberately, to front only the essential facts of life, and see if I could not learn what it had to teach, and not, when I came to die, discover that I had not lived," he seems to be offering a reason for a claim that was embedded in his action. The claim, in Habermas' terms, seems to be something like a validity claim that his action was right, appropriate. His neighbors understood this as a claim on them. However, Thoreau and his interlocutors seem to be in strong disagreement over what claim is being made. "Going to the woods" seems to mean one thing to Thoreau, a very different thing to his respondents. There is little doubt that *Walden* is full of arguments. The argument that it is right to go to the woods because there it is possible to live deliberately includes an explicit claim (It is right to go to the woods), an implicit question (Why? What good is there in moving into the woods?) and an explicit reason (because it is possible to live deliberately there). However, it is not clear that Thoreau's real claim is the one his interlocutors are responding to, that his apparent interlocutors are his real interlocutors, or who the audience for this exchange really is. To attempt to clarify these matters is to plunge into the depths of *Walden*.

Other Approaches to Claiming

So far, I have emphasized the social-historical background which is the medium in which claims take shape, partly in order to make clear the ethical character of claim making. However, the ethical realities of making claims go even deeper than this. It is also possible to understand our making claims to one another as a way in which we claim one another (instead of disowning one another), and to understand our claiming one another as a way in which we take responsibility for one another. I have tried to point out something like this fact by speaking of the "deference" we ordinarily pay to one another's acts of claiming. However, it is also possible to understand these actions more expansively as ways in which we take responsibility for ourselves, and so become what we are. The coincidence here of a deeply social concept of reason with a frankly romantic notion of self-creation by way of reason makes it possible to overcome some of the useless dilemmas found in the literature of rhetoric and composition—specifically the polarized and abstract dispute between theorists and teachers who focus on the experiences of individual writers and those who focus on the social and cultural frameworks within which individuals write.[6] In order to develop and clarify my own approach further, I want to call on Emmanuel Levinas' concepts of proximity and responsibility, and to elaborate these ideas in more detail yet, I want to use Stanley Cavell's concepts of claiming and disowning.

It is unusual to call on philosophers of this sort in a discussion of the rhetoric of argumentation. Teachers of composition, as well as teachers of critical thinking and informal logic, usually take argumentation to be the domain of psychologists or logicians. For example, in *Thinking, Reasoning, and Writing*, Elaine P. Maimon and her collaborators call on developmental psychologists and informal logicians to help English professors teach written reasoning. The developmental psychologists provide a framework for objectifying writers in terms of developmental stages which explain why they behave the way they do. According to these psychologists, the development of writers should aim at and culminate in a final stage, in which maturity is reached, or in which one behaves more like an "expert" than a "novice." Such schemes have been criticized from a number of angles, and to my way of thinking the criticisms have been devastating.[7] However, my own indifference toward such theories has a different source: they do not deal with the questions I am concerned with. Primarily, they do not ask what written reasoning is or what good it is for us. They do not seriously ask whether and why it is worth teaching. They do not ask about its ideology, its provenance, or its purpose. They simply take too much for granted. They are not interested in an approach to teaching which might call into question what reasoning is; they simply want to take the reality of mature and expert reasoning for granted as something settled, and reproduce those abilities in students. I don't. In fact, I suspect that the objectification of individuals and reasoning in developmental psychology occludes what is most important about individual and social transformation in education, as well as what is most appealing about reasoning.

Professors of English have also turned to informal logicians for help with the teaching of written reasoning. Most teachers of composition are probably familiar with Stephen Toulmin's model of ordinary argumentation. Some know the work of Michael Scriven, or are familiar with the "fallacies" approach to teaching informal logic, or have read in the philosophical literature on critical thinking. I will discuss some of this material in more detail in later chapters; however, here, too, these people are not asking the questions I believe to be the most important. Informal logicians still concern themselves with propositions and beliefs and premises and their relations, and not with the study of reasoning as a way we assume our identities and give shape to our ethical and social lives. They do not recognize the importance of understanding reasoning as the medium of our self-creation. And they do not see the relation between argumentation and such remote matters. They rarely refer to the fact that reason can be a substitute for force, and so rarely theorize the relationship between argumentation and conflict. Although they often say that one needs to "think critically" in order to evaluate the surrounding society, they do not offer a theory of reason that would give the idea of social criticism philosophical standing.

There are people in English studies who do. I think first of all of Wayne Booth, who relies neither on psychology nor on informal logic to develop his rhetoric of reading and writing. Instead Booth (126–37) calls on philosophical pragmatists like George Herbert Mead and John Dewey, and philosophical rhetoricians such as Richard McKeon, to help him develop his famous notion of the self as a field of selves. I call on Levinas and Cavell here for a different kind of help with a somewhat similar project.

EMMANUEL LEVINAS

Emmanuel Levinas' writing can be understood as a sustained critique of the ideas that ontology has a priority over ethics and that cognition has a priority over the responsibility we take for one another. Such a reversal makes up an important part of my own concept of a pragmatic rhetoric of reason. Like Habermas, Levinas recognizes very clearly that reasoning depends on the ability to question, but he ties explicit questioning to cognition, and to the process whereby ontology takes precedence over ethics. In order to delve deeper, and to hold the idea of research accountable to its own principle, he asks, "Why does research take the form of a question?"(24).

This is a difficult if not impossible inquiry because it attempts to use a question to understand whether or not using questions is the appropriate manner of understanding something. This suggests that Levinas is not really challenging the usefulness of cognition and the form of research to which it is tied, but rather is trying to located its motive. I take this to be identical to one of the aims of a pragmatic rhetoric of reason: to redescribe argumentation and its motives in ways that do not depend on traditional philosophical models of rationality.

In a Heideggerian move, Levinas finds a kind of answer in the act of questioning, in the idea that there are motives for questioning that are audible in questioning itself: "If one is deaf to the petition that sounds in questioning and even under the apparent silence of the thought that questions itself, everything in a question will be oriented to truth and will come from the essence of being. Then one will have to stay with the design of this ontology, even if in certain of its implications, inflexions of forgotten voices resound"(26). These voices are, to use Levinas' terms, the ethical realities of the *saying* which get occluded by the *said*. They have to do with our experience of one another before as well as in the making of claims and the raising of questions. These forgotten voices could be the voices of affection, love, hesitation, aggression, hope, resistance, suffering, joy. In any case, they signal an experience which is intimate and interpersonal and thus best understood in ethical terms; they are the voices of the experience of our ongoing socialization, our being claimed before we are able to understand claims as claims. According to Levinas, every explicit claim and every explicit question arise from this experience.

Levinas takes these voices as evidence that the origins of reason and knowledge lie in our ethical lives with one another: "The 'birth' of being in the questioning where the cognitive subject stands would thus refer to a *before the questioning,* to the anarchy of responsibility." Thus, "Being would not derive from cognition"; rather, being and cognition would both derive from "proximity." "Proximity" in turn is understood as "a certain modality of my responsibility for the other, this response preceding any question, this saying before the said"(26).

Taking on this responsibility for one another is not something we do on the basis of reasoning; it is already something we are, and something that enables reasoning. The background and condition for whatever ontological identity we manage to achieve, for whatever self we succeed in becoming, is our already being a kind of ethical responsiveness to the presence of other people. According to Levinas, the responsibility we take on in this responsiveness cannot be justified. It is not itself motivated in the ordinary sense: "This passion is absolute in that it takes hold without any *a priori.* The consciousness is affected . . . before forming an image of what is coming to it, affected in spite of itself." This "ethical" origin of reason is not itself an activity of reason. It is, as I have been saying, an experience of being claimed, and of responding to that being claimed, rather than an experience of hearing claims themselves.

This being affected "in spite of itself," this proximity of others, is, Levinas believes, something which troubles us. It is, to use his words, as if we were "persecuted" from the very beginning, forced to take responsibility for something we had no part in setting up. This attitude carries over into Levinas' social-ethical interpretation of communication. To distinguish the cognitive/ontological interpretation of communication, which focuses on a relatively context-free message, from the ethical interpretation of communication, Levinas draws a line between the "saying" and the "said." The said might be, for example, a proposition, but the saying is understood as a mode of responsibility, a modification of the proximity that comes before all action. Saying is responding to a neighbor (47). It is to begin to take responsibility for the others with whom one is entangled, and whose nearness one feels as a kind of persecution. Saying begins the task of taking responsibility.

Because he conceives of proximity as a kind of persecution, Levinas understands saying as a kind of "exposure" to the other. He emphasizes the passivity of saying by describing it as a self-sacrifice to the other. Saying, as a disclosure of one's being-in-the-world, is self-disclosure—a way of making oneself intelligible. This interpretation of laying oneself open before someone else can also be understood as an interpretive dislodging of the subject from its sphere of privilege and privacy. For in saying, one gives up one's established self-identity, and in the act of sacrifice becomes "otherwise than being." In saying, one finds an ethical existing which cannot be captured in traditional conceptions of subjectivity. The existing that is "otherwise than being" is an existing that takes place only in ethical activity, in the sociality of saying.

There are some obvious parallels here between my attempt to understand the phenomenon of claiming in a postphilosphical way and Levinas' attempt to describe the preontological, ethical character of "saying." We both emphasize the senses in which we are already claimed by one another before anything is said, and so we reject the idea of a reified subject forming intentions in a private language and a private domain. We both believe that what is said, in my case, what is claimed, is best understood as a feature of an action—for Levinas, saying, for me, claiming. And we both emphasize the senses in which saying is an act that makes one vulnerable to others, instead of emphasizing the senses in which saying and claiming might be understood as just more acts of aggression or persecution. Levinas also begins to develop a concept of the self that does not depend on reifying ontological notions—subjective or objective—but instead relies on concepts of ethical realities which are understood to be generative of selfhood, and in this project, too, we are in agreement. Such ideas take us worlds beyond the developmental schemes and logical models on which teachers of writing have become so dependent. They also allow us to begin to explore reason and argumentation without having to rely on notions of *mind* or of the *presence* of an ideal signified.

However, there are some important differences here as well. The most significant difference concerns Levinas' basic mood, expressed in metaphors of suffering and pain. He uses the language of persecution to describe our sociality, and he uses the language of pain to describe saying. In addition to "exposure," he speaks of stripping, denuding, wounding, and death (48ff.). I myself believe that Levinas' moods and metaphors are dominated by suffering and pain in a way that is not called for simply by the phenomena themselves. I say this with some trepidation, knowing that Levinas' actual life has given us moods and metaphors that make a strong claim on our attention. Given Levinas' life, and given the responsibility he takes on in the dedication to *Otherwise than Being or*

Beyond Essence,[8] I would not venture to criticize his writing. However, his moods and his vocabulary do not make an absolute claim.

To take what appears at first to be an opposite case, I believe the same is true of Heidegger. Heidegger's heavy moods and his language of guilt and dread and death are perhaps appropriate for him, and follow from a serious responsiveness to early-twentieth-century European history. However, different times and people must be responsive to different events. I find it interesting that the claim of Pascal is very great on both Heidegger and Levinas, and yet Pascal exposes our foibles with a much lighter wit, and no less deeply.

Since I grew up in southern California in the 1950s and 1960s in an atmosphere of historically extraordinary personal freedom and what appeared to be limitless horizons—the real achievements, I realize, of much historical suffering—my own moods are very different. There is always the painful side of saying, and of socialization. However, those of us for whom the memory of suffering is not an overriding obligation need not continue to theorize on the basis of such suffering.

In fact, one can make an argument that we have in part an opposite obligation. It took tremendous historical suffering and labor to create the environment many of us enjoyed as children and grew to take responsibility for as adults. We may have an obligation, then, to theorize also on the basis of this historical accomplishment, as a way of giving thanks, and taking advantage of our freedom to think something new.

For there are joys of socialization too. Claims are not only self-exposures; they are also motivated by delights, and a desire to share them. Some claims may be exhibitionistic in a pleasant way; others may be almost unself-conscious, sheerly to disclose the world in some way, without the sound of a forgotten voice urging us not to. And the proximity of others can be experienced not only as a persecution, but as a kind of human shelter, a discovery of a communal habitation, in which one's self-disclosures take on many different meanings, few of them dangerous or frightening. The loss of private subjectivity and the launching off into the unprotected explicitness of saying can, in the right circumstances, be experienced as liberation, as a movement toward both a better self and a better modality of selfhood.

I want to explore these possibilities further by taking up some of the ideas of Stanley Cavell, who lets himself be influenced by Heidegger and European philosophy, but who appropriates this thought in an American context, by way of Emerson and Thoreau and Hollywood. However, I want to conclude this discussion of Levinas with an account of and response to his story about the intellectual redemption of this suffering by the "rationality of peace." I want to do this in order to tie this phenomenologically inclined account of claiming to the discussion of how arguments can still be evaluated and judged, a discussion I offer later in the book. Levinas' account is similar in important ways to Chaim Perelman's and my own, for it gives a central place to the idea of justice in reasoning.[9] In fact, it paves the way for an understanding of arguments as primarily justice-preserving rather than primarily truth-preserving. As a cognitive term, "truth" must be derived from an ethical term, "justice." Again, such an approach will take us worlds away from the logic- and truth-based theories with which most teachers of writing and critical thinking are familiar. However, if my account of our present philosophical and cultural situation is accurate, such theories are no longer persuasive anyway. A rhetoric of reason which conceives of reason as grounded in ethical realities rather than logical ones may prove much more helpful in guiding our actions.

According to Levinas, we are from the beginning in a kind of struggle with one another. We are in a situation and in possession of ways of being that we have not created, that are unmotivated and unjustified. We have already been claimed and have claimed others in ways that have never been spoken. We have been active in an ethical domain without the aid of ethical understanding.

The project of discourse, of saying, is to take responsibility for this situation, which means taking responsibility both for oneself and for those others who are undifferentiated from oneself in the sphere of proximity. The aim of taking responsibility is to redeem this suffering and wounding, to achieve justice in sorting out the ways in which we affect (and effect) one another. The idea of reason is the idea of justice and peace as the goal of discourse: "Responsibility for the others or communication is the adventure that bears all the discourse of science and philosophy. Thus this responsibility would be the very rationality of reason or its universality, a rationality of peace" (160). The motivation for reasoning is a desire for justice and peace, relief from persecution and suffering. In addition, it is a desire for a modality of selfhood which is neither private, enclosed subjectivity nor expulsion from privacy into a domain of social objectification. Levinas calls this modality of selfhood "otherwise than being," and its proper medium is the rationality of peace.

The refusal to reason is motivated by the counterconcept to responsibility: indifference (166). Indifference is a kind of skepticism, a refusal to take up the project of a rationality of peace, a disclaiming of our responsibility for one another. Levinas links this indifference with a failure to experience the transcendence of the other, the irreducibility of the other's selfhood to concepts or narratives. By contrast, the experience of the transcendence of the other is part of the overcoming of indifference and part of the beginning of reasoning: "The difference in proximity between the one and the other, between me and a neighbor, turns into non-indifference, precisely into my responsibility. Non-indifference, humanity, the one-for-the-other is the very signifyingness of signification, the intelligibility of the intelligible, and thus reason "(166). Signification is not understood in the metaphysical/epistemological way that deconstruction explores and undoes. Instead, this one-for-the-other is an essentially ethical phenomenon. It requires an overcoming of resentment, an ur-compassion for the other, even forgiveness: "The non-indifference of responsibility . . . is the source of all compassion. It is responsibility for the very outrage that the other, who qua other excludes me, inflicts on me, for the persecution with which, before any intention, he persecutes me" (166).

To the degree that Levinas is right, educators whose charge is to teach reasoning face an immense challenge. If the ability to reason rests on an assumption of ethical responsibility which requires compassion and forgiveness, then we confront students who face not simply "cognitive" difficulties but ethical ones. Moral imagination, the ability to recognize the otherness of the other, and "compassion," a willingness to take responsibility for the other, lie at the heart of the project of reason. Such imagination and responsibility may be difficult indeed. However, if Levinas is right, the cultivation of this imagination and responsibility is not only the road to peace and justice, and the way to a new self and a new modality of selfhood; it is also the road of reason. There are no guarantees that this process is an easy one, or that it can undo the sufferings of the past. On the contrary, it is perhaps the most difficult of human tasks, and may in some instances require a memory of and sensitivity to suffering that is extraordinary. It also calls for an end to resentment—not an easy thing to ask of other people.

No wonder that people form communities of fellow sufferers to begin the process of reasoning outward. Such associations are in many instances the only practical hope for people whose identities are dominated by the resentment of cruel and violent experiences of proximity. They form a kind of Tocquevillean civic group which allows the survivor of pain to escape isolation, reason with certain others, and so begin a process of education that will allow the individual to reason in a greater variety of contexts. The danger of such communities is that they can perpetuate themselves in a separatist withdrawal that institutionalizes their resentments. If Levinas is right about the desirability of a modality of selfhood that is "otherwise than being," then one would think that the goal of every rhetorical community would *to some degree* and *in some respects* be its own obsolescence, expressed in its constant self-transformation, or its launching of its members on to new communities.

For teachers, these are very practical problems. Every day we face people who want to be more than they are, people who are in my experience surprisingly willing to take responsibility for one another. There is not in any educational institution I know of the opportunity to usher these students through the different communities that would allow them to maximize their abilities to reason. However, if we take this greatest development of their individual abilities as a goal, then we do generate the idea of a community of responsibility in which these abilities can develop without needless obstructions. The way to this goal, the dangers that must be risked and the compromises that must be made with other communities in order to bring individual students closer to this goal, are a matter that is different for each individual, each group of students, each teacher, each institution. However, the goal itself, the achievement of a rationality of peace, seems to me a more than worthy one.

Levinas' rationality of peace is the overcoming of the pain and injustice of proximity and saying, a kind of redemption of suffering. In some ways, the idea seems to depend on the "pain and suffering" concept of claiming and being claimed. However, there are other ways in which this is not so. A rationality of peace is also the goal of anyone who sees discourse as a field of conflicts which need to be resolved in a just way, without violence. Reason and argumentation are ways to resolve these conflicts, which needn't always be thought of as extraordinarily painful. Many of our conflicts with one another are enjoyable. We enter into some of them for the sheer exhilaration of the possibility of transforming ourselves by holding ourselves accountable to one another. Others we are forced into by social exigencies. Argumentation is the peaceful settling of these discursive conflicts. Where there is no conflict of any kind, there is no reason. I intend to develop this idea of a rationality of peace further in the chapter on argument and conflict. Here, I want simply to mark out the lines of agreement and difference between Levinas and me, in order to develop and clarify my own approach, and to differentiate it further from the standard treatment.

STANLEY CAVELL

Stanley Cavell has strong reservations about argumentation, and has devoted much of his recent writing to "reading" rather than argumentation; however, he also has a concept of claiming that is relevant to this discussion. It is worth comparing Levinas and Cavell on this issue, and to use this comparison to elaborate further the nature of claims in arguments.

Again, discussions of reasoning and argumentation in logic, in psychology, and in rhetoric and composition give almost no consideration to the nature of claims and claiming. They simply take for granted a claim's cognitive status as a proposition. This widespread obliviousness to the nature of claiming is really remarkable given the agreement one finds in some philosophical treatments of reasoning which focus exactly on the event of claiming. In the case of the current discussion, it is remarkable how much agreement there is between Levinas and Cavell, and how radically at odds their thinking is with dominant notions of claims in arguments.

A good place to begin with Cavell is with his notion of knowledge as a kind of acknowledgment: "I do not propose the idea of acknowledging as an alternative to knowing but rather as an interpretation of it" (*Quest* 8). Cavell plays with the different meanings and senses of "acknowledgment"; however, his uses of the word usually call on the ideas of recognition and responsibility. A counterconcept in Cavell's lexicon is "disowning." Knowledge as acknowledgment is a mode of responsibility for oneself and an owning up to and recognition of one's connections with others. Knowledge is thus a practical term, an ethical one. Just as, for Levinas, it is responsibility that "bears all the discourse of science and philosophy, [and is] the very rationality of reason," so for Cavell knowledge is an owning up to one's life and one's relationships.

Cavell takes the romance of knowledge to be the opposite of the tragedy that skepticism plays out. The tragedy of skepticism is set in motion by a failure to acknowledge, by a refusal of responsibility. Cavell's best treatments of this idea are in his Shakespeare criticism, where he traces the consequences of Lear's disowning of Cordelia and Leontes' disowning of Hermione and their son. Cavell's provocative readings of *King Lear* and *The Winter's Tale* show how Lear's madness and Leontes' radical and destructive suspiciousness are also epistemological disorders, instances of skepticism which follow from a failure to acknowledge one's child, or one's wife, as one's own, and so a failure to acknowledge oneself, as father, or husband.

When Cavell says that acknowledgment is an interpretation of knowledge, he means that reasoning permits of being understood in ethical terms. Skepticism is an actual practical response to our condition, and not simply a doctrine. We are all skeptics to some degree, playing out a lack of responsibility and acknowledgment in our lives. We slip into skepticism on an everyday basis: "Thoreau calls this everyday condition quiet desperation; Emerson says silent melancholy; Coleridge and

Wordsworth are apt to say despondency or dejection; Heidegger speaks of it as our bedimmed averageness; Wittgenstein as our bewitchment" (*Quest* 9). As we have seen, Levinas calls it indifference. Skepticism in this sense is a part of our condition.

In terms of argumentation, skepticism is a refusal to argue, to experience claims as claims, a refusal to recognize that reason and knowledge are dependent on and are peaceful and hopeful modifications of the ways we are already implicated in one another's lives. To recognize these claims, and to take responsibility for them in arguments, is to be responsive to and responsible for those others who have already claimed us (Levinas' "persecution"), as well as to take responsibility for ourselves.

For Cavell and for Levinas, we take responsibility for others and for ourselves at the same moment as the same act. For Levinas, we move into a new mode of selfhood when we assume responsibility for others, a mode that is otherwise than being. For Cavell, acknowledging others is the only path to self-acknowledgment. In Cavell's reading of *The Winter's Tale*, Leontes cannot acknowledge himself (as the father he is) unless he acknowledges his son (as his son). In order to take responsibility for ourselves, we must acknowledge the claims others have made on us.

In argumentation, understood pragmatically and rhetorically, we do this by making claims explicit, and hearing them as questionable. Hearing them as questionable gives us the option of affirming or denying them. Affirming or denying them on the basis of reasons gives us a way of taking responsibility for our affirmations and denials. As I will show later, what counts as a reason for us will itself be an acknowledgment of our solidarity with or alienation from people who count or discount our reasons as acceptable. Thus, letting something count as a reason is a way of acknowledging or disowning our connection to other people, too.

It's worth staying with the idea of skepticism a while because it may be one way to understand the resistance to argumentation among teachers of writing, many of whom are trained in skeptical versions of literary theory and philosophy. There is a kind of truth to skepticism, says Cavell: "It names our wish (and the possibility of our wishing) to strip ourselves of the responsibility we have in meaning (or in failing to mean) one thing, or one way, rather than another" (*Quest* 135). Cavell makes this remark in the context of a discussion of the philosophical undecidability of the meaning of any utterance. Skepticism's response to the experience of this undecidability is to abandon the project of warranting knowledge and instead to provide exposés of the way this epistemological conundrum permeates communication. This approach makes reasoning and argumentation, the attempt to justify claiming one thing rather than another, seem to be indefensible.

However, Cavell believes that this fact of undecidability is just the fact of our condition, and is the starting point to which both philosophical skepticism and the claim of reason are a response. "Skepticism is our philosophical access to the human wish to deny the conditions of humanity" (*Quest* 138). Skepticism holds human beings to a superhuman standard. There is a kind of nobility in this wish, and it takes many forms. Cavell points out that there is a streak of skepticism in Christianity's nihilistic wish to overcome the human condition, and in Nietzsche's similar longing for an *Übermensch*. In fact, throughout Cavell's writings there is a kind of admiration of skepticism for the strength of its longing. However, Cavell's usual judgment is that it is destructive of human possibilities: "Skepticism is neither true nor false but a standing human threat to the human" (*Conditions* 24). Usually, he characterizes it as a refusal to acknowledge, a refusal of birth, of the human, an urge not to start the world. Subjectivism as a form of skepticism is, as in Levinas, a form of this refusal, a retreat to the safety of an enclosed sphere, a denial of the responsibility of reason.

Like Levinas, Cavell recognizes that acknowledgment can be threatening. To leave the shelter of an imagined subjectivity and launch forth into responsibility for making and hearing claims as a way of being oneself is a kind of danger: "Against annihilation, ceasing to exist as the one I am, there is no safeguard . . . its safeguard is the recognition by and of others . . . If this recognition of and by others strikes you as threatening your life, you will be perplexed. [What is important is] to acknowledge your unauthorized life as it is, taking an interest in it. Some will, I think, wish to say that there is no way one's life is; to me this betokens a refusal to try putting it into (provisional) words (a refusal to struggle for its authorship)" (*Quest* 144). Here is the Levinasian fear of exposure and death, and the realization that one's life is in the hands of others. Cavell's idea of acknowledging one's "unauthorized" life is like Levinas' "unjustified" taking on of responsibility. The question is whether one will *say* or not, whether one will make claims and hear them, or retreat into skepticism.

Acknowledging makes several demands of us. First, it makes the romantic demand that we be "willing to continue to be born, to be natal, hence mortal" (*Quest* 143). Acknowledging means entertaining the idea that one's self is not a settled matter, not something one has, like a thing. Again, Levinas describes this modality of selfhood as "otherwise than being." Cavell prefers to speak of siding with one's next or further self in a continuous process of dying and being born.

Second, acknowledging demands of us a concept of the possibility of education and continuous education. An educator plays the role of the philosophical friend, "the figure, let us say, whose conviction of one's moral intelligibility draws one to discover it, to find words and deeds in which to express it, in which to enter the conversation of justice" (*Conditions* 32). This figure, whom Cavell finds in the philosophical friend, and in the marriage partner in Hollywood comedies of remarriage, is the one who makes a bridge for us to our next self, who claims us, makes claims on us, in the sense of calling us forth into new ways of becoming morally intelligible to ourselves.

Do we have the courage and imagination to think of the teaching of written reasoning in this light? In Chapter 4 I will argue that the teaching of written reasoning does ask students to become different from what they have been, to undergo transformation. If Cavell is right, this is not an accidental effect of making claims; it is the very heart of education. Each of us provides a stage for a number of explicitly conflicting voices, as well as for a number of "forgotten" voices, the "background" of the previous chapter. In argumentation, the explicit voices speak in the roles of claimant, respondent, and audience. In making warranted claims, we move out in one direction rather than another, become a disclosure of one way rather than another way. As Cavell puts it: "Becoming intelligible to oneself may accordingly present itself as discovering which among the voices contending to express your nature are ones for you to own here, now" (*Conditions* xxxvi). To own some of these voices and not others is to become intelligible as one kind of self rather than another. Education is learning to hear the claims of these voices and to reason about these claims as a process of being called to one's next self.

Cavell recognizes that there is a serious danger in thinking of education this way. He describes it as the urge to "impose the maximization of one's private conception of good on all others, regardless of their talents or tastes or visions of the good" (*Conditions* 46). Here is the totalizing reified universality of the fascist classroom. I suppose that for some people it is the rejection of this picture of education that leads to skepticism and to the pedagogy of skepticism.

Cavell himself offers two ways to avoid this danger, and both of them have for me a direct relevance to the teaching of written reasoning. First, he points out the importance of "the exemplar," the "friend" who calls one to one's next self. This exemplar of one's own best possibilities illuminates one's own beyond. The friend is the bridge to one's next self. Finding this friend is always an individual matter because he or she calls one to one's own better self. Cavell emphasizes the distinction between a "specimen" and an "exemplar":

> The biological association of "specimens" suggests that the
> grounds for identifying them (hence for assessing their value) are

specifiable independently of the instance in view, of its effect on you; its value depends upon this independence; specimens are samples, as of a class, genus, or whole; one either is or is not a specimen. Whereas the acceptance of an exemplar, as access to another realm (call it the realm of culture; Nietzsche says, echoing a favorite image of Emerson's, that it generates "a new circle of duties"), is not grounded in the relation between the instance and a class of instances it stands for but in the relation between the instance and the individual other—for example, myself—for whom it does the standing, for whom it is a sign, upon whom I delegate something.[10]

This exemplar is figured, according to Cavell, in Aristotle's idea of the friend as "another myself," and in Nietzsche's and Emerson's notion of the friend as being also one's enemy in the sense of an enemy of one's present attainments.

In these senses, the exemplar/friend/enemy is the interlocutor in argumentation, the one who responds to my claims, who challenges them, and leads me to give reasons. I do not address my claims to just anyone, and I do not take just anyone's challenges and responses as significant or worthy of reply. The interlocutor befriends me by fielding my claims with respect, becomes my friend/enemy by challenging my claims, and functions as my exemplar by calling me to give the reasons for my claim. As we will see, giving reasons is an act in which I move into one form of life or another.

Such a conception of the exemplary interlocutor, who is known by his or her effects on some particular individual, is a challenge to the blind totalizing of making a specimen of the exemplar, and ignoring the good of individual students. Since the idea of an exemplar is a dynamic and changing one (the exemplar is an exemplar only insofar as it is in a particular relationship to an individual), it cannot be captured once and for all in some curricular or educational program.

Another protection against such blindness is the idea of what Nietzsche calls a "mighty community," which Cavell understands as a community which promotes the kind of friendship and exemplifying we have been discussing here. What marks this community is its own being in constant transformation in its movement toward its unattained perfection. Cavell writes, "Obviously it is not a present but an eventual community, so everything depends on how it is to be reached" (*Conditions* 53). This places any educational process itself into the same stream of transformation that transforms individuals.

Obviously, such a community cannot reach a state of being once and

Part Two: Reconstructing Argumentation

for all. The question is not even, as Cavell puts it, "how it is to be reached," but instead how it does its reaching. I will try to show that this "mighty community" can be understood to be a community of argumentation,[11] in which we make claims on and to one another (we refuse skepticism), challenge one another's claims (we befriend one another), and discover and give reasons (and so project forms of selfhood and community).

Such a conception of argumentation and its teaching lies some distance from the concerns of the developmental psychologists and informal logicians who just now have the attention of teachers of writing. I can't see any good reason for this. In Chapter 1 I developed the idea of rhetoric as a postphilosophical understanding of discourse that breaks with foundationalism and correspondence theories of truth by recognizing audiences as the measures of arguments and conceiving of reason as having essentially ethical motivations. Levinas and Cavell are clearly participants in the project of thinking through this concept of rhetoric in a way that developmental psychology and informal logic are not. If teachers of writing in higher education are to teach written reasoning seriously, they may want to take the idea of rhetoric more seriously as a means of understanding reasoning itself.

The Claimant and Reasons

Not only do claimants make claims, they also offer reasons for the claims they make. I will examine the idea of a reason more carefully in the chapters on audience, but since it is the claimant who offers reasons, I want to introduce a few of the main ideas here.

A claim itself is not an argument; a claim with a reason for making the claim is. But what is the reason for a reason? A reason is an answer to a question. If a claim were not questioned or challenged in some way, there would be no need to offer a reason to support it. Again, most assertions just stand without needing to be held up by reasons. They do not happen as part of the unfolding of an argument. They develop into arguments only when they are questioned. In this respect, argument is a form of conflict and conflict resolution, and the conflict it enables is a mutual conflict. Although I will discuss the nature of this conflict in detail in a later chapter, it is important to catch a glimpse of it here.

Mere assertions which do not develop into arguments are also instances of conflict. They are attempts by someone to persuade someone else to share an experience, a way of seeing, a way of revealing things. I take it for granted that issuing an invitation to share an experience is usually an attempt to make it more likely that the other person will indeed share the experience. We do not issue invitations out of indifference to the actions of other people; we issue invitations in the hope that we will influence the people to whom we issue them. (Of course, sometimes our apparent invitation is not our real one.) In this sense, an invitation, an assertion, is already a kind of persuasion. There are proper and effective ways to issue such invitations (there is a *rhetoric* of invitation), and there are improper and ineffective ways. And in any persuasion, there is already a kind of conflict: a conflict between things as they are and things as the claimant wishes them to be. Further, this conflict is already social. A claimant wants other people to experience things differently from the way they ordinarily would. Thus, there is a conflict between the claimant's purposes and the ordinary purposes of other people.

However, this conflict is not mutual if the assertion does not develop into an argument. If the audience for the assertion just defers to the claimant, and agrees to share the experience, then the conflict is resolved through this deference to the aims of the claimant. There are many different kinds of deference one can pay to assertions, and many different kinds of only apparent deference. One can field a claim with relative indifference, or with different degrees of unexpressed resistance. Silence may not be simple deference. For example, one could argue with oneself about someone else's claim without actually responding expressly to the claimant. However, this would be a case of unexpressed mutual conflict, of only apparent deference. Of course, silence may also be a mode of resistance.

When a conflict becomes mutual, when someone who fields a claim questions the claim, then a respondent emerges, and the possibility of reasoning arises. When the claimant makes a response to the respondent by offering a reason for the claim, an argument appears. These are the minimal conditions for there being an argument. There must be a claim, there must be some challenge to that claim, and there must be a response to the challenge in the form of a reason for the claim, a reason offered to settle the conflict. In written argumentation, the challenge is often implicit, but it can usually be made explicit, although this will be a matter of interpretation. This much, then, is an argument; it contains the essential features of a conflict and an attempt at resolving it by way of reasoning. Whether a reason counts as a reason, and whether it is convincing or not, are dependent on the judgment of an audience, and thus—and I am following Perelman here—the worth of an argument is a function of the quality of the audience which would assent to it, the quality of the form of life and selfhood to which following the argument would lead. The demand for a warrant, a rule which permits one to move from reason to claim, is not an essential feature of an argument, although in rhetorical situations in which the level of conflict is high, a demand for a warrant and perhaps for backing is very likely.[12] I am tempted to say here that the enthymeme is in itself a complete argument, and that other schemes of argumentation are just elaborations on the enthymeme. However, this is the case only if we understand the enthymeme not as an abbreviation of anything, but as something complete in itself. The explicit claim/implicit question/explicit reason complex is a complete argument. It is not a shortened syllogism. It is missing no parts. It is not less rational because it is less elaborate.

So an argument from particular to particular is still an argument because it involves an explicit claim, an implicit challenge, and an explicit reason for making the claim—even if it won't convince many audiences. It functions as an argument as long as someone accepts it as an argument. For Thoreau, the wish to live deliberately is a sufficient reason for going to the woods. The strength of this argument does not depend on a warrant which states that whoever wishes to live deliberately should go to the woods; it depends rather on how desirable it is to be "Thoreau." *Walden* is an elaboration of the form of life that results when one allows oneself to be convinced by the argument, an elaboration of what it means to be "Thoreau."

To recognize a reason as a reason, to be convinced by it, is to project oneself into a way of life. This is why the offering of reasons always immediately generates the concept of an audience which would be persuaded by such reasons. Although the claimant offers the reasons in an argument, only the audience bears final responsibility for their being convincing or not, for the degree to which they count as good reasons. Thus, I will continue the discussion of reasons when I treat the role of the audience and the evaluation of arguments.

Summary

In Chapter 1, I described the dissolution of the traditional concepts of reason and argument, and sketched the background and the motivations for reconstructing the theory of argumentation as a pragmatic rhetoric of reason. At the beginning of this chapter, I sketched the outlines of such a rhetorical theory, one which would meet the real social and individual needs a theory of reasoning must meet. The theory depends on a concept of argument as internally dialogical, and thus elaborates a theory of reason as a communicative activity.

In this chapter, I have also developed a theory of claiming as a replacement for the traditional theory of the proposition. To understand claims, one need not resort to a theory of propositions which would isolate the claim from the act of claiming, the said from the saying, the signified from communication. Instead, one can understand claims as being intrinsically linked to actions and their motives—in fact, as being themselves speech actions. In turn, these speech actions are always embedded in ethical, social, and historical contexts which allow them to show up as claims.

Further, claims are themselves implicit calls for response and criticism, as Habermas has shown in some detail. Not only are they embedded in and motivated by ethical, social, political, and historical backgrounds and interests, they are also essentially linked to questions, to challenges. Insofar as their being questionable is not understood, they fail to be claims. The traditional theory of propositions fails to grasp these rhetorical conditions for the advent of claims. Logical theories presuppose (to put it in logical terms) both the background conditions for the intelligibility of argumentative propositions, and the interlocutors and audience which both grasp the propositions as claims and recognize their argumentative status. However, logical theories presuppose these things "unconsciously," without recognizing the way an explicit acknowledgment of them would radically transform the theory of argumentation.

Because logical theories misinterpret claims as propositions, they fail to situate the theory of argumentation in the appropriate ethical and social and philosophical contexts. Instead, they imagine that logical rules have a status that is independent of any of these contexts, a kind of necessary existence in a domain that is free from ethical, social, and historical uncertainty. I have argued here that such an approach has been vitiated by a broad consensus in contemporary philosophy, as well as by people's ordinary intuitions about arguing.

However, I have also claimed that such a situation offers an opportunity to think reason and argument anew, to turn toward a rhetoric rather than a traditional logic of reason. I have claimed that a rhetorical approach can explain the successes of reasoning and argument without occluding the ethical, social, and deep human dimensions of reason. I have discussed, clarified, and developed (and criticized) Emmanuel Levinas' attempts to disclose the ethical dimensions of reasoning in his concentration on the saying rather than the said, in his accounts of responsibility and indifference, and in his hope for a rationality of peace. I have tried to deepen and extend this approach to claiming by looking closely at Stanley Cavell's claim that acknowledgment, disowning, friendship, and skepticism are critical terms for any theory of reason.

The claims I am making about reason and argument are in one sense "philosophical" ones, and are prompted in large part by the contemporary situation of philosophy. However, genuine philosophical problems, and genuine responses to them, are not the property of philosophers alone. All disciplines and professions have their philosophical dimensions. Every claim to reason carries philosophical understandings along with it. Although much of the orientation of a rhetoric of reason is necessarily philosophical, the aims of this book are much more specific and pragmatic than the aims of traditional philosophy.

Most generally, as I have said, a rhetoric of reason attempts to fulfill specific human needs: the need to reconcile conflicts in a peaceful way, the need to give meaning to social criticism, the need to explain the aims of higher education as something more than the realizing of parochial interests. In addition, a rhetoric of reason must explain reason's claim to offer a better life for individuals; it must account for rationality's power to transform. Levinas' rationality of peace is an obvious attempt to explain the conciliatory powers of reason and the universality of the social interests for which it speaks. His conception of the ways in which "saying" throws us into new modalities of selfhood is a likewise obvious effort to reveal the transformative powers of reason. Levinas and Cavell both emphasize the ethical and transformational character of reasoning. Cavell also elaborates in some detail a theory of education which follows from an ethical-transformational concept of reason, and in fact has as its goal the process of the transformation of knowledge in a community of friendship.

More specifically, I am concerned with the philosophical dimensions of the teaching of written reasoning. Courses in composition are a more central and more influential part of the curriculum in North American colleges and universities than philosophy courses. What students come to believe about reasoning, they often come to believe in these courses. The mindfulness with which they practice reasoning is often acquired (or not acquired) in these courses. If they experience their own reasoning as an attempt to measure up to a timeless logical standard whose rules are formal and universal and are the special possession of their teachers, they will fail to understand the real powers and limitations of reason. They will have no experience of the real claim of reason on their lives and in their society.

I am strongly convinced that such concerns are not remote matters. If my sketch of a rhetoric of reason indicates anything at all so far, it indicates that an experience of reasoning is an experience of the ethical and social bonds which hold people together in communities. It is also an experience of a form of selfhood that enables personal transformation. Where the experiences of friendship and community fail, reason fails.

Where reason fails, individuals cannot find paths to meaningful change. We don't have to look far to discover instances of what happens when people find it impossible or undesirable to reason with each other or with themselves.

The teaching of written reasoning in rhetoric and composition courses has been held hostage by logic and psychology, whose conceptions of reason are inadequate not only because they are absolute, but also because they fail to inspire a love of and delight in the experience of reason. I am doing everything I can here to set the captive free, to say a rhetoric of reason that will have some attractions for those of us whose regard for our students runs deeper than our theories know.

3 QUESTIONING

I insist on the difference [between discussion and polemics] as something essential: a whole morality is at stake, the morality that concerns the search for truth and the relation to the other. In the serious play of questions and answers, in the work of reciprocal elucidation, the rights of each person are in some sense immanent in the discussion. They depend only on the dialogue situation. The person asking the questions is merely exercising the right that has been given to him: to remain unconvinced, to perceive a contradiction, to require more information . . . As for the person answering the questions, he too exercises a right that does not go beyond the discussion itself; by the logic of his own discourse he is tied to the questioning of the other.
—Michel Foucault, "Polemics, Politics, and Problematizations"

Whose Question?

In the preceding chapter, I showed in some detail how questioning was an essential feature of claiming. Since the questioner's role in argumentation is usually suppressed in logic-based theories of reasoning, a theory of questioning has not traditionally played a role in accounts of argumentation. Some logicians have recently turned their attention toward dialogue games, and this attention has included a focus on the questions that are asked in such games. Yet rarely is questioning understood as an essential part of an argument itself. Rather, the "rational discussions" of question-and-answer form that interest logicians are understood in terms of their *containing* arguments. Their main problems are knowing how to extract genuine arguments from such discussions and then how to analyze them in accordance with logical standards. My own approach is exactly the opposite of the "dialogue games" approach. My approach to argumentation conceives of an argument as containing or, better, *being* a specific kind of "rational discussion." This discussion takes place between a claimant and a respondent/questioner in the presence of an audience.

Questioning has also become a central theme for Michel Meyer's philosophy of "problematology." Problematology is a complicated and systematic approach to issues of knowledge, reason, and argumentation which assigns a very important place to the question. Meyer (4) believes that the history of philosophy from Plato on is a forgetting of the fact that a proposition is an answer to a question. According to Meyer, propositions are responses to situations and the questions that arise from them. Thus propositions, as answers, are intelligible only in a pragmatic, "problematological" context. Drawing on work of Gunther Grewendorf, J. L. Driver tries to sketch this context. She claims that answers are intelligible only in terms of: (1) the knowledge situation of the questioner; (2) the questioner's purposes; and (3) the usefulness of the answer relative to these purposes (Meyer 245–46). Obviously, this is a serious attempt to understand reason dialogically and contextually. I accept wholeheartedly the idea of this context as it applies to answers, that is, to reasons given in response to a question that follows a claim.

However, Meyer and his followers draw more extensive conclusions from this. Thinking of all propositions as answers, Meyer ends up implying that making a claim is tantamount to asking someone else to ask the question to which the claim is an answer (138–39). Once propositions are understood as answers instead of claims, the logic of Meyer's move is inevitable. The question would always come first, and claims would always come second, as answers.

The problem with Meyer's move is that it ignores the phenomenon of the claim and of claiming, which is, as we have seen, in very important respects different from that of questions and questioning. I agree with Meyer—and this is a significant agreement—that some propositions are always the answers to questions. For example, reasons offered in an argument are always answers. I agree, too, that *sometimes* making a claim is an attempt to get a respondent to ask the question to which the claim is an answer. However, a claim is not *necessarily* best understood as an answer to a question. It is certainly not best understood as *simply* the answer to a question. Although claims may be understood by highlighting this dimension, there is also much that this particular kind of highlighting occludes.

Perhaps my objection can best be explained this way. To put my point in Meyer's language, we are always answered before we have questions. Each of us has already grown up into answers to which the questions have been forgotten. In order to reason about these "answers," we may indeed want to do historical research into the original "questions" or "problems" to which our cultural heritage and our socialization are an answer. That is, we may want to do what Nietzsche called "antiquar-

Part Two: Reconstructing Argumentation

ian" history. However, this is not the only way to be reasonable. We might instead want to understand our social and cultural background as something to which we ourselves pose the questions. We may want to see it as having claimed us in our own time, and we may want to put questions of our own time to it in order to accomplish our own purposes rather than just determine how well someone else's purposes have been met. These two projects may overlap at important points. We may want to recover the questions of the past in order to evaluate their relevance to our own time and our own best questions. However, this overlapping project is itself best understood as a project of discovering the ways in which we have been claimed, and then ourselves making those claims explicit by questioning them. Thus, a central disagreement between Meyer and me is that he seems to believe that the questions that are essential in reasoning about propositions have already been asked, and that our task is to discover them. I believe that we are at least sometimes ourselves the important questioners, questioners who are representative of a newly emerging audience.

Consider an example. Suppose that someone says, "Children should be considered incompetent until proven otherwise." Suppose the speaker or writer imagines himself to be speaking out of a situation in which a presumption of competence has led to what he takes to be deleterious policies toward children. Suppose, for example, that child labor has been justified on the basis of a presumption of competence: children are willing and able to work; let's not put laws or policies in place which would presume that they are incompetent to choose for themselves. The statement about the presumption of incompetence may be an answer to a question something like, "How can we prevent the cruelties of child labor?" Answer: "We must assume something like incompetence on the part of children to decide for themselves, and decide by law that they are not permitted to work."

However, in a situation in which child labor laws are already in place, and in which children suffer flagrant rights abuses by those who are responsible for their care, and in which these abuses are justified on the basis of the presumption of incompetence, is it reasonable to say that we must continue to understand the claim about incompetence as an answer to the question about child labor? Not at all. It may be that our own question, a new question, to which the proposition is *not* an answer, is the one we really need in order to understand the *claim* being made on us. Suppose our new question is: "Why should we continue the presumption of incompetence when it leads to widespread and flagrant violations of children's rights?" This question reveals the proposition as a *claim* on us, and on our society, in a way that I believe is more useful than understanding the proposition *simply* as an answer to a past question. It is the reason or reasoning which follows this new question which is more properly understood as an answer.

This is, of course, a very complicated issue. I have tried to sketch some lines of agreement and disagreement between Meyer's influential account of questioning and my own; however, more thorough treatment of this issue will have to occur in specific discussions in the following chapters. Meyer's privileging of the question is closely related to Heidegger's and Gadamer's work on questioning. Since I continue to develop some of my own ideas in connection with theirs, much of what follows will have some bearing on Meyer's theory of problematology. I will reserve my most serious confrontation with the idea of privileging questioning for the chapter on argumentation and ideology. I will say now that although my own account of questioning differs from Meyer's, it seems to me impossible to develop a theory of argumentation without privileging questioning in a strong way. If one follows the Heideggerian/Gadamerian/Meyerian path of believing that questioning is in every way prior to other ways of acting, then this is not a problem. If, however, one believes, as I do, that people are at least as affirmative as interrogative, then one sees the ways in which the Heideggerian path leads away from a disclosure of the senses in which people are affirmative. This means that argumentation promotes a kind of ideology that must be, from a theoretical point of view, recognized and described, and from a practical standpoint, countered.

The Respondent as Questioner

Although I have distinguished the roles of claimant and respondent, and thus distinguished claims and reasons from questions, these distinctions are best understood as *distinctions in discursive roles,* and are made in order to highlight the dialogical aspects of an argument, not in order to establish the deep priority relations between questioning and claiming. From one angle, it can appear that questioning has a priority; from another angle, claiming can appear to have a priority. Actually, as we have seen, claims and questions have a logical relation to one another, and depend on one another; a claim is an implicit plan of its own questionability. Further, it is a question that first allows a claim to emerge as a claim, and it is a question that makes possible the emergence of a reason as a reason. I will consider these claims in order.

Again, most assertions do not get into arguments; most are not called into question. Most invitations to share experiences are simply accepted or ignored to some degree or other. In this sense, affirmations precede questions; we are answered before we ask. Most affirmations are never even made explicit. We grow up into the competences that allow us to share experiences as members of a society; we adopt without reflection the ways of seeing, understanding, and acting that make the groups we belong to what they are. We learn the language and discourse, the stories and songs, the skills and gestures that provide us with the shared background which is necessary for us to communicate and reason together. Even explicit assertions are usually not questioned. They are part of an everyday sharing of experience, and the deference we pay to most assertors is a sign of our trust and willingness to share one another's disclosures of the world. This kind of growing up into a way of being is an inheriting of a domain of what is unquestionable and mostly unthought.

In this sense, before we are able to hear a claim as a claim—that is, before there can be a claim—we are already claimed by others. We have already adopted a shared way of experience, a common way of life. Heidegger says about our way of being that we are *"aufeinander angewiesen Sein"* (*Concept of Time* 240)—signed over to one another. We are already claimed by others before we are able to experience a claim as a claim—already *called* into being by others before our own being becomes an issue for us. It is only when our being becomes an issue for us, only when we are moved by questions, that a claim can come into being for us. As we have seen, to hear an assertion or an affirmation as a claim is to hear it as something questionable. This means that one must move into the role of questioner in order for a claim to appear as a claim. Questions allow claims to come forth as claims, and questions depend upon there being a questioner.

The emergence of a questioner is not a simple matter. First of all, to understand oneself as a questioner is to place oneself in a privileged role, maybe even a superior one. Hans Robert Jauss points out the following thought-provoking fact: "The first question in biblical history posed to a human being is a question leveled by God, the Lord and Creator, at Adam, his creation. It is a question that passes down from above, a question emanating from the highest authority and directed at its unequal image. It begins the interrogation concerning Adam and Eve's misdeed and results in their expulsion from Paradise . . ." (52). Jauss goes on to make clear, with several examples, that questioning is typically a privilege of the powerful. And there is obvious truth in what Jauss says. Questioning one's superiors is often taken to be a sign of impertinence or rebellion. Even questioning one's equals can be taken to be a sign of mistrust or disapproval. In contrast, the questioning of one's subordinates is taken to be almost a duty of power.

We should not think of power here in simple terms of one person's ability to influence another's actions. The image of the Creator-Questioner and the creature-respondent suggests that questioning is actually a creative action—that questions occur "before" there are human beings. This is one angle from which questioning can be understood to have a priority. If human beings are such that they have no essential nature, then it is in questioning themselves that they enact the kind of being they have. Becoming self-conscious by way of questioning oneself is, in the biblical myth, connected with the expulsion from paradise and the origin of human beings as they are. "Adam, where art thou?" elicits "Where *am I?*" Most parents playfully question infants, and model the role of questioner, long before the infants can ask questions themselves. If Jauss is right, they are calling their children forth as human beings, as self-questioning creatures.

Questioning takes one out of the usual roles of deference and places one in a role of privilege, a creator's role. This means that to hear a claim as a claim—and not, for example, as an order, or command or threat—is to assume a position of privilege. This has interesting consequences for our conception of how universal argumentative rationality really is, as well as for teaching and for the aims of education.

In general, all people have the ability to enter the role of the questioner. More particularly, though, we are socialized and individuated in ways that limit our ability to question and that assign our rights as questioners to particular domains. It may be that some groups are identified by the deep competences they have that affect their ability to enter the role of the questioner. In the Scollons' work with Athabaskan- and English-speaking Alaskans, they found that English speakers believed that Athabaskans avoided asking direct questions and asked questions in "unusual places." Athabaskans believed that English speakers asked too many questions (36).

If Jauss is right, it may be that people who have a sense of themselves as having more of a certain kind of authority or power than others are more likely to pose questions, and thus more likely to understand assertions as claims—i.e., as questionable in a process of argumentation. If this sense of oneself is the kind of deep competence that is not easily separable from what one *is*, then to say that argumentative rationality is universally accessible misses something important.

This in turn has consequences for the way we think of the teaching of argumentation and reasoning—especially in relation to critical thinking and reading and to written argumentation. Every teacher knows how profoundly difficult it is for some students to locate the claims a writer is making. The challenge in such instances is to help to make a claim come to life *as a claim* for a person who cannot hear a claim's being made. The person who cannot hear a claim's being made in a piece of writing is in an important respect insensible to writing as writing. The problem is that the unclaimed reader has not questioned the writing in a way that would allow the claim to come forth as a claim. Until an assertion is understood as something questionable, its being a claim stays closed off to us.[1]

However, if someone sees the questioner's role as in some particular case socially inappropriate, or if the role conflicts with the deep competences a person has grown up in, then it is unlikely that the person will respond directly to a teacher's report about a claim in some piece of writing—even if the teacher makes explicit the ways in which the claim is questionable. In some cases, some people may resist the very role of questioner, and thus make it impossible for the claim to come forth as a claim for them.

The social and cultural variability in the questioner's role has strong implications for how we think of the purposes of education and of appropriate ways of accomplishing those purposes. A closer focus on the realities of education is appropriate here.

The question I want to explore concerns whether college writing programs should have as their goal the development of argumentative reasoning in students. However, a prior question concerns the appropriate means of accomplishing this goal. The question of means has a priority because what argumentative reasoning is, in practice, will be determined partly by the means through which such reasoning is developed. In Cavellian-Nietzschean terms, the process of reaching a "mighty community" is the only form a "mighty community" can ever take.

People will not learn to hear claims, and thus will not comprehend the relation between claims and reasons for claims, will not understand arguments as arguments, unless they can ask the questions that allow claims to appear as claims. However, the identities of people are often closely connected to their resistance to some kinds of questioning and their inclinations toward others. If the teaching of argumentation is taught in a formal way, as a kind of logic, one can shortcut the entire event of questioning to focus on the formal relations between claims and reasons, conclusions and premises. One can pretend that one is teaching reasoning when not a single student ever experiences a claim as a claim. In such cases, students dutifully memorize formal rules and calculate relations, but they do not learn to argue. Instruction in logic usually conceals the event of the claim. It solves the problem of having to confront the serious differences among people by ignoring them.

However, it is not clear how one can respect these differences and still teach argumentative reasoning. Suppose one teaches argumentation by making explicit the question which calls forth a claim and inviting students to ask the question themselves. One may be inviting them to give up part of what makes them what they are. One may be asking them to give up a self-understanding that is so deep that it is related to their very competence to ask some questions seriously. In such cases, the natural response to instruction is resistance. To teachers, such resistance may appear as a lack of intelligence, a lack of reasoning ability. Some students may even internalize such interpretations of their lack of performance.

It is not difficult to imagine examples. Devoutly religious students may not easily be able to separate themselves from their religious beliefs. They may believe that separating themselves from their convictions, even in imagination, is seriously undesirable, a sin against God. Let's imagine such a student to be an evangelical Christian. Let's imagine that he enrolls in a "Bible as Literature" course in college. He believes that the Bible is the Word of God. He believes that when he reads the Bible, it is not just an action of his own, but the action of God speaking to him, changing him, through the Scripture. His professor tries to persuade him to ask questions which seem to him not only irrelevant but symptoms of a rebellious attitude toward God: who were the historical authors of such and such chapters? What oral traditions were they drawing on? Who edited their writings? Why is one kind of transgression against God emphasized in one place and another kind someplace else? Which social and political interests did such emphases serve? To invite this student to ask these questions is to ask him to set aside his faith for a while in order to take on the identity of the literary critic. However, such identity switching is for him, as it is for many people, not something one does simply on invitation. For him, it is not something he can do without, for a moment, setting aside his faith.

Or imagine a young woman in a political science course. Imagine that she has been raised to experience the overt challenging of male assertions about politics as something inappropriate for a woman, as something seriously uncomfortable for herself and slightly distasteful when she sees other women do it. Suppose the practice in her family and among her friends was for the women to facilitate and pacify these discussions among men and to withdraw when this was no longer possible. Imagine that they usually addressed the claims made in such discussions only among themselves and often only indirectly, in stories about people they actually knew. Now imagine that this young woman is asked to take the questioner's role in a class discussion about principles of distributive justice in which the main interlocutors are males. To do this, she must give up the roles in which she has competence, and take on roles which make her uncomfortable and seem to her improper. She must make for herself a new social identity. Thus, when she is called on to speak, she opts to say "I don't know," or to make a brief reply to get off the hook. This seems more reasonable to her than suddenly to give up everything she knows about how to act.

Surely, there are many such stories we could tell about students' resistance to instruction. Although silences and resistance are often interpreted as signs of an unwillingness or inability to learn, they are often significant of differences of this kind. How can the teaching of argumentation respect these differences and still develop in students the ability to fill the questioner's role, to allow claims to come forth as claims?

I want to say right out that I believe that to learn is to change and that to learn to argue means learning to take the questioner's position. This means that people who are not practiced at this social-cognitive role, whose self-conception conflicts with its demands, or who find it uncomfortable will have to change if they are to learn to write and reason better, in more ways and in more contexts, than they already do. I see no way around it. There is no guarantee that an education will leave people and social groups untouched. People who do not experience challenges to their beliefs, their social roles, their self-understandings, are probably not receiving much of an education. However, educators must not be oblivious to what they are asking of students. Sometimes they are asking people to become something very different from what they are, to take on new identities.

How is it possible to make this demand of students and still respect the differences they bring to the classroom? First, we can recognize that students who are different in their attitudes toward the questioner's role are not for that reason deficient in their intelligence or in their general abilities. Since students are different in this way, we must find ways to persevere with them for as long as they will persevere with us; they approach argumentation from very different positions, and some begin much further away from certain questioners' roles than others. It is naive to believe that because they do not all reach the same goal on the same schedule they are not all making significant progress toward it. I realize that this raises difficult policy issues, but at least it changes the considerations which should guide policy deliberations. Actually, these considerations have more immediate relevance for teachers as they design assignment sequences, conference with students, and comment on their papers, for they provide a useful way of conceptualizing the difficulties students are having, and provide grounds for hope in what may look to others like hopeless situations.

We can also respect the resistance of our students.[2] One way of doing this is to make explicit the conflicts between the ordinary self-understanding of students and the new self-understanding in which they are being invited to participate. To do this is to make questionable both ways of understanding what is questionable and what is not. This invites both the teacher and the student to enter into a domain of questioning they would ordinarily resist. The mutuality of this kind of questioning signals a respect often missing from classrooms. However, this respect is the respect of reason, the respect of a rationality of peace. This mutuality and respect are oriented by the idea that the teacher and the student are alike in what is most important from the standpoint of reason: the ability to call oneself into question.

There is no escaping this. The respect necessary for mutual communication and learning is a particular and determinate kind of respect. There are other kinds of respect that help to achieve other goals.[3] In the practice of this respect, the teacher of written reasoning is at an advantage because what is being taught and learned is written reasoning itself. In a course on the history of the U.S. Constitution, students must be held accountable for learning a tradition of argumentation with which they may not themselves be comfortable—probably without having the chance to examine the differences between their own sense of what is questionable and the senses that have guided Supreme Court decisions. (Still, it would be nice to imagine such courses differently.) However, in a course on written reasoning, making such differences the issue is a genuine possibility. Teachers of writing are not responsible for transmitting knowledge in exactly the same way as teachers in other disciplines. Students who take writing courses in which the real conflicts at issue in their writing are the subject matter of the course may be much more likely to be successful writers later, in courses where such conflicts are no longer the main issue.

Of course, dealing with such conflicts is never complete; they arise in new ways in new contexts, and the more diverse the student population, the deeper and more frequent such conflicts are. This is why written reasoning needs to be taught at all levels of the curriculum and in training programs outside of the university or college. Written reasoning is not simply a matter of mastering basic skills and then applying them to new situations. It is also a matter of developing new kinds and levels of competence in new contexts. More specifically, it is coming to know what kinds of claiming and questioning are appropriate in different circumstances. It is knowing which voices need to be heard. We strengthen people's ability to do this in writing courses in strong and direct ways, but the process is never complete.

We can also learn to respect students' silences. It is a reasonable goal to try to have students participate in discussions in roughly equal ways and measures by making sure that they fill, in roughly equal ways, the different discursive roles available in discussions and arguments. However, when this does not happen, one must carefully measure the power one uses to try to achieve this goal. It is of little use to force silent students to speak when they are intensely uncomfortable with speaking. They may be learning and changing slowly, orchestrating inner arguments, but they may be unable to negotiate a change in social identity for some time. Why not respect the fact that they are engaged in a serious process, one which calls into question not just their beliefs but their identities? These are not educational-psychological recommendations based on theories of personality and motivation and on questions about what the most "effective" teaching strategies are. They are recommendations which follow from an understanding of the philosophical and ethical realities of teaching argumentation and from a simple principle of respect for the people we teach.

These remarks can be put into perspective by way of a helpful distinction. We can distinguish between the goal of developing reasoning abilities in students and the goal of turning them into rationalists. To develop their ability to reason is in part to strengthen their abilities to enter questioners' roles. To turn them into rationalists is to have them enter these roles in all cases without discretion. A respect for difference is in part a recognition that rationality not only is one good among many but also is a good only when it is in balance with other goods. Reason is fire. The proper amount, at the proper time and place, contained in the right way by other elements, can be a great help to human beings. However, the endless and unconstrained questioning of absolutely everything is fire out of control, and consumes everything it touches. Every organization of human effort, every society, every discipline and profession, is in part a distinction between what is questionable and what is not, a containment of reason's fire. To experience our students' resistance to rationality in this light is to appreciate the fact that the identities they have achieved are no small accomplishments.

The fact that students do not all enter a classroom with equal access to questioners' roles is not a problem that can be solved. We cannot, through instruction and inducements, expect to change people's social identities in a term's time—even if we imagined that this was a desirable goal. However, we can exacerbate the problems that arise in the teaching of reasoning by suppressing the fact that we are asking people to change their self-understanding. This fact is completely covered up by traditional logic-based attempts to teach argumentation. It is covered up in most models of informal logic. It is mostly ignored in the teaching of critical thinking and English composition. It is distorted in developmental psychologists' ideological schemes of hierarchies of moral and intellectual development.

The blindnesses of these approaches can become especially serious in ethnically and socially diverse classrooms. The first victims of the cover-up are teachers themselves, who misunderstand the nature and seriousness of what they are asking of students when they ask them to enter questioners' roles. The other victims are the students, who experience the hidden conflicts but who believe that they are beside the point, that they are significant of personal problems or inabilities. As the director of writing programs at two different universities, I have seen such conflicts escalate to the point where real teaching and learning become impossible, where the teacher believes that a student is so resistant that he is not teachable and where a student believes that a teacher dislikes him personally and has discriminated against him because of his beliefs. These blind conflicts help no one.

Everything here depends on the fact that it is a question that allows a claim to come forth as a claim. Before we experience a claim as a claim we have already been claimed without knowing it. To be a member of a group or a society is to be claimed by a particular way of experiencing what is. As long as one is claimed in this way, one belongs to that group or society. To experience that group's claim *as a claim*, that is, to realize the questionableness of the claim, is to that degree no longer to be simply claimed by the group, no longer to belong only to it. When we ask students to enter the questioner's role in a way that makes this claiming explicit and questionable, we are asking them to give up what they have up to that point understood to be their deepest loyalties. This is an ethical and political challenge with broad ramifications. To teach argumentation is to stand in the middle of the conflict precipitated by this challenge.

The Respondent as Interlocutor

There are a number of actions open to people who have discovered their being claimed by others and who experience this being claimed as to some degree questionable. For example, people can ignore or resist being claimed to different degrees and in many different ways—

by not listening, by not taking seriously, by forgetting, by changing the subject, by traveling, by fighting.

To question a claim is no longer simply to defer or to ignore or resist but to pay attention, and to regard either one's interlocutor or one's audience (as well as oneself) with a measure of respect. Without this respect, or trust, or love—this attachment—what would be the motivation for hearing a claim as a claim? Why would one attempt to reason about the claim? What good could come of it? Rhetoricians from Aristotle to Chaim Perelman have recognized that to argue with someone is to show a sign of deep respect. One does not argue with just anyone. As Aristotle says at the end of his *Topics*, "You ought not to practice dialectics or hold a discussion with just anybody . . . You should not readily join issue with casual persons; this can only result in a debased kind of discussion" (164b). Perelman and Olbrechts-Tyteca tell this story: "We must not forget that by listening to someone we display a willingness to eventually accept his point of view [recall here Cavell's account of the friend, and Aristotle's description of the friend as "another myself"]. There is great significance in the attitude of a Churchill forbidding British diplomats even to listen to any peace proposals German emissaries might try to convey . . . because [it] prevent[ed] . . . the existence of the conditions preliminary to possible argumentation" (17). Thus, respondents pose questions and thereby disclose claims when they themselves have become questionable in some way, when the ordinary deference to being claimed is no longer desirable, *and* when there is some hope that reasoning about the claim with someone can achieve some good. The good could be the mutual resolution of a conflict that would otherwise come to violence. Or it could be (even at the same time) that a new version of ourselves is attracting us out of our usual deferrals to those around us and toward a new respect for our(new)selves. The interesting thing about argumentation, and the way in which it differs from other forms of resistance to being claimed, is that it charts a course to one's new self *via* a respectful engagement with the experience and reasoning of other people.

This kind of engagement is not possible if one's resistance to being claimed by a group is too strong. For even though one can make a claim explicit, make it come forth as a claim, through entering the questioner's role, most of what happens when one argues is *not* made explicit. One is always claimed by much more than one can make explicit in a claim. If one is resistant to the entire background in the light of which an argument takes place, one probably does not have the requisite respect for the experience and reasoning of one's interlocutors and audience to argue meaningfully.

At the same time, as we have seen, one must also have both a dissatisfaction with one's ordinary deferring self and some hope in a new self that is to be gained by way of reasoning, by way of taking responsibility for one's being claimed and for claiming.

Responses and Questions

There are different kinds of responses that may be made to a claim in the course of an argument. Here are the three that seem the most common: (1) a call for reasons, (2) a call for clarification, and (3) a countercall, a counterclaim that conflicts with the original claim and sets up a kind of antiphony. Imagine the claim: *The American democracy is in a state of decline.* If the validity claims implicit in an assertion are called into question, then this typically takes the form of a call for reasons, for example: "Why (for what reasons) do you claim that American democracy is in decline?" Here, the truth of the statement is being questioned, and the questioner asks for good reasons to believe that the claim is true. As we have seen, one could also question the sincerity of the claimant by asking for evidence that the claim is a sincere belief of the one putting it forth. And one could also ask for reasons which would support the implicit claim that the assertion was an appropriate one to make on the occasion. All of these questions are calls for reasons.

However, the validity claim of intelligibility usually has a different status from the others. When it is called into question, the questioner is asking not just for reasons but for clarification. For example, if the questioner replies, "But what do you mean by 'democracy'?" the claimant could reasonably respond by saying, "When I say 'democracy,' I mean that it is not the nation or the land or even the *republic* that is in decline, but democratic practices. By 'democracy' I mean not simply a representative form of government but a government in which citizens take themselves to be informed participants."

Calls for clarification are in a special sense prior to calls for reasons because what is at stake in a call for clarification is the claim itself. If it is not clear what the claim is, then it may not be clear in what respect it is questionable. This becomes apparent in actual arguments which proceed with an assumption that the meaning of the terms is clear but stop when the reasons offered in support of a claim seem not to support the claim being made. For example, suppose our claimant in the above example supported the claim by saying that citizens vote on the basis of a more narrow range of interests than in the past and that an ever smaller percentage of them vote at all. The interlocutor could respond: "I see.

What you mean is not *decline* but *change*. American democracy can change in these ways without our having to see it as a decline. In order for the democracy to *decline*, you would have to show that democratic opportunities have declined and not simply that these opportunities are being used by free individuals in new ways." Until an agreement about the use of "decline" could be reached, the giving of reasons for the claim could not proceed. Instead, an argument could take place about the proper use of "decline," or an exploratory dialogue in search of a new word could begin. Until some clarification was reached, the argument about the claim, or a new version of it, could not proceed.

Validity claims about appropriateness and sincerity may also have a priority to the giving of reasons in support of an explicit claim—although intelligibility claims are prior to either of them. Arguments about the appropriateness of introducing certain kinds of claims and lines of argument are common in negotiations. Very often, the relevance and appropriateness of making claims about certain topics must be established before argumentation can proceed. And it is also true that in some contexts we do not wish to reason with people unless we believe that they are expressing their sincere beliefs. In any case, however, a call for clarification has a somewhat different status from other questions and responses. A call for clarification brings a particular claim into focus, distinguishes it from other possible claims, and thereby makes the meaning of an emerging choice stand out more clearly against a background of assumptions and competences.

Responding to a claim by offering a counterclaim is yet a different kind of response. If someone responds to our exampled assertion by saying: *On the contrary, the American democracy is thriving,* we have a very different situation. To offer a counterclaim is to attempt to set up mutual calls and responses and parallel courses of argumentation. The classic written form of this kind of parallel argumentation is found in the *Dissoi Logoi*—a form that has not introduced a tradition because the major but not sole social purpose of argumentation is to resolve conflicts. Consequently, most counterclaims, with the counterarguments that support them, are incorporated into and subordinated to argumentation that supports a primary claim. Counterclaims and their arguments may lead to clarification or qualification of a primary claim, and in most written argumentation this mutual influence of claims and arguments is taken to be an important part of argumentation's ability to make new knowledge, to inquire, and to resolve conflicts. However, writing rarely reflects parallel lines of argument.

Interestingly enough, this does not seem to be a requirement in the argumentation that takes place in fiction, poetry, and in film. Plays and novels are full of examples of competing and apparently equally compelling arguments being presented to someone who faces a choice. An advantage fiction has over argumentation is that the consequences of making a choice, of submitting to one argument or another, can be tracked in a story. The consequences can then become parts of new arguments that can be used to reevaluate the choice, and in retrospect and in some cases understand in a new way the previous arguments which failed to enable the better choice.

Further, fictional genres seem better able to show the meaningfulness of contradictory claims and equally compelling arguments. In the film *Adam's Rib*, Katharine Hepburn's and Spencer Tracy's characters argue opposite sides in a court case, and appeal, respectively, to the spirit of the law and the letter of the law. The argument is generalized in their marriage and in their lives—although we learn that in the best marriage this argument, in its many versions, is also internal to each character. The argument can never be definitively settled on one side or another. In fact, this "difference" in its many forms, these incompatible claims and parallel arguments, make possible what mutual journeying and newness there is in marriage, or in law, or in life.

This capacity of fiction and film to elaborate parallel lines of argumentation without resolution is similar to the way argumentation is turned loose in research and inquiry. This "turning loose" of argumentation also pushes it toward its limits, and often makes it a means or mechanism in another kind of discourse rather than a genre of its own. Most written argumentation is aimed at resolution rather than self-perpetuation. This is because argumentative reasoning is used for the purpose of making choices and resolving conflicts. It is when one is faced with a choice, when a conflict of disclosures, interests, plans must be resolved nonviolently, in language, that argumentation finds its proper place as a genre. In the chapter that follows, I will attempt to explain exactly how argumentation functions as the peaceful discursive resolution of conflict. In Chapter 8, I will explore the uses of argument for inquiry and discovery.

Once again, the most important fact about the place of questions in arguments is that the role of the questioner is usually ignored. Typically, the relation between a claim and a reason is understood to be a logical one. The "movement" from premises to conclusions is understood to be generated by logical rules of implicature which are effective independently of human motives and actions. Modern writing practices intensify the occlusion of the question by presenting arguments in a monovocal frame. In a dialogical theory that is also pragmatic and rhetorical, questioning is shown to be internal to argumentation. As a way of summing up these important points, I want to consider one final example.

Here is a written argument from Ludwig Wittgenstein's *On Certainty:* "155. In certain circumstances, one cannot make a *mistake*. ('Can' is here used logically, and the proposition does not say that in these circumstances one can say nothing false.) If Moore were to pronounce the opposite of those propositions which he declares certain, we would not just not share his opinion; rather, we would regard him as demented." Wittgenstein makes his claim in the first sentence: "In certain circumstances one cannot make a mistake." The next sentence is best understood as a reply to a respondent, an answer. In this case, the implicit respondent has asked for clarification: is this a logical claim or an empirical claim? To understand Wittgenstein's second sentence, one must indeed be able to understand the question to which his clarification is a reply. One must grasp the distinction between a logical "cannot" and an empirical "cannot," and one must know why the question is appropriate to ask in this instance. Wittgenstein himself is arguing with someone for whom this clarification is necessary; he is recognizing the immediate question that will come to this reader's/interlocutor's mind, and is showing a respect for his or her responses.

The reason in support of his claim, offered in the third sentence, is more complicated, and is formulated in response to a more complicated question or set of questions. A reader can think of many possibilities here. However, the silent questioner has obviously challenged the claim; the claim needs a reason. I can imagine Wittgenstein's implicit interlocutor saying something like: "But it's always possible to be mistaken about anything; you yourself realize that no knowledge is completely justifiable on self-evident foundations. You yourself say that justifying just comes to an end. Doesn't this mean we could be mistaken about anything? Are you saying that some knowledge is absolute? Can you give me an example of one of these situations in which it is impossible to make a mistake?"

Wittgenstein's response to something like this challenge is to write: "If Moore were to pronounce the opposite of those propositions which he declares certain, we would not just not share his opinion; rather, we would regard him as demented [*geistesgestört*]." Obviously, Wittgenstein is writing to an audience who knows which of Moore's propositions he has in mind—say, the one with which Wittgenstein begins *On Certainty:* "I know that here is a hand," when one is looking at one's own hand. Wittgenstein's answer, then, is: here is a situation in which one cannot be mistaken. We would not use the concept of a "mistake" to describe what could go wrong here. If I were wrong about my own hand—

say, if I thought one of my student's hands was my own, or if I thought the telephone was my hand—I would not have made a "mistake." I would be in more serious trouble. The reason to assent to the claim is that some instances of going wrong about what one knows are better described as being demented than being mistaken.

To understand Wittgenstein's argument more completely, we would have to imagine more thoroughly the audience for whom it was offered. Such an audience would know more about the consequences of assenting to Wittgenstein's claim, and know more about its connection with other claims he wants to make. The point here is that in order to reason in writing, Wittgenstein must know how to fill the interlocutor's role; he must know how to raise questions for his own claims. The quality of his argumentation will be dependent on the quality of the interlocutor he can imagine, because his answers, his reasons, will be answers to the questions of that interlocutor. Without such an interlocutor, one cannot reason. To imagine this kind of interlocutor is to imagine oneself as someone else.

This brings to mind—who else but—Socrates, who, at the conclusion of his discussion with the wealthy sophist Hippias in the *Greater Hippias* (304D–E), tells Hippias that he is lucky not to be tormented the way Socrates himself is: "I am called every bad name by that man who is always cross-questioning me. He is a very close relative of mine and lives in the same house, and when I go home and he hears me give utterance to these opinions he asks me whether I am not ashamed of my audacity in talking about a beautiful way of life, when questioning makes it evident that I do not even know the meaning of the word 'beauty' . . . It is my lot, you see, to be reviled by . . . him. However, I suppose all this must be endured. I may get some good from it—stranger things have happened."

The conversation between Socrates and his "houseguest" takes the form of a conflict, something Plato emphasizes in this passage. The point is that the conversation of reason itself is a conflict. This conflict is unpleasant in some ways, but there is no question that Socrates and Plato see this internal conflict as both the life of reason and an essential feature of a good life. In the *Apology,* the idea is even more explicit. There Socrates tells the assembly about the "divine guide" he has had since childhood: "It is a kind of voice which, whenever I hear it, always turns me back from something I was about to do" (31D). This questioning, challenging voice sets up the conflict which finds a medium in the dialogue of argument. Experiencing this conflict is sometimes unpleasant. But as Socrates says, it may do us some good; stranger things have happened.

4   ARGUMENT AND CONFLICT

Argument as Conflict

In Chapter 1, I emphasized the way traditional concepts of reason had provided a way to resolve conflicts peacefully, had offered a court of appeal beyond the authority of any actual social power, and had helped to make clear the goals of higher education. I mentioned that part of the measure of a rhetorical theory of reason would be its success at accomplishing these same purposes. In order to understand how a pragmatic rhetoric of reason can explain argumentation's ability to meet these demands, it is necessary to understand more thoroughly how argumentation is itself a form of conflict. I also discussed the commonly held view that the aim of argumentation is actually to defeat and overcome an opponent. That view takes argumentation to be aggressive, coercive, hostile, and domineering. In this chapter, I intend to develop in detail an account of the senses in which argumentation is conflict, but conflict of a very different sort from that imagined in the "argument is aggression" view.

I want to begin with the results of Chapters 2 and 3, regarding the role of claims and questions in arguments. It has already become clear that argument is a kind of social conflict. One reason argumentative communication is a kind of conflict has to do with the role of claims in arguments. Just bringing different voices together in a single discourse illuminates differences, but does not necessarily allow for conflict. We could simply juxtapose different understandings of the world without their being in competition or conflict with one another. However, to make a claim is both to reject a host of incompatible assertions and to bring the claim to bear on someone, and thus to create the potential for conflict. The potential is actualized when, for example, someone puts forth an incompatible counterassertion, or directly challenges the claim. Different versions of reality come into conflict in argumentation by way of being asserted. In assertions, we make claims on one another. Thus, the conflict in argumentation is essentially social.

A demand for a justification is also a kind of social conflict. It originates in, depends on, and transforms an original social difference. This conflict takes place as a central feature of written argumentation; a claim is made and a justification accompanies it, as if one were in conflict with an absent interlocutor. And not only argumentative debates between actual groups and individuals are forms of social conflict, but even when we are engaged in self-deliberation we are engaged in a process which is social and conflictual in form. We divide into roles, and into explicitly different ways of understanding something, in order to reason.

Thus, I propose that argument is a kind of social conflict, and that in important ways it resembles violent conflict. Conflict takes a particular form in argumentation; it is nonviolent and it tends toward a specific kind of resolution—explicit agreement on a claim—but it is conflict nonetheless. In fact, although I won't have much to say about it, discourse itself can be understood to be conflictual, with the level and kind of conflict varying across the fields of discourse. Although I am interested in this continuum of conflict in discourse, and will have to move outside of argumentation in order to mark its boundaries, this chapter will focus on the specific levels and kinds of conflict that make argumentation what it is. However, to mistake this close connection between argumentation and violence as somehow implicating argumentation in a social project based on a deep structure of aggression and domination is to miss the critical ethical difference between violence and reason. Because of this difference, the teaching of argumentation has a unique ethical importance. I will be able to redeem this claim about argumentation's unique ethical importance only later in the book.

In the meantime, it is necessary to do something to prevent an undesirable ethos from being projected here, and ruining what merit there is in my arguments, so I will say this. First, although war and argumentation share a process of conflict that is remarkably similar, the media of this conflict are hugely dissimilar—to the extent that where war is a process of violence, argumentation is not only nonviolent action, but in principle the renunciation of violence. It is, in fact, the great alternative to violence. But if it is a genuine alternative, a substitute for violence, it must itself be a way of having conflict, one which is capable of guiding conflict to resolution in a mutually satisfactory way.

Second, although as pacifists point out, war takes no small amount of cooperation between opposing forces, it is certainly true that argumentation requires enormously more cooperation than war. It presupposes such deep ethical commonality that it seems to some degree misleading to focus on its conflictual features. And this is certainly correct. I hope my attention to conflict in argumentation does not block a clear view of its cooperative dimensions. Some forms of conflict are possible only on the basis of deep and continuing cooperation among participants. Nevertheless, without conflict there is no argumentation, no inquiry, nothing new to talk about. As William Carlos Williams says:

> Dissonance
> (if you are interested)
> leads to discovery.

Thinking of argument as conflict is one way of being interested in discovery.

Finally, I also want to point out that the resolution of argumentative conflict is a particular kind of peace—a peace that can be established only through conflict. It is not the kind of pacification that allows all forms of being-in-the-world to coexist indifferently. It is not the end of all argumentative conflict; that would be the opposite of conflict, a kind of hegemonic peace, the peace of indifference and skepticism. The resolution of conflict through argumentation does not produce this kind of peace. It is never final, never complete. It always settles on a particular use of language, a particular way of showing something. This is the feature which links it to choice, and to our need to understand our choices as following from reasons.

The Problem of Epideictic

To begin this conceptualization of argument as a process of social conflict and resolution, I want to consider Chaim Perelman and Lucie Olbrechts-Tyteca's remarks on argumentation and violence in *The New Rhetoric*. They title one section of their treatise "Argumentation and Violence," and throughout *The New Rhetoric* they remark on the ways in which violence and argumentation are like and unlike. They begin by observing that argumentation and violence can be considered as the same process aimed at the same end except that in argumentation argument is substituted for force (54). Then they claim that the aggressor in argumentation is the person who initiates a specifically argumentative debate. (However, they oversimplify the act of claiming here. As we have seen, there are many ways in which the claimant is the opposite of an aggressor.) They contrast the aggressor to the one who, instead of initiating a debate, strengthens established values—and for Perelman and Olbrechts-Tyteca this occurs especially in epideictic rhetoric. This strengthener is not like someone engaged in violent conflict at all. Instead, this person is like "the guardian of dikes under constant assault by the ocean" (55).

So, in trying to enlist *The New Rhetoric* for help in building this theory, we encounter a first obstacle. Epideictic seems to lack the connection with social conflict, and looks more like a struggle with nature. We could solve this problem by refusing to think of epideictic as argumentation and instead saying that it is a form of discourse which is a precursor to argumentation, makes argumentation possible, but doesn't itself offer arguments. Its purpose is, as the New Rhetoricians say, to strengthen the agreements on which argumentation depends, but not to offer arguments themselves. The problem, though, is that to be consistent one would have to throw out the figures and techniques which constitute epideictic, and refuse them to argumentation proper. However, this would tend to lead to styleless argument, an impossibility for a natural language and for real arguments. So the better choice is to try to show how epideictic, too, is a form of social conflict—without giving up Perelman and Olbrechts-Tyteca's insight.

As usual, the New Rhetoricians are onto something profound. Their remarks suggest a very important point, one which must be conceded, but is not what it first appears. Although all argumentation is like violent social conflict, and is itself a form of social conflict, a certain kind of persuasion—call it "epideictic"—is also involved in securing the necessary conditions for argumentative social conflict, in fact for the congealing of any social identity at all. So epideictic has a kind of natural necessity; it is an establishment of the possibility of explicit argumentative social conflict. In this sense, then, it is more like sustaining a natural territory within which social solidarity and determinate conflicts can arise than like those conflicts themselves. However, it is also a kind of implicit social conflict, and is used in attempts to change the way other people experience arguments, in fact to expand the domain within which argumentation is effective.

To put it in more general terms, explicit social conflict is always a matter of a determinate particular against a determinate particular—one claim or set of claims against another. In the same way, argumentation is an explicit conflict of particular claims. But epideictic, even though it is always this too, is not only this. It is also discourse which promotes determinateness over against indeterminateness, social solidarity over against the dissolving of social unity. *The New Rhetoric* insists that it is existing social solidarity, understood rhetorically as settled agreements, which enables argumentation as a way of resolving conflicts. Without the maintenance of these agreements through epideictic discourse, the domain of argumentation would lose ground to violent methods of settling disputes. Thus, this unique kind of rhetoric sustains the "natural" conditions for more familiar kinds of argumentation. The metaphor of a sea of unconstrained intelligibility against which we protect ourselves with artifactual dikes of unquestioned agreements is exactly appropriate.

The concept of epideictic is probably too little appreciated by philosophers, literary theorists, and social critics. It provides a rhetorical way of understanding issues which have a broad importance in the study of discourse. Great amounts of agreement and identification are necessary to enable complex discursive conflicts. It is useful and important to ask, in many contexts, what the relation is between the quantity and kind of agreement and the quantity and kind of conflict in any discursive situation, as well as what a desirable balance would be, given one's purposes. Less agreement on fewer things leads to less explicit differentiation, and less communication about differences. It also means that conflicts are less likely to be settled through discourse. More agreement on more things leads to greater particularity and determinateness, and thus more *difference* in argumentation, as well as to an appearance of greater universality.

However, this latter is only an appearance. The agreements it is possible to make *in general,* the different kinds of identification it is possible to achieve, cannot be measured. To make an agreement is to resolve a conflict—in one way, and not in another. Every agreement achieved represents a loss of some possibilities. Yet this rarely appears to be the case once the agreements are in force, for by then the challenges have fallen silent. Their possibility is not taken seriously; in William James's words, they are not living options. With fewer agreements, one denies fewer possibilities, but has less determinateness and complexity in discourse, and fewer resources for reasoning and arguing.

This helps to frame what has become a pressing question for those who study language use and teach it to others. Can we sustain the practical agreements our society has achieved—its particular kinds of identification, its "we"—purely for the sake of the determinateness and complexity they give our society, purely for the sake of the particular goods they have allowed us to achieve, without appealing to some other justification for these agreements, some language-independent truth or good in which these agreements are rooted? The nurturing of epideictic rhetoric is, from a rhetorical point of view, a source of hope for sustaining the identification of people with one another. It promotes the possibility of a rationality of peace. It can also insulate societies from other traditions, and enclose them in fairly static systems of self-differentiation. The problem is to find an angle from which to evaluate that which makes it possible for one to make evaluations. One way societies preserve this possibility is to cultivate incompatible values and ways of understanding. A society can pursue multiple competing epideictics at once, if it is lucky, and if the commitment to continuing argumentation is strong across the different epideictic communities. However, as we have seen, the commitment to continuing argumentation is itself a commitment to particular ethical ideals, ideals which must be shared for argumentation to succeed.

Unfortunately, epideictic rhetoric rarely appears in this sort of discussion except in extreme circumstances among small groups and on the outer margins of society. Following Deleuze and Guattari, Victor Vitanza ironically promotes an anti-epideictical rhetoric of dissolution as a way of resisting the accumulation of destructive power in the state and other agencies of totalizing social control. However, like deconstruction, these efforts always depend on the agreements they work to undo, and insofar as these efforts gain any voice in society, they make use of epideictic, and transform this conflict about whether there should be social solidarity into a more ordinary argumentative conflict between different social groups. Epideictic is, after all, and even in its negative forms an agreement-building activity rather than a Babel-inducing one. Deleuze and Guattari, as well as Vitanza, face Nietzsche's practical impasse of having to use an ascetic practice to undo the effects of ascetic practices.

Epideictic as a genre tends to strengthen existing agreements rather than create new ones, and so guarantees the conditions of argumentation rather than directly participating in it. To this extent, *The New Rhetoric's* natural metaphor is helpful. However, epideictic is called for only when existing social solidarity is too weak for one's argumentative purposes. This situation motivates acts of epideictic discourse, which can always be taken as carrying a general claim: we should have a stronger attachment to certain shared understandings. The claim doesn't appear explicitly in the discourse, as it does in ordinary argumentation, but it is still carried by the discourse. Epideictic is designed not to gain agreement on an explicit claim that there should be stronger social solidarity, but rather actually to strengthen that solidarity. This is why epideictic discourse tends to rely on techniques like amplification and presence, and generally on the perlocutionary force of utterances for its success.

In the terms I have been using, epideictic discourse is a way of strengthening certain claims on people without making those claims explicit. If the claim one is attempting to strengthen is called into question by one's audience and thus made explicit, one's epideictic efforts have failed. One is left with having to resort to explicit argumentation to accomplish one's purposes. In this sense, we have all been claimed epideictically before we are able to argue. *The New Rhetoric* even identifies epideictic discourse with the discourse of primary education. Educators of young children, it says, "must proceed by means of affirmations, without entering into a discussion in which the pros and cons are freely debated" (54). Thus, it emphasizes the priority of affirming to questioning, a priority which, as we have seen, some contemporary theorists of argumentation have neglected.[1]

However, what would the situation be for educators who lived in a society in which argumentation itself was held in the highest regard? Would it be possible to strengthen the attachment of students to argumentation without allowing them to practice it? Wouldn't the aim be instead to find that balance between epideictic and explicit argumentation which would best achieve the goal of a community of argumentation? And wouldn't a community of argumentation be a community in which one was already claimed by the implicit conflict of epideictic but was learning to make some of that claiming explicit and so learning to claim oneself?

In any case, the deliberate use of epideictic is clearly motivated by social conflict. And, in fact, in some respects epideictic is more violent than ordinary argumentation. For just as in war a great deal depends on keeping one's intent hidden from one's enemy,[2] so in epideictic discourse one often keeps one's affective goal concealed from the audience. This allows one to strengthen attachment to certain values without having to make explicit claims, offer reasons, or entertain objections. So epideictic, too, can be understood as a form of social conflict—conflict between those who want to strengthen traditional truths and values and those whose attachment to such truths and values is relatively weak.

I should at least point out here that this has some counterintuitive consequences for our understanding of fiction and poetry and drama. According to the measure I am using here, these genres claim us more aggressively than argumentation because they rarely make any of their claims explicit. We can argue with the claims they make on us, to the degree that we can locate them, and can interpret their answers to our challenges. However, like epideictic, they make their claims implicitly in order to make them more forcefully, and part of their effect on us (their changing us) depends on our simply going along, without questioning every claim.

It is interesting to ask what place the teaching and learning of epideictic discourse should have in college writing programs devoted to the teaching of written reasoning. As I have mentioned, the techniques on which epideictic relies do not differ from the techniques used by other forms of written reasoning. And epideictic is often necessary in order to reason with audiences whose adherence to particular ideas must be strengthened before an argument will have the intended effect.

It seems obvious that any serious curriculum in written reasoning will have to take epideictic seriously—even if not under that name. Proficiency at epideictic requires judgment about when ideas need to be strengthened and to what degree. It requires imagination about what stories and scenes and sounds will create strong feelings of identity in an audience. It requires an ability to amplify, to put ideas into images, to call up moods and feelings—abilities which are too often understood to be in conflict with one's ability to reason instead of in support of it. A curriculum which takes epideictic seriously as a part of written reasoning is a broad and comprehensive writing curriculum—not in the sense of trying to teach the plethora of different purposes for which people write, but in the sense of recognizing that many different "kinds" of writing can be used to reason.

Ways of Conflict

With epideictic discourse, in which claims are hidden or implicit, it is not immediately obvious that we are witnessing conflict. With ordinary argumentation, in which a claim and support for the claim are offered explicitly, the conflict is much more obvious. Consider again the New Rhetoricians' claim that violence and war have the same goal as argumentation, the resolution of conflict—violence and war by way of force, argumentation proper by way of reasoning. In the case of war, conflict is between societies making competing claims on territory, sovereignty, and so on. In the case of argumentation, the conflict seems to be between claims themselves. However, the conflict is between the claims not as propositions, but as speech acts which proffer choices which are incompatible with each other. More deeply yet, conflicting claims open up incompatible ways of being. This conflict can still be conceptualized as social conflict; it's just that *in argumentation force is exerted through the medium of language as reasoning, and thus finally in reasons themselves.* Claims, questions about claims, objections, modifications of claims, counterclaims—these are offered by people, by social groups. If no one offered claims and counterclaims, there would be no argumentation.

In this sense, conflict is prior to argumentation. Questions at issue in argumentation are conflicts which are already present among people— claimings and responses to those claimings which are occurring in many different preargumentative ways. Claims and questions do not appear out of nowhere, as the result of a school exercise in invention. Rather, they are explicit forms of claimings and resistances to those claimings that already surround us and permeate us. Sometimes we have to "discover" these conflicts in the sense of making them explicit as claims and questions about those claims. However, the conflicts are already there in implicit and sometimes explicit ways. When certain social-historical and ethical conditions are met, and where we have the right sort of perception and imagination, we can bring these conflicts into language, with the hope of examining, exploring, clarifying, and perhaps resolving them reasonably. Arguments are simply conflicts which have been contained in reasonable language.

In what follows, I explore six ways in which argumentation can be understood as conflict, and I show how a social-conflictual theory of the process of argument can contribute to the theory of argumentation.

The Parties to Conflict

First, one can ask, Who are the parties to this argumentative conflict? They may be actual people or social groups, and when they are, it is very important to know who they are. Argumentative conflicts represent different social interests; a claimant or respondent's ethos could depend heavily on what interests he or she is understood to be representing. However, within argumentative discourse these parties may also be understood generally in terms of the roles they play as expressed in the speech acts in which they engage: claimant, respondent, and audience (or judge). The audience is made up of those people the speaker, or writer, wishes to influence by the argumentation. The goal of argumentation is to convince an audience to accept an explicit claim by way of an argument. It is the audience, the reader, who resolves the conflict. Thus, although the conflict in argumentation appears to be between a claimant and a respondent, unless the respondent is also the audience, this is only an appearance. Some conflicts between claimants and respondents may be staged for the sake of a third party. In that case, the real claim would be on the audience and *not* the respondent. We must locate the conflict among these parties, or we cannot understand argumentation as argumentation.

Written argumentation severs the direct connection between the intended audience and the actual audience. Readers may take arguments into their own hands even though they are not the intended audience. In such instances, the interpretation of an argument may evolve in ways the writer had not anticipated. Here, the deconstructionist rule of iterability holds sway. However, someone is still making a claim by setting forth an argument. This someone may be the inhabitant of a speech role brought to life in the act of reading or thinking. It may be someone who cites an argument from another writer. It may be a publisher or editor. Writing creates a number of questions for any theory of how arguments are to be interpreted. However, *someone* must be understood as making a claim which is intended to be supported to *someone's* satisfaction.

There are the further questions of the relation of the writer of the argumentation and the reader of the argumentation to these roles, and also questions of the relation of the implied writer and reader to the real people writing and reading. Sometimes a writer may speak through the claimant, sometimes through the respondent. Whether and in what sense the writer is a member of the audience is often important for audiences, and readers, to know. After all, we usually want to know how sincerely arguments are being offered. Claimants who use arguments by which they are not themselves convinced present special problems. It is not always obvious who is speaking when a reason is given. Audiences often speak through interlocutors, and skillful arguers script audiences into dialogues in careful ways, knowing when an audience should side with a claimant, when with a respondent, when with neither. However, regardless of these many important and interesting complications—and there are many more—unless there is explicit conflict within the argumentation in the three roles mentioned, one doesn't have an explicit argument, and to show that there is an implicit argument would require making it explicit by describing these roles. The sorting out of these many roles and their possibilities is of immense importance both for writing arguments and for interpreting them.

Thus, the essentials of the conflict are simple enough. The most apparent conflict is between the assertor and the challenger; they are in overt disagreement about a claim. They will settle this dispute by argumentation which will be judged by the influence it has on an audience, which sits as judge of the dispute. However, this means that there is a second and more basic conflict between, on the one hand, an audience, which must be in need of influence for there to be an argumentative situation, and, on the other, the assertor and challenger, who try to influence the state of the audience. The audience is active in any influence assertions and challenges and justifications have in the development of an argument, and in any resolution of conflict. Without the need to influence an audience, and without the responses of the audience at every point, there would be no argumentation.

In general, the conclusions of an argument are representations of the intended audience response. However, I want to emphasize the role of the interlocutors here, too. For just as audiences may be classified as universal or particular, as well as specialized, so can interlocutors. Given this, I would like to supplement one of Perelman and Olbrechts-Tyteca's claims. They claim that the worth of an argument is dependent on the quality of the audience which would assent to it. By worth, they mean how convincing an argument should be for us. I would like to say that the quality of an argument, meaning something like how interesting or significant it is, is dependent on the quality of the interlocutors. However, again, claimant, respondent (or questioner), and audience are discursive roles; they are distinguished by the kinds of speech actions they take and the particular functions they are assigned in argumentation. One person could fulfill all these roles, or several people could fulfill just one. However, each role calls forth the others. A claim is made on an audience, and calls forth a response. A questioner responds to a claimant on behalf of an audience. An audience influences whether and how a claim should be made, and what the appropriate responses to a claim are.

The Focus of Conflict

Second, one can ask what the parties are in conflict *about*, and classify arguments in terms of the issues around which conflicts revolve. This has been the approach of stasis theory and its attempts to classify the kinds of conflict involved in argumentation. Stasis questions are generalized forms of questioning that typically arise in argumentative situations, typical forms of interlocutor response. In every argument, there is a point at issue, and unless one identifies this conflict, one can neither create nor understand an argument.

However, understanding argument as conflict can also bring to the theory of argument an alertness to the covert conflicts going on beneath the claims being thematized in argumentation. And this can raise new questions about who the parties to the conflict really are, and what their disagreement is about. As we have seen, we are already claimed by a background that is not made explicit in the claims we make. We always affirm more than we can say. As in the theory of war, there can be conflict about what a conflict is really about.

For example, Clausewitz believed that the state was an autonomous entity and that power struggles occurred between nations. Thus, war was a direct expression of one nation seeking to force another nation to conform to its will and its national interests. Yet, according to Lenin, the struggle expressed in war was actually a struggle between ruling classes—special interests. The real power struggle, the real conflict, was not thematized in war. The real unity was not a nation, but classes which ran across national boundaries.

Discursive conflict raises similar questions. The language use involved in argumentation always belongs to a particular way of understanding, and does not always thematize the primary conflicts operating in it. To thematize these underlying conflicts could threaten the status of the argumentation, and could reveal the extent to which an ideal speech situation has not been achieved. Just as ruling classes would find it difficult to wage national wars if the working classes became more class-identified than nation-identified, so it would be difficult to carry on argumentation about an ostensible conflict if the interlocutors believed an underlying conflict were the primary one. Here, perhaps, are more of Levinas' forgotten voices, responding to conflicts that are rarely or never made explicit in argumentative situations. A theory of argumentation, a rhetoric of reason, must acknowledge and help to identify multiple levels and kinds of conflict in argumentation. Identifying hidden conflicts—that is, identifying unfocused as well as focused conflicts—does not simply vitiate explicit argumentation about thematized conflicts. However, it can reduce the degree to which we find such argumentation convincing, or the number of situations in which we would find its reasons compelling.

Obviously, there are many underlying conflicts of this sort. In an ideal argumentative situation, there should be no internal or external constraints on people's abilities to speak, and there should be a rough equality in power among the participants.[3] However, the procedures of argumentation often reflect inequalities among participants and potential participants, and do serve as constraints. These procedures sometimes become part of the process of argumentation itself, as when males interrupt females more often than females interrupt males, or when males are able to set the topic of a discussion and females aren't. These inequalities also infiltrate discourse in sexist usage and in discrimination against nonprestige dialects. Thus, while argumentation may thematize one conflict, it may not at all recognize that the language use it engages in to thematize that conflict is itself conflictual and furthers *without argument* the interests of one party to the conflict. Thus, the other party continues to lose no matter what agreement is reached about the thematized conflict.

In writing, these conflicts become even more hidden and obscure because the challenges of the respondent do not appear in writing. One can easily enough study the explicit citations and references made by a writer, but it is much more difficult to find the implicit respondents, and to determine what interests they represent. If readers believe that the proper respondents are not being given voice, they will conclude that the relevant facts and challenges have not been taken into account, and will be unconvinced by the argumentation. Thus, different claims will generate different respondents for different audiences, and the differences between audiences will be measured partly by their judgments about the focus of the conflict.

Not only are there implicit respondents, there are also implicit motivations for claims. These motivations are connected to our having been claimed prior to our ability to understand or make claims ourselves. Other people's interests are written into the discourses we use in argumentation. Their conflicts and the conflicts they produce in us are preserved and concealed in our uses of language. Once we have identified these conflicts, they can be expressed in claims and challenges to claims, and they can be brought before an audience. However, while they are hidden they are simply carried along with our language use. Thus, all argumentation realizes aims which it cannot thematize; all argumentation carries unfocused conflicts with it. If one believes that there should or could be a form of discourse which is completely transparent, and that reason requires such a discourse, one will find here a fatal flaw in argumentation. However, if one believes that every saying leaves something unsaid, and every choice depends on something unchosen, one will instead find here just the fact of human condition.

The questions of who the parties to the conflict are and what the conflict is really about are obviously related. One's answer to one question will influence one's answer to the other question. And these questions themselves could clearly be matters of conflict. In fact, it might in some situations be advantageous for a writer to screen or disguise the real parties to a conflict or to try to hide some of the unthematized conflicts in some discourse. Again, whether a writer can succeed in this will depend on the audience which receives the argumentation.

The Intensity of Conflict

Third, the intensity of argumentative conflict may also be considered. Intensity of conflict can be measured by the degree to which a party to an argument is willing to give up other claims and beliefs and values in order to defend or attack the claim in question. This is especially clear in cases of moral argumentation in which people have conflicting commonsense beliefs. A typical move in argumentation is for a challenger to point out that in defending a claim an assertor has come into conflict with other commonly held beliefs. For example, any argument which tries to defend an absolute moral principle will come into conflict with the utilitarian principle that an action's rightness can be measured by its consequences. In a high-intensity conflict of this kind, one finds an increase in the extent to which all other beliefs will be sacrificed to support the main claim.

Here is a version of an example that is sometimes used in this kind of argument:

Imagine that you are a strict deontologist about ethical rules—
that is, you believe that there are some ethical rules which it is
always right to follow, never right to break. Let us say that one
of these rules is a prohibition against lying. Imagine that a
psychopathic murderer comes to your door, and asks whether
there are any children in the house. You have heard about this
murderer, and you know he can overpower you and will kill the
children in your home if you tell him the truth. In fact, you have
five children in your home at the time. According to you, since it
is *always* wrong to lie, the moral thing to do seems to be to permit
the murders to occur.

The example is odd, but it does make a point. Most of us follow a number of ethical rules, and on occasion they come into conflict. In the case
of the example, many other rules might come into play: prevent murder,
protect children from those who would harm them, act so as to increase
the happiness of others, use your common sense, and so on. Any of these
might lead one to override the rule about lying, to make an exception.

In order to defend a claim that it is always wrong to lie, one would have
to give up one's allegiance to a great many other rules or values one also
believes in. Arguments carried to high levels of intensity are corrosive of
people's argumentative resources. Such arguments may begin with interlocutors holding and sharing a number of incompatible beliefs, values,
and rules. Such shared resources are usually brought into play in useful and appropriate ways in situations of relatively low intensity. High-
intensity conflicts force such incompatibilities out into the open, cause
them to appear as intolerable contradictions, and lead arguers to drop
their allegiance to some beliefs in order to defend a single claim.

The similarity to war is hard to ignore. Nations which go to war on
principle may find themselves sacrificing other principles in unforeseen
ways in order to preserve an absolute allegiance to the principle for which
they went to war. Conflicts of high intensity are obviously destructive
of human lives and natural resources. However, they are also destructive of cultural resources, destructive of the delicate balances of incompatible cultural understandings, values, and beliefs achieved within
a nation, destructive of its background capacity for reasoning, for resolving conflicts.

On the other hand, there are those who believe that war also has for
this very reason a salutary effect on nations. Hegel argued in the *Philosophy of Right* that states which experienced prolonged periods of peace
suffered corruption and needed the purifying experience of war. Hegel's idea was that unless a nation was required to make sacrifices, to

give up some goods for others, it would not preserve itself because it would not stand for anything. If every national principle can be compromised, a nation no longer has any identity beyond its most powerful factions and subgroups. Corporations or other nations end up taking power over it. Hegel believed that war helped a nation to purify itself of "corruption" of this kind, to defend itself and thus to protect its people from other powers and keep them under the protection of its principles.

It would be too easy to reject Hegel's point of view out of hand. After all, we all oppose war nowadays, and any principled defense of war seems depraved—especially given our current destructive capacities. It would be easy, too, just to assert the opposite of what Hegel says here. I can imagine someone saying that what Hegel calls corruption is actually health, that we must move beyond the politics of identity, in which a nation decides its identity by force, and through the destruction or suppression of competing principles and interests. Better to have a thriving, pluralistic society with subgroups pursuing numerous incompatible purposes within the context of a weak national state. Better to pursue a postmodern politics of fragmentation.

Such a response to Hegel has an obvious appeal, but it misses Hegel's point. As long as there is any state at all, it must have some character. Some dispensation of powers and rights and goods will take shape among a people; some conceptions of good are always being sacrificed. High-intensity conflicts among competing organizations of power allow agents to make choices about which goods will be sacrificed and which won't. "War" is Hegel's word for such high-intensity conflicts in the lives of nations, conflicts in which hierarchies of goods are established explicitly and by choice instead of covertly through the accidental struggle of the most powerful competing forces within the state. The state is supposed to represent the interests of all its people, and not just the special interests of its most powerful groups. One may not believe that any actually existing state does this, but it is hard to deny Hegel's claim that such matters are being decided one way or another as long as a nation exists. In fact, any social group with any particular identity will have to go through some analogous process in the course of its development.

Still, high-intensity conflicts may be developed independently of actual war. William James begins his "The Moral Equivalent of War" by nearly paraphrasing some of Hegel's remarks on war made in *The Philosophy of History*. James agrees that war demands commitment and sacrifice of us, and that this improves our lives and our societies. A life without having to make sacrifices is a life of "degeneration." War calls for the development of virtues that are also important in peacetime, but war *forces* the development of such virtues and increases their strength.

James believes that the projects of pacifistic societies should be capable of developing such virtues in its members, but he believes that such virtues are more difficult to develop in peacetime than in war. Nevertheless, he urges us to pursue lives of peace with the commitment that war claims of us.

James is facing what Nietzsche thinks of as the problem of nihilism. Once one has seen the highest values devalue themselves (in this case, the value of the nation and war), how does one prevent nihilism, degeneration? What claim can ideals make on us? How can we have conflicts of any intensity at all? It seems important to be capable of such conflicts, to be able to live a life which can be understood to have some significance, to make one's choices and consequent sacrifices meaningful.[4]

There is a similar problem in argumentation itself. I have already pointed out the obvious ways in which arguments of high intensity can be destructive, even foolish. However, they can also be immensely clarifying. Intensifying conflict is one way we achieve clarity, one way we demand integrity of ourselves and one another. If we hold a number of incompatible beliefs, and use one in one situation, one in another, we never achieve clarity about what we really believe; we never really become one person, responsible for our beliefs. When we allow other people to express incompatible views, we fail to recognize them as people of whom we expect integrity. High-intensity arguments, in which people are expected to sacrifice some beliefs for others, lead to this kind of clarity and integrity.

Again, it would be foolish to expect this kind of self-transparency and integrity in all situations; however, it would also be senseless to do away with it altogether. Becoming clearer about what we really believe and cherish is a kind of growth. Achieving integrity in these matters is a kind of loyalty, and makes us reliable to those who depend on us. If our children, our partners, our friends could not know what we believed or what our loyalties were from one day to the next, our relationships with them would be very different from what they are. The possibility of trust and confidence which continue over time and across different situations makes life very different from what it would otherwise be.

The Level of Conflict

High-intensity conflict tends to force up the *level* of conflict. The level of conflict can be understood in terms of the *generality* of the claims being defended. As the level of the conflict escalates, fewer and fewer claims can withstand the absolute scrutiny and high level of challenges forced on them. Skeptics tend to force up the level of argumentative conflicts to quite abstract heights. Perelman and Olbrechts-Tyteca track the level of conflict up to a universal audience. As we shall see later, Stephen Toulmin's model of argumentation is actually a tool for tracking the level of conflict in argumentation.

Low-level conflicts are conflicts about very particular matters, matters which are not obviously connected with general principles, and so they tend to be low-intensity conflicts. For example, a conflict about whether a community should build a swimming pool or a skateboard park would usually be a low-level conflict. Nothing very general hangs on the choice. People involved in the conflict would probably not have to sacrifice important beliefs and values in order to make their cases. Participants in the argumentation would probably not have to make appeals to general principles about which there might be conflict.

To put it in Perelman and Olbrechts-Tyteca's terms, most low-level conflicts are conflicts which are decided by relatively particular audiences. Certain facts, values, customs, understandings are assumed to hold for the particular audience involved in the conflict. If a community outside of Seattle, Washington, in the 1990s is deciding whether to build a swimming pool or a skateboard park, it is probably not relevant how people today in Tanzania would respond to the arguments, or how people in seventeenth-century Massachusetts would have judged the strength of the reasons offered. It is assumed that general truths and values are not at stake in the conflict.

Argumentation at a higher level of conflict tends to make its appeals to broader audiences. When people argue about whether freedom or justice is more important as an organizing principle of government, they could reasonably appeal to the judgments of people in very different societies and historical periods. More general principles are usually judged by more general audiences.

However, this apparent symmetry of intensity and level is the result of what is only a strong correlation. One can always imagine exceptions. One can imagine very-high-intensity conflicts which are also very low level. For example, imagine the following. A friend has been imprisoned unjustly in a foreign country. It would be a great risk, and a great expense and sacrifice, to attempt to help him. One would have to sacrifice one's allegiance to a number of principles in order to attempt to gain the freedom of one's friend. One might have to sacrifice principles that command one's loyalty to family or to co-workers or to clients or patients or to other friends. One might have to break other promises, commitments, in order to decide to help one's friend.

One might do all of this not because one holds to the general principle, *Friendship is the highest value*, or the maxim, *Sacrifice all other principles for the sake of friendship*, but rather because of one's loyalty to *this particular friend*. In such a case, the intensity of the conflict in one's reasoning is very high, but the level of the claim being defended, *I should help* this *friend at all costs*, is very low. In fact, the reasoning here is probably judged by a very particular audience: oneself alone. It is for this reason nonetheless argumentation. The fact that there is no warrant for *I should help* this *friend at all costs* is just a sign that the level of conflict is not high. The statement still serves as a reason for one's actions—even though it is a sufficient reason only for the one who utters it, the audience whose way of life is at stake.

Thus, although intensity and level are generally correlated, there is no necessity in the correlation. Level and intensity are distinct. Some people will find this result counterintuitive. They will claim that a reason that counts as a reason for only one person is not a reason at all. In Toulmin's terms, they will claim that it is only a warrant that connects a reason to a claim and thus establishes an argument. However, such objections betray an allegiance to a logical interpretation of reasoning and a refusal to allow audiences to be the judges of the merits of arguments. A pragmatic rhetoric of reason recognizes that all reasoning stops somewhere, in the satisfaction of some audience or other. A rhetoric of reason does not absolutize any particular audience, and is not prejudiced against individuals as audiences. The task is to describe the audience for whom an argument is effective. Adhering to particular reasons is the making of a particular form of life. We can understand the actions of someone who would sacrifice everything for a friend even if we would not recommend these actions to everyone, or reason in a similar fashion ourselves. We need not say the actions were "irrational" in order to reject the claim the reasoning might appear to make on us. Our reasons articulate our loyalties, and our own loyalties may lie elsewhere.

On the other hand, if we could succeed in getting this person into a higher level conflict about what deserves our loyalty, we might find ourselves engaged in reasoning which would have a broader claim over our collective actions.

The Means of Conflict

Fifth, one can also examine the means of conflict—the medium in which it is contained. In violence and war, we have relatively uncontained conflict—at least from the standpoint of discourse. In nonviolent action and classic civil disobedience, we see a more confined rhet-

Part Two: Reconstructing Argumentation

oric at play, a containing of violence in more symbolic conflict. Conflict is further contained when it is expressed only in discourse, even if it is discourse which is not yet argumentation. For example, in threats, lies, slander, insults, pleas, manifestos, nonnegotiable demands, and so on, we find a kind of discursive conflict which has its own rhetoric, but which is not yet argumentation. This is the sort of discourse to which Wayne Booth objects so strenuously in the introduction to *Modern Dogma and the Rhetoric of Assent.* Booth calls the parties to such discourse "combatants," because they have failed to contain their conflict in arguments, and thus their discourse resembles violence more than reasoning.

And certainly the conflict to which Booth is referring was not neatly contained. It is this idea of the containment of conflict to which a rhetoric of reason must pay special attention. However, it is also the intensity of the conflict to which Booth is objecting. Booth's book is written out of the milieu of the social conflict of the late sixties and early seventies. The conflict is intense because certain issues have taken on an overriding importance in the minds of the combatants, who are ready to sacrifice a number of hitherto established beliefs and practices to overthrow or suppress their opponents. The urge to action outside the usual forms of reasoning is a sign that there aren't enough agreements to enable meaningful argumentation. High-intensity conflicts often cannot be contained in argumentation; the commitment to one's own goals overrides the more delicate commitments and agreements and ethical bonds on which argumentation depends. Booth is right in trying to develop an account of a more expansive argumentative rhetoric which would include in reasonable discourse more than just arguments which yielded high degrees of certainty. But, to follow Aristotle and Churchill and Perelman, there is wisdom in knowing what one is willing to argue about and what one is not willing to surrender to public opinion. Sometimes our loyalties are so deep that they are not up for public reasoning. Some actions are so unthinkable that we don't have to reason about them.

One can find relatively uncontained conflict across the entire spectrum of discourse, and at all levels and degrees of intensity. But one has argumentation proper when force is contained in reasons. This is the essential insight of Habermas' attempt to develop the concept of an ideal speech situation, an imaginary situation in which all force has been eliminated except for the force of the better reasons. In such a situation, conflict has been contained in argumentation proper. All the particular structural constraints on argumentation are removed; there are no internal or external constraints. Everyone has an equal opportunity to argue and to be heard. Everyone's arguments are to be taken equally seriously. No one attempts to dominate or act merely strategically—either consciously or unconsciously. There are no threats, no inequalities, no corrupt procedures. Of course, this is an imaginary situation, it never really exists, but we can use this ideal to set a goal for our argumentation, to measure it, and to criticize arguments which take place in conditions which stray too far from this ideal.

I believe that in argumentation we have the greatest containment of conflict found in any of our discourse practices. This is why argumentation is so closely connected to our concept of reason; reason is supposed to be a nonviolent way of resolving conflicts. This does not mean that the level and intensity of conflict in argumentation are lower than in other discourse practices. In fact, I think that one can reduce the level and intensity of conflict in discourse practices that are nonargumentative further than would be possible in argumentation. Argumentation is animated by and depends on conflict in ways that make it different from other kinds of discourse. However, even in argumentation, one can reduce the intensity of conflict. This happens when argumentative reasoning is used for purposes of inquiry and in exploratory discourse. The aim of such discourse is not agreement so much as the discovery and articulation of ways of understanding. In this kind of argumentation, a more nonantagonistic questioner is present, one who asks questions that further a line of inquiry without constantly escalating the level of conflict and without trying to force closure on the claims being entertained. Such reasoning may take place in search of audiences, as a way of discovering them. In such situations, the conflict has a tendency both to slip out of its confinement to what are obviously reasons and to move into a domain where conflict is much more like play than combat. Interestingly enough, the function of ordinary-level argumentative conflict seems to be to reduce actual social conflict, while exploratory argumentation seems to assume a situation in which social conflict is already reduced.

The Purpose of Conflict

Sixth, and finally, there are different goals of the conflict resolution processes found in discourse. The goal of argumentation is to increase the adherence of an audience to a claim. This is the goal of argumentation as such, as a process, but this does not mean that people do not have other motivations for arguing. They always do. People rarely argue just for the sake of arguing. They engage in it for much the same purpose for which they engage in other conflicts; they expect to gain something from it. They may be more or less committed to achieving their goal. If they are very committed, the intensity and level of conflict may be forced up. If the commitment is absolute, the conflict it engenders will probably not be able to be contained in argumentation. Argumentation, then, is a means to other ends. But it is always a risky method, and is riskier the more the argumentative situation approaches the conditions of an ideal speech situation.

One of the most remarkable things about argumentation is that we learn when we engage in it; as our beliefs and goals are challenged by others, we often see fit to modify them, or take up new purposes altogether. Once we agree to argue, and to go on arguing, we enter a process whose outcome we cannot determine ahead of time, one in which our purposes are never completely secure.

Objections and Clarifications

If what I have said so far is right, then an important way not to defend but to clarify and develop my own account is to consider the challenges which could be made to it. I will begin by responding to the objection that I have offered no way to understand what an *argument* is, and I will explain how a rhetorical theory can still give a reasonable account of this. Then I will consider a particular kind of counterclaim, a structural model designed to analyze and evaluate arguments—Stephen Toulmin's famous model of the layout of arguments. I intend to show that everything that is useful about this model can be understood in terms of a rhetorical theory of argument as process, and that the parts of it that cannot are, in fact, misleading. Finally, I want to consider Lakoff and Johnson's claim that *Argument is war* is a metaphor in the light of my own claim that argument actually is a kind of social conflict, and show what the metaphorical interpretation of the relation misses.

THE IDEA OF AN ARGUMENT

Can we still make sense of the notion of *an* argument if we conceptualize argument as a process of conflict? Yes, but the only reason for isolating an argument this way is to evaluate it as something that is finished and must be measured by a conventionalized standard. And for both theoretical and pedagogical reasons, I want to give some reasons against doing this. First, one can evaluate argumentative discourse *without* isolating arguments from the process of argumentation. We can evaluate arguments without resorting to formal models by identifying the kind of audience which has the authority to judge their merits. I will devote all of Part II of this book to showing how audiences can serve as the measures of argumentation. Further, though, when we isolate an argument, we remove it from a context of argumentation, a rhetorical situation, a host of arguments with which it interacts, a continuing conversation, and redescribe it in terms which come from elsewhere; in short, we change it. Sometimes, we distort the argumentation by conceptualizing it as an argument. This happens especially when we start finding "fallacies"—as if writers of arguments were attempting logical proofs and had simply misapplied rules. Further yet, written arguments are sometimes embedded in imaginary contexts, and it is not at all clear how they should be interpreted. For example, are the argumentative utterances of the characters in a Platonic dialogue unambiguous candidates for isolation and analysis? What is their relation to what we might want to ask about the argument of the dialogue? Isolating arguments could in some cases take us further away from what is actually being said.

Nevertheless, it does make sense to ask, What is the argument? and to tell people that it is not exactly clear what their argument is. It makes sense because what isolated arguments schematized according to logical or quasi-logical models *really are* are representations of the way an idealized audience would conceptualize the argumentation. Thus, in trying to say what an argument is, I am describing a view I believe any audience *must* take in order to understand argumentation *as* argumentation.

So, again, the minimal conditions for there being an argument are that there must be a claim, there must be some challenge to that claim, and there must be a response to the challenge in the form of a reason for making the claim, a reason offered to settle the conflict. The demand for a warrant, a rule which permits one to move from reason to claim, is not an essential feature of an argument, although in rhetorical situations in which the level of conflict is high, a demand for a warrant and perhaps for backing is very likely. So an argument from particular to particular is still an argument because it involves an explicit claim, an implicit challenge, and an explicit reason for making the claim . . . even if it won't convince many audiences. It functions as an argument as long as someone accepts it as an argument.

STEPHEN TOULMIN

I want to consider Stephen Toulmin's model of argumentation as a kind of counterclaim to what I have proposed here, and use an understanding of argument as a process of social conflict to interpret and evaluate Toulmin's model of the layout of arguments. Of all the "models" of logical form with which I am familiar, Toulmin's comes the closest to being a model of the process of argumentation. The model is an attempt to capture the *structure of arguments,* and so it is spatialized and represented synchronically in a way that enables us to analyze arguments we have isolated from argumentation. And yet when Toulmin explains and justifies the model, he resorts to a description of the process which the model arrests. Thus, according to Toulmin, when one wants to analyze the force of an argument, one must imagine two parties in a process of conflict: an assertor and a questioner. An assertor makes a claim; a questioner challenges the claim by asking for clarification, or more properly to get the argument going, justification. The assertor then gives grounds for the claim. This questioner can be intransigent and engage in an argumentative escalation of the conflict by asking for a warrant that makes the grounds good reasons for the claim. If a warrant is offered by the assertor, the questioner can escalate the conflict still further by asking for backing for the warrant. Backing usually takes the form of general scientific principles, legislation, some established body of professional knowledge. Backing is specific to argumentative domains, and is linked to the various rational enterprises operating in a society. Toulmin also includes modal qualifiers and conditions of rebuttal to get the model to conform to ordinary argumentation, in which arguments rarely go through in unqualified fashion. These qualifiers, too, are represented as responses to a questioner who challenges the unconditionality of the claims made by an assertor.[5]

What I find most noteworthy in Toulmin's scheme is that it is not really so much a formal model of argument as a map, a method, for tracking conflict in argumentation, and identifying the levels of demand for justification an argument reaches, the level at which the conflict must be resolved. As a measure of argumentation, it is a representation of the point of view of a very generalized and idealized audience of competent professionals whose demands for justification are very high, but limited by professional identities and standards of professional competence. This is obvious by looking at the kind of "backing" Toulmin's imagined interlocutors offer.

The questions this raises are: why has Toulmin arrested the process of argumentation in a spatialized scheme, and why does he limit the level of justification to backing? And the answers are (1) he wants a way to evaluate arguments that makes it look as if they are being evaluated formally, in terms of the internal relations of the parts of the argument. That is, he wants this to look to some degree like logic. And (2) the reason he limits the demand for justification to backing is that his idealized audience is basically an institutional figure—someone whose rationality is institutionally determined by the rational enterprise to which he or she is committed, who raises no questions about it, and who, in fact, doesn't know how to. This latter point can be seen clearly in Toulmin's account of moral reasoning, in which backing plays almost no role. Moral arguments, he claims, are usually settled at the level of the warrant. At the level of backing, we resort to individual preferences—or in more explicit terms, to dogmatism. If we did take general questions about established morality and professional competence seriously, it would mean, Toulmin says, and I quote, "pursuing them either in rhetorical or philosophical terms." End of discussion.[6]

But there are real disadvantages to this project. Above all, it's basically misleading. The model is supposed to be a neutral tool for analyzing and evaluating arguments, but it actually represents an audience which makes particular kinds of demands on a writer. The kind of audience which would exact a measure of the sort represented in the complete model has a level of universality higher than that demanded by most audiences, but—and this is the second disadvantage, the reasoning is also arbitrarily limited. That is, it pretends to model rationality itself, but it provides no way of understanding reasoning that attempts to appraise the rationality of the various rational enterprises themselves or of settling between the competing claims the different enterprises may make.

This misrepresentation is not only not necessary but arbitrarily reduces the domain of argumentation and gives up on any effort to conceptualize that domain in a more expansive way. Toulmin offers a model that looks like a completely decontextualized formal and universal means of evaluating arguments, but it actually reifies one particular version of what is universal and cuts off any reasoning which would try to discover the particular character of that universality.

Thus, what is best about Toulmin's model can be understood in terms of the process I have described in the preceding chapters. A rhetoric of reason leaves Toulmin everything he really needs, and it prevents the misunderstandings to which his model could lead. I am not objecting to Toulmin's sketches of the "basic patterns" of arguments or of their "layout." They are useful in many ways. I am instead trying to understand what they are. One difficulty here is that Toulmin's account lacks a theory of claiming—a theory of argumentation as action, an account of the senses in which reasoning is a way of being, a means of acknowledging oneself and others. What the account is also missing is a recognition of the fact that the ascending hierarchy of appeals is a representation of one kind of audience and not a representation of rationality as such. *How much* reasoning we demand in a particular situation depends on our judgments about what is appropriate. Toulmin can't really explain why we sometimes *appropriately* refuse to recognize an appeal to the level of backing—the level of professional knowledge—why we sometimes give greater weight to the commonsense claims of a lower level of conflict. To explain these things would require a theory of audience—a theory of the way in which reasoning is a way of becoming a certain kind of person, a person who recognizes a certain way of life as worthy, and whose standards of rationality are an expression of the judgments of the person he or she would like to be or become. And even when Toulmin seems to recognize this, as he almost does with his acknowledging that sometimes backing is just an appeal to a chosen "way of life," he still fails to acknowledge the variability of the audiences which judge whether such an appeal needs to be made at all and whether it is legitimate or not.[7]

LAKOFF AND JOHNSON

Next, I want to consider George Lakoff and Mark Johnson's claim that the relation of conflict and argument is a metaphorical one. The most important point about Lakoff and Johnson's concept of metaphor as it applies to "Argument is war" is that we don't just talk about arguments in terms of war. What we do in arguing is partially structured by the concept of war. This is why Lakoff and Johnson call their book *Metaphors We Live By*. We can, they say, actually win or lose arguments. We conceptualize interlocutors as opponents. We attack their positions and defend our own. We use strategies. We abandon indefensible positions. Lakoff and Johnson say that this metaphor is in the concept, and thus that the talk about argumentation as war is in one sense literal. We act according to the metaphor, and the metaphor enables thinking which otherwise would not be possible. This is a quite different account of the connection between conflict and argument from the one I have offered.

Lakoff and Johnson make it sound as if war and argument are ontologically entangled with one another, or at least that they have overlapping features, but this is clearly *not* what they mean. They say: "*The essence of metaphor is understanding and experiencing one kind of thing in terms of another.* It is not that arguments are a subspecies of war. Arguments and wars are different kinds of things—verbal discourse and armed conflict—and the actions performed are different kinds of actions. But argument is partially structured, understood, performed, and talked about in terms of war" (5). Thus, although war and argument are two different kinds of thing, our concept of one structures the way we think of, talk about, and perform the other. However, if what we *do* in arguing is partially structured by the concept of war, then it's hard to see how arguing and war are two different kinds of things. After all, arguing is what we do in arguing; it is a kind of action we take. If the kind of action we take in argumentation is warlike, then the metaphor structures not only our concept of argument, but argument itself. Of course then we don't have two different sorts of things, so the relation between them can't be described as metaphorical. It is not so much that they are *like* each other as that they are, in some respects, the same kind of thing. However, this is what Lakoff and Johnson deny.

Lakoff and Johnson could try to get out of this difficulty by saying that the way in which the war metaphor structures argument is not an essential way, that argument would still be argument if it were not structured by the metaphor of war. But they are reluctant to make this case. They invite us to imagine a culture where argument is viewed as dance, with roles choreographed according to aesthetic purposes. They conclude that "It would seem strange even to call what they are doing 'arguing.'" And they say that the neutral thing to say would be that "we have a discourse form structured in terms of battle and they have one structured in terms of dance" (5). Here it seems that there is no such thing as argument apart from the war metaphor; so they resort to the term "discourse form." Notice the slip. Now, it is not that we have a *concept* structured in terms of a metaphor, but an actual *discourse form* which is so structured. It seems clear that Lakoff and Johnson cannot maintain their primary claim that war and argumentation are two completely different kinds of things.

This can be seen even more clearly in their account of the way conversation passes into argument. They say that conversations pass into arguments when they start to be structured in terms of the war metaphor. This is, then, what makes a conversation an argument (77ff.). But if the metaphor is what makes conversation an argument, it is what makes an argument an argument. Thus, again, the metaphorical structuring and the thing being structured cannot be kept distinct. The reason for this is that the relation between argument and war is not simply metaphorical. Argument and war are both forms of human conflict, and they both aim toward a resolution of conflict, although usually toward very different kinds of resolutions. The difference is in the way the conflict is contained—whether it can be contained in language use, and then further whether it can be contained in reasoning. This difference between the force of reasons and physical force is enormous, and has enormous consequences for human lives and societies, but it should not completely blind us to the senses in which argument and war are processes of human conflict that share many features. Recognizing these gives one an even deeper sense of wonder at the fact that there are rhetorical practices at all, that human conflict *can* be contained in discourse, and that a relative peace can be achieved and sustained through discursive means.[8]

The exact logic of the relation between war and argumentation is not easy to make clear. Trying to make it clear gets me into another conflict with Lakoff and Johnson.

Lakoff and Johnson hold that structural metaphors like "Argument is war" are *grounded;* that is, that one of the terms comes from a domain in which we have a direct experience, usually a physical one, of that to which the term refers.[9] They say that the "Argument is war" metaphor is grounded in that it allows us to conceptualize what a rational argument is in terms of something that we understand more readily: physical conflict. They explain that "Fighting is found everywhere in the animal kingdom and nowhere so much as among human animals" (64). They conclude that there is a "lineage" that runs from argument "back to its origins in physical combat" (64). But these notions of origin and grounding and lineage raise more questions than they answer. The idea that there is an original domain of direct experience and immediate meanings from which, in some linear fashion, meaning flows into indirect and derivative signs is deeply questionable.

This is because physical conflict is itself already rhetorical, already a kind of symbolic action, already understood in terms of argument. Nowhere is this clearer than in Clausewitz's dictum that "War is just policy carried on by other means." Here, the metaphorical "lineage" runs in exactly the opposite direction: the reasoning carried on under the normal conditions of peace allows us to conceptualize what rationality there is in war. Thus, the origin and grounding of our understanding of war lie in reasoning and rational activity. However, Clausewitz did not really see it so simply. He also saw the senses in which "Peace is the continuation of struggle by other means." The point is that there is in both physical combat and argumentative reasoning something like conflict. And this conflict has a rhetoric, a way of signifying that is more like discourse than like an immediate and direct experience of brute force.

This is overt in many of the features of war. In bluffing, ambushing, and deceit in general, there is an attempt to persuade an opponent to draw certain conclusions. And this is the stuff of war. Again, as Sun Tzu says, "All warfare is based on deception. Hence, when able to attack, we must seem unable; when using our forces, we must seem inactive; when we are near, we must make the enemy believe we are far away; when far away, we must make him believe we are near. Hold out baits to entice the enemy. Feign disorder and crush him . . . Attack him where he is un-prepared, appear where you are not expected" (11). The actions we take in conflict are designed to function as reasons for opponents to think in a certain way or take a certain action in response. Force is not simply immediate. Force in human conflict is significant, and the study of war is in part a study of the rhetoric of force. Brute force is not significant in this way. Brute force does not make a claim on us. It is not questionable the way an act of claiming is. It is not a communicative event.

Thus, it is not that physical conflict is a pure experience of immediate physical meanings which we lift in order to conceptualize argument. This ground or direct experience is not really direct or immediate at all; it, too, is a matter of signification, interpretation, and all the indirection and mediating these involve. Physical conflict is not the ground of argumentation. If anything, it would be more proper to say that argumentation is the ground of physical conflict, and that war and fighting would be impossible without it.

However, I find it more helpful to say that conflict has different objects, is contained in different ways, and that it has different levels and intensities, different goals and resolutions. The question of whether there is something unsayable about conflict—that is, the question of whether conflict is something apart from that in which it is "contained," is of course not easily answerable, if it is answerable at all. But whatever it is, it not only allows us to conceptualize argument and physical conflict in terms of each other; it also makes each of them possible: both the destructive conflict of war and violence and the discourse that not only sustains peace, but animates the rational inquiry that leads to new forms of life. I hereby admit to having some slight metaphysical proclivities toward thinking that conflict is in some sense real;[10] however, all I am urging here is that conflict is much more generative, all-pervading, and constructive than we are usually inclined to think. Considered from one angle, the angle of argumentation, conflict is a way of having peace and renewal.

Conclusion: Back to Teaching

Let me conclude this chapter by tying some of these themes back together with the project of teaching written reasoning to see if there is any early yield. Again, the only "yield" this theory intends to offer teachers is a new way of thinking about what they are doing when they teach argumentation—not a set of directives for how actually to do it. I do not believe that the important variables in good teaching can be controlled by adopting theory-driven lesson plans. I do believe that some of the greatest threats to education are skepticism and smallness of spirit. Again, one of the purposes of developing a rhetoric of reason is to give a spirited response to skepticism on its own ground, and so to give confidence and hope to teachers of written reasoning. However, a rhetorical angle on reasoning does suggest particular views of what happens when we teach, and it would be neglectful not to point them out.

First, one of the advantages of conceptualizing writing as a process of conflict is that it allows teachers to think of that process as a field for their own action. It is not just that teachers *intervene* in that process, although that is the way it is often put, but that they become participants in it. To conceptualize argument as a process of social conflict structured by these roles of assertor and questioner is to show us what social roles are already there in this process for teachers or commentators to inhabit. Writers don't know whether claims are clear or whether they stand unless they can hear the relevant challenges that can be made to them. Thus, teachers can play the role not only of the ultimate audience-arbiter of the effectiveness of arguments, but also of participant-interlocutor, voicing relevant questions, questions which themselves generate clarifications, reasons, qualifications, and more reasons. Part of teaching argumentation is having the ability to recognize and to play the relevant roles within a dispute, so voices can come to life for a student who has not been exposed to them, or for some reason cannot hear them. Students who cannot "develop" their ideas are students who cannot hear the voices of the relevant interlocutors.

However, immediate qualifications are necessary. Students can also be overwhelmed with the voices a teacher brings to bear on their claims. Helping students to find the appropriate interlocutors is a process that requires a kind of judgment that cannot be simply handed from one person to another. If Cavell is right, finding the appropriate interlocutor/ friend/enemy is, in fact, almost everything, in reasoning as in life. Recognizing this can cause us to flee to simpler, more manageable and teachable models of argumentation, or it can disclose the teaching of reasoning as an activity that is very rarely glimpsed as what it really is. Persistently asking which stasis is at stake in a student's reasoning is, in my own experience, a very successful action to take with students. However, I have also seen this done mechanically, without any real grasp of what a student was trying to communicate. Timeliness and appropriateness and seeing things from the students' points of view are everything in the teaching of written reasoning.

Looking at argumentation as social conflict also suggests one of the functions reading fulfills in developing arguments, and explains what research in preparing an argument can be. One function is quite simply finding the voices to argue with, discovering voices which stem from other forms of life, other sets of experiences, other basic beliefs. Of course, it takes a good reader to give voice to what comes in print, but this is one way for a teacher to teach reading, too. This means reading and researching for something more than simple background knowledge. It means looking for claims, especially conflicting claims. It means searching for the voices that call one's own claims into question. It means making judgments about which of the many voices one encounters can be brought together into productive conversation. And it means doing so in a way that is most helpful for the individual student in question, which means individual students must be taught to do this for themselves. Again, in my own experience, this means that yes/no, point/counterpoint issues are nearly worthless for teaching written reasoning. Issues which permit several different reasonable approaches, many different kinds of voices, are much more productive of learning.

Third, a pragmatic-rhetorical angle on reasoning gives students a way of conceptualizing written argumentation in terms of its function. The goal is not to produce an argument, but to resolve social conflicts, to lead different voices toward agreement. This seems to me an eminently more motivating reason to write than to make the production of an argument an abstract end in itself, one to be evaluated in terms of its meeting certain formal criteria.

Fourth, "anticipating objections" is no longer simply one of the "parts" of an argumentative discourse, or something one does at the end of a speech or essay. Conflict, disagreement, the voices of difference, are the sources and springs of argumentation. Invention begins with conflict and disagreement rather than setting them aside as problems to be solved *after* an argument has been formulated. This means that audience and interlocutor are involved in the reasoning and writing process from the very beginning—maybe not explicitly, but their roles must be filled nevertheless. Teachers who think of reason in rhetorical terms will find ways of recognizing and using the primacy of interlocutor and audience in the process of writing. In fact, this gives teachers a way to explain to students how valuable they can be to each other in the process of developing their arguments.

Fifth, this way of thinking of the teaching and learning of argumentation illuminates its ethical features—and this in several respects. First, it conceptualizes argument as an alternative to arbitrary power, violence, and war. Second, it alerts us to the many social conflicts that may be operating in discourse, thematized or not. Third, it brings us into contact with ways of thinking and reasoning that are different from our own, and provides a powerful means for deeper mutual understanding.

Finally, it also gives students new ways of establishing their own identities. If what I have said is right, then our identities as reasoners, as people who engage in written argumentation, is partly constituted by those others to whom we give voice in our reasoning. Which others we give voice to, how much we let them speak, what we let them speak about, how we subordinate them to each other—all this will make up our own identity as thinkers, as arguers, as people with voices of our own.

Such an understanding of the teaching of written reasoning may not in itself deliver us completely from the reluctance and skepticism that threaten us, but I believe it clears our path a little.

PART THREE

EVALUATING

ARGUMENTS

5 AUDIENCES AND ARGUMENTS

Introduction

Chapter 1 of this book explored the current philosophical situation of theories of reason, and showed how the collapse of traditional models of argumentative reasoning called for a new rhetorical account of reason and argument. The following chapters sketched the general outlines of such a theory, and then began to try to fill in the outline.

The reconstruction of argumentation offered in the chapters on claiming and questioning answered a fairly straightforward question: if reasoning is not best understood in traditional metaphysical or logical or psychological categories, then what categories are appropriate for clarifying what happens when people argue? Throughout Part I, I tried to avoid any reductive account of argumentation. Instead, I focused on the senses in which claiming and questioning and justifying are actions we already understand in deep and complicated ways in everyday life. I tried to elaborate and develop and clarify these understandings by interpreting claiming and questioning as speech actions which take place in ethically rich environments. I also tried to show the consequences of such an approach by persistently posing questions about education in general and the teaching of written reasoning in particular.

Again, this attempt to hold a relatively nonmethodological, nonreductionist discussion about reasoning, one that takes the idea of rhetoric as its angle on argument, can be measured only against pragmatic standards. Logic and psychology and metaphysics have failed to explain what happens when people argue, or at least have failed to explain it in a way that makes the teaching of written reasoning attractive and justifiable. A rhetoric of reason can be measured by the degree to which it accounts for the possibility of reasoning, reveals it as something worthy and attractive, and shows how it meets the needs that the traditional concept of reason can no longer meet.

However, a primary obstacle still stands in the way of a convincing rhetoric of reason. This obstacle is rhetoric's prima facie inability to offer a standard for the evaluation of arguments that has anything near the clarity and force and universality of logical standards. Part III confronts this obstacle by showing how audiences can be the measures of arguments in ways that meet the objections that logician-critics have made against rhetoric. So in this chapter I begin to develop a theory of audience as a sufficient measure of the strength of arguments. I start by constructing a concept of audience in general and then dividing audiences into a few basic kinds. I continue by developing the idea of a universal audience—an idea which allows a rhetoric of reason to make a distinction between arguments that are more generally valid and arguments that are effective only for more particular audiences. The concept of rhetorical universality plays a critical role in the rhetoric of reason. In the final chapter of the book, I will show how the concept helps rhetoric to satisfy the needs of reason that were discussed in Chapter 1.

In Chapter 6, I will show how audience-based standards of rationality can also account for our concept of what it is to be unreasonable, and so I offer a new rhetorical theory of fallacies, one that sharply contrasts with the recent theoretical attempts of informal logicians. In Chapter 7, I step back from the project for a moment to evaluate not arguments but argumentation itself, to acknowledge that argumentation carries an ideology, and to try to clarify its ideological commitments.

The Concept of Audience

Although the purpose of this chapter is to show how a reception theory of rationality can meet the objections that logicians and philosophers might make to it, it is necessary also to develop the general concept of audience at work here, in order to prevent misunderstandings. Since I will be speaking of the audience primarily in its role of evaluating arguments, I want to stress very strongly that *audience plays a role at every instant and in every feature of any argument.*

It is easy to see how features of argumentation like background information, clarifications, illustrations, and so on are ways of meeting the needs of audiences. However, it is not usually seen as clearly that the kernel of an argument, the claim/reason, is just as completely dependent on an audience as any other features of argumentation. I mentioned in Chapter 4 that the primary conflict at play in argumentation is the conflict between a claimant and an audience. The claimant understands the audience to be in need of change, so there is a conflict set up between the audience as it is and the audience as the claimant would like it to be. Or, put differently, there is a conflict between the claimant's disclosure of things and the audience's.

So the first fact of argumentative conflict is that a claim is made *on an audience.* If there were not an audience in need of change—change in knowledge, perspective, intent, sympathy, mood, awareness, any kind of change—there would be no claim, no argumentation. Further, as we have seen, it is the audience which will determine the way the claim is expressed, the occasion on which it is expressed, the language in which it finds expression—in fact, unless the claim is made in the appropriate way, it will not even *be* a claim for the audience in question. It is not as if one can construct an argument, and then present it to an audience for evaluation. It is the audience-claimant pair, in conflict, which first creates the need for and possibility of reason and argument. Again, this audience may be oneself, or one other person, or a very large group. The audience may be conceptualized in terms of individual, highly idiosyncratic responses, or in terms of psychological types, or demographic characteristics, or shared interpretive and evaluative conventions, or many other things. However, audiences shape arguments from the very beginning, from the very motivations for reasoning argumentatively.

The audience also influences the particular speech actions of the respondent, or the interlocutor. The interlocutor may or may not respond to a claim in the way that the audience would, but the interlocutor should respond in a way that the audience can recognize as *relevant* to its eventually judging the argumentation. Thus, the implicit question or objection in written arguments is also influenced by, if not made by, the audience.

Above all, the audience has a say in what counts as a reason for a claim. The most important knowledge a writer or speaker must have of an audience is a knowledge of what, for that audience, will count as a reason for and what will count as a reason against. Reasons count in different ways for different audiences. To mistake one's audience can be to fail to reason successfully. For it is the audience which is the measure of the worth of arguments.

However, a major question arises at this point. How do we know which audience is the real audience for any particular piece of argumentation? How do we know which audience is the appropriate judge of some piece of reasoning? The answer to the question of audience may be found only by way of a careful identification of the claimant. For it is the claimant who intends to make a claim on someone and to support the claim with reasons. The speech action of making a claim depends on the possibility of identifying the person on whom the claim is made. Thus, the audience that will judge an argument will be those on whom the claimant is making a claim. It is this audience which must decide whether and to what degree to accept or refuse the claim.

As we know all too well, though, things are not this easy. It is no simple matter to know on whom the claimant is making a claim, or even who the real claimant is. Arguments and audiences are linked to many kinds and levels of claimant. In Plato's *Protagoras,* Socrates may be making a claim on Protagoras, and Protagoras may be both interlocutor and audience within the scene in which the argumentation takes place. In one sense, then, Socrates may intend to influence Protagoras with his argumentation. However, it is possible that Socrates has no hope or intention of actually convincing Protagoras of anything. Rather, it may be that he is using Protagoras as an interlocutor for an argument whose real audience is the group of men and boys gathered around the pair. However, these men, too, may be only an apparent audience; in fact, there is good evidence in the dialogue that Socrates has a low regard for their judgments. Socrates could be making his real claim on young Hippocrates, who is intended to be the judge of the argumentation, and who has given Socrates a motivation for arguing with the great sophist in the first place. Or, since Socrates is telling the story of the dialogue to an unnamed companion, it could be that the real claim in question is being made on this companion—that Socrates is giving an account of the arguments in order to let them have their proper influence on the proper audience.

Of course, it could be that Socrates is not the claimant at all. It could be that Plato is the claimant, and he could intend a quite different audience for the dialogue he has written. Each argument in the dialogue might make up part of a much larger argument intended for an audience which is never characterized or addressed in the text itself. Beyond this, it could be that the dialogue comes to make new claims in later historical periods, claims Plato could not easily have foreseen. The dialogue may be cited today as having a bearing on contemporary issues, and so the new claimant may actually be one of our contemporaries, who is affirming the dialogue in a new way. Or *we* may read the dialogue as making this new claim, and we may ourselves be the new audience. In fact, part of learning to reason is learning to hold the dialogue of reason with ourselves, to fill the various speech roles that make up an argument.

Further, a whole host of claims may accrue to a historical text as it is passed along through the centuries. Consequently, a text such as a Platonic dialogue may be experienced as making a complicated, inconsistent system of claims, the result of the interpretations and arguments and editions and translations that have become internal to our experience of the text itself. As I said before, we are claimed, even by a single text, way beyond our ability to make claims explicit.

However, even given all these difficulties that stand in the way of agreeing on an interpretation of an argument—i.e., identifying the claim, claimant, and audience—there are some relatively simple and helpful ways to understand how audiences function as judges of arguments. (I want to consider only arguments which are intended to be successful; arguments which are meant to fail call for a different treatment.) Every reading of an argument yields an implied audience, and by this I mean the audience on whom the claim is understood to be made and in terms of which the argumentation is supposed to develop. In a charitable reading, this implied audience is also the audience for whom the argument is persuasive, the audience which allows itself to be influenced by the reasoning.

These facts illuminate the two most important principles of a rhetorical theory of argument evaluation. First, audiences are the measures of arguments. One knows the degree to which an argument has succeeded with an audience when one knows the degree to which the audience really does fill the role of the implied reader and end up being persuaded by the reasoning. Second, audiences must themselves be judged. We can always imagine an audience for whom a particular piece of reasoning is successful. To know, for ourselves, the worth of a piece of reasoning, we must know the quality of the people who would assent to it, or the quality of the lives such people would lead. The worth of an argument is directly determined by the worth of the life it informs. The evaluation of arguments rests on the same shifting, complicated, inconsistent, everyday sense of what is good, what is worthwhile, what is desirable, that human beings have tried to systematize in theories in all the disciplines and professions and spheres of life that lay claim to a rational justification.

Am I taking a stand, then, on the side of the "invoked" or "fictional" audience over against the "addressed" or "real" audience? Not at all. In one sense, neither "invoked" nor "addressed" captures the profundity of what happens in argumentation. There is a sense in which audience is more an event than a collection of people—real or imagined. That is, audience is something that happens in time, as an event in people's lives, in their talking and writing and communicating in general. We are constantly becoming one audience or another, constantly abandoning audiences we have been in the past. Even talk of *event* does not go far enough. Audiences are not just isolated events in our lives; audience is a mode of being, one of the ways human beings *are*. Audience is one of the ways we make possible ways of being our own, one of the ways we learn and change. By moving into what is, for us, a new audience, we move into a new way of understanding and judging, new kinds of experiences.

A written argument is addressed to someone, or to some group, which already has a way of being an audience, and this shapes everything about the argumentation—whether the writer "consciously" imagines these people or not. In addition, though, a claimant is trying to change these people, and so must clear a new way of understanding and judging for them to enter. To say that the writer must "imagine" this new audience puts it way too psychologically, as if it were simply a private, inner event. From one angle, it is readers who are in conflict with the implied audience, and they are measuring its attractiveness as a way of being through the probing and testing of an interlocutor—an event that is being orchestrated or conducted, as well and as much as possible, by the writer.

Thus, it is misleading to take a stand, in the teaching of writing, on the side of having students focus either on the "addressed" or the "invoked" audience.[1] Influences run in all directions. Readers and writers are shaped by the actual ways of being of other people at every stage in the reading and writing process. And readers and writers are influenced by an implied way of being just as thoroughly—one way or the other, if they are reading and writing well. The event of audience occurs everywhere in this process of conflicts and resolutions. In what follows I have deferred—in order to avoid awkward neologistic phrases—to our usual ways of speaking of audiences as if they were groups of people with particular characteristics. However, readers should be mindful of the fact that the concept of audience *as a way of being* runs through all the reasoning here.

The task a rhetoric of reason faces is to develop a theory of audience which can both take these approaches and yet still give hope that reason can resolve important conflicts—conflicts that might otherwise grow violent, or conflicts about what higher education is, or conflicts about what kinds of societies we should have, and how we should live.

Kinds of Audience

There are many different ways to divide audiences into kinds. For the purpose of demonstrating the complexity of interpreting arguments, one can imagine almost countless ways of categorizing audiences. However, for the purpose of showing how a rhetoric of reason can maintain a special hold on the claim of *reason*, it is not necessary to imagine so many kinds of audience. I intend to outline only a few general categories of audience in order to defend the claims I want to make about reason and argumentation. The categories I have chosen are taken from Chaim Perelman and Lucie Olbrechts-Tyteca's *The New Rhetoric*, although I have changed them both to suit my purposes and to clarify their role in evaluating arguments. The bulk of my discussion is taken up with an effort to clarify the idea of a best audience, a paragon or "universal" audience—the argumentative equivalent of reader response theory's "ideal reader." Here I go fairly deeply into *The New Rhetoric's* very

complicated and in many ways profound (and profoundly misunder-
stood) attempts to reconstruct the universality of reason's claims in
rhetorical terms.

The most important of the distinctions *The New Rhetoric* draws between kinds of audience is the distinction between a particular audience and a universal audience.[2] This distinction between audiences is
made in order to distinguish between argumentation which appeals only
to particular groups with particular characteristics in particular places
at particular times and argumentation which attempts to transcend such
particularity and make its appeals more broadly. By developing an
account of the differences between universal audiences and particular
ones, Perelman and Olbrechts-Tyteca believe they can better distinguish between merely effective and genuinely valid argumentation.
One of the advantages of this line of approach is that they can thereby
avoid the more vicious dualisms which sometimes afflict theories of argumentation—for example, the dualism of reason and emotion which
assigns moods and emotions roles to play in persuasion and in effective argumentation, but none in convincing and in genuine argumentation. The approach also carefully avoids similar divisions of mind and
body, form and content, objective and subjective, intellect and will.

Particular audiences are constituted by agreements not only on facts
but also on concrete values, interests, and objectives. If one addressed
the members of an audience as adherents of a particular religion, or as
members of particular political groups or parties, one would be addressing them as a particular audience. On the other hand, if one addressed them simply as reasonable people, and did not rely on their
adherence to the concrete values of a particular religion or political
group, one would be addressing them as a more universal audience. The
problem in attempting to develop such an approach is that one faces an
obvious dilemma: the "universal" audience is either an empty concept—too vague and general to be of any real use in evaluating arguments—or it is not really "universal" at all, but just another particular
audience disguising its interests as universal truths. The problem is to
develop a criterion for validity that avoids this dilemma of being either
universal but empty or concrete but particular. And the strategy a rhetoric of reason adopts is to make universality a thoroughly rhetorical
idea—a feature of an audience, a matter of degree, and something which
finds different concrete fulfillments in different rhetorical situations. This
strategy of thinking of rationality or universality as a feature of audiences rather than arguments is not altogether new.

Socrates says in the *Phaedrus* (273E) that a worthy rhetoric would employ techniques capable of convincing the gods themselves. However,

the most systematic and persistent attempt to develop this kind of theory occurs in modern political thought—in social contract theory. A central concern of modern political theory is to find an audience whose members evaluate one another's arguments in a way that ensures that the most worthy argument will be the most effective one.

In Hobbes, Locke, and Rousseau, human beings are themselves to have the authority for deciding what rules shall order their societies. They imagine human beings not as they are, but as they were or would be in a state of nature. They justify the social contract on the basis of the deliberations individuals would go through in a state of nature and the rules they would adopt in such a state. The advantage of imagining a state of nature is that individuals in such a state have universal human features and follow natural laws. They are not susceptible to appeals made to them as members of particular groups or classes. Thus, the arguments by which they are persuaded have more universal worth than the arguments that persuade actual individuals in actual societies. Of course, such theories seem to have a mythic or literary cast to contemporary political theorists. And they are all bedeviled by a moral valorizing of nature which many people simply will not accept.

A more contemporary effort of this sort is made in John Rawls's *A Theory of Justice*, in which he tries to imagine an audience whose deliberations will result in their adopting genuine principles of justice. However, instead of imagining a state of nature, he imagines a hypothetical situation of equal liberty, what he calls the "original position." In such a position, writes Rawls, "No one knows his place in society, his class position or social status, nor does anyone know his fortune in the distribution of natural assets and abilities, his intelligence, strength and the like. I shall even assume that the parties do not know their conceptions of the good or their special psychological propensities. The principles of justice are chosen behind a veil of ignorance" (12). Because the reasoning which goes on within the original position is addressed to an audience which has only universal human features and no particular ones, the principles of justice which emerge from such deliberation have a general scope and not merely a particular one.

A Basic Problem with the Approach

The same general strategy has been recently adopted by Jürgen Habermas, and since his attempt is one of the most contemporary, and since it is explicitly a part of a theory of communication which has already had a great influence on communication theorists, rhetoricians, and literary theorists, I want to use it as an example of the general problem such attempts face.

Habermas holds to a consensus theory of truth, but he needs a way to distinguish a "rational" consensus from a merely de facto one, and thus truth from mere agreement. He comes up with a criterion similar in some respects to Perelman and Olbrechts-Tyteca's. The criterion of truth is not mere agreement, but agreement under certain conditions— conditions under which all the particular structural constraints on argumentation are removed and the cooperative search for truth is the only motive in play. There must be no internal or external constraints. Everyone must have an equal opportunity to argue and be heard. Everyone's arguments must be taken equally seriously. No one may attempt to dominate or act merely strategically—either consciously or unconsciously.[3]

Habermas realizes that this is never the concrete situation in which argumentation takes place. It is a counterfactual ideal. Yet he claims that it is a supposition we make when we speak of truth claims' being rationally grounded in argumentation, because if we can argue that the outcome of an argument was influenced by other motives, that an audience was acting strategically or neurotically, that some member was threatened by force, and so on, then this would call the truth claim into question—the consensus would not be understood to be a rational one.

However, Habermas came to realize that there was a serious problem with his concept of an "ideal speech situation." The problem has to do with the emptiness of the motivations of the participants in it, their lack of any other motivation than reaching a consensus on truth. As Habermas writes, "Is it possible that one day an emancipated human race could encounter itself within an expanded space of discursive formation of will and yet be robbed of the light in which it is capable of interpreting its life as something good? The revenge of a culture exploited over millennia for the legitimation of domination would then take this form: right at the moment of overcoming age-old repressions it would harbor no violence, but it would have no content either."[4] As a consequence of this, Habermas has come to limit the relevance of the "ideal speech situation" to deliberations about social justice, and he is left with the great problem of how rationally to ground claims about all those social goods, actions, and ideals that are *not* simply matters of procedure.

And this is the general problem for theories that attempt to ground conceptions of reasonableness and validity in conceptions of ideal audiences. The argumentation that is persuasive for such abstractly conceived audiences can be conducted only in the most abstract and formal terms. The agreements such audiences are capable of reaching never concern the concrete and substantive kinds of issues such audiences were designed to deal with.

Similar objections have been made to *The New Rhetoric*'s concept of a universal audience. They have been made most explicitly and systematically by John Ray, who charges that the concept is "excessively formal and abstract," and that it "loses all validity when it is concerned with particular situations." He claims further that it is supposed to be an "infallible rational standard," "transcendental," and "not determined by empirical experience."[5]

In this chapter, I want to explain more clearly just what the concept of a universal audience is by showing how universal audiences are constructed and how they are used. Then I want to show how, when properly understood, the concept of a universal audience avoids the dilemma of being either universal but empty or concrete but particular.

How to Construct a Universal Audience

The New Rhetoric's concept of a universal audience is profound and complicated. I want to clarify and develop its account, first by looking at the rules it gives for constructing a universal audience, and second by examining the uses it suggests for the concept.

What is most interesting about the rules for constructing a universal audience is that they are not systematic and in fact could often yield conflicting results. There are no priority rules about when to follow one rule rather than another, no limiting of particular rules to particular situations or anything of the sort. Instead, Perelman and Olbrechts-Tyteca simply offer these rules, sometimes only implicitly, and without ever bringing a consideration of them together at one time and place. Thus, what they are really offering us is not so much a system of rules for constructing *the* universal audience as a number of techniques for constructing universal *audiences*—techniques which *themselves* have variable persuasive force as justifications for the universal audience one is constructing. This is because constructing a universal audience is not really much different from inventing arguments to defend one's conception of universality. For in every move toward universality, there lies a technique for achieving universality. This technique itself can be understood as part of an argument for the concept of universality it yields. That is, if one's concept of universality is called into question, then the first line of defense is to show how it follows from what is ordinarily taken to be a universality-producing technique.

All constructions of universal audiences begin with particular audiences. One has a particular audience in mind, and one performs certain imaginative operations on it in order to give it a universal character. One way to do this is to set aside all the particular, local features of the audience and consider only those features of the audience one considers universal. Another similar method is to exclude from the particular audience all those members who are prejudiced or lack imagination or sympathy or are irrational or incompetent at following argumentation, and to include only those who are relatively unprejudiced and have the proper competence.[6] This rationality and competence qualification is further specified in a number of ways.[7] To be competent, one must be "disposed to hear" the argumentation[8] and must "submit to the data of experience" (TNR 31). One must also have the proper information and training, and in addition one must also have "duly reflected" (TNR 34).

Another way is to add particular audiences together—to be sure that one's argumentation appeals not only to one particular audience, but to many, or even all particular audiences (RR 14). By adding audiences together this way, one could eventually come to the whole of humanity—if such universality were required by the argumentation.[9] Another technique is to imagine one's argumentation addressed not only to the particular audience one faces at the moment, but to similar audiences at other times, in later years, say. Arguments of this sort frequently make appeals to history and ask their audiences to imagine themselves in their historical roles. According to classical philosophers, the most universal of audiences is the "timeless" one, and the more one's arguments have a timeless appeal the more universal they are usually taken to be (TNR 32).

A way to test and strengthen one's construction of a universal audience is to let other audiences criticize it (TNR 35). For example, if the particular audience one has universalized can corroborate one's judgment about what really are its universal features, then one's concept has greater validity and strength in argumentation than it would otherwise have. For example, pollsters have pretty well established that California voters vote for or against candidates on the basis of race. In constructing a universal audience of California voters, one would reject this characteristic. And my guess is that California voters would see the reason in this—that they would say, yes, race is a factor in how we vote, but we recognize that in some important sense it probably shouldn't be and that political argumentation shouldn't make appeals of this sort.

Once again, these methods are not systematic, and can lead to conflicting results. For example, one party may believe that a specialized audience represents the real universal audience for some particular argument. The opponent of the argument may deny this, and claim that the public represents the real universal audience. Thus, one writer may appeal more to the "competence, training, and knowledge" criteria, and make them very strong criteria, while another may appeal to the criterion of adding audiences together, or letting "everyone" decide. This dispute takes a very concrete form in the conflict over the status of expert testimony in judicial hearings, and in the conflict about whether we should select a jury of experts to decide cases which seem to require specialized knowledge. In such conflicts, reasoning can fail because each side measures the reasoning differently. Perelman believes that in such situations we should postpone argumentation until, through dialogue, question and answer, exploratory discourse, we come to a deeper mutual understanding and uncover agreements that can allow us to continue the argumentation (RR 16–17).

There is now a well-marked history of universality in which men are naturally taken to be members of a universal audience and women are taken to be swayed more by their particular predilections than by universal considerations. In the history of universality, what is taken as universal and what is taken as particular often follow the lines of power that divide male from female, conquerors from conquered, rich from poor, jailers from prisoners, sane from insane, adults from children, and on and on—although these lines never divide things as neatly as one might sometimes imagine.

A rhetorical theory cannot itself manufacture out of the air a concept of universality which will meet the demands of justice and satisfy all people everywhere. Rather, it depends on the ways actual people in actual historical societies reach reasonable agreements with one another, how they reach concrete understandings of universality. However, as a theory of reason, it also depends on a theory of justice. I will discuss this in more detail a little later. Very briefly, however, an understanding of justice is embedded in any concept of reason or universality. In the construction of a universal audience, we disqualify some people and we empower others. This is an action whose justice must be defended. It must be defended before yet another audience, to which I will come in a moment.

The Uses of Universal Audiences

Perelman and Olbrechts-Tyteca use the concept of a universal audience for several different purposes. First, they use it to distinguish persuading from convincing (TNR 26ff.). This is a critical problem in rhetorical theory, and it is usually taken on by resorting to any of a number of controversial dualisms, especially the dualism of reason/emotion.[10] Second, they use the concept to distinguish effective from valid argumentation, and thus de facto agreement from de jure agreement (TNR 463). Third, they use the concept of a universal audience to distinguish between fact and value. That is, a fact is supposed to be that to which a universal audience assents, while a value is that to which only particular audiences adhere (TNR 66). Their aim in making this distinction is to identify which agreements stand fast in argumentation. According to *The New Rhetoric*, argumentation is founded on agreement, and moves from original agreements to new agreements. In any rhetorical situation, certain agreements stand fast, or argumentation is not possible. Thus, there is a rhetorical way to distinguish the domain of the real (what stands fast) from the domain of the preferred, as well as from presumptions and hypotheses about the real (about which one can argue without undermining the rhetorical situation).

This is a radical rhetorical approach to the fact/value distinction, and it is worth entertaining the view for a moment, if for no other reason than that it offers such a sweeping vista. Values are simply those things on which human groups disagree, and which in fact define different groups as the groups they are. We expect that people will divide into different groups when it comes to adhering to values, and we recognize this as legitimate. We don't really expect other societies to share our values completely. However, facts are those matters about which we do expect such agreement. Facts have a universal claim on human beings or else they are not facts. This is a simple and stunning account. Obviously, the "we" in this account is a liberal European of late modern times.

The New Rhetoric acknowledges that values can attain the status of facts—i.e., that ethical life isn't limited to the "subjective" features of valuing and preferring: "An agreement about the conception of reality is linked to a social and historical situation which fundamentally conditions any distinction that one might wish to draw between judgments of reality and value judgments" (TNR 513). And again, "The status of statements evolves: when inserted into a system of beliefs for which universal validity is claimed, values may be treated as facts or truths" (TNR 76). When Perelman and Olbrechts-Tyteca refer to "universal values," as they do on occasion, they mean values that have attained the status of facts or truths—that is, the adherence of a universal audience.

Another important use of the concept of a universal audience is to identify the audience for philosophical argumentation, scientific argumentation, and argumentation about morality.[11] In all these kinds of argumentation, there is an implicit claim that one's arguments ought to be persuasive for more than a particular audience, that the one who is arguing is appealing to universal standards of reason.[12] Perelman and Olbrechts-Tyteca also believe that the concept can be used to solve the problems one faces in composite audiences. That is, when an actual audience consists of a number of different particular audiences who ordinarily do not assent to the same arguments, one can construct from them a universal audience, and address one's arguments to it (TNR 31).

Finally, a universal audience may be used as a standard of relevance. Although arguments can be persuasive for particular audiences even if they are one-sided and omit any recognition of opposing arguments, an argument that is convincing, one which gains the assent of a universal audience, must give a proper hearing and proper credit to all sides of an argument, or all relevant arguments (TNR 119).

Living Universality

Now that we have a clear notion of what the concept of a universal audience is, how to construct it, and what its uses are, we can better understand the senses in which it is always something more than an abstract and empty concept. In fact, we can see how the concept succeeds in helping us pass through the universal but empty or concrete but particular dilemma. Actually, universality is something that constantly changes and is always new.

Consider first the senses in which the universal audience always has some degree of cultural specificity—for it always does. This audience does not gather in some nonhistorical sphere, isolated from and immune to human activities and mortal weaknesses. It is rather always a universal of a particular, a concrete generality. It represents a *sensus communis* rather than being an abstraction that stands above the agreements reached by actually existing groups.[13] That this is the way the concept was understood by Perelman and Olbrechts-Tyteca can be seen clearly in some specific passages from *The New Rhetoric*.

First: "Everyone constitutes the universal audience from what he knows of his fellow men, in such a way as to transcend the few oppositions he is aware of. Each individual, each culture, has thus its own conception of the universal audience" (TNR 33). In other words, any conception of a universal audience has a specific content that comes from the fact that it is constructed by a specific author within the agreements that make argumentation possible within or among specific cultures. Thus, the universal audience is not a pure, not a transcendental concept. There is always something empirical in it, something which comes from the experience of an author and the traditions of a culture. As Perelman and Olbrechts-Tyteca say, "The universal audience is no less than others a concrete audience, *which changes with time,* along with the speaker's conception of it" (TNR 491, emphasis added). However, this statement must be qualified. For certainly, the universal audience lacks the actual existence of concrete audiences, and is to this extent ideal— after all, as Perelman and Olbrechts-Tyteca also write, the agreement of a universal audience is not a fact but a unanimity imagined by an author (TNR 31).

Second, what follows from this is: "Each speaker's universal audience can from an external standpoint be regarded as a particular audience" (TNR 30). This is a very important transformation of the concept of universality; every concept of universality is to some extent local, and one can always move out of the locality within which it holds sway. That is, if we move outside the rhetorical situation for which someone has constructed a universal audience, we can see the senses in which the construction lacks universality. We can imaginatively take the external point of view by employing the techniques for constructing a universal audience and carrying them farther than the author has. For example, we can imagine an argument's being addressed to a broader group of audiences, imagine its strength in a different historical context, and so on. We could add eleventh-century Egyptians to the audience, or ancient Olmecs, or blind people, or clergy, or hermaphrodites, or any other group we believe the speaker or writer may have neglected. If one takes the external point of view, one sets up a new rhetorical situation and thus imagines a new universal audience.

The brilliance of *The New Rhetoric* lies in its creation of a concept of universality that can tolerate such transformations. One can always take the view from a distance, and show that some definite concept of universality is not truly universal. But despite that kind of abstract and external criticism, Perelman and Olbrechts-Tyteca insist that "It nonetheless remains true that, *for each speaker at each moment,* there exists an audience transcending all others" (TNR 30).

Third, I mentioned before that one can strengthen one's conception of a universal audience by letting other audiences criticize it. As *The New Rhetoric* says, "Audiences are not independent of one another . . . particular audiences are capable of validating the universal audiences which characterize them . . . Audiences pass judgment on one another" (TNR 35). This too is a way in which the content and specificity of the universal audience are preserved. The universal audience is constructed by performing imaginative operations on a particular audience. It is always the universal of a particular. If this particular audience completely rejected the universal audience constructed from it, it would weaken the argument that the conception of the universal audience is the right one. Thus, the particular audience has a role in validating the universal audience, in keeping it from losing its relation to the particular audience in question. Of course, the particular audience cannot be the only audience which has a role in validating the conception of a universal audience. After all, the construction of a universal audience is itself a judgment on the insufficiencies of the particular audience. Rather, there is always another audience to which an appeal is made in such cases, and I shall come to this shortly.

Just before that, however, it should be pointed out that the fact that the universal audience is not a pure concept, the fact that it lacks the necessity and absolute universality to qualify it as "transcendental," does nothing to cast doubt on its universalizing tendency. The techniques for constructing a universal audience are universalizing techniques. Their being limited by what is taken for granted in a specific rhetorical community does not mean that they do not yield increasing degrees of universality. The imaginative expansion of audiences across cultures and across time and the application of notions like competence and rationality are clear indications of this. Rather, it means that they do not yield a merely formal, abstract concept of an audience, an audience which would assent to nothing but formal proofs, analytical statements, and empty platitudes.

The universality of a universal audience is limited by the good that one can achieve by way of participating in argumentation in a particular rhetorical situation. Agreement may be a part of such a good, but such a good is more often *that for the sake of which the agreement is sought*. We argue for the purpose of accomplishing something, making our lives better in some way. We do this in real situations, from our particular perspectives, not as disembodied minds. We criticize our societies in order to improve them. We reason with one another in order to avoid violent conflicts in the pursuit of incompatible goals. We never argue without some interest in the outcome. I can see only relative merit in the objections that the view from nowhere could raise to this practice. And I can see little sense in underestimating the small goods that *can* be achieved, by turning loose on such goods a critical, generalizing impulse that will settle for nothing less than absolute universal good, and which eventually overpowers any conception of a concrete good whatsoever.

In this regard, I believe that Perelman and Olbrechts-Tyteca have failed to clarify the senses in which universal audiences always do adhere to concrete goods. Recall that they distinguish between facts and values by dividing audiences into universal and particular. They claim that universal audiences agree on facts alone, while particular audiences adhere to common facts and values. They admit that values can sometimes come to hold the status of facts, and that the line between facts and values varies from audience to audience. And although there is nothing inconsistent about what they say, it does fail to capture the sense in which all universal audiences still embody a concept of what is good, and not just a concept of what is true. I admit that because of the way they have defined facts and values, this concept of what is good may have come to have the status of a fact when a universal audience adheres to it.

However, viewed from outside, from a "more universal" perspective, that fact may still be a value, that universal audience still a particular one. In fact, from far enough "outside," almost all facts show themselves to be values. Universal audiences appear more as embodiments of a concept of what is good than embodiments of a concept of what is true, or factual. This is even more strongly so if, as *The New Rhetoric* says, one can *always* take the external view. If this is so, then *every* universal audience can be identified as an agreement on concrete values. For this reason, *The New Rhetoric*'s universal audience is sometimes better understood as a *paragon* audience. From within the rhetorical situation from which a universal audience arises, universality is its defining feature. However, viewed from "outside," relative universality is only one of the features of a paragon audience, and not the only defining feature. From a distance, local concepts of universality are also agreements on concrete values.

The point I am making is not intended to undermine the account in *The New Rhetoric*. Again, I believe that the treatise offers a profoundly helpful theory of universality. I want only to make clearer the ways it underplays the senses in which it is right to say that universal audiences are held together by commitments to concepts of what is good—the senses in which Perelman and Olbrechts-Tyteca are really thinking of a paragon audience without recognizing it.

Beyond Universality

A final way to gain some insight into the sense in which a universal or paragon audience is both concrete and universal is to consider a concept which is as far as I know completely neglected in philosophy and rhetorical theory. This is the concept of an undefined universal audience. The concept has a very specific and very important use. Here is the single passage from *The New Rhetoric* in which it is mentioned: "It is the undefined universal audience that is invoked to pass judgment on what is the concept of the universal audience appropriate to . . . a concrete audience, to examine . . . the manner in which it was composed, which are the individuals who comprise it, according to the adopted criterion, and whether this criterion is legitimate" (TNR 35). It cannot be just a particular audience which passes such judgment, or there would be no difference between the particular and universal audience. Rather, the undefined universal audience is the audience for our construction of a universal audience. This should not sound strange because as we have seen such a construction itself employs argumentative techniques, and implicitly contains a claim that the universal audience we have constructed is the appropriate one. This claim and argument do not hang in empty space/time; they are offered to an undefined universal audience—one to which we appeal, but one which we cannot make definite.

This can also be approached from a different angle. Once we know that we construct the universal audience within individual and cultural constraints, "as a way to transcend the few oppositions we are aware of"—once this is known, then don't we also know that our concept of the universal audience is always to some degree insufficient? Don't we recognize that there are arguments of some strength which oppose our construction—even if we don't know what they are? Don't we know that, in appealing to an undefined universal audience to validate our construction, we have recognized that in some sense the universal audience is not—even for us—the universal audience? Don't we recognize that there are always universal audiences beyond our universal audience?

The difficulty one faces in trying to conceive of such an audience is that it is defined as undefined, known only as what is unknown. However, although the undefined universal audience is unknown, it is never absolutely unknown. Rather, it is a determinate unknown in the sense that the move from a concrete audience to a universal audience sets out in a particular direction and thus begins to articulate an ideal. Of course this is always to some degree indeterminate, a matter of interpretation, full of historical ambiguities.

Yet the direction established, the preconceptual *sense* we have of the undefined universal audience is determinate enough so that we know this audience when we encounter it; we know it when it does become determinate, when it does come to appearance. For example, there are those occasions on which an audience responds in ways we had not anticipated, and in fact goes beyond our own reasoning and our own ideas. Sometimes, an audience evaluates our reasoning *in ways we could not have foreseen—but which we nevertheless recognize as legitimate.* How is it that we can recognize such unforeseeable audience responses as legitimate? Because we *do* have a knowledge of the undefined universal audience—not an explicit conceptual knowledge, but the kind of knowledge which allows us to recognize the legitimacy of its responses once they do find a voice.

This kind of knowledge should not be underestimated. The substitution of a direction, a vector, an ever-better emergent newness for a comprehensively and conceptually grasped universal audience means that this audience is never grasped directly, but only indirectly—often in feelings, inclinations, reservations, hopes, and hunches. I believe it is also at play in our logically underdetermined ability to make practical and aesthetic judgments.[14] But to comport oneself toward this undefined universal audience, even if one does not understand exactly what it is, is a relatively familiar kind of comportment. I take Socrates to be expressing something of this idea when he says that he is more satisfied with losing arguments than with winning them, because when he loses an argument—when an interlocutor responds in an unanticipated but legitimate way—then he learns something new; otherwise, he is left in his ignorance.[15] For Socrates, an encounter with this audience brings change, newness, learning.

So the undefined universal audience is both unforeseeable and anticipated—something we both know and don't know. It is at once an unknown ideal and something potentially concrete. It becomes concrete in actual audience responses. Yet once it becomes concrete and definite in this way, it can no longer fulfill the role of the undefined. Instead, it adds further determinations to our concept of a universal or paragon audience—it becomes a part of it. It is as if paragon audiences come to be out of and through the undefined paragon audience, but the undefined paragon audience itself forever withdraws into indefiniteness.

We can draw a number of conclusions from this discussion. First, rhetoric has a philosophical moment which cannot be eliminated except at great cost. This distinguishes rhetoric from any kind of social science and especially from psychology. The idea of a universal audience introduces an instability into rhetoric which makes rhetoric's domain more like history than psychology, except that the instability in rhetoric is a philosophical one, a matter not simply of what is true, but of the *measure* of the truth yielded by argumentation. An advanced psychology may someday be able to measure the effectiveness of arguments—at least in principle—but it could never measure their validity. Reason is as alive as human beings, as weak and strong and as changeable as they are.

This account of universality in rhetoric also "solves" or rather places at its proper place—in actual human interaction, which means within actual historical practices—the problem of avoiding the dilemma between empty universality and concrete particularity. It is a practical historical task to create and preserve societies with the proper balance between universalizing rationality and the goods of particular traditions. A rhetoric of reason is well adapted to this balance at the theoretical level, but it takes no historical action.

Finally, a rhetoric of reason offers a theory of rationality which neither disguises nor undervalues the particular *ethical* interest of reason. For the universalizing interest of reason is essentially an ethical one, and has a strong orientation toward the future. On this, both Habermas and *The New Rhetoric* are in strong agreement. As Habermas came to say, "I prefer to speak of an *anticipation* of an ideal speech situation . . . The anticipation of the ideal speech situation has the significance of a *constitutive illusion* which is at the same time an appearance of a form of life" (emphasis added).[16] Or, as Perelman puts it, an appeal to universal values, which is always an appeal to a universal audience, is indicative of an *aspiration* for agreement (RR 27). In the end, any appeal to a universal audience signals such an aspiration, and thus announces a willingness to go on seeing one's opponent's side, to go on testing one's reasoning against more and more demanding measures, to make universal agreement one's aim.

And if the universal audience represents an aspiration for agreement, then rationality in the strong sense of valid argumentation is itself such an aspiration. But as Perelman knew at least from the time of *The New Rhetoric*, the good of universal agreement is just one good, and it must be measured and balanced by other conflicting goods. Sometimes the goods about which we disagree are more important to us than our eventually reaching agreement with people who do not share our moral concerns. This is why Habermas' attempt to ground rationality in communication fails—it gives an absolute primacy to truth, and limits its ideal audience to rational motivations alone in the sense of motivations to reach a consensus about truth.[17] And this is precisely where a more radical rhetoric of reason succeeds. It meets the philosophical objection to rhetoric head-on by developing a new concept of universality. However, unlike modern philosophy, it does this without succumbing to an empty rationalism or resorting to metaphysical dualisms. Following the lead of *The New Rhetoric*, a rhetoric of reason fulfills philosophy's original aspiration in a philosophically oriented rhetoric theory *which includes a rhetoric of philosophy*, and provides, so to speak, a way out of rhetoric from within rhetoric itself.

Transversal and Universal

"The universal audience" is a hard term to sell. Despite the limits set on the term; despite the instability and unpredictability of the undefined universal audience, the source of universality; despite even the identification of the use of "universality" as an action motivated by hope rather than an intellection with purely cognitive motivations, the term vibrates with notions of necessity, apriorism, and reification. In order to prevent these associations from misleading, I have tried to emphasize the changeableness and variability of this audience, and I have tried to show the senses in which "paragon" often better captures its main feature. However, given the need for all these explanations and qualifications, one might think it better just to drop the term and work with a new word.

The best candidate I know of for this role is "transversal," especially as it is developed by Calvin Schrag in his *The Resources of Rationality*. The context in which Schrag develops this notion is much the same as the postmodern context I tried to sketch earlier in this work. Schrag is fully aware of the philosophical paradoxes and reflexivity involved in reasoning about reason. He warns at the very start of his discussion that a concept of transversal rationality must itself be transversal. That is, rationality must be described neither in empiricist-foundationalist nor in rationalist-transcendental fashion. Instead, he finds transversal rationality active within different spheres but never in exactly the same way. Instead transversality is different in its different guises, and describing it is always a matter of adapting one's accounts to those differences without ever hoping to resolve them in a general concept.

Schrag begins his exposition by offering Felix Guattari's description of communicative activity in a psychiatric hospital as an example of transversality at work. In Guattari's hospital, the reasoning employed in decision making is spread across many groups at many different sites and with very different kinds of power. Each even has its own kind of rationale for its decisions. These groups are in dialogue with each other, reasoning across group boundaries and not only within them. The decisions arrived at in this way are, says Schrag, a "praxial accomplishment," informed by knowledge and understanding but not deduced from theoretical truths or simply handed down by experts from an epistemological "above."

Schrag claims that the move to transversality is motivated by a desire to resist the power of modern subjectivity, its "theoretico-epistemological paradigm," its administrative arrogance, its misrecognition of the differences among people, and its obliviousness to the actual lives they lead. He mentions Foucault as a major figure in this move to transversality: "Foucault has generalized transversal praxis to encompass the play of power relations that congeal into a variety of social forms, such as the 'opposition to the power of men over women, of parents over children, of psychiatry over the mentally ill, of medicine over the population, of administration over the ways people live.' The specific forms of these power relations vary from political situation to political situation, but the struggles through which the forms are defined display common concerns and motivations. Foucault speaks of them as 'transversal struggles'" (154). The literal meaning of "transversal" for Foucault seems to be something like "transgovernmental power." He says in "The Subject and Power" that "transversal struggles . . . are not limited to one country . . . they are not confined to a particular political or economic form of government" (211). Foucault is here offering one more description of his post-Marxian approach to power and conflict. The apparent conflicts defined by governmental power, in terms of which human life is administered, are not the conflicts which are most important to the people being governed. Instead a number of conflicts cut across the lines of official separation and conflict, unifying people who are in apparent conflict and separating those who are apparent allies. Transversal struggles are these other struggles that go on within and across the more officially organized conflict boundaries. They also require a "micropolitics" instead of a political science or a vanguard. They employ multiple rationales and degrees of accommodation and adjustment that are fugitive to any single overarching theory or the knowledge of any one group.

Schrag is very sympathetic to this move to a notion of transversal rationality. However, he finds it to be limited by its primarily reactive motivation. The move is compelling as a rejection of logocentric, theoretico-epistemological models of rationality, but the notions of "transversal rationality" are sketchy and vague. Schrag's aim is to offer a more constructive concept of transversality and so to give a better account of the "resources of rationality." To this point, Schrag's project aligns fairly closely with my own. A rhetoric of reason begins with the same recognition that modern, epistemologically oriented theories of reasoning are just no longer convincing. It finds reasoning operating within groups which, in the course of argumentation, arrive at agreements on their own terms, without the need for a metaphysical-logical foundation for rationality.

However, a rhetoric of reason specifies the dialogical openness operating within argumentation, and finds that the social need for conceptions of universality is ineluctable. The word "transversal" is supposed to "split the difference" between pure universality with its vertical metaphorical structure and pure heterogeneity with its strong horizontality. Schrag recognizes the need to offer a constructive notion of how communication is possible across (trans) groups with deep differences, but he wants to avoid the metaphorical limits of verticality/universality. He cannot disentangle "universality" from the concept of "necessity" and its sense of overarchingness. One cannot blame him. As he points out, his real problem is with "the metaphysically sedimented grammar of universality" which links the word to a legion of metaphysical powers.

Whether it is better to try to shake off these entanglements by using "universal" in new ways, as Perelman has done, or to drop the term as hopelessly contaminated and turn to a new one, as Schrag has done, is difficult to say. My own inclinations are with Perelman, and this for three reasons. First, as Perelman points out, our history and our argumentation are already suffused with and dependent on notions of universality. Philosophy, moral discourse, international law, and religious language all depend on communication which is supposed to be compelling for—or at least is addressed to—"everyone." Theories of communication must have a way of understanding the "rationality" that is at work in such communication—and not just say that it is dependent on philosophical errors. Using the concept of a "universal audience" to explain such discourse seems to me to deepen our understanding of this communication in ways that neither epistemological-criteriological nor transversalistic approaches can.

Second, transversality fails to capture the pragmatically open intentions of reasoning that attempts to succeed before a universal audience. Schrag's comments on Merleau-Ponty are instructive here. He admires Merleau-Ponty's attempt to revise the grammar of universality, but concludes that Merleau-Ponty occupied only a "halfway house" in "the journey from the universal to the transversal." He quotes Merleau-Ponty: "The universal: no longer the overarching universal of a strictly objective method, but a sort of lateral universal which we acquire through ethnological experience and its incessant testing of the self through the other person and the other person through the self. It is a question of constructing a general system of reference in which the point of view of the native, the point of view of the civilized man, and the mistaken views each has of the other can find a place—that is, of constituting a more comprehensive experience which becomes in principle accessible to men of a different time and country."[18] Thus, for Merleau-Ponty, this lateral communication results in something which goes further than simply satisfying the different groups across which the communication actually occurs. Instead, the "more comprehensive experience" which results becomes in principle "accessible" to groups and individuals who are not present, not yet clearly imagined. An audience emerges that judges "transversality" itself, and how far-reaching it is. Merleau-Ponty's attempt at going "halfway" by preserving a flexible notion of universality not only aligns "grammatically" with Perelman's work on universality, but also preserves the open-ended aspiration that one's reasoning will satisfy others who are not actual interlocutors.

Judith Butler describes what is essentially this same problem in *Gender Trouble:* "Universality" is a pressing problem for feminist theory because feminist theory has mostly analyzed "universality" in strongly ideology-critical terms. The "universal" has been unmasked as male, as denying female (and other forms of) particularity. Yet the social and political need for universality keeps returning: "Theories of feminist identity that elaborate predicates of color, sexuality, ethnicity, class, and able-bodiedness invariably close with an embarrassed 'etc.' at the end of the list. Through this horizontal trajectory of adjectives, these positions strive to encompass a situated subject, but invariably fail to be complete. This failure, however, is instructive: what political impetus is to be derived from the exasperated 'etc.' that so often occurs at the end of such lines?" (143).

I would say that the "etc." is universality's way of asserting itself in theorizing which has for the most part denied it a place. There is no final list of identity predicates, yet the moral imperative of recognition (its universality) demands that we add the "etc.," that we not exclude any identity that might deserve "recognition." However, this is exactly what universality in the rhetorical sense is: not the annihilation of all particular identities in the assertion of a reified and abstract one, but the demand of the "etc." The aspiration for a universal audience, for Merleau-Ponty's "accessible in principle," is a recognition of the moral imperative not to leave "anyone" out, the hope of recognizing an audience of "everyone." To end a list of identity predicates without the "etc." is to reify some particular identity, to "essentialize." It is to put an end to the historical elaboration of human identities and the development of the social and political frameworks within which such identities can be recognized. The use of the "etc." is the recognition of the need to use some concept of "universality," to develop some idea of human being (or, in rhetorical theory, of an audience) that is not simply particular and complete.

A third reason to preserve claims to universality is to keep argumentation open to criticism. Clarifying the indefinite scope of philosophical, moral, international-legal, and religious claims by pointing out that they project an audience of "everyone"—of people yet unborn, of people yet unknown to those who are making the claims—makes that reasoning vulnerable to criticism in a powerful and important way. If an argument is set forth with an explicitly transversal scope, then its proper judges are in those groups across which the argument cuts. Critics from outside those groups have no standing, and critics within those groups cannot appeal to the fact that people outside those groups might judge matters differently. However, when an argument is known to project its claims to a universal audience, critics can raise objections that certain groups of people or certain features of their identities have been left out—that the reasoning does not have the scope imagined. This is important not only for criticism but for universalizing discourses themselves. Those discourses can renew themselves and adapt to changing situations only by developing new reasoning that responds to the challenges of critics.[19]

It is difficult to imagine doing away with universalizing discourses; they meet needs that are strong enough to defeat any campaign to repress them. Better, I think, to acknowledge them with a revealing name, and theorize them more adequately—which means, in part, comprehending their vital interdependence with their criticism.

The Rhetoric of Logic

I want to carry this argument a little further by briefly outlining the general direction in which a rhetoric of logic would develop. A thorough interpretation of logical rules in rhetorical terms would take volumes, as well as years of work, but the general approach can be fairly easily understood and sketched. I have argued throughout this book that logic has serious insufficiencies as a theory of reason and argumentation. Now that we have developed the concept of a universal audience, we can explain further the senses in which logic has a serious misunderstanding of itself. My claim is that logical principles and rules are best understood as expressions of how a universal audience judges arguments. The goal of logic is to develop a very spare concept of universality, one that we would be hard-pressed to challenge because to challenge it would immediately call our own reasonableness, sanity, education, and intelligence into question. At our current evolutionary and historical-cultural location, we have a relatively well-defined idea of what counts as a competent human being. In its most stripped-down form, it is captured in some basic rules of reason that typically get taught in logic courses, or in logic-based courses in writing. On the other hand, it is also the case that the ideal logical subject also embodies some extreme and abnormal characteristics, and these have to do mostly with the assumptions that open up the logical point of view.

Again, I have no hope of elaborating this idea in anything like the detail called for. However, I can begin to develop a few examples which support this claim. To start, I want to make a couple of very important qualifications. First, when I say "logic," I am to some degree oversimplifying. In contemporary philosophy, there are many different "logics," and there are competing philosophical accounts of their status and their relations. However, I did not invent this simplification. The existence of many logics and the philosophical conflicts about them are not publicized in introductory courses in logic, in introductory logic textbooks, or in the kind of logic that gets exported to English composition, critical thinking, and speech communication courses. The oversimplification of logic is institutionalized—and I believe that it works against students. A rhetoric of reason could begin to bring some order and clarity to the teaching of logic, as well as to the teaching of speech and writing.

Second, the informal logic and critical thinking movements have already begun to reform and rejuvenate the teaching of logic. The motivations for and the evolution of a book like Howard Kahane's *Logic and Contemporary Rhetoric* is a good example of this kind of change. However, such books are still moored to a logical foundation that is inadequate. I will discuss this more thoroughly in the next chapter. Here, I want simply to recognize that the teaching of logic is in flux, and has changed for the better over the last twenty years.

In light of the rhetorical standpoint I have developed so far, the logical point of view should be seeming more and more strange, more and more dependent on implausible assumptions and unasked questions. Logicians sometimes take the genuine confusion of undergraduates who, in the words of their teachers (I have heard them), "can't think abstractly" to be an intellectual deficit. I believe the ability to take the logical point of view is a mental advantage; however, I also believe that the fact that many people do not take it is due more to logic's having suppressed some basic questions than to the innate incapacities of students. Actually, many of the obstacles students have are identical to the problems philosophers of logic make careers of. Students do not see what formalized arguments have to do with real arguments in a natural language. They constantly complain that formalized versions of arguments do not capture the real reasoning going on in argumentation. In the philosophy of logic, philosophers take the relation of logic and natural languages to be a profound philosophical problem; in introductory courses, most professors do not present it this way. My own belief is that students often have *philosophical* difficulties with what they are taught in introductory logic courses, or in writing courses in which an English professor or graduate student tries to introduce them to formal reasoning. What the basic problem boils down to is that students—as well as philosophers of logic—are not clear about just what the claim of logic is, or who is making the claim. More specifically, they are not clear about why they should take the logical point of view. Again, philosophers take such questions very seriously in their own work, much less seriously in introductory courses.[20]

To cast some light on these problems, I want to consider very briefly some features of the universal audience that logic posits as the appropriate evaluator of proofs. First, the audience for logical proofs is infinite. This point has been well made by John Woods in a different context. Perfectly logical minds are not limited by memory, attention, or time. From a logical point of view, the aim of reasoning is to construct a valid proof. For some purposes, it would take enormous amounts of time to do this. But an ideally logical agent has an infinite amount of time to make such calculations—even about relatively insignificant matters. From a logical point of view, there is no place to stop and say: "Enough is enough. It's time to make a decision and get on with other things." The ideal audience posited by logic does not operate under the constraints of having a limited amount of time on which there are competing demands.

Obviously, there are clear advantages to being unlimited; logic's universal audience does capture an important feature of our ordinary notions of reason and universality. It takes some of our abilities and imagines them as much more powerful than they are, removes many of the limits on them, and creates the idea of a kind of superhuman mind. However, just as obviously, there is a difference between this audience and many other conceptions of the paragon audience. A paragon audience is often thought of in much more human terms. Often, it must know how to weigh the significance of different issues and give the proper amount of attention to each. It must know when an argument is good enough, given the circumstances. For the logically infinite audience, everything has equal significance; reasoning is evaluated only in terms of the formal relations among already formalized propositions. Obviously, such an audience is not the best judge of the reasoning of human beings, who live a relatively short time, and who frequently change their ideas about what is worthwhile.

I should at least point out that this difference between the universal audience of logic and the paragon audience of rhetoric is one way of understanding contemporary controversies in cognitive science and artificial intelligence. In trying to construct models of intelligence, or intelligent machines, we face exactly this problem. How can a mere increase in sheer calculating power ever make possible expert systems which must discriminate between what is significant and what is not? We can program machines to recognize a hierarchy of important tasks, and have them distribute most of their power to those more important tasks. We can even program them to change priorities when conditions change in specified ways. The difficulty is not a technical one. The problem is that a paragon audience—the one whose expertise and judgment and sense of what is important we would like the machine to imitate— is constantly changing in ways we cannot foresee, and so cannot program into even a highly capable machine. This is the whole point of the undefined universal audience—an extremely important concept for rhetorical theory. It helps to explain why there is a limit to our ability to predict changes in what counts as reasonable. Theories of education which ground themselves in some current model from psychology— even in its most advanced forms in cognitive science and AI—will always find themselves falling behind.

Much more briefly, let me treat two further features of logic's universal audience. Logic assumes that natural language can be translated into abstract symbols, into formal propositions. It does this partly to disambiguate natural language, partly to remove anything but its formal features. By doing this, logic gains univocity, simplicity, and the power that comes from treating propositions in purely formal fashion. People can very quickly reach agreement about the formal relations among propositions, much less quickly about the strength of natural language arguments. The universal audience of logic is a reflection of this fact.

However, the limitations of this audience are obvious: it is oblivious to the ambiguities and resonances and moods of natural language since these are lost in the translation into a formal language. This audience also lacks any sense of the importance or meaning of what is being argued. In some situations, real people will not reach agreement about how to translate between natural and formal languages. Some paragon audiences will refuse altogether to argue about some issues. Again, the point is not that logic's universal audience is somehow *wrong* or misconceived. The point is that from some angles it is a very particular audience, not a universal one. It embodies many of our notions of reasonableness; it fails to embody others.

The last feature of this audience I'll treat here is its refusal to allow contradictions. It's a basic principle of logic that one may not both assert a proposition and deny it; one may not contradict oneself. This stricture is referred to as the principle of noncontradiction or the law of the excluded middle. Proving the negation of a proposition is tantamount to disproving its assertion. An audience which permitted contradictions would not be the universal audience to which logical proofs appeal.

The ideal audience who judges arguments this way has a specific kind of integrity, a well-integrated ego. It does not have multiple personalities. It does not believe different things at different times in the course of reasoning; it does not change. It does not sometimes believe that history is a story of human progress, sometimes disbelieve it. It certainly does not believe something and disbelieve it at the *same* time. Of course, it is odd to speak of this audience's believing anything at all because it thinks symbolically. It approves or disapproves the formally generated movement from proposition to proposition. However, where these propositions contradict one another, it throws up a flag—and it does this consistently.

This ideal of consistency and integrity is a particular ideal. We do not always expect perfect consistency of one another. We know that we often hold contradictory beliefs; we know that we often change our minds about things, too. I believe we may even expect that a paragon audience would hold some contradictory beliefs. Our recognition of true moral dilemmas shows that we understand the paragon audience to adhere to contradictory principles of ethics. In fact, for moral pluralists, such contradictions are just a fact. For example, if I believe that it is wrong to lie, and I also believe that it is right to choose the act which, overall, has the best consequences, I will end up having to say that some actions are both right and wrong.

Or consider the trap Michael Dukakis fell into in the 1988 U.S. presidential debates. It was well-known that Dukakis did not favor capital punishment. He was challenged by a panelist to say what he would do if his wife and daughter were assaulted and raped. He replied in a way that was consistent with his announced principles. His reply was widely regarded by the public as "bloodless." Some commentators took this to mean not just that the public disagreed with him about capital punishment, but also that he showed too much integrity, too much consistency with principle. He did not permit any obvious human emotions and judgments to conflict with his principles. The conclusion of many commentators was that Dukakis would have been better off with the public if he had admitted that his own feelings and judgments conflicted *to some degree* with his principle. Better to suffer some conflict with oneself, most people seem to think, than to be coolly logical.[21]

From a logical point of view, such judgments are impermissible. Logic's universal audience will not permit such reasoning. However, the members of a paragon audience of moral pluralists might. They would be able to say that some actions are both right and wrong, permissible and impermissible. They would say that facing such dilemmas is part of what it means to be a human being in a world of incompatible goods. In fact, they would say that the consistency and integrity demanded of logic's universal audience are the consistency and integrity of a Creon or a Lear, who would have been better off allowing themselves some contradictory beliefs.

Again, my point is that the universal audience of logic is one audience among others. Its judgments will sometimes conflict with the judgments of other paragon audiences. One of the purposes of a rhetoric of reason is to describe these ideal audiences and to show how they articulate certain ideals of rationality and of what it means to be human. The universality of logic's ideal audience is very high. If we take the logical point of view, we can accomplish a great deal in the way of reaching agreements. However, such an ideal and such a view are not absolute, and do not contain all other ideals and views.

The idea of a universal or paragon audience meets some of the objections that philosophers and logician-critics have made to rhetoric. Specifically, it expands the concept of audience to embrace and even surpass traditional models of rationality. The fact that audiences are the final measures of arguments does not mean that all arguments are just aiming for effectiveness or success in some low or easy sense. There are audiences which are very demanding. In fact, rhetoric's recognition of the differences which still separate the most demanding audiences conceivable is good evidence that its criteria for universality can be even more exacting than traditional logical ones.

A rhetoric of reason describes the varying standards that are at play in the evaluation of reasoning. It acknowledges the genuinely universalizing moments in reasoning, and it recognizes reasoning as a realm in which paragon ways of being human are set forth and explored and tested against other ideals. In the final chapter of this book, I will explain how this new way of conceptualizing universality helps to redeem the promise of higher education and give new purpose to core courses in composition, critical thinking, and informal logic.

6

BEING UNREASONABLE

A RHETORIC OF FALLACIES

In the previous chapter, I tried to show how a reception theory of rationality could offer standards for the evaluation of reasoning that are at least as exacting as those of traditional logic—and in some respects even more demanding. I want to continue that effort in this chapter by outlining a new, rhetorical theory of fallacies. A rhetorical theory of fallacies succeeds in two ways that logic-based theories of fallacies have failed. First, rhetoric can show the way past the "basic problem" of fallacy theory. The basic problem for informal logicians is that there are situations in which there is nothing "fallacious" about a fallacy. In some instances, "fallacies" are admitted by everyone to be legitimate ways of reasoning. Second, a rhetoric of fallacies can reconnect informal logic with the larger concerns of philosophy and the broader world of human concerns in general. The severing of the language of logic from the language of human concerns has led to more and more powerful kinds of formal reasoning.[1] However, the cost has been the loss of any relation of logic to the actual choices made by individuals and societies.

The attempt to find a logic of everyday reasoning has enormous consequences for education. By default, the schemes and models and rules of logicians have been adopted in countless English composition and critical thinking and speech communication courses. In English composition, the schemes, formulas, and vocabulary of informal logic have become commonplace. Many if not most of the composition books on my shelves contain references to "fallacies," and although not all the accounts in these books match exactly the accounts of informal logicians, they all appear to be trying to make the match as close as possible.[2] For all the theoretical denials, the assumptions of most teachers of writing are still deeply Ramist: there is no rhetoric of reason. Instead, philosophers and logicians are the authorities on reasoning. Teachers of writing look to philosophy and specifically to logic for knowledge about good reasoning. This leaves the teaching of writing, the inheritor (with speech communication) of the rhetorical tradition, with a very weak concept of rhetoric. It is little wonder that composition so often defaults either to expressionist ideals of eloquence, on the one hand, or to imi-

tative appropriations of disciplinary conventions, on the other. Reason
is the property of other disciplines, not rhetoric, not writing.

However, the results of importing a default logic of reason from philosophy have been, at best, doubtful.[3] For twenty-five years, informal
logicians have tried to break out of the formal-logical prison in which
they have been trapped. They have tried to reestablish a link between
the concerns of logic and the social, political, personal, and broader
philosophical concerns we have as human beings. They have tried to do
so while still holding on to logical models of rationality. There are many
reasons to believe that educated common sense and open public deliberation are richer and more adequate for reasoning about the actual
choices we face than are the abstract models and categories of logicians.
But it is only by way of rhetoric that logic can be brought back to life
and reconnected to those broader concerns.

In fact, I believe that the logical theory of fallacies has had directly
harmful effects on the teaching of writing. One of the strongest prejudices of new teachers of writing is that they must search for "fallacies"
in their students' papers. Somewhere in their educations, they have
learned a list of informal fallacies, and when they become teachers of
writing they believe that, at last, they have found the appropriate place
to use this knowledge. So they dutifully point out to students the "fallacies" in their reasoning, writing the names of the fallacies in the margins of their papers.

I believe that this practice is indefensible. Written reasoning is not
typically an attempt to construct a proof, so breaches of rules will not
ordinarily invalidate the reasoning. And where the identification of fallacies is not an attempt to identify a rule violation, it must be clarified
and justified in light of the basic problem of fallacy theory—i.e., one must
say why, *in the particular situation in which it is found,* some technique of
reasoning is "fallacious." For what is most notable about the "informal
fallacies" is that there are situations in which there is nothing wrong
with them at all.

Few teachers of writing have a theory of fallacies that would support
their logical marginalia. Few students really grasp what was inadequate
about their reasoning when they encounter such marginalia. A rhetorical theory of fallacies can help teachers understand their own actions
better, and so aid students in understanding why someone might take
their arguments to be unreasonable.

However, for informal logicians and fallacy theorists to cut their ties
to logic would be almost unthinkable. Before I outline a rhetorical theory of fallacies, I want to explore this fact. I intend to do this by examining the mostly unexplored conflict between rhetoric and philosophy

that has made the contemporary philosophical scene what it is. The break with foundationalist logic that enables a rhetoric of reason has failed to take place within the field of informal logic. Instead, informal logic has maintained a partly contradictory dependence on formal logic, and this is a dependency it seems unable to give up. It's worthwhile understanding why this is so.

Rhetoric and Philosophy

The first fact about any attempt to use rhetorical theory to understand the problems of what has come to be called "informal logic" is that it is likely to be ignored. There are some obvious causes of this. First, the informal logic movement, although international in scope, is, in sheer numbers, a North American phenomenon. The bibliographies are dominated by North American philosophers, with some contributions from speech communication and English composition. Further, the movement is fueled by an educational demand for courses in critical thinking and informal logic. Practitioners and scholars in these areas have formed a discourse community which is informed by their training, their more immediate practical concerns, and the general intellectual environment of North American universities. Their training most likely never included even an introduction to rhetoric. The practical demands on them to teach introductory undergraduate courses in critical thinking do not allow them to teach rhetorical theory in their courses. In addition, except for the journal *Philosophy and Rhetoric*, the history of rhetoric and rhetorical theory are not even a small part of the North American philosophical environment, even in the field of argumentation.

However, there is another reason for this nonreception. Rhetoricians work within a different philosophical framework from that of most American philosophers, and their theories are sometimes radically at odds with most of the assumptions made by philosophers of argumentation in North America today. The two points are related. Consider, for example, Perelman and Olbrechts-Tyteca's *The New Rhetoric*, whose primary accomplishment is to have overcome the difference between philosophy and rhetoric—a distinction that is essential to the self-understanding of the informal logic movement and most of its work on fallacies. One can see that the tradition from which the book draws is different simply by scanning its index. Cicero, Herennius, Isocrates, Quintilian, Whately—these names are not frequently encountered in North American philosophical scholarship. They belong to the indexes

of books in speech communication or classics—not books by philosophers on argumentation. However, beyond this, even the traditional
philosophical literature cited in the book is immensely broad in scope,
with representatives from all eras and very diverse traditions. For Perelman and Olbrechts-Tyteca, a treatise on argumentation is a work that
involves one in making judgments about major philosophical issues that
have received attention throughout the entire history of philosophy and
across cultures. As they say at the beginning, the treatise is not simply
an argumentation manual but marks "a break with a concept of reason
. . . which has set its mark on Western philosophy for the last three centuries" (1).

This takes us directly to the second point. Most American philosophers working on argumentation are thinking within the framework
bequeathed to them by the tradition from which a rhetoric of reason has
broken. It is a framework against which they are struggling, and which
they have modified in important ways, but overall they have shown
themselves in principle unwilling to break with it, even when this leads
to continuing incoherencies and inconsistencies in their thought and
practice. The central issue here is the relation between logic and argumentation, and the closely connected question of rhetoric—whether it
is within the province of philosophers (or vice versa), and what its relation with logic is.

On this question, there is a fundamental rift between most American
philosophers and the approach of this book. The informal logic movement has attempted to be quite clear in its commitments on these issues.
It has insisted that the standard for argumentation must be some kind
of *logic*. This position is documented in the introduction to *Informal
Logic: The First International Symposium*. There the informal logic movement is defined by a "conviction that there are standards, norms or
advice for argument evaluation that are at once logical—not purely
rhetorical or domain specific—and at the same time not captured by
the categories of deductive validity, soundness and inductive strength."

Ralph H. Johnson, certainly a leader in the establishment of informal
logic, has recently reinforced this defining conviction of informal logic
in his reevaluation of C. L. Hamblin's already classic 1970 work, *Fallacies*. The upshot of Johnson's criticism is that in substituting a dialectical
standard for the evaluation of arguments for an alethic or epistemic one,
Hamblin has crossed the divide from logic over into rhetoric. The very
idea of this transgression seems to be a shocking one, and Johnson
broaches the issue with great delicacy: "I think what Hamblin has
done—perhaps without knowing it—is replace *the logical criterion of
goodness with the rhetorical criterion of effectiveness*" (285). (Apparently,

the idea that Hamblin could do this while fully alert cannot be seriously entertained.) When Johnson first introduces the idea that acceptance is Hamblin's criterion for the worth of an argument, he asks, "Does this make anyone besides me nervous?" (283). Johnson concludes by referring to his discovery simply as a "suspicion," as if some more definite charge would betray a lack of discretion: "My suspicion is that what Hamblin's proposal for dialectical criteria captures is not so much logical as rhetorical virtue" (286).

Johnson's judgments and fears reflect well the professional philosopher's attitude toward the distinction between philosophy and rhetoric. Put quite simply, philosophy itself, and thus the professional identity of philosophers, depend on a strict distinction between philosophy and rhetoric. A philosopher who blurs the line can be suspected of not being fully conscious, and any serious entertaining of the idea that the line is not what it appears to be is ground for philosophical nervousness.

A rhetoric of reason breaks sharply with such a philosophical orientation and attitude. It requires a clean break with the tradition that grounds reason in logic and conceptualizes argumentation in terms of logical models. From the standpoint of a rhetoric of reason, there are two essential differences between logic and rhetoric. First, logic has been primarily concerned with proof and demonstration. What really distinguishes "proof" from "argumentation" is that proofs and logical demonstrations are bivalent; they are either valid or invalid, sound or unsound; either they go through or they don't. Rhetoric, on the other hand, is concerned with, as Perelman and Olbrechts-Tyteca put it, "the discursive techniques allowing us to induce or to increase the mind's adherence to the theses presented for its assent. What is characteristic of the adherence of minds is its variable intensity . . ." (4). This abolishes the rule of bivalence. Arguments can be better or worse, stronger or weaker, even more or less valid. It's all a matter of degree. No truth tables here.

Second, from a logical point of view, the concept of validity can be explained in terms of logical form. Certain formal relations among propositions communicate truth from premises to conclusions and so establish validity. However, a rhetoric of reason conceives of validity quite differently. The general measure of the strength of arguments is the audiences at whose assent the arguments aim, the ways of life to which they lead. The distinction between merely effective argumentation and valid argumentation is made by distinguishing between the audiences for which argumentation is effective, between the forms of life different kinds of argumentation enable. A merely effective argument is effective only for particular audiences. A valid argument is effective for a universal or paragon audience, an audience which embodies our conceptions of a reasonable way of life. Thus, the worth of an argument is dependent upon the quality of the life to which assenting to it would lead—or, in other terms, upon the quality of the audience which would be convinced by it. Again, "universality" or "paragonhood" is a matter of degree as well as kind, and what will count as universal is determined by the particular rhetorical situation.

Philosophy has traditionally been concerned with the universal features of reasoning—i.e., with Reason—with discourse that should persuade everyone and not just people with particular interests and biases. The distinction between philosophy and rhetoric depends on some kind of distinction of this sort. However, this very distinction is a rhetorical one. Logic is typically taken to be the norm for discourse, and this confers on philosophy its normative status in relation to natural language, and thus its superiority to rhetoric. However, this norm is itself, from a rhetorical point of view, founded in an ideal audience, which determines the norm. Thus, logic is grounded in reception, in a form of life, some possible way of being human and making judgments. Whether or not one speaks logically will be decided by how effective one's speech is with this audience. This means that the distinction between philosophy and rhetoric is itself a rhetorical one, and that philosophy is a special branch of rhetoric.

These features of a rhetoric of reason are stumbling blocks for many philosophers who are engaged in the study of informal argumentation. To accept these ideas may seem tantamount to forsaking philosophy itself. However, I believe just the opposite is true, that a rhetoric of reason points the way to a renewal of philosophy. It makes possible the reinterpretation of philosophy as the criticism of the partiality of certain supposed universal audiences and the articulation of more convincing conceptions of universality. It offers this interpretation in full recognition of the fact that philosophy expresses an aspiration for human solidarity and not a doctrine of human essence. Such an approach could reveal philosophy's worth in a new way.

It is true that some wings of the informal logic movement have seemed to begin to migrate in the direction of rhetoric. This seems especially true of contemporary work on the "dialogue structure of argumentation."[4] However, I do not believe that the situation of informal logic has been essentially changed by its recent attention to dialogues. From Hamblin through Hintikka and Walton, the investigation of dialogues has been consistently formal. The ruling model is still one that comes from formal logic. The goal of the analysis of argumentative dialogues has been to establish a set of formal rules whose violation could be considered an act of unreason, the commission of a fallacy.

There are certain advantages to the new dialogical theories. First, in Hamblin's case especially, the approach makes it possible to begin to specify the dialogical circumstances in which a logical breach (e.g., inconsistency) is not really a fault in reasoning. Second, the analysis of dialogues opens up a new domain of rule breaking. One can break not only logical rules, but also dialogue rules. This is especially important for those fallacies which have to do not with what makes an argument fallacious, but with what makes certain speech acts inappropriate in an argumentative dialogue and with what sometimes prevents a dialogue from producing an argument at all. For example, fallacies relating to questions and to relevance are better treated as violations of these kinds of rules.

However, although there are advantages in this approach, there are serious disadvantages as well. First, there seems to be no philosophical grounding for dialogue rules. Either the rules are stipulative—almost like the axioms of competing mathematical systems—or they are simple translations of logical rules into dialogue rules. But why follow dialogue rules? What is the source of their authority? It is worth recalling that in Plato's dialogues the judges and enforcers of the rules of dialogue, even to the point of determining who the interlocutors should be, are the members of the audience. And, in Plato, the quality of the argumentation *as argumentation* is almost always directly dependent on the audience involved.

Second, what dialogue rules have been proposed are still *formal rules.* Thus, fallacies are still conceived of as violations of rules. This preserves the expectation of bivalence in the evaluation of arguments, and prevents our understanding the senses in which arguments can be weaker because less reasonable and stronger because more reasonable. Third, although the attempt to identify different dialogue games gives a way to distinguish situations in which an argumentative move is fallacious and situations in which it is not, it does not typically provide a way to understand the relations among different dialogue games, and thus it yields no understanding of whether it is more or less reasonable to play one game rather than another at some place and time. Because formal dialectics does not accomplish this, it cannot really distinguish cases in which an argumentative move should be considered a fallacy from cases in which it should not.

A rhetorical theory of argumentation provides a much more promising avenue of approach. In the remainder of this chapter, I want to sketch in a general way how a rhetoric of reason could contribute toward settling the vexing problem of informal fallacies. Thus, in what follows, I will offer a reinterpretation of the nature of fallacious reasoning, and give a few examples of how a rhetoric of reason would treat specific fallacies. I hope to show that one can make serious philosophical sense of what have been called informal fallacies by following through on the principles of a rhetoric of reason.

The Basic Problem and the New Theory

As Douglas Walton has written, "The basic problem with fallacies has always been that, once you look at them closely, you can see that in each case the type of argument alleged to be "fallacious" can evidently, in some instances, be a correct—or at least not unreasonable—form of argument, or kind of move to make in argument" (3–4). Given this "basic problem," one might ask a more basic question: are there really *fallacies* at all? From a rhetorical point of view, the answer might seem to be no. After all, there are no rules to break; there are only audiences—audiences with which one succeeds and audiences with which one fails, to some degree or other. However, if we hold closely to the concept of audience as it was developed in the previous chapter, and use it to frame some of the general questions of fallacy theory, we can uncover a consistent and very helpful explanation of what is wrong with so-called fallacies—an explanation that is part of a larger account of what it means to argue reasonably or unreasonably.

I want to begin with C. L. Hamblin's to-the-point definition of a fallacy: "A fallacious argument, as almost every account from Aristotle onward tells you, is one that *seems to be valid* but *is not* so" (12; compare Aristotle, *On Sophistical Refutations* 164a–165a; *Rhetoric* 1400b). In order to understand the sense a rhetorical theory would make of such a definition, one must recall rhetoric's rather profound notion of validity: a valid argument is one which wins the assent of a universal audience. A merely effective argument succeeds only with a particular audience.

If we interpret the "valid" of Hamblin's definition in rhetorical terms, we radically transform the traditional framework for understanding fallacies: a fallacious argument is one that seems to persuade a universal audience, but does not. Instead, it persuades only a particular audience. Thus, in the case of a fallacy, we have an instance of a particular audience's mistaking itself for a universal audience. The general feature of unreasonable argumentation is just this fact that a person or group which reasons in a way it assumes to be universal actually reasons in a way that is particular either to an individual or to some group of people. To commit a fallacy is to mistake the scope of the effectiveness of an argument. To use informal-logical terms, all fallacies are specific versions of the universalist fallacy.

This leads to some interesting results. For example, one cannot commit a fallacy when addressing a genuinely universal audience. Since a universal audience is the standard for what is as opposed to what merely *seems to be*, things cannot merely *seem to be* to a universal audience. The *seems to be* is always a *seems to be* for some particular audience or other. Neither can there be a fallacy when a particular audience is addressed *as* a particular audience. In such a case, no one believes that the argumentation is pretending to be valid; it is merely trying to be effective. In order for there to be a fallacy, a particular audience must seem to itself capable of judging as a universal audience, and yet be unable to do so. It must misunderstand its own receptivity to an argument as being more representative than it really is.

This explanation of what is fallacious about fallacies provides a way to solve the "basic problem" of fallacy theory. The problem is to find a way to determine in which instances a traditional "fallacy" is reasonable and in which instances it is not. The approach of informal logic has still been to look for formal features or rules of reasoning, or of the dialogues in which reasoning occurs, in order to distinguish some of these instances from others. A rhetorical approach is quite different. A traditional "fallacy" may be invalid, but still effective and so not unreasonable, when it persuades a particular audience but cannot convince a universal one. Thus, it may be perfectly reasonable to argue "fallaciously" with a particular audience. Clearly, this means that it is not the formal features of the "fallacy" that cause it to be unreasonable.

Thus, a rhetoric of reason cannot provide a list of fallacies, or a classification of fallacies, based on the different kinds of logical breaches involved. What it could offer in place of traditional fallacy theory is a classification of different kinds of audience and accounts of the ways in which arguments can go wrong for these audiences, accounts which include descriptions of the types of counterargument that might decrease the effectiveness of specific argument types. In fact, this is exactly what Perelman and Olbrechts-Tyteca have given us in *The New Rhetoric*. I want to extend their approach to a consideration of some particular classes of fallacy.

There are three very general ways arguments can go wrong. First, the essential enabling conditions of argumentation may not be in place. Second, the basic premises and starting points of an argument may not be understood in common. Third, the particular techniques of argumentation may not be effective for all the interlocutors in the same way. An

Part Three: Evaluating Arguments

exhaustive analysis of these three ways in which reasoning goes wrong would require an entire book that would essentially rewrite all of fallacy theory. Here, I will give only a few examples of each kind of argument criticism under headings taken from traditional fallacy theory.

AD BACULUM

First, to the degree that the conditions for argumentation are not in place, it could be successfully argued that what seems to be an argument is really not. For example, argumentation requires not only a common language and a means of communication, but also a respect for one's interlocutor, a modesty or willingness to change on the part of the initiator of the argument, and the renunciation of violence by all parties. This is not simply a matter of fallacious reasoning, but a matter of whether or not the conditions of discourse are themselves conducive to argumentation. To the extent that they are not, it could be argued that argumentation does not take place.

What has been called *argumentum ad baculum* is best understood in this context. If argumentation is a conflict in which the use of force has been renounced, then to the degree that force is used or threatened the discursive conflict is not an argument. Thus, *ad baculum* is not in the strict sense a fallacy because it is not an argument. However, we can use a rhetorical approach here to reveal more about what is unreasonable in the *ad baculum*. From a rhetorical point of view, the most general feature of "fallacious" reasoning is that a particular audience mistakes itself for a universal one. In this case, a discourse *seems to be* argumentation to a particular audience, but a universal audience sees that it is really not argumentation at all. Thus, the judge of the argument about force in the case of a true *ad baculum* must be a particular audience which mistakes itself for a universal one. Its being a particular audience makes the use or threat of force opaque to it, so that the discourse *seems to be* argumentation. However, this audience assumes that it is a universal audience and knows the threat of force when it sees it, that there is no difference between seeming and being for it, and so there are no grounds for saying the discourse is not argumentation.

Consider an example: Armed police stop your train and board it. They announce to the passengers that they are searching for drugs. They walk up to you and ask permission to search your luggage. You ask why. They say that it would help them a great deal in their efforts to stop drug trafficking if you would comply. You consider matters for a moment, then decide to agree to the search.

The practical reasoning here is this: you should agree to the search because it will help stop drug trafficking. Is this a case of *ad baculum*? There are different ways force may be threatened here. The police are armed, and that in itself could be taken to be a threat. There are several of them and one of you in close quarters, and they are asking you to do something you would rather not do. That could be taken to be a threatening situation. There may be additional factors. They may be larger than you. They may speak loudly in a commanding tone. They may take what you consider to be a threatening posture, and they may have threatening expressions on their faces. They may move through the train in a way that says they are commanding and not requesting. As other passengers around you uncomfortably consent to be searched, you may feel less and less that refusing the request is a real option.

Rhetorical theory offers several different approaches to this example. First, let's imagine that both the police and you believe very strongly that the war on drugs requires extreme measures, even the overriding of some civil liberties. The police intend to intimidate you into consent by their speech and behavior. You recognize their intent, are pleased at their aggressive pursuit of drug traffickers, and, having nothing to hide, consent to the search. In such circumstances, this would not be an instance of *ad baculum*. There is nothing which *seems* to be an argument to either the police or you. There is simply a threat which is perceived as a threat.

Consider different circumstances. Imagine that the police involved sincerely believe that they are *not* acting in a threatening manner. Imagine that nevertheless almost all of the passengers feel that the request and the explanation are more of a threat than a request backed up by a reason. In such a situation, there would be grounds for saying that the apparent argumentation of the police is not really argumentation at all. This is a good example of what accounts of *ad baculum* are really trying to get at: a situation in which a particular audience (the police) mistakes itself for a universal one, mistakes its reception of a discourse as being the only accurate one.

There are complications here. For example, what if the passengers were exceptionally cowardly or paranoid, and perceived threats where most people would not? Would the example still hold? In such a case, everything would depend on whom we take the universal audience for the argumentation to be. If the universal audience is "most people," then we could take a poll to decide the issue. In this instance, the passengers would win and the example would hold. When the U.S. Supreme Court decided a similar case, it ruled that the passengers, though perhaps made uncomfortable, could refuse the search without facing retaliation. The members of the Court were working with a conception of how a model

176

Part Three: Evaluating Arguments

citizen would respond in this case, and it was their idea of the model citizen—neither exceptionally courageous nor exceptionally cowardly—that decided the case for them. In this instance, it was the model citizen who was the imagined universal audience for the argument of the police.

Thus, an interlocutor's simply feeling threatened in an argumentative situation does not completely undermine the framework of argumentation. There may also be at play in the mind of the audience some conception of how threatened a person should feel, given the circumstances. Such a measure makes it possible to evaluate argumentation even in cases where a particular audience might be self-deceived about whether it really is threatened by force or whether it is threatened by something else, perhaps by the direction of the reasoning itself, or perhaps by something the reasoning reminds it of.

To clarify this further, consider a very different example: A husband and wife are trying to reason together about how to educate their children. The husband announces the conclusions he has reached, and gives his reasons. He also remarks that he cannot leave the matter up in the air any longer because he is losing his peace of mind. He takes the remark to be a sincere expression of his devotion to his children's education. His wife takes it to be a threat that if his plans are not accepted he will become angry. She opposes his plans but is too afraid of his anger to state her own arguments.

Is this an instance of *ad baculum*? The question is, who is the audience to whom an appeal is made in this case? It cannot be the ideal citizen or even the rational person. What is at stake is not how children in general should be educated, but how this particular couple should educate its own children. Neither can it be only one of the partners; that would be, in this case, a failure to reason together and reach an agreement—the reason for trying to construct a framework for argumentation. The audience in this case must be the concrete universality of both partners. This may ring oddly because we do not ordinarily think of universality in these terms. However, from a rhetorical point of view, universality is always a matter of degree, and is always relative to the particular argumentative situation. One of its uses is to overcome the heterogeneity of composite audiences, of which this couple is a small example. The framework of argumentation is undermined here by the husband's assuming that his reception of his remark as an expression of devotion is the way his wife should receive the remark as well. He believes his reception has relatively universal validity when it does not. There is no appeal being made here to an audience beyond the concretely universal one. The wife need not object that any rational person would interpret the remark as a threat. The point is that *she* does, and this is enough

high
persuasive

to undermine the framework for argumentation between her and her husband.

This account of the framework of argumentation makes possible a serious philosophical understanding of what has been called *argumentum ad baculum*. The approach avoids the basic problem of fallacy theory while at the same time connecting informal logic to substantive philosophical questions about the degree of universality to be found in specific human experiences—in this case, in the reception of discourse as argumentation.

EQUIVOCATION

Equivocation has been thought to be something like a fallacy since at least the time of Aristotle, who classified it as one of the fallacies dependent on language (*Rhetoric* 1401a). Equivocation, says Walton, "resides in the fallacious deployment of ambiguity in arguments" (242). So, in the case of a fallacy, the *appearance* of validity is created by equivocation. The *reality* is that some single sentence expresses more than one proposition and that the argument is invalid. Most of Walton's chapter-length discussion of equivocation is devoted to an analysis of formal and near-formal arguments which are assumed to be either valid or invalid. Ambiguity is taken to be the root problem, and techniques of disambiguation are taken to be the main cure.

It is difficult to imagine two approaches to the place of ambiguity in argument that are more different from one another than Walton's logical approach and a pragmatic-rhetorical one. In this case, I want to use Perelman and Olbrechts-Tyteca's insights into the rhetoric of ambiguity to construct a rhetorical account of equivocation. Perelman and Olbrechts-Tyteca discuss ambiguity in part 2 of *The New Rhetoric* under the heading "The Starting Point of Argument." Perhaps the central issue dividing rhetoricians from Walton and other informal logicians is the whole matter of there being some expectation of clear univocality in argumentation. According to *The New Rhetoric*, "A notion can be considered univocal only if its field of application is wholly determined, which is possible only in a formal system from which every unforeseen element has been excluded" (130). And: "In most cases, the impression of clarity, linked with univocity, is the product of ignorance or of lack of imagination" (125). The doctrine of univocality, which belongs to the idea of demonstration, and not argumentation, is dependent on the assumption that we have rational intuitions of clear and distinct ideas (130).

A rhetoric of reason rejects the idea of such rational intuitions and adopts instead a theory which depends on a recognition of the need for interpretation, interpretation which is grounded in the fact that ambiguity is inherent in every part of the argumentative situation. Not only words and sentences can be ambiguous and require interpretation, but also actions, events, and things themselves. This is quite different from any fallacy theory whose prototype of ambiguity is a strict homonymy in which the fallacy is "dependent on language." Not only is language ambiguous, so is everything else. Perelman and Olbrechts-Tyteca give the example of how the same action can be understood as "tightening a bolt, assembling a vehicle, earning a living, or helping the export drive" (121). Interpretive choices of this sort make up the "starting point" of argumentation because unless agreements can be reached on these interpretations, argumentation cannot begin. Of course, very often the real problems arise only in the course of argumentation, when the consequences of adopting certain provisional agreements begin to appear, and one party withdraws its initial assent.

Not only is the phenomenon of ambiguity deeper and more pervasive than is sometimes recognized in informal logic, but ambiguity and argumentation are interdependent—each a condition for the other. It is the strain that argumentation places on language that causes us to make distinctions where previously we thought that our meaning was clear. And it is what *The New Rhetoric* calls the "plasticity of notions" that makes possible whole domains of argumentation. This plasticity is different from the "fuzzy categories" by which linguists, philosophers, and cognitive scientists have recently been distracted. The point is not that concepts have indistinct extensional boundaries; rather, it is that concepts change as they are applied in new ways. In fact, this capacity of concepts to undergo transformation in new situations is one of the sources of new knowledge, new ways of understanding.

In light of this fact, Perelman and Olbrechts-Tyteca are driven to say that ambiguity is *constitutive* of the sphere of argumentation: "It is precisely because the notions used in argumentation are not univocal . . . that the conclusions of an argument are not binding" (132). The point is crucial. An essential distinction between demonstration and argumentation is that the former is compelling, while the latter admits of degrees of adherence. The idea is that judgments about ambiguity are themselves "degreed," and that this is reflected in our degree of adherence to the claims of arguments. In its formal demands for univocity, logic closes off the world of argumentation.

There is a famous philosophical argument which is offered by John Stuart Mill in his little book *Utilitarianism*. The argument has received a great amount of attention from philosophers, many of whom believe that the argument commits the fallacy of equivocation, and thus fails. Here is the argument: "The only proof capable of being given that an object is visible is that people actually see it. The only proof that a sound is audible is that people hear it; and so of the other sources of our experience. In like manner, I apprehend, the sole evidence it is possible to produce that anything is desirable is that people do actually desire it" (37). Many philosophers have charged that Mill equivocates on the meaning of "desirable." They spot the sense in which being "visible" or "audible" is disanalogous to being "desirable," and they use this to establish two distinct meanings for "desirable": (1) capable of being desired, and (2) worthy of being desired. They charge that Mill's argument trades on this ambiguity, that just because something is desired does not mean that it *should* be desired. And they usually have lots of examples. You can certainly think of your own.

However, when Mill "equivocates" by saying that "the sole evidence it is possible to produce that anything is desirable is that people do actually desire it," he is not, from a rhetorical point of view, really offering a "proof." Rather, he is offering an argument which depends on an ambiguity in "desirable." If we reject *any* connection between "desirable" as "worthy of desire" and "desirable" as "is actually desired," then the argument will have no persuasive force for us. On the other hand, if we believe that "worthy of desire" and "is actually desired" are identical in meaning, Mill's discourse begins to look like a compelling proof. If we adopt what seems to me the commonsense idea that there is *some* connection between how worthy of desire something is and how much it is actually desired, then whether one is persuaded by Mill's argument will be a matter of degree, and will depend greatly on the relative persuasiveness of competing arguments. That is, it seems to me reasonable that in most cases the fact that a thing is desired counts to some degree as prima facie evidence for its desirability. However, this evidence will have to stand up against evidence to the contrary.

Let's consider, then, how, from a rhetorical point of view, the deployment of ambiguity *could* be an example of a "fallacy." I want to consider what the philosopher G. E. Moore called the "naturalistic fallacy." I hope to show that Moore's reservations about this "fallacy" were reasonable, but that a rhetorical framework can provide a more helpful analysis of it—and of Moore's own "open question" argument.

According to *The New Rhetoric*, there are certain abstract values which win the adherence of a universal audience: truth, goodness, beauty (76), justice, liberty, wisdom (134). There are also concrete values "attaching to a living being, a specific group, or a particular object, considered as a unique entity" (77). Perelman and Olbrechts-Tyteca give the examples of "France" and "the Church." Insofar as argumentation

Principle of fallacy

relies on adherence to abstract values, it can appeal to a universal audience. Insofar as it relies on adherence to concrete values, its appeals will be persuasive only for a particular audience. Abstract values are able to attract universal adherence only because of their vagueness. One can depend on this adherence only as long as one does not disambiguate the general concept by linking it with a concrete value.

Abstract values are of critical importance in difficult argumentative situations. As Perelman and Olbrechts-Tyteca put it, they "make possible the crystallization of a global effort of good will." Agreements about ambiguous notions are "evidence of the fact that one has decided to transcend particular agreements, at least in intention, and that one recognizes the importance attaching to the universal agreement which these values make it possible to achieve" (76). They think of this quite literally in terms of international agreements about human rights. The "principal merit" of using ambiguous notions in this context is that "it encourages a continuation of the dialogue" (134).

What can go wrong in such situations is not that someone uses terms ambiguously; on the contrary, that is what enables the argumentation. Rather, "fallacies" arise when an audience conflates a concrete value with a universal one, and thus imagines itself a universal audience when it is really only a particular one. Let's look at the naturalistic fallacy and the open question argument in this light.[5]

Very briefly, Moore believes that *good* is a simple, indefinable, non-natural property. He believes that most moral theories try to show the identity of good with some specific natural property, that they try to define what is extraordinary and indefinable in terms of something of which they have a more ordinary experience. For example, the classic attempt to define *good* as that which gives pleasure would be an attempt of this sort. However, Moore believes that it would always make sense to ask whether the definition is right, whether, in this case, "giving pleasure" is really good. The fact that it always makes sense to ask this kind of question gives power to Moore's "open question" argument: "good" cannot be defined because it's always an open question whether or not the proposed definition is right. Thus, to offer such definitions is to commit a fallacy, the "naturalistic fallacy."

First, let's admit that in the way Moore describes the fallacy it has to do more with definitions than with arguments. However, such definitions make up part of the starting point of argumentation, and we can assume that what was "fallacious" about such definitions was that they were deployed in arguments which became, for that reason, unconvincing. Second, let's admit, along with Bernard Williams, that this may be the most "spectacular misnomer" in the history of philosophy (121). For the crux of the argument does not really depend on good's being a non-natural property. As Moore writes, "Even if it were a natural object, that would not alter the nature of the fallacy . . ." (14).

What Alasdair MacIntyre calls Moore's "one genuine argument" in support of his position is the "open question" argument (250). Whenever someone attempts to define "good," by saying that "x is good, and whenever we say 'good' we mean x," one can always ask, "is x really good?" And this question, says Moore, will always be meaningful. Whether the good is pleasure, or freedom, or a renewal of religious devotion, or wealth, or whatever, the question always makes sense.

From a rhetorical point of view, the way to explain this is to recognize that *good* functions as an abstract value, while its definiens functions as a more concrete value. "Good" can characterize in a very abstract way a great number of other values. However, to *identify* the good with any of these less abstract values is to identify an abstract value with a concrete one. Because "good" is more abstract than its definiens, the open question argument works; there is always something more to *good* than any concrete value. Thus, one commits the "naturalistic fallacy" whenever one defines good in terms of a concrete value.

Moore was perceptive in calling this kind of defining a fallacy, for it has the general feature which all fallacies have when we consider them in a rhetorical framework. They all involve a particular audience's mistaking itself for a universal one. In this case, a concrete value, which is a value only for a particular audience, is identified with an abstract one, which holds for a universal audience. Human groups—nations, religions, neighborhood alliances and gangs—can often be understood by the way they specify the content of abstract values. Such commitments bind people together as particular audiences for argumentation, as particular rhetorical communities. These communities reason in such a way that "good" actually *means* the good of some tradition, some group, some very specific idea.

A rhetoric of reason would provide no grounds for saying, from within such a rhetorical community, that such reasoning was fallacious. However, if such a group came to believe that its reasoning was compelling for all people everywhere, it would have mistaken itself for a universal audience, and so have become unreasonable. As *The New Rhetoric* puts it, abstract values "can be regarded as valid for a universal audience only on condition that their content not be specified; as soon as we try to go into details, we meet only the adherence of particular audiences" (76).

This approach to ambiguity is radically different from the usual treatment. Ambiguity is an essential condition for argumentation, and equivocation is the argumentative use of the fluidity of concepts for reasoning about issues which do not permit demonstration. However, there are instances of equivocation in which a particular audience interprets an ambiguous term in a specific way, and mistakes this interpretation for a universally acceptable one. These instances of equivocation could legitimately be called unreasonable, and thus seem to be what fallacy theorists are looking for when they try to solve the "basic problem" of determining which instances of equivocation are "fallacious" and which are not.

THE FALLACIES OF COMPOSITION AND DIVISION

According to the fallacies of composition and division, what is true of a part may therefore be asserted to be true of a whole (composition), and what is true of a whole may therefore be asserted to be true of a part (division). Some of the examples given in the philosophical literature are so artificial that it is hard to imagine their *seeming* valid to anyone. One often finds this example: all of the parts of this machine are light; therefore, this machine is light. Nevertheless, ways of analyzing such "fallacies" have been provided. What is typically said to distinguish fallacious composition from valid composition is that in valid compositions one has a premise that permits the inference. In invalid compositions, one does not. This seems to be the conclusion of both Richard Cole (cited in Hamblin 21) and Douglas Walton (214-15), who suggests a solution similar to one reported by Quine (cited in Hamblin 19). Hamblin rightly objects that this makes every fallacy of this sort a formal one (21). I want to set this class of such fallacies aside. These arguments seem to lack even the appearance of validity, and they are widely treated as formal breaches.

However, there is another class of these fallacies which typically regards not machines and their parts but human groups and their individual members. For example: all the citizens in this city pay their debts; therefore, the city will pay its debts. According to Hamblin (18-19), Schipper and Schuh claim that the argument includes an equivocation: does "city" refer to the whole or to each part?

However, the charge of ambiguity begs the question. Most people know that a "city" is in some respects distinct from its individual citizens. Just because the life expectancy of the inhabitants is seventy-five years, this does not mean that the city can be expected to perish after about seventy-five years, and no one would ever imagine this inference's being valid. Similarly, no one who would assent to the argument in question really believes that it is a proof; no one believes that it is logically impossible for a city not to pay its debts. Rather, the question concerns the degree to which one can know something about the quality of a city by being familiar with the qualities of its inhabitants. In the remote past, if a city was small, had no past indebtedness, and had a culture of fiscal responsibility among its inhabitants, one can imagine that this fact could be included as evidence that the city was likely to be reliable. In any case, the question seems to be one of relevance—of how *close* the connection between the city and its inhabitants really is, i.e., whether it is close enough, in this specific respect, to make the reasoning persuasive.

Cohen and Nagel offer a similar example (cited in Hamblin 18), and treat it in a similar way: the soldiers of a given regiment are strong; therefore, the regiment is strong. They locate the ambiguity in "strong" and disallow the reasoning on the grounds of formal failure. Once again, however, this begs the question. The real question is whether there is a connection between the strength of the individual soldiers and the strength of the regiment, what the nature of that connection is, and how strong it is. Here, it seems that the possible connections are more obvious than in the above example. For example, the individual soldiers of one regiment could be healthy, well fed, and well rested, and thus individually strong. The soldiers of another regiment could be diseased and deprived of supplies of food, fresh water, and sleep, and thus individually weak. *Ceteris paribus,* these facts would be prima facie good reasons for saying that one regiment was strong while the other was weak.

A rhetorical approach to this sort of argument allows us to speak much more accurately about its strengths and weaknesses than does fallacy theory. In the first place, we should once again point out that argumentation is *dependent* on ambiguity. An ambiguity in one's concepts allows one to connect, by argumentative techniques, what is not obviously or necessarily connected. The question is how convincing such connections can be made to be.

Once again, Perelman and Olbrechts-Tyteca have worked out the rudiments of a sound rhetorical approach to this problem. They describe this kind of argument in at least two places in *The New Rhetoric.* In the section on quasi-logical arguments, they deal with "Inclusion of the Part in the Whole" and "Division of the Whole into Parts." They offer the following from Locke as an example of "what is true of the whole is true of the part": "For whatsoever is not lawful for the whole church cannot by any ecclesiastical right become lawful to any of its members" (231). In the section titled "The Group and Its members," they consider these relations not simply in quasi-logical terms as the relations of wholes and parts, but rather as relations of interaction, in which our concept of the individual influences our concept of the group to which he or she belongs, and vice versa. This interaction can be used to raise or lower our estimation of either the individual or the group. I will focus on this kind of argumentation here.

Many arguments that appear to have the form of "what is true of the whole is true of the part," and vice versa, can be better understood in terms of interaction between the group and its members. Our concepts of individuals and their qualities are changed as we learn which groups they do or do not belong to. This is not simply a matter of deducing something about individuals on the basis of group membership. Nor is it a matter of generalizing about groups based on the qualities of individual members. Rather, our idea of the individual and our idea of the group *interact*; they are malleable concepts, and they influence one another.

This interaction is used in argumentation in many ways. The high achievements of individual members of a group can reflect well on an entire group. The disreputable actions of others can reflect badly on the group as a whole. Some people stress the failures and indiscretions of individual psychiatrists in order to disqualify them all. The question is, when is it reasonable to argue in such a fashion and when is it "fallacious"?

To answer this, we must return to our definition of "fallacies" as arguments which seem to convince a universal audience but do not. The concept of a universal audience has a particularly surprising application here. For here we could ask whether a member of a truly universal audience could belong to a particular audience as well. Wouldn't the charge to further general human interests conflict with allegiance to some particular human group? Wouldn't a universal audience/paragon way of life have to be understood as being *not* essentially obligated to or constrained by loyalty to a particular group? If this were the case, and if we imagined people as rational, this could put a stop to all group/member interaction in argumentation.

This actually seems to be the guiding assumption in law insofar as it moves in the direction of substituting individual for collective responsibility. In the voir dire process in criminal jury trials, prospective jurors are often questioned about whether they have attitudes about groups to which the defendant belongs which would prejudice them against the defendant. The idea is that the defendant should be considered as an individual detached from all groups and that group/member interaction should be disallowed in reasoning about guilt and innocence unless such interaction can be established within the strictures of legal procedure.

Would a universal audience, which tries to understand itself as capable of setting aside its group memberships, not extend the presumption of this ability to others as well? That is, would not a universal audience refuse to alter its conception of an individual on the basis of group memberships? If this were the case, would not all such argumentation fail for a universal audience and thus be fallacious if it gave the appearance of so succeeding? This would mean that only particular audiences use the concept of group/member interaction for the purposes of argumentation. And it *is* the case that we seem to reason one way about groups to which we belong and a different way about groups of which we have a low opinion. Members of the latter groups are more or less automatically contaminated by their membership. Members of our own groups are affected positively by their membership. A universal audience, which belongs to no other group, would not reason in such a way.

The difficulty here is that not everyone shares this conception of universality. Some people believe that, at least in most rhetorical situations, it is impossible to imagine a human being as distinct from the groups to which he or she belongs. They believe that to be human at all is to be a member of some cultural group and for that group to have determined fairly thoroughly whatever individuality one has. Such people would not usually universalize beyond the bounds of some cultural group. Thus, group/member interaction as an argumentative technique *would* convince the most universal audience imaginable. However, for people with a strong concept of individuality, such reasoning would count as fallacious. It would be a clear example of a particular audience's taking itself to be universal, an example of argumentation which seems to be valid but really isn't.

A rhetoric of reason provides no way of deciding which group is right. Unless the two groups share a conception of a universal or paragon audience, the conflict cannot be settled by way of argumentation. This may seem to put the rhetorical approach in the same category as the approach of informal logic, since one cannot say when such argumentation is fallacious and when it is not. However, this is not the case. A rhetoric of reason can judge when the argumentation is fallacious *for some audience* in some context. And, from a rhetorical point of view, this is the most anyone can reasonably claim to do.

Conclusion

The conflict about when argumentation is valid and when it is fallacious is often a conflict about what human beings are, about which features of human beings can be taken to be universal. I take it to be a strength when a rhetorician, or logician in the broadest sense, shows how reason is the enactment of an idea of what it is to be human. From a rhetorical point of view, argumentation which appeals to a paragon audience is always such an enactment. Since fallacies are instances of argumentation that seem to convince a universal audience but really do not, they are windows on our concepts of what it means to be human. The most interesting and intractable dilemmas that fallacy theory faces are conflicts about what it means to be human, about what universal audience is really appropriate for the argumentation in question.

Such an understanding of fallacy theory could reconnect informal logic both to the vital questions of the philosophical tradition and to the real problems of our societies. In an age of resurgent nationalisms, reactivated ethnic conflict, and intransigent racism, questions about universality and rationality have obvious practical importance. The development of feminist theory has increased the grounds for having doubts about past conceptions of universality and reason. Questions about which groups are persuaded by what kinds of reasoning and why, and some idea of what it is reasonable to hope about discovering common grounds for evaluating argumentation, are among the most provoking issues of our time.[6] In the end, a rhetorical theory of argumentation does not rest on some particular reified conception of universality. To practice argumentation is not to assume that there is in some already established sense a common human nature to which one is appealing. It is rather a practice of hope, an agreement to go on reasoning with people who are different from oneself. This is tantamount to acting on a desire to *create* something in common, in order to live together in a mutually beneficial way.

To connect the theory of argumentation with such aspirations while at the same time clarifying and resolving a number of fallacy theory's traditional problems seems to me no small achievement. A rhetoric of reason is informal logic's neglected opportunity.

And insofar as college writing programs have adopted informal logic as their approach to written reasoning, they have squandered their birthright for some dubious philosophical pottage. College writing courses are the inheritors of the rhetorical tradition. They stand at the gateway to higher education, at the core of the curriculum, the few courses that the entire faculty of a university can agree are worthwhile for all students. They make a claim to cultivate in students a general intellectual ability, the ability to reason in writing. This ability is not valuable simply in the context of a single discipline or profession, but has a general value. It is the ability of someone who has been educated to be not only a specialist but a citizen, a critic of specialized knowledge and not just an agent of it. It is the ability of a literate, educated individual, an ability which depends on deep common sense. To restrict the concept of reason to mathematical or formal reasoning, or to take that as the foundation for all models of reasoning, is to repeat the mistakes of those epochs which turned their backs on rhetoric, and to some extent on reason itself. A rhetoric of reason restores a heritage to college composition, and thus lights up a path to its future.

7 ARGUMENT AND IDEOLOGY

EVALUATING ARGUMENTATION

The last function of reason is to recognize that there are an infinity of things which surpass it.
—Pascal

The utopian image of the argumentative society is not a straightforward one. The celebration of argumentation involves a celebration of differences and, thereby, of unresolved dilemmas . . . This means that the theme praising argument cannot expect, in all consistency, to have its own unopposed argumentative triumph.
—Michael Billig

The Ideology of Argumentation

In the previous two chapters, I tried to show how a rhetoric of reason could provide a satisfactory account of what happens when we evaluate arguments. In this chapter, I would like to step back from the idea of evaluating arguments, and consider how argumentation itself might be evaluated. After all, we not only evaluate arguments but also make judgments about when, where, and to what degree it is appropriate to reason argumentatively with one another. In one sense, I have been evaluating argumentation throughout this entire book. My goal has been to open a perspective on argumentation that discloses its worthiness to be a central concern of courses in written reasoning, critical thinking, and speech communication. In particular, I have opened this perspective in order to help teachers of writing understand written reasoning as something preeminently worthwhile.

Yet although I have tried to answer questions and respond to objections as a way of thinking through the theory and developing it, I realize that there are probably systematic objections or patterns of questioning building up in some readers. I say this because I myself have experienced the force of such objections and questions while writing the previous chapters. I believe it was C. S. Lewis who said somewhere that it could undermine one's faith to write as an apologist. A doctrine never seemed as indefensible, he said, as when he was writing in its defense. At times, I have felt the same way trying to write this defense of argumentation. In this chapter, I will keep writing in argumentation's defense, but I also want to acknowledge argumentation's limits, and I want to let some difficulties stand, without my trying to defend argumentation against all challenges. In fact, I want to issue a few of these challenges myself.

I also want to reaffirm my general position. This project grew out of my concrete experience as a philosopher who directs a composition program and teaches writing and rhetorical theory. Even from a standpoint which recognizes argumentation's ideological obtuseness and its limits as a form of communication, one can still make the judgment that written reasoning is, of all the things one could teach in a writing course, the most worthwhile. It's been said more than once that good teachers can be known by the number of important things they refuse to teach. Writing courses and textbooks often lack focus and purpose; they simply try to cover too much. Writing teachers usually have only a term or two to help students develop their abilities. They must make choices about what to teach, about which goals are the most important. They must decide *not* to teach many kinds of writing that are very important, very worthwhile. Even given the limits of argumentative discourse, I believe that written reasoning is the most important kind of written discourse to cultivate in students in colleges and universities. I will make my most general case for this in the last chapter.

The following discussion of ideology divides into three sections. First, I show how the ideological nature of argumentation limits its usefulness. In this section, I treat the ideology of argumentation in fairly general, philosophical terms. Following this, I broach the question of gender and argumentation. This topic requires a book of its own, but I would like at least to open up some conversation between feminist theory and a rhetorical approach to the idea of reason. Third, I try to begin to identify the ways argumentation is and is not culture-specific, and I try to outline some of the senses in which the teaching and practice of argumentation further a particular cultural formation. Again, I can do this only in the most general terms.

The Limits of Argumentation

The limits of argumentation may be drawn along several lines. First, argumentation concerns only that which is made explicit

Part Three: Evaluating Arguments

in claims. Not every affirmation can or may be made explicit. Insofar as we allow argumentative discourse to determine our understanding of what exists, what is desirable, what is possible, we exclude many very important features of our experience, features that cannot be made explicit in assertions and claims. From an argumentative point of view, what cannot be shaped into a claim can be neither justified nor criticized. It falls outside the scope of argumentation, outside its ability to disclose, examine support, reconcile.

From the perspective of a rhetoric of reason, what can and can't be shaped into a claim is understood in light of the concept of audience. This is true even of the "background" which cannot be made explicit in communication. In Chapter 2, I offered evidence that all communication is dependent on a background of deep competences. These competences are not beliefs that we hold, but features of our being, features of our identities as participants in a particular culture, a particular society in a particular place at a particular time. When we speak or write, we affirm these competences to use a particular language in a particular way, and so affirm the appropriateness of particular discourses and all that belongs with them. Argumentation does not thematize these affirmations. It does not disclose them. It depends on their being shared by interlocutors and audiences, and it takes place in the communicative clearing they have opened up. However, these competences are not themselves the conclusions of arguments—at least not the conclusions of arguments offered by the people who depend on the competences.

Thus, argumentation affirms without argument the appropriateness of particular competences, particular ways of disclosing the world. It is only within the communicative clearing opened up by these competences that reasoning can reveal what it does. All reasoning is regional. All argumentation furthers a particular perspective on what is real, what is possible, and what is worthwhile.

What is opaque to argumentation is different in each argumentative situation. Each audience has particular competences. As we move outside particular situations, and look at particular formations of argumentative discourse from different or more universal positions, we can see the ideology in them. From such positions, we can certainly argue about that ideology. In this respect, which specific ideology argumentation furthers depends on the audience before which one makes a claim about ideology. After all, most claims about ideology have to be defended to be convincing. Although all argumentation is in general ideological, the specific ways in which any particular example of argumentation is ideological vary from particular audience to particular audience.

Some things, like deep competences, cannot be thematized in argumentation because we are unable to call them into question without undermining the very framework within which we call things into question. There are other cases in which we are unable to call certain things into question because it is improper to discuss them, improper to make them the content of claims and questions, improper to expose them this way to the available audiences. Argumentation is ideological in the way it assigns these things to a realm of unreason. For again, what cannot be claimed cannot be justified or criticized. Argumentation is limited to the available audiences. Their abilities and sympathies and strengths delimit the sphere of argumentation. There are some things about which we simply cannot reason, not even with ourselves—often, especially not with ourselves.

Sometimes the impropriety is a matter of impermissibility. We all know that it is impermissible to discuss certain things in some contexts. Some issues may not be discussed in front of children. Some assertions make one liable to legal action, or could provoke violence or some other kind of revenge. Some topics are shocking or offensive for some audiences. Even where it is not strictly impermissible or obviously dangerous to discuss some ideas, it may be so to some degree or other. In such a case, the conditions for reasoning may be partly secured, but partly not.

Consider an example. Recently, I read an article about the practice of the ritual infliction of pain in a performance context. Public pain rituals were being defended by participants as ways of transcending ordinary consciousness, and rising to new forms of trust and awareness. The defenders of such performances gave examples of pain rituals in many different cultures in many different historical periods. They presented testimony from other participants about the rejuvenating and mind-expanding effects of the rituals.

Obviously, there is argumentation going on in this article. However, there are many people who would not experience the writing this way. The article mentioned that one spectator at a recent performance rushed from the room because she had to vomit, and she did not return. Many people will have some degree of the same reaction when reading about such performances. In such cases, the reactions of the audience are such that argumentation is either not possible, or possible only to a very small degree. One can't reason about things for which one's audience has such strong feelings of revulsion. In such settings, these matters are mostly outside the domain of reason and argumentation.

It is also impossible to argue about matters which are not living issues. There are some things people just don't care to argue about. For example, many people will simply not care to spend much time considering the arguments that they should participate in public pain rituals. For most of us, this is just not something to which we're going to devote much thought. For every audience, there will be many such matters. Even our concept of the universal or paragon audience will be constrained by what we consider significant and worth our time. Every conception of reason carries such an ideology with it. Every instance of argumentation establishes a domain of what is arguable and what is not.

There are other reasons it may not be possible to make some ideas explicit in claims. Some ideas are private or personal or secret, and shaping them into claims which can be defended before an audience changes their meaning. Ideas which are private do not have to be defended because they do not make claims on someone who questions them. They can just stand. They are sometimes almost indistinguishable from us, more a part of what we are than part of a set of beliefs we hold. Of course, we can question our private ideas, but then we have formed a kind of public domain in our imagination, and we take sides for and against our ideas—we separate ourselves from them. Argumentation makes private ideas appear irrational, indefensible. Argumentation supports ideas, legitimates them, by forcing them into some kind of conversation with a questioner/respondent. This makes what is private to some degree public; it weakens the sphere of privacy. Argumentative conflicts can be resolved only by deferring to audiences which have a less private, more universal angle on the conflict. If what is indefensible by argumentation is for that reason irrational and illegitimate, argumentation furthers an ideology that is destructive of the sphere of privacy. Reason is a social force that makes everything a matter of some kind of public deliberation.

Another difficulty with shaping ideas into claims is that some ideas are not only private but also just not clear or simple enough to put into claims. Imagine a scene that evokes in you the strongest sense of deep well-being and happiness. For me, it might be hiking alone above the timberline on a bright September day, with views of the peaks of the High Cascades. Or it might be a summer picnic at the arboretum, talking with friends, watching the children running up the forest paths, playing and calling out that they have found a turtle or a snake. Or it could be walking through a strange city, and having insights at each corner into the accumulated labor and hope of its citizens—how they had together made a city that was vibrant and peaceful, with a sense of a future. However, the claim I would want to make about such experiences escapes me. I want to affirm such experiences, and let myself be claimed by the sense of well-being they evoke, but I can't come close to describing everything that is happening to make such an experience what it is. Nothing I can say seems to warrant the depth of my response to the situation. Nothing seems to justify rationally the sense of wonder and gratitude I have at such moments for simply being alive, there in the wild wonder of it all.

From Plato's *Thaeatetus* to the opening arguments of Hegel's *Phenomenology of Mind* to Wittgenstein's "private language" argument in the *Philosophical Investigations,* philosophy has relentlessly attacked all claims about such experiences. All three of these major philosophical works interpret references to such experiences as knowledge claims, and all three take such claims to be unwarranted. The arguments are subtle, and differ from one another in important ways, but all three depend on interpreting references to such experience as claims. Once one attempts to put such experiences into explicit, univocal language, one must meet public criteria both for applying general concepts and for supporting claims about such experiences. As Hegel points out, there is no escape to highly general language, like "this" or "now," for although these try to capture everything about an experience, they really succeed in capturing *every* this or now, and so fail to differentiate the significant experience from any other experience.

I was fortunate enough to study Hegel's *Phenomenology* with Herbert Marcuse in the last graduate seminar he ever offered. I was assigned to present Hegel's arguments in the opening chapters of the *Phenomenology.* After correcting my pronunciation of *aisthesis,* Marcuse asked a single question about my oral presentation of Hegel's arguments. Is it really correct, he asked, to say that whatever cannot be said is therefore unimportant and so dismissible? He went on to suggest that perhaps we all did have *some* understanding of what we mean by "this" and "now." It was not an understanding we could defend or make explicit, but it was not *nothing.* If it were, we would be in serious trouble. Now, there are ways of interpreting Hegel's *Phenomenology* that recognize this fact, but for me this recognition was a turning point. Much of the history of philosophy is a history of a struggle against claims to private, special knowledge, claims to revelation, claims to know something ineffable.[1] Philosophical argumentation forces us into conversation with a very general audience, and demands that we make and defend our claims before this skeptical gathering. Yet why should we have to do this? Why should every feature of our experience that cannot be justified in a public domain be for that reason dismissed as irrational?

I don't want to exaggerate the point. I argued in the chapters on claiming and questioning that launching out of this relatively private domain of prerational experience is a way of finding both new selves and new modes of selfhood. Making claims on other people is a way of holding oneself accountable to them, a transforming of oneself by way of a loyalty to others. There are ways of renewing these experiences even in this process of transformation and argumentation, so the loss of their immediacy is never once and for all. However, argumentation does carry an ideology. It furthers the dissolution of a private domain, and it is corrosive of some very important features of human experience.

As a last example of something which is not easy to put into a claim, I want to discuss a set of actions which are in general appropriate but individually indefensible. There are actions and gestures which are immediate for us, and which define our competence as particular kinds of people. Think, for instance, of the way we sometimes put our arms around each other in order to communicate comfort and love. Rarely do we reason about such things. In fact, if we discovered that someone needed to reason about such things, we would probably believe that the person was in some way underdeveloped, or unsocialized. One part of cultural competence is knowing how to take actions of this sort immediately, without having to think of arguments for putting one's arm around another person. Once we make such actions the subject of arguments, it changes their character. If we had to defend the action of putting our arms around other people to comfort them, it would tend to undermine the action of giving comfort immediately.

I take it for granted that in any culture there are some immediate actions of this kind, actions which not only do not need to be defended but actually cannot be defended because to defend them is to change their character, to change them into something questionable, something which needs to be defended. Now it is true that such actions can be defended in general; that is, we can argue that in general it is good that people comfort one another without having to reason about it. However, even in this case too much argument is corrosive of the practice. If such arguments occur, it is because there are questions about whether it is good to go on comforting one another in this way. Recognizing that such questions need to be answered weakens the degree of immediacy available in putting one's arm around another person. Questioning the gesture of comfort, either before the action, or retrospectively, or in general, undermines the immediacy of the practice. And in all societies, there are many such practices that depend on this relatively unquestioned immediacy.

Argumentation has consequences. Within its domain, certain experiences cannot come to expression; they fall outside the scope of rationality. Whether because they are private, or unclear, or improper, or unthinkable, these matters are not eligible for argumentation. In addition, argumentation affirms competences it does not and cannot make explicit; argumentation does not thematize everything it affirms. And finally, the meaning of some claims can change when forced out into the openness of an argumentative realm. The practice of certain actions can be undermined by being questioned, even if it is eventually justified. In all these ways, argumentation furthers very particular ways of disclosing the world and understanding things. It promotes certain kinds of action and undermines others. It makes some forms of life seem desirable and deprives others of any justification.

Now, there is an obvious objection to this claim about the ideology of argumentation. The objection goes like this. It is not *argumentation* or *reason* which promotes a particular ideology, but rather the audiences that judge argumentation and the claimants who are influenced by them. It is *audiences* that disallow certain claims, find them shocking or improper; *audiences* that misconstrue private claims made in a public context; *audiences* that lack imagination and enforce unrealistic standards of clarity; *audiences* that demand justification of things which should be taken for granted. If we imagined a tolerant, sympathetic, imaginative, charitable audience, we could imagine argumentation which did not suffer from the ideological disabilities just described.

This is a powerful objection. It is a version of the objection Perelman and Olbrechts-Tyteca make to Aristotle's concept of rhetoric. They accuse Aristotle of undervaluing rhetoric by limiting its domain to audiences which are deficient in certain reasoning abilities. "But why not allow," they ask, "that argumentations can be addressed to every kind of audience?"[2] They develop the concept of a universal audience as a way of imagining audiences that are qualified for all kinds of argumentation, the kinds of argumentation Aristotle would probably have assigned to dialectic rather than rhetoric.

The challenge that this objection must meet is to imagine a paragon audience, an audience which is not ideological. However, as we have seen, any audience can be seen to lack paragon universality if we distance ourselves from the context for which the audience is said to be universal. In the same way, any audience may be shown to be ideological if we distance ourselves from the situation in which the audience is thought to be ideology-free. An audience may be ideology-free as far as the purposes of the parties in conflict go, but the audience may be judged to be strongly ideological by outsiders. What is unimaginable for one group is not necessarily unimaginable for another.

Let's try to imagine an ideology-free audience and see where we land. Let's attempt this with the easiest problem. It seems simple enough to imagine an audience before which it is permissible to make any claim, raise any question. Modern, liberal societies usually provide spheres which encourage the development of such audiences. Universities, for example, are often thought to be more open in this respect than schools or churches or city councils. Let's consider the easiest form of impermissibility, too. Let's consider an audience which is not shocked or repulsed by any claim. Lawyers and doctors are sometimes supposed to take this posture. During my graduate training in philosophy, I often thought I was being trained in this kind of openness, trained to examine dispassionately every caller, any claim. I even thought I noticed that graduate students who showed themselves incapable of this detachment were treated condescendingly, by their peers as well as by their professors. So there seems to be a social need to develop our capacity to imagine ourselves as such an audience, at least in particular professions for particular purposes. And it doesn't appear altogether impossible to do so.

However, we seem to have escaped from one ideology into another. An audience for which everything is thinkable is an audience of a particular kind. It is a universal audience, one which has been constructed quantitatively by adding together all the things which we can imagine as thinkable for all the audiences we can imagine. However, it is not necessarily a paragon audience in the sense of being ideology-free. This audience has a very particular sense of what is desirable, what is worthwhile. It *excludes* any limitations we might want to draw on what is thinkable. To accept its position, its judgment, is to abandon ourselves to a domain in which everything is thinkable.

For some of us, this would be a strongly undesirable position to take. Our moral identities depend on there being some things that are unthinkable for us. You can use your own imagination to test the boundaries of what is and isn't thinkable for you. For me, an hour with an Amnesty International Report provides plenty of testing. I find my everyday emotions and beliefs and hopes undermined by too much time with a report of this sort. I think what is for me usually unthinkable. The more I try to understand what motivates torture, what social forces and what kinds of self-understanding tolerate and promote it, the more I find myself losing touch with my everyday moral identity, an identity sustained and strengthened by a particular kind of social life. Now, it is important to have a flexible moral personality, one which can integrate new knowledge, develop new sympathies, and which is not destroyed or undermined when exposed to very different forms of life. And there are certainly psychosocial differences in any community when it comes to this kind of flexibility. Certain roles carry a responsibility for moral frontier work. Someone must do the work of Amnesty International. Someone must investigate and prosecute crimes. Someone must perform and assist at abortions. However, such work is not completely cost-free. And although the costs can be reduced by controlling psychosocial variables, the problem is not just psychological. The changes we suffer when we must entertain the unthinkable are changes to the ideals of rationality which hold sway over our lives. And this means that they are changes in the kind and degree of solidarity we have with other people, and perhaps changes altogether in which people we have solidarity with.

This truth is given powerful dramatic expression in a fine film called *Manhunter,* a kind of forerunner to *Silence of the Lambs.* We first meet the main character on the beach, with his family. The setting is serene. He is happy enough, but he seems still to be recovering from some kind of mental or emotional collapse. He is approached on the beach by men in suits. It turns out that he is a detective of unusual abilities, and they need his help in tracking down a serial, multiple murderer. After expressing great reluctance, he is finally persuaded to help, and he is taken away. His unusual ability turns out to be an uncanny power to imaginatively enter the minds of criminals. He visits the scene of a murder not once or twice but over and over again, and not to collect information, but to slowly locate and enter the perceptions and thoughts, the experience of the killer.

As terrible new thoughts become possible for him, old thoughts become unthinkable. He loses touch with his old identity, becomes incapable of communicating with his wife and child, and begins to lose his own mind. The central tension is between two incompatible domains of what is thinkable, and the question is whether the criminal can be caught before the detective is completely lost in the unthinkable, unable to recover himself and find the ordinary again.

The point is that our moral identities are sustained by the fact that some things are unthinkable for us—at least to some degree or other.[3] When our moral identities are challenged through unconstrained questioning before an audience for which everything is thinkable, they simply cannot be defended without being changed.

Thus, there is a question about whether the paragon audience should be an audience for which everything is thinkable or an audience which knows in each case what should be thinkable and what should be left unthought.[4] For there is a legitimate question about the degree to which we should, in each case, hold fast to our moral identities, and the degree to which we should expose them to unconstrained questioning. This question cannot be reasoned about before an audience which has already made a commitment on the issue. A paragon audience which has made such a commitment already represents a certain ideology.

This result will be troubling only to those who believe that reason can or should be absolutely ideology-free, absolutely neutral with respect to what kind of life is worth living. It will be troubling only to those who believe that an absolutely ideology-free position is a useful position to take. However, such beliefs have little connection with the real uses of reason. Reasoning makes possible a way of overcoming conflicts and reaching agreements. This requires only the degree of universality, the degree of ideology-freeness, needed to resolve some particular conflict. The belief that we need better concepts of universality than we have, less ideologically loaded concepts of the paragon audience than we are using now, is perfectly consonant with a rhetoric of reason. A rhetoric of reason interprets the concepts of universal and paragon audiences as aspirations for agreement, hopes for reconciling conflicting parties in peaceful ways. Better concepts of universality mean hopes that are more inclusive and expansive in the reconciliation for which they aim. Once reason achieves this reconciliation, it has reached the level of ideology-freeness required for the situation. This is all that can be asked of argumentation. To ask for more is to misunderstand the limits of argumentation and to risk destroying what moral identities human beings have managed to achieve.

I said at the beginning of this section that the limits of argumentation may be drawn along several lines. One way to schematize the respects in which argumentation is ideological is to think of the ideology of claiming, the ideology of questioning, and the ideology of reaching agreement. In the above section, I discussed primarily the ideology of claiming, and examined the ways in which the requirements of claiming furthered an ideology. I began to touch on the ideology of questioning, and I will continue this now. After this, I will examine the ideology implicit in argumentation's focus on reaching agreement. Since the general idea about the ideology of argumentation has already been developed, I will treat these specific ideas more briefly.

Argumentation privileges questioning over affirming in important ways. As we have just seen, and as I argued explicitly in Chapter 3, claiming itself is a kind of deferring to questioning. Every making of a claim in an argument is at the same time a concession that the claim is questionable. That is why an argument is necessary. We don't argue about unquestionable affirmations. And yet, as we have seen, to say something is questionable is to take a particular point of view, to make a particular judgment. To argue about something at all is already to have made a judgment about its questionability.

Argumentation's privileging of questioning can be seen in another way. In argumentation, we typically defend claims and not questions. A claim is made. A question is asked. Now, what requires justification, the question or the claim? Ordinarily, the claimant must support the claim. The questioner need not justify the question. There is an asymmetry here in the demands we make on claims and questions. It is only in fairly extraordinary situations that questions can themselves be called into question, and when they are it *interrupts* the argumentation rather than furthering it. One obvious reason for this is that questions are often implicit in arguments, hidden in the relation between a claim and a reason. Just recovering them and making them explicit can be a difficult work of interpretation. Since all this work and potential controversy stand between the claim and the reason, it is experienced as an interruption of argumentation's natural work of supporting claims with reasons and so creating agreements.

In addition, questions are typically justified in ways that are very different from the ways we justify claims. More important, we do not really justify *questions* at all. Not only is the question usually implicit in written argumentation, but what needs justifying in a question is also implicit. What needs justifying is not the question itself, but an implicit *validity claim*. The validity claim at stake in asking a question is usually the claim that the question is appropriate and relevant in the argumentative situation. But with this identification of the validity claim, we have lost the *question* completely. We have converted it into a claim in order to make it questionable. The question itself is fugitive to interrogation. Even when we seem to justify a question, what we justify is rather the *claim* that the question was an appropriate one.

Argumentation does not make it impossible to call questions into question by questioning their implicit validity claims. However, it does make it relatively hard. It is harder to examine what is implicit; easier to examine what is explicit. Since argumentation—and especially written argumentation—tends to leave questions implicit, and since questions are called into question by way of raising doubts about *implicit* validity claims, argumentation tends by its very nature to privilege the question over the claim, to make the claim of the question harder to question. This is one of argumentation's great strengths; it provides a powerful way to "think critically" about claims. However, it gains this power by making it relatively difficult to think critically about critique itself.

Even if one overcomes this difficulty, and learns to ferret out questions with the single-mindedness and perseverance with which most students are now trained to ferret out "presuppositions" and "assumptions," it is still the case that argumentation is a kind of questioning, and so an affirming of questioning as a way of knowing. All argumentation depends on questioning, and justifies claims by way of answering questions. Its way of knowing is the way of the question. There is no escape from this within the domain of reasoning. No questioning of questioning itself.

In Chapter 2, I cited Emmanuel Levinas as having asked, "Why does research take the form of a question?" I pointed out that what is unusual about this approach is that it uses a question to attempt to understand whether questioning is the best way of understanding. If the rhetoric of reason I developed in Part I of this book is correct, there is no escape from the question within the domain of reason. However, this does not mean that we must be oblivious to this fact. Argumentation furthers an ideology, and the more we are aware of argumentation's limits in this regard, the healthier our appreciation of argumentation can be. Not everything should be exposed to the corrosive effects of reasoning. Many human accomplishments are too subtle, too tenuous to treat this way. No one questions everything. Aristotle knew that there were some things we just don't argue about—and this goes for any "we." Or, as Wittgenstein says, there are some things about which we cannot be mistaken (*On Certainty* no. 155). To argue is to say, "I could be mistaken, and I will give a special privilege to the question of whether I am mistaken or not."

Thus, argumentation, as a form of discourse, is closely allied with modern suspiciousness and doubt, with interrogation, and with a will to power.[5] However, if I am right, this aggression of argumentation is located not in the act of claiming or in the assertion, or in the reason, but in the question, which is itself fugitive to the kind of rational doubt it makes possible.

Another way to understand the ideological limits of argumentation is to examine argumentation's privileging of agreement and consensus. I developed this idea in some detail in the chapters on conflict and audience, but it bears repeating in this context. Typically, arguments resolve conflicts by settling on one claim rather than another. Arguments reach at least provisional conclusions. The whole purpose of arguing is to resolve conflicts, disagreements, by reaching conclusions on which people can agree.

However, this means that argumentation privileges sameness over difference, consensus over dissensus. Differences which are brought within the domain of reason are understood as something to be overcome. Again, this is not because argumentation posits a single way of understanding, or a metaphysical domain of Truth to which all people must conform. Rather, it is because argumentation is concerned with differences as *conflicts*. And its purpose and virtue lie in the resolution of conflicts. Resolving conflicts is what argumentation is for.

Clearly, though, a way of understanding that marks difference as something which needs to be overcome in agreements is just one way of understanding difference—a highly ideological one. On the basis of this recognition, we could launch a real attack on the teaching of argumentation. We could claim that we need to do more to *protect* and *preserve* the differences among individuals and human groups. We need to let them be. The last thing we need to do is to promote a kind of discourse which automatically conceptualizes difference as something which needs to be overcome in sameness.

Post-Enlightenment thinkers have warned over and over that modern reason has an imperialistic, leveling tendency. It has global ambitions. It is an agent in the annihilation of tribal peoples, local cultures, distinct traditions. It measures everything by the same standard, and transforms each place into every other. In situations of social conflict, it can force minorities out into a public forum dominated by audiences that do not value their differences.

As teachers of students who may come from diverse cultures, and have very different kinds of lives, perhaps argumentation really is the last thing we should teach. Why force all students into the same rhetorical community, and lead them into reaching agreements with one another? Why not explore and magnify their differences? After all, one of the things they need to learn is how different they really are from one another. They need to learn how race, class, and gender have shaped and will continue to shape their experience. They need to know how people who are different from them disclose the world and understand the things in it. We have too many students who are too quick to reach agreements with one another, and too quick to imagine that they have reached agreements with yet other audiences. They need to learn more about the differences among people before they arrogate to themselves the responsibility for overcoming these differences.

Thus, what we need in writing courses are the kinds of discourse that let these differences come forth and appear in lively and moving ways. Students need to go on learning, as we all do, that it is not necessary to reach agreement on everything, that we can be different from one another and that there is nothing wrong with this. Differences are not obstacles; they don't have to be "overcome."

Perhaps, then, we don't need courses in "critical thinking" nearly as much as we need courses in suspending critical thought in order to reach deeper understandings. Perhaps we need composition courses that teach and encourage what Peter Elbow calls "rendering." Rendering is the written sharing of experience. Its aim is not to overcome conflicts through explicit reasoning, but to deepen one another's understanding of what it's like to be the other person. Rendering can give differences their due. It is not bent on representing differences as conflicts. In fact, it suggests that it may be better to live with differences than overcome them.

202

These are powerful objections to the teaching of argumentation, and they deserve a response. Although my full response to them can come only in the final chapter, after the discussion of "Argument as Inquiry," I will address them to some degree in just a moment. First, however, I need to complete the general account of argumentation's ideology of agreement by showing how this ideology is connected with the ideas of choice and power.

Differences become conflicts only when choices must be made. It is the need to choose which deprives us of the luxury of simply letting differences be. Of course, it is possible to write without being constrained by this need to make a choice. I mentioned earlier the famous *Dissoi Logoi*, in which "twofold arguments" are set forth. In this kind of writing, arguments for and arguments against a thesis stand pretty much just juxtaposed. We can imagine many other forms of writing that refuse to make a choice between alternatives. We can imagine voices making incompatible claims side by side, perhaps in columns on the same page, without the claiming on one side's ever being called into question by the claiming on the other side. We can imagine essays which include "twofold" or "threefold" arguments without deciding among them. There are many, many ways to uncover differences without treating them as conflicts in need of resolution.

However, when differences do come into conflict, and when these conflicts must be resolved, when some choice must be made, argumentation can be called in to play the role of the third party, the mediator. Through the process of responding to challenges by examining, clarifying, qualifying, modifying, and supporting claims, it shapes agreements. I discussed the dynamics of conflict in argumentation in Chapter 4. In Chapter 5, I developed the idea that the aim of argumentation is agreement. Here, I want to emphasize again that agreement is in many ways an important good, but it is only one of the many goods people seek. Making a choice is sometimes exactly what is called for; at other times, a choice may not be necessary.

It is the idea of choice that connects the practice of argumentation to power. Typically, people with power make choices; people who lack power lack choices. The history of rhetoric is linked in interesting ways to the shifts and increases and decreases in the ways choices are distributed in societies. In most standard histories of rhetoric, the need for training in argument arises coincidentally with changes in the legal organization of Greek cities. It was, in George Kennedy's words, "the needs of the democracies in Sicily and Greece" which engendered technical rhetoric (16). This link between shifting the power of choice to a public and the coincident development of that public's need for argumentation is obvious everywhere in the history of rhetoric. And this link is effective both as the size of the enfranchised group grows and as it decreases. Kennedy's history of rhetoric is famous for tracking just this link in the movement from a "primary" rhetoric, concerned with argumentation and persuasion in civic life, to a "secondary rhetoric," which developed when and where the opportunities for practicing primary rhetoric became unavailable.

Obviously, the power of choice is distributed unevenly. The choices available to people, and the degree of availability, break down along every imaginable line: age, health, race, gender, class, culture, region, education, historical period. Argumentation as a form of discourse will be cultivated most intensely where it is most useful. Among individuals without much power to choose, argumentation may not seem to be a very important kind of discourse. Among people who do not have effective responsibility for mediating conflicts and settling social disputes, argumentation may not seem very useful. However, among those responsible for making choices, or enabling them in others, it could easily be thought to be the most important form of writing and speech available. Among those who are responsible for mediating social conflicts, argumentation will seem indispensable. And so it does seem, in law, in politics, in research, in international affairs, in most public spheres in which disagreements arise.

For this reason, argumentation is linked to powerful social groups, groups responsible for making choices. Argumentation is linked to a particular kind of power—limited power, not absolute power. Monarchs and dictators do not need to argue.[6] To the degree that decisions do not need to be justified, choices need not follow from reasons. However, where choices need to be justified, argumentation is necessary. And where the expectation of justification is very high, the ability to argue is itself a form of power. So people who are trained for public life are typically trained in argumentation, and spheres of public power are defined by the kinds of argumentative discourse that go on in them.

However, outside of these spheres, the need for argumentation is not as obvious or as strong. Families do not resolve internal disputes in the same way as countries. Not only are there obvious inequalities in power and abilities within families (children are smaller than adults, and infants cannot speak or write), but the expectations of justification are not present to the same degree. Although agreements may be desirable, there are many situations in which parents do not expect to have to reach agreements with their children in order to legitimate their choices. Further, in domains where people are held together by love, they may resolve conflicts in ways that do not require argumentation. From a "rational" point of view, these ways of resolving conflicts will always be vulnerable to criticism. This is why societies typically try to preserve some form of privacy for families, and this is also why such privacy is always a matter of controversy.

To the degree that people lack the power to make choices for themselves, or resolve their own disputes, or participate in the resolution of public conflicts, discourses other than argumentation will have primary power among them. Sometimes, some people speak in such a way that they enable other people to argue, but do not argue themselves. Other times, people try to prevent direct argumentation. Often, people tell stories rather than offer explicit arguments. And, of course, sometimes people magnify the differences among human groups in order to deepen mutual understanding and prevent premature argumentative agreements.

I want to return now to the earlier arguments against the claim that written reasoning should be the central focus of college writing courses. The argument went like this: what we need are not more agreements and stronger ways of reaching them, but deeper understandings of our differences and more powerful ways of communicating them. My response to this argument is twofold. First, I am going to argue that even given this choice there are still powerful reasons for opting to teach argumentation. Second, I am going to show how the disjunction between "rendering" and argumentation is in any case unnecessary, how the idea of written argumentation includes the idea of powerful renderings. Thus, I am going to make a case for a *curriculum* that is inclusive and flexible. If I were arguing simply to persuade, I could easily omit the first part of this response. After all, if the disjunction is unnecessary, why deal with it at all? However, if the theory I have been assembling is sound, then responding to objections is a way of clarifying and developing my own ideas. And responding to this objection on its own terms allows me to do this in what I think are some important respects—even beyond my defense of the theory.

To some degree, the choice between rendering and reasoning is a real one, especially if the choice concerns the purpose of teaching writing in colleges and universities. And given the choice, there are several fairly strong reasons for choosing to teach written reasoning. To begin with, there are many other courses and departments in which students are exposed to powerful differences and strong renderings: Anthropology courses, history courses, women's studies courses, ethnic studies courses, language courses, international studies courses, religious studies courses—one could go on and on. The college curriculum is full of powerful ways of understanding and representing differences. Not the least of these are the ways differences are amplified and explored in literature courses and in creative writing programs. The *purpose* of a huge part of the college curriculum is to give students a deep exposure both to difference and to ways of representing it.

However, there are very few courses which enable *students themselves* to *make choices* about these differences, to reconcile conflicts, to take responsibility for mediating disputes, and thus to develop *new* voices of their own. Courses in written reasoning grant to all students a position that is usually reserved only for elite groups—a position of responsibility for making reasoned choices and for defending them before a public audience. Writing courses are the primary sites for cultivating the capacity of students to become agents in their own educations. Too often the responsibility for serious written reasoning is reserved for the few—for students writing honors theses, or students in special programs. The great majority of students in large universities rarely get the opportunity to imagine themselves in positions of responsibility, able to mediate genuine disputes about knowledge and policy and to justify judgments about what is worthwhile.

The fairly common assumption that the responsibility for genuine, extended written reasoning should not be given to just any student came home to me forcefully recently in discussions in my own department and on my own campus. In a small planning group, someone urged that the department think of curricular reform in terms of what English majors should be able to *do* rather than what courses they were expected to have sat through. He proposed that the department require a senior essay of each of its majors. He also proposed that the essay be written in a senior-level course taught by professors, and that the entire professorial faculty participate in teaching sections of the course. Good reasons were offered for and against the proposal, but one of the reasons offered against the proposal was that it would turn the English department into an honors college. It took me a while to grasp that this could be counted as a reason *against* the proposal. However, in retrospect, it is obvious. We do not ordinarily think of students as agents of their own education to this degree. We do not expect them to take responsibility for an extended piece of written reasoning. We expect that after four years of sitting through our courses, they could well be unable to write an acceptable essay.

This expectation is alive everywhere in large public universities. Some departments have actually reduced the amount of writing required in upper-division courses because the students are just not up to writing at the appropriate level. Instead, these departments offer multiple-choice examinations. At my last institution, I discovered that students' writing had actually regressed between the conclusion of the first-year writing sequence and their entering upper-division courses. It turned out that some of them had written no papers at all between the end of their first-year writing courses and their entry into my upper-division, advanced writing course. Professors do not ask for written reasoning because they are afraid of what they will receive, and they do not believe that it is their responsibility to teach writing.

However, if the students cannot reason in writing about what they are learning in their courses, what good can be gained by having them take the courses at all? How can they retain information they can do nothing with? And why *should* they? How will they ever be prepared to reason clearly enough to write in the professions, to complete reports and policy recommendations, to make the countless adaptations and changes they will need to make to be successful in their lives and in their careers?

I will give two more reasons for favoring written reasoning over rendering in college writing courses. First, although it is important to recognize and understand differences which are not conflicts, it is more important to learn how to resolve the conflicts we face. And we do face conflicts. In the United States, we face intransigent racism, and we must make choices at every level, from the personal to the international, about how to resolve the conflicts caused by racism. We face conflicts about gender issues that confront us with serious choices at every level. We face conflicts about ethnicity, about sexual orientation and the law, about the rights of children, about economic policies, about labor and the environment. We face conflicts about what knowledge is and whose claims about knowledge warrant assent. We face conflict in almost every part of our lives and our society.

These conflicts are both dangers and opportunities. They are dangers insofar as they prevent us from cooperating together for our mutual good. They are dangers insofar as they lead us to resolve our problems by resorting to force and violence. They are dangers insofar as they lead the victims of unfair resolutions of conflict into skepticism, mistrust, rage, and despair. However, they are opportunities insofar as they offer us the possibility of transformation, of new selves, new knowledge, new agreements. They are opportunities insofar as they offer paths out of our old selves, and call us toward a new, more inclusive ideal of reason, a new paragon audience. The only way to redeem these opportunities is to cultivate our ability to have real arguments with one another, to teach and learn the dialogue of reason.

Second, the curriculum of rendering and difference is already a curriculum permeated by choice and power. Deciding what to render, deciding what aspects of experience to disclose, requires choice. It requires deciding also what *not* to render, what is not as important to bring to the attention of others. Further, every representation of difference also contains difference. After all, every rendering can be called into question—especially when one person's renderings are taken to be representative of a group's experience. However, these choices and the reasons that support them are often hidden from students. Why not give students access, somewhere in the curriculum, to the processes that produce the representations they are offered? There is, after all, great conflict about what kinds of generalizations can be made about the experiences of different human groups. Why not give students access to concepts of difference by allowing them to examine the reasoning that leads to different renderings of experience?

However, in deep and important respects, this disjunction between rendering and argumentation, between letting differences be (or magnifying them) and resolving conflicts, is seriously misleading. First, the question is not whether we should let differences be, by rendering them, or whether we should rather transform them into agreements, by reasoning about them. To render experience to an audience for some purpose is already to transform experience. Not only is that which is rendered constantly changing, but the rendering itself is an agent in the change. The pace of this change is accelerated in relation to the amount of rendering going on in a society. For better or worse, we live in a period and in a society of rapid and frequent communication. Our individuality, our sense of self, undergoes accelerated change because of this. Ethnic groups, religious groups, neighborhoods, our identities as men and women—these forms of identity which are relatively slow to change in periods and in places where communication is less frequent, less rapid, and less widespread—all undergo rapid transformation in high-communication societies.

The future of experience, the experience of the relatively nondominant as well as the relatively dominant, lies in the capacity for transformation in a high-communication world. Our abilities to dialogue with and change in response to those who are different from us are what will preserve and renew that which is most important for us.

From the point of view of a rhetoric of argumentation, human beings exist partly as ways of having conflict. Through conflict, we renew and transform our individual selves as well as the groups to which we belong, and on whom we depend, in part, for our identities. The teaching of written reasoning has a primary importance in education because the vitality of our differences depends on our willingness to reason with one another and transform ourselves by way of creating new common ground.

Again, this is a position that carries an ideology. The teaching of written reasoning tends to work against all fundamentalisms, all segregation. People who have a strong sense of a *settled* ethnic or racial identity, or a *settled* religious identity, or a settled identity of any kind, should find an education in reasoning uncomfortable and unsettling. Those whose overriding aim is to protect and strengthen these settled identities are right to believe that most colleges and universities are prejudiced against their interests. It is perfectly reasonable for them to want to build independent, private colleges and universities.

The goal of a college curriculum which grants a central place to the teaching and learning of reasoning is not to make the classroom "safe" for people with diverse backgrounds. Rather, it is to make it equally dangerous and demanding for everyone, something most colleges and universities have failed to do. Instead, they have simply defaulted to the divisions and prejudices of the larger society. The teaching of written reasoning is a way of strengthening our ability to have genuine conflicts, to create an educational setting that is equally dangerous for all, and so relatively safe for everyone. Writing courses can be one powerful agent in the transformation of higher education. And they can be powerful in this way by enabling *all* students to bring their own transformative powers into the classroom in written reasoning. In fact, there are no more important courses in the college curriculum, no better site for the hope that *education itself* can make a difference.

Second, the disjunction between rendering and reasoning, between communicating differences and reconciling differing parties, is a false disjunction because written argumentation includes and in fact depends on the ability to render, to describe, to create presence in writing. Earlier, I showed why the teaching of epideictic rhetoric is an essential part of any curriculum in written reasoning. Epideictic is the means by which we strengthen an audience's attachment to certain ideas without having to make explicit claims about those ideas. Instead, we tell stories, paint pictures, describe feelings, recall past events, and generally increase the presence, the felt power, of shared beliefs.

As I said before, this requires judgment about which ideas need to be strengthened and to what degree. It requires imagination about which past events, which stories and scenes, which images and sounds will deepen the identity between the claimant and the audience. It requires, too, the ability to amplify—to put ideas into images, stories, into language that can appeal more directly to our sensibility.

Further, to write good arguments requires rendering conflicts accurately—and accuracy is determined by the audience. In Chapter 4, I explored the fact that it is not always an easy matter to grasp exactly what an argumentative conflict is about, or who the parties to the conflict really are. Neither is it always easy to measure the intensity of the conflict. These matters can often be captured better by rendering than by explicit claims. We can sometimes gain a much fuller understanding of conflict when it is rendered in concrete images and specific details and from very particular points of view. Often, this goes under the name of "background information," but it is more than that. Classical order includes not only a narration (of the facts, of background information), but also an exordium. However, I believe that it is best to think of the classical divisions as functions that need to be fulfilled rather than as distinct parts of a spoken or written argument. The exordium is an introduction part of whose aim is to create in the audience an appropriate mood, the appropriate receptivity for the argument. This can be done in the actual narration, the background, that shows the conflict for what it is. That is, the rendering of the conflict can itself include an attempt to show how deep the conflict is, why it is worth caring about. I said earlier that a rhetoric of reason refuses the distinction between reason and emotion. Instead, it recognizes that emotions allow reasons to appear as reasons. It is rendering a conflict in its fullness that both motivates us to reason about it and allows some reasons to appear stronger than others.[7]

These requirements are not incidental to a curriculum in written reasoning. It is necessary to strengthen shared ideas in order to reach the starting point of argumentation. It is necessary to render conflicts accurately in order to gain an audience's trust and goodwill, to strengthen certain emotions to open up the conflict in its fullness. A curriculum in written reasoning would have to include practice in rendering and aim at a well-developed understanding of how rendering is used in written reasoning. The disjunction between rendering differences in order to deepen our understanding of them and reasoning about them in order to resolve our conflicts is not only unnecessary, but when it comes to any actual curriculum in written reasoning, quite impossible.

Still, it must be admitted that argumentation aims at agreement and consensus. Insofar as arguments do not lead to new agreements of *some* kind (this need not be a resolution of the *thematized* conflict), they fail to reach their aim. This is part of the ideology of argumentation. When we are interested in holding fast to our differences, and not interested in reaching new agreements with people who are different from us, we will turn to other kinds of communication, or away from communication altogether.

These, then, are some of the general limits of argumentation, the respects in which argumentation carries a particular ideology that one may to some degree and for some purposes reject.

Argumentation and Gender

The ideological limits of argumentation may also be clarified in the context of more specific ideological controversies. The question of the relation between reason and gender has been one of the main focuses of feminist theory of the last 10–15 years. By now, it appears that almost every conceivable position has been taken on this question, even though every year a new interpretation of the controversy appears. There is no way to address the depth and variety of positions taken in a short subchapter such as this. Yet it seems imperative to acknowledge the question of gender in some kind of explicit and developed way. The alternative is to leave responses to the question implicit in the theory, and so appear to be neglecting the question altogether.

The primary difficulty is to know *which* feminist theory to open up an explicit dialogue with. Sandra Harding has pointed out that there are competing contemporary feminist epistemologies—epistemologies which are closely related to concepts of rationality. *Feminist empiricists* believe that traditional epistemological methods are essentially sound. The problem, from their point of view, is that we have had bad science and bad reasoning because of sexist and androcentric biases. Historically, men have had the positions of power in large-scale rational and scientific enterprises. As men come to recognize and remedy their biases, and as feminist women take positions of power in the production of knowledge, society will produce better science, less corrupted by sexist and androcentric distortions. *Feminist standpoint theorists* believe that science and reason are always shaped by gender. They believe that the deep differences between the lives of men and women influence the basic ways one understands the world. Concepts and concerns drawn from women's lives and activities will be very different from those drawn from men's. There is no "remedying" these differences. Rather, science is improved not by having all its practitioners achieve a unitary, bias-free consciousness, but by assuring the participation of different groups, whose different standpoints will yield fuller knowledge than a single one can.

In addition to these, there is full, *radical feminist postmodernism*, which is sometimes characterized as gender skepticism. This position further radicalizes the feminist impulse to reject traditional androcentric thought by identifying that thought with dualistic and hierarchical categorization patterns. However, a first victim of the deconstruction of these categories is gender itself, with its man/woman dichotomy. Sometimes, these critics point out that gender thinking leaves out hermaphrodites and other not easily categorizable people, and in general forces everyone and everything onto one side or other of a dichotomy. Another feature of gender skepticism is the recognition that age, race, class, health, and a host of other differences fracture the reality of gender. The idea of "woman" suppresses and distorts its subdifferences every bit as effectively, if not as broadly, as the universalist concept of "man."

In addition to these very different feminist or postfeminist epistemologies, there are very different feminist positions on what the response to gendered concepts of science and reason should be. Genevieve Lloyd has pretty persuasively shown how the concept of reason in the history of Western philosophy has been gendered as male. However, what should the response to this be? Is the traditional "reasonable man" somehow wrongly or "accidentally" gendered? Are women consequently wrongly gendered by being denied access to this "subject position"? Should men and women both aspire to the traditional concept of reason? Or is this an impossible demand, one that would exacerbate in hurtful ways the split consciousness of women who already suffer from all the contradictory expectations that follow from their gender? Should there instead be different expectations for men and women, two ideals of reason, and some kind of separatist organization of male and female education? There are, of course, many positions, many conflicts. The point is that agreeing on an analysis of the gendering of reason still will not solve problems about what kind of social and educational response follows from that agreement.

Christine Di Stefano has rightly pointed out that many of the controversies in feminist theory come down to the question: How basic are gender differences? Since this is a question that I can't imagine ever having an answer to, I think she is right to say that this is another way of "asking how basic *we want them to be* for particular purposes and ends" (66). In this regard, the theory I have been developing depends on a particular answer to this question. Gender differences cannot be so basic that they vitiate the aspirations for reasonable agreement that the theory describes. If a rhetoric of reason is strongly gendered as male, and if gender differences are "basic" in the strongest sense, then the theory excludes women, and cannot provide a nonviolent way of resolving conflict, a rationale for higher education, or a justification of social criticism—except among men.

Let's ask, then, whether the rhetorical concept of reason is strongly gendered. I want to begin by pointing out that in many ways the theory was developed in an implicit dialogue with feminist critiques of traditional concepts of reason. The critique of modern concepts of rationality in Chapter 1 parallels feminist critiques of modern subjectivity as strongly gendered. In attempting to filter out the influence of the body, the senses, emotions, interests, and history, Descartes and his many followers were effectively excluding everything "feminine" from the practice of reason.[8] In a rhetoric of reason, none of these exclusions are in force, at least not in principle. One could object that even using the word "reason" invokes the whole history of the term, and so the strongly gendered undertones it carries.[9] To some degree, this is certainly right. However, there is just no "safe" language to turn to. Gender is certainly basic enough to permeate most of our language. Yet "reason" itself is a fractured term. There are many contrasting and contradictory concepts of reason in the Western tradition. What I am trying to do is strengthen those ideals of reason in which reason is contrasted with violence rather than with the senses or the emotions.[10] In *this* tradition, the promise of reason is closely connected with nonviolence and with freedom. I want to understand why such a promise has seemed plausible. And I want to redeem, as far as I can, those promises of reason according to which reason promotes freedom and nonviolence.

One way to test the success of these efforts is to examine the central ideas of claiming, questioning, and agreeing that make up the heart of the theory in light of some concerns and objections developed by feminist theorists. In this context, it might also prove useful to further scrutinize the idea of universality developed in Chapters 6 and 7. I want to provide only an outline of the course such a test might take. In each case, I believe I have modified the concept of reason in a way that mitigates its having been gendered as male.

First, the rejection of the idea that reasoning can make everything explicit, or that all the conflicts operating in argumentation can be grasped at once, is a recognition that argumentation always takes place in a context in which differences are at play, never completely under control. Argumentation can *always* be criticized. Insofar as suppressed gender conflicts are influencing the argumentation toward one outcome or another, one can reasonably say that an important conflict is being resolved not by reason but coercively, by way of unthematized constraints.

In addition, however, claims are made only about what *can* to some degree be made explicit. If the split between what can and cannot be made explicit is a gendered one, then claiming itself is fundamentally gendered. Some French feminists and their followers have argued that the feminine is the domain of the body and its silence. What is discursive always takes place in the phallogocentric domain of language. Thus, the central and most basic conflict of gender is fugitive to reasoning: the interlocutor does not speak. Again, I do believe that there are dimensions of human experience that are fugitive to explicit articulation and reasoning. There are conflicts that cannot be brought to clarity and mutual understanding. If these dimensions of experience are strongly gendered, then it may be that "women" have inarticulable depths of experience that "men" lack, or at least that are different from "men's." If that is the case, then they will, in claiming, experience an inarticulable conflict that men will not.

Obviously, this is not a "problem" that a theory can "solve." A rhetoric of reason acknowledges that not all experience can be made explicit in claims and that not all conflicts can be resolved by reasoning. However, I do not believe that this undermines the attempts to justify the teaching of written reasoning as a central purpose of a higher education. The claim of the theory is not to "solve" all problems. Insofar as it is worthwhile for people to learn to resolve the conflicts they *can* resolve by way of language, nonviolently, it is worthwhile to cultivate our abilities to reason in writing. If some conflicts are the result of matters about which we have no choice, then these conflicts are facts of our condition, not conflicts that can be resolved at all—theoretically or otherwise. Again, however, I believe that the classroom must be a place where everyone feels equally uncomfortable, equally safe. If it is true that most women face specific inarticulable conflicts that most men do not, then it is a challenge to educators to develop a response to this fact that ensures, as far as possible, a rough equality in the dialogue of reason. If one is *not* persuaded by the reasoning of the French feminists, one will not think of this difficulty in the same way.

Actually, though, the concept of the claim is an explicit rejection of the concept of a proposition, and so a continuation of the deconstruction of modernity's gendered hierarchy of a historyless domain of disembodied reason and a historical domain of bodies, senses, emotions, materiality, interests. The concept of a claim also reveals the twofold character of asserting. A claim is not only an assertion; insofar as it contains its own questionability, it is also a kind of self-effacing, an announcement of its own vulnerability. Its being a claim depends on this doubleness, this refusal of a split that could be gendered. Further, the concept of claiming is thoroughly social. We make claims on one another as a way of acknowledging one another and taking responsibility for one another. As I said in the discussion of Levinas, it is this taking responsibility that *enables* reasoning. This concept of interpersonal responsibility has typically been both gendered and excluded from the concept of reason. A rhetoric of reason includes responsibility and acknowledgment as definitive features of argumentation. In these ways, reasoning is not so much genderless as gender-complex. It makes de-

mands on gender-simple people to occupy several different and sometimes conflicting places on a continuum of gendered activities. I believe
that genuine claiming (claiming that leads to mutually satisfactory reasoning) may in fact make more demands on gender-simple men than
on gender-simple women, for it depends on just these "feminine" qualities, qualities that are often absent when argumentative forms are used
as a cover for other aims.

Against expectations, perhaps, the idea of questioning may remain
more male-gendered than the idea of claiming. If the right to question
is, as I have suggested, connected with a specific kind of social power,
then insofar as this social power is gendered, the right to question is too.
Since it is the question that actualizes the conflict implicit in the claim,
questioning is a way of engaging the conflict, and overt participation in
conflict, too, may be strongly gendered.

Again, I see no way around this. The idea of "woman" developed
partly as a way of excluding women from education, from power, and
from public life. As a consequence, gender-simple women who receive
an education in reasoning will experience the "umcomfortableness" and
conflicts that some more gender-complex women know as a way of life.
I would like to say, again, that the educational aspiration of a rhetoric
of reason is a classroom that is, overall, equally uncomfortable to all,
and not uncomfortable only for specific groups of people. Knowing that
one group is more vulnerable than others to discomfort and exclusion
is important for teachers of written reasoning who share this aspiration.
Our classrooms must, overall, achieve a *rough* equality in the distribution of discomfort for argumentation to take place—or at least, the most
equality possible given the circumstances.

Argumentation is also, as we have seen, ideologically slanted toward
agreement. This is because its main purpose and legitimation lie in resolving conflicts. However, I would again like to deny that this entails an
obliteration of important differences. The question that always precedes
argumentation is: is this an issue about which we need or want to reach
agreements? There are many differences among people that do not need
to be "resolved," many differences which should perhaps be deepened
so that many forms of life may flourish. Argumentation comes into play
when conflicts need to be resolved. In addition, it is possible to *argue* that
some specific difference need *not* be thought of as a *conflict*, to use argumentation to expand the depth and range of difference instead of to decrease it. It is true, however, that once one enters into argumentation, the
aim is a certain kind of agreement with someone about something.

Finally, the idea of universality has come in for very rough treatment
from feminist theorists. What has counted as universal has been men's

experience; the traditional concepts of reason and of a rational subject, both supposed to be universal, have instead been unmasked as male. When a concept of universality is promoted, it seems at least to obscure gender differences, and probably generalizes specifically masculine traits. Even the aspiration for universality can be interpreted as a hope that gender will somehow disappear. Insofar as reasoning, or a theory of reason, attempts to make universal statements, it attempts to suppress gender differences.

I have two general responses to this. First, the idea of rhetorical universality developed in Chapters 5 and 6 is very different from traditional philosophical concepts of universality. In a rhetorical approach, universality is always a matter of degree and is always judged by an undefined universal audience. Universality also develops along different lines; there are different and sometimes incompatible ways of achieving more universal standpoints. Universality is an achievement of particular people at particular times and for particular purposes.

Second, the aspiration for universality of this sort is not necessarily an attempt to abolish or suppress gender differences. However, it is an attempt to achieve a way of evaluating arguments that is acceptable to everyone, regardless of gender or beliefs about gender. At times, it may also be representative of a willingness to put certain conflicts aside in order to resolve others. If one believes that gender conflicts should be thematized on every occasion and in every context, and that no one should ever set them aside, then one will not participate in this kind of effort.

I want to conclude this section by more explicitly revealing my own beliefs about these matters, for they are certainly influencing this discussion in ways I cannot completely control. I believe that race, class, and gender have become our categories of difference because power and choice are distributed unequally along those lines. (Although I believe that children are our single most oppressed class of people, they do not even get into this kind of discussion, and there are interesting rhetorical reasons for this.) These categories are used to shatter the old, universal voice of "reason," which had class, race, and gender biases that deprived people of choice and power. The point, as I see it, is to develop a new concept of reason that will to some degree accomplish what the old idea tried to accomplish, but without repeating its exclusions.

It is true that the ideals of reason have been formulated by a relatively small group of privileged males, and that the ideals have arisen from their privileged experience and interests. However, part of this experience was to have choice and some power. Part of it was to have an education in world affairs, in history, science, technology, languages. And

Part Three: Evaluating Arguments

this experience has always been centrally shaped by reasonable dialogues and argumentation with other people, a use of language that
typically requires education and a particular kind of environment. The
need to reason together to resolve conflicts is something that will be
shared by whatever groups are enfranchised with choice and power and
are concerned at all with exercising that power legitimately. The question is whether we still think of ourselves as aiming at extending this
choice and power to more people, or whether we are so disillusioned by
its historical exclusions that we reject this aspiration altogether.

We inhabit a web of power in which we work and live, and we do our
best to redeem the small part of it about which we have some choice.
Our good work will always be distorted by these conditions, and our
efforts will always have unforeseeable outcomes. There are no safe positions. However, there are fragile hopes and promises of reason that have
been handed down to us and for which we now bear the responsibility.

Argumentation and Multiculturalism

There are other differences among people that are also
important when assessing the ideology of a theory of rationality; however, I believe that most of them can be understood along the lines I have
offered above. Race and class issues are similar, in many respects, to the
issue of gender—at least when it comes to theories of reason. I have
treated gender issues in depth because feminist theorists have focused
in a sustained way on the concept of reason in ways that other theorists
of difference have not. They have in fact absorbed many of the controversies about race and class and brought them to bear on the concept of
reason. By contrast, philosophy, as a professional field, has shown relatively little interest in clarifying itself in the light of contemporary concepts of cultural variation or in developing any sound body of compar-
ative philosophy. Ethnophilosophy, as practiced by anthropologists, has
focused much more on "worldviews" than on reasoning and argumentation. And rhetorical theory and the history of rhetoric are still solidly
ensconced in a profoundly traditional and European self-understanding. Given these conditions, the discussion of argumentation and gender will, for now, have to represent the way a rhetoric of reason accounts
for its ideological implications for specific groups.

However, as a way of concluding this account of argumentation and
ideology, I want to bring the rhetoric of reason into some relation to the
current discussion of multiculturalism. The general question the idea of
multiculturalism poses to the theory I have worked out here is: is argu-

mentation culturally specific, one more way of eroding and misrecognizing the unique identities of particular cultures? The answer is yes, it is culturally specific, to some degree. And yes, as I said, it *can* be corrosive of particular identities, but it need not be. And yet no, because preserving identity depends on the kind of transformation and recognition argumentation promotes.

To justify these answers, I would like to make use of some of Charles Taylor's ideas, taken from his "The Politics of Recognition." Taylor points out that the demand for recognition found in discussions of multiculturalism is a thoroughly modern idea, the result of particular social-historical changes. More than a couple of hundred years ago, our current discussion of multiculturalism would have made little sense. Recognition was built into one's socially derived identity, one's social role. However, with the modern development of the idea of authenticity, the idea that one's identity is both inwardly derived and socially negotiated, the possibility of misrecognition arises. Recognition of one's unique identity must be won. Misrecognition, the mirroring back of a confining or demeaning picture, can be positively harmful. Misrecognition can be internalized, and can become debilitating. Thus, the need to be recognized, and not misrecognized, becomes a vital need.

According to Taylor, the politics of equal recognition has come to mean two things. First, the politics of universalism promotes equal respect for all individuals as individuals. The basis of this respect is the capacity and the desire of individual human beings to shape their own lives, to live, to change, to make choices in whatever ways they see fit. Second, the politics of difference demands the recognition not only of individuals, but also of the unique identity of particular groups. The charge the politics of difference makes against the politics of universalism is that it is a politics of assimilation that misrecognizes and thus harms particular groups. The "individual" respected by the politics of universalism is not a member of a particular culture. The focus of this second kind of respect is not an individual's *potential* for forming an identity, but rather what has been made of that potential—a respect for actually existing cultures. It is a demand for this kind of respect that animates many of the current discussions about multiculturalism.

This demand affects writing courses, or courses in reasoning, in a familiar way. Insofar as there is a reading list, some people will demand that their particular groups be recognized in that list. This demand will sometimes conflict with the judgments people make about the *worth* of readings on the list. In the best of cases, this conflict will be worked through argumentatively, with each party learning from the other, and changing its criteria for selecting readings accordingly.

However, the demand could affect courses in written reasoning in a different way. One can imagine the charge that argumentation itself is culturally specific in a way that misrecognizes and disrespects the particular communicative styles of different cultures. Even if argumentation is a relatively universal practice, the occasions on which one argues, what one argues about, the frequency with which one argues, the people with whom one argues, how explicitly one argues, how far one carries an argument—all these things may vary strongly from culture to culture. Different ways of resolving particular conflicts may be preferred by different cultural groups. Violence may be a legitimate way of settling some disputes. Hierarchical social relations may strongly structure argumentative discourse among some peoples. Traditional practices may preclude some kinds of argumentation, or limit it to a specific subgroup. Some conflicts may be tolerable for some groups, not for others. Some things may be said among one people, not among others.

As I have said, argumentation is a culturally specific practice, and the claim that it is good to cultivate people's abilities to argue carries a certain ideology. Argumentation is only one way of resolving conflicts. It refuses violence. It tends to judge the influence of social hierarchy on communication as illegitimate. It assumes a respect for individuals. It promotes agreements. It tends toward publicity. It is sometimes corrosive of what is very private or unique to a particular group. It tends to place the politics of commonality above the politics of difference. In these ways and others, the teaching of written reasoning can fail the demands of that brand of multiculturalism which asks for equal recognition of some group of existing cultures.

So, from one angle, the view I have been promoting so far has been a quasi-ethnocentric one. I have admitted that argumentation and the teaching of argumentation further an ideology, and I have tried to make that ideology as appealing and all-embracing as possible. However, I have also tried to show how argumentation can lead one away from ethnocentrism, and toward new ideas of universality. In this sense, I have been working against ethnocentrism. However, I am left with the fact that argumentation itself depends on and promotes a particular kind of culture—and has no concept of how its alliance with that culture could be evaluated. Again, the features of this culture are very general and very inclusive, and yet it is obvious that there are many existing individuals and social groups who would oppose it. In the end, the value of argumentation is connected to the value of that culture. People who are repulsed by the ideas of transformation, nonviolence, cooperation, and agreement will be repulsed by the ideology of argumentation, and the reasons one could give for preferring it.

However, those of us who are committed to reason, and its culture, should keep contending voices alive in our thoughts. For example, we can be alive to the possibility that argumentation is not an eternal and universal agency of nonviolent transformation, but might itself be transformed by yet another agency with many of the same aims. Loyalty, friendship, love, and forgiveness are also agencies of transformation and reconciliation. That is, transformation and reconciliation can occur in many ways, and in fact do occur in different ways across cultures and time. Argumentation is an adaptation to conditions which appear to be natural, eternal, necessary, and yet we know that they are not. It is not impossible to think that argumentation could itself be transformed by some more powerful agency of reconciliation.

PART FOUR

ARGUMENT, INQUIRY,

AND EDUCATION

8   ARGUMENT AS INQUIRY

The Idea of Inquiry

So far, I have developed a theory according to which the aims of argumentation are understood primarily in terms of the agreements and the resolution of conflict reached through the process of argumentation. I have emphasized the self- and socially transformative features of this process, at times to the relative neglect of questions about knowledge, research, and inquiry. This is because my first aim is to convince teachers of writing and critical thinking in colleges and universities that argumentation is deeply connected to these kinds of transformation and so worth pursuing seriously in courses in the core curriculum. I attempt this convincing against the background expectation that many readers, especially those with primarily literary training, will believe that argumentation fails in these regards. However, I would like to move on now to show in more detail how a rhetoric of reason can also cast light on the idea of inquiry itself. For to the degree that I have succeeded in my first aim, some readers may suspect that I have failed in another— the aim of showing how a rhetoric of reason can clarify the ways argumentative reason makes discovery possible, the ways it helps create new knowledge. I said in Chapter 1 that the processes of reasoning in first-year composition courses are not essentially different from those in advanced fields of research. I want to support that claim in this chapter. The last thing I would want would be for a reader to have the impression that rhetoric makes claims on students alone, or perhaps on scholars in the humanities, but not on scientific inquiry.

Two Kinds of Reasoning:
Some Historical Angles

The distinction between *genuine* reasoning (usually conceived of as logical or scientific reasoning) and *rhetorical* reasoning is responsible for a schism that has bedeviled the history of rhetoric and distorted the history of philosophy. Needless to say, it has also had a deleterious effect on education. A pragmatic rhetoric of reason refuses to recognize this split or to accept the schism of rhetoric and philosophy that has resulted from it. In fact, one of the major efforts of this book is to effect a rapprochement between philosophy and rhetoric that can be brought to bear on the immense challenges faced by teachers of writing. Such a rapprochement is also intended to make possible some recovery of the notion of courses which belong to a general, core curriculum at the level of higher education, courses which can make a claim to be in the service of interests shared by all. In order to clarify what is at stake in this rapprochement, and to understand how deep the schism between different kinds of reasoning has become, it is necessary to recall, at least in outline, the central role the schism has played in the history of rhetoric and philosophy. In many ways the history of this distinction just is that history. And so any attempt to overcome the distinction should plot itself, at least to some degree, against the history of the distinction.

PLATO

Interestingly, Plato took a very strong stand against making a distinction between rhetoric and philosophy. In the *Phaedrus,* he argues that any rhetoric which is distinct from genuine dialectic is not an art or ability at all. Genuine rhetoric, as the art of speaking or writing, is not something different from dialectic. Socrates' main argument for this position is what could be called the "completeness" argument—the argument that so-called rhetoric is just an incomplete version of philosophy. The completeness argument works in two ways. First, it works by commonsense analogies with medicine, tragedy writing, and music, in which an incomplete knowledge of medicine, tragedy, and music is contrasted to a complete one. Second, the argument works by identifying the purpose of speech and writing as "healing" or "leading the soul," and then shows how so-called rhetoric cannot accomplish this purpose and so is not a true art of speaking and writing.

At *Phaedrus* 268A–B, Socrates imagines someone saying: "I know how to apply various drugs to people, so as to make them warm or, if I wish, cold, and I can make them vomit, if I like, or can make their bowels move, and all that sort of thing; and because of this knowledge I claim that I am a physician and can make any other man a physician, to whom I impart the knowledge of these things." Phaedrus rightly replies to Socrates that such a person would also have to know "whom he ought to cause to do these things, and when, and how much." Socrates goes on to develop other analogies. He describes the pseudotragedian who knows how to write individual speeches but not how to combine the speeches to produce a tragedy. He also describes a "musician" who claims to know harmony because he can produce the highest and lowest notes. The commonsense reaction to such people is, as Phaedrus says, to laugh at them and think them crazy.

Claims that rhetoric is an art are taken to be analogous to the claims of these other pretenders. Clearly, Plato has technical, handbook rhetoric in mind when he has Socrates imagine Adrastus or Pericles saying: "Phaedrus and Socrates, we ought not to be angry, but lenient, if certain persons who are ignorant of dialectics have been unable to define the nature of rhetoric and on this account have thought, when they possessed the knowledge that is a necessary preliminary to rhetoric, that they had discovered rhetoric, and believe that by teaching these preliminaries to others they have taught them rhetoric completely . . ." (269B–C). This version of the completeness argument depends only on one's agreeing that rhetoric has a purpose. Knowing the elements or "preliminaries" of rhetoric without knowing how to use them to accomplish the purpose of rhetoric is, obviously, not having knowledge of rhetoric. For this argument to be convincing, one need not agree with Socrates about what the purpose is.

The completeness argument works the other way around when Socrates argues that the art of speaking and writing—rhetoric insofar as it is *not* distinguished from dialectic—has a particular purpose. This version of the argument *does* depend on one's agreeing with Socrates about the purpose of rhetoric, and what Socrates says about this is rather stunning: "The way of the art of healing is much the same as that of rhetoric . . . In both cases you must analyze a nature, in one that of the body and in the other that of the soul . . . to impart health and strength to the body by prescribing medicine and diet, or by proper discourses and training to give to the soul the desired conviction and virtue" (270B). This view of the purpose of rhetoric leads to some very interesting Socratic speeches and to some accounts of rhetoric which are probably unsurpassed in the tradition. In a speech at 271C–272B we come across one. It is, says Socrates, the specific power of language (*logou dunamis*) to lead souls by persuasion (*psychagogia*). Thus, the one who knows the art of using language knows how to lead souls. So rhetoricians must know what kinds of people there are, what kinds of language use there are, and how the different uses of language affect the different kinds of people. They must also learn to recognize the different kinds of people when they meet them as well as be able actually to speak to them in the appropriate way. Add to this, says Socrates, a knowledge of timeliness, and one has a more complete understanding of rhetoric than most rhetoricians have.

What is remarkable about this passage is the way it grounds rhetoric

Part Four: Argument, Inquiry, and Education

and philosophy and science in an ethical/educational project and not *primarily* an epistemological one. That is, the passage contains an implicit denial that there are two essentially different kinds of reason, one inferior, one superior; or that there is an ethical/practical kind of reasoning, on the one hand, and a theoretical-scientific kind of reasoning, on the other. Instead, all discourse is understood to be subordinated to the overriding purpose of *psychagogia*. The superficial understanding of Plato's objection to rhetoric is that it is inferior to dialectic because it is concerned only with producing opinions while dialectic is aimed at a true knowledge of things.[1] However, the primary concern in this passage is with *psychagogia*. So-called rhetoric knows how to affect other people through language; it understands that language is a kind of power. However, it does not understand what this power is for; it does not grasp that rhetoric is a kind of healing, a leading of souls into conviction and virtue. And so it is incomplete—no "art" at all, just a knowledge of some "preliminaries," some elements. Rhetoric in its completeness is indistinguishable from philosophical dialectic, which in turn is indistinguishable from *psychagogia*, a kind of mutual teaching and learning. Ultimately, insofar as the purpose of language use is concerned, the propositional content of a speech or something written is not of the first importance; what is of first importance is whether and how the soul is led.

In the context of argumentation, the point is to understand what kind of conflict, at what level and what intensity, is appropriate for someone at some place and time, given the goal of guiding that person's soul. As Socrates warns, too much argumentative conflict at an early age can cause one to become a misologist—a hater of arguments. In the *Thaeatetus*, at 163C, Socrates restrains himself from raising objections to young Thaeatetus' answers because he fears that such objections will check the young man's philosophical growth. The leading of someone's soul is a highly individualized activity, finely tuned to issues of timeliness and context. One cannot simply set out in search of the abstractly "best" arguments, without a knowledge of one's interlocutors.

This is the framework in which Plato's famous warnings about writing must be understood. The measure of speech or writing is the measure of the degree to which it accomplishes its purpose of leading a soul well. Since this leading is so highly individualized, and since it is the effect of language on a particular person which is being measured, one can judge the meaning and clarity of language only in terms of this effect. The problem with writing is that people tend to believe that it is genuine *logos*, that it has a power that can be measured or appreciated in itself, apart from the way it actually influences someone's soul at some time and place. Thus, Socrates says:

> He who thinks, then, that he has left behind him any art in writing, and he who receives it in the belief that anything in writing will be clear and certain,[2] would be an utterly simple person, and in truth ignorant of the prophecy of Ammon, if he thinks written words are of any use except to remind him who knows the matter about which they are written . . . You might think [written words] spoke as if they had intelligence, but if you question them, wishing to know about their sayings, they always say only one and the same thing. And every word, when once it is written, is bandied about, alike among those who understand and those who have no interest in it, and it knows not to whom to speak or not to speak; when ill-treated or unjustly reviled it always needs its father to help it; for it has no power to help or protect itself. (275C–E)

This last line is very important. The power *(dunatos)* writing lacks is the specific power *(dunamis)* of logos, of language. Writing is weak in this sense because it is not as finely responsive as speech to the needs of leading a particular soul in a particular way at a particular time and place. It is not that writing is merely an imitation or simulacrum of an original "presence" found in speech. Speech, too, can go astray, can fail to lead the soul—as Socrates frequently shows. Rather, it is that writing is less fit for the purpose of language than speech. In the *Phaedrus*, writing is, as Derrida makes unforgettable, a drug that can be a medicine or a kind of poison, and is usually something of both. It is not that writing is absolutely powerless when it comes to leading souls; it is that it is less powerful, less useful, less adaptable, and so more capable of misleading—a medicine prone to misuse.[3]

This speech sets up the important passage in which Socrates introduces the idea of a kind of logos that is "better and more powerful" than writing, and describes it as "the word which is written with intelligence in the soul of the learner, which is able to defend itself and knows to whom it should speak, and before whom to be silent." At this point, it is Phaedrus who is allowed to utter the Magnificat: "You mean the living and breathing word of him who knows, of which the written word may justly be called the image" (276A). Compared to this logos, both speech and writing, as well as signing, would be "images." Here, the proper medium of language is the soul. Written or spoken logoi have the power of participating in this living logos, but Socrates would have us distinguish between language that is lived in this way and language that is not. Thus we have something very near to the Heideggerian idea that language is a feature of the being of human beings—one of the ways we exist—or to the Wittgensteinian idea that a language is a form of life. Rhetoric is *psychagogia* in a deep way.

This recognition allows Socrates and Phaedrus to come to the question of "Why write?" to place writing in its appropriate psychagogical context. One must always write playfully—the analogy Socrates uses here is gardening—and one may write for two different audiences: for oneself, to treasure up reminders for oneself when old age brings forgetfulness; and for others who are also trying to follow the path one has followed (276D). The purpose is still *psychagogia:* one may lose one's way in old age, and need leading; and others may be on one's trail, and they may need a map of the way. The preferred method of such teaching is also still dialectical, and when it is done properly it is described as sowing, in a fitting soul, "intelligent words which are able to help themselves and him who planted them, which are not fruitless, but yield seed from which there spring up in other minds other words capable of continuing the process forever, and which make their possessor happy, to the farthest possible limit of human happiness" (276E–277A). However, there is in the end no disqualification of writing from participating in this process. Quite the opposite. Socrates has undone one understanding of writing in order to replace it with another. Once one understands that writing, on its own, is silent and powerless, one can grasp its proper role, its context, its purpose. At the conclusion of Socrates' and Phaedrus' discussion of writing, Socrates gives a speech which the nymphs at the sacred place tell him to repeat to all writers: "If [a writer] has composed his writings with knowledge of the truth, and is able to support them by discussion of that which he has written, and has the power to show by his own speech that the written words are of little worth, such a man ought not to derive his title from such writings, but from the serious pursuit which underlies them . . . The epithet 'wise' is too great and befits God alone; but the name 'philosopher,' that is, 'lover of wisdom,' or something of the sort would be more fitting and modest for such a man" (278C–D). Plato wants to distinguish sharply between genuinely philosophical writers and all the others because he wants to justify calling these philosophical writers "philosophers."

Let me highlight a few of the main points here. First, Plato's theory is a radical reception theory. Writing on its own has the appearance of being meaningful, but only in the context of a soul that can be influenced by it can it actually be meaningful. Second, writing's decontextualized scene deprives it of speech's more finely tuned power to lead individual souls well. However, third, this does not mean that writing cannot participate in philosophical *psychagogia*. It can do so if it operates with a frank recognition of its limitations—and if it works dialectically.

It is quite reasonable to assume that Plato's own writing is an attempt to acknowledge these limits, to remedy, to some degree, the dangers of writing. Written dialogues can be understood as an effort to keep a reader's attention on the process of *psychagogia* as it affects the individual souls of interlocutors. Reading a dialogue requires that one identify in varying degrees with different interlocutors at different times, or to imagine an independent role for oneself in the dialogue. The point of a Platonic dialogue is not so much to get Plato's doctrine (although the history of Plato commentary is inevitably full of such attempts—after all, even this writing is a drug) as to follow a trail, to make one's way into and through a conversation, and to emerge with conviction (not belief) and virtue (not rules).[4]

In the reading I have offered here, I have identified with poor Phaedrus, whose soul is bewitched by writing and professional writers, and who believes that rhetoric is something which can be separated from questions about how one should live. I take this identification to be useful for those of us who live with rooms full of books and who teach for pay.

From one angle, the rhetoric of reason I have argued for here can be seen as a response to Plato's challenge. I have tried to resituate written argumentation in its dialectical scene, to identify its interlocutors and their actions, to bring written argumentation back into this work of *psychagogia*, to understand it as a process of transformation by way of conflict, as a process of finding ways to new selves. I have also tried to refuse the distinction between logic and rhetoric, or dialectic and rhetoric, or reason and rhetoric, or philosophy and rhetoric. Instead, I have tried to comprehend all these pairs within the framework of a theory which conceives of argumentation's purpose as the nonviolent resolution of conflict and the making possible of social criticism and higher education. I have also tried to unite this interest with an interest in scholarly and scientific inquiry, with research and with reasoning in general. The whole aim of a rhetoric of reason is Platonic in this sense: it wants to bring all reasoning into a conversation about its purposes and about its relation to what is good.

In the end, Plato's Socrates tells us not about two kinds of reason; there is, after all, one art of discourse, whose purpose is to lead the soul. However, the histories of rhetoric and philosophy have certainly not developed along Platonic lines. Philosophers have typically accepted Plato's denunciation of (incomplete) rhetoric as a kind of fraud, and viewed his success in distinguishing between philosophy and rhetoric as a kind of grounding moment for philosophy. They have typically ignored the argument of the *Phaedrus* that philosophy and (complete) rhetoric might both be essentially the same activity. Rhetoricians have usually understood Plato as the enemy of rhetoric rather than as its friend because they have read him in much the same way as have many philosophers.[5] As a consequence, they have looked to the older Sophists or more often to Aristotle as the defender of an art of rhetoric, and have discovered their own founding moments there. As someone who is arguing for a rapprochement of philosophy and rhetoric, I find each of these reactions to be unfortunate and unnecessary.

ARISTOTLE

Aristotle does seem to have distinguished rhetoric as a separate art of language, and thus seems to reinforce the idea of essentially different kinds of reasoning. He contrasts rhetoric to dialectic and to "scientific" instruction and reasoning—and certainly to philosophy. Where Plato wrote of a general "art of logos" which was finally understood to be possible only on the basis of a love of wisdom, Aristotle is much more inclined to speak of specific arts of reasoning and to distinguish them from one another. Because Aristotle writes of a specifically rhetorical *techne,* historians of rhetoric often describe Aristotle as having rescued rhetoric from Plato's attacks and set rhetoric on solid, independent ground. However, this description is not only based on a deep misunderstanding of Plato, it is also responsible for a concept of rhetoric that is decisively severed from philosophy, a concept that has led to a steady decline of rhetoric's status in the modern period. This strong distinction is also responsible, in part, for a concept of philosophy that has proven itself incapable of weathering twentieth-century intellectual history.

The primary difficulty in understanding the differences between Plato's and Aristotle's views of rhetoric is that they use major defining terms in very different ways. It is certainly not correct to say that Plato believed that there was no true art *(techne)* of rhetoric but that Aristotle thought that there was. It is more accurate to say that Aristotle denied that there was a *general* art of logos of the sort Socrates speaks of in the *Phaedrus.* Aristotle believed that the "logical" arts broke down into different kinds, one of which was rhetoric. From a Platonic view, this means that Aristotle denied that there was anything like a *dunamis* of logos or a purpose for the power that language has.

It would be interesting to be able to press Aristotle on this point. After all, in the *Nicomachean Ethics* he writes of a good at which all things aim. He describes this good as happiness or well-being *(eudaimonia)*. All the different arts have their separate ends, but these ends are themselves means to other ends, leading finally to an end that is not itself a means to other ends: happiness, which in its highest form is philosophical activity. This suggests that although each art has a distinct end, these ends have their own further ends; thus, the arts of language and reasoning *do* in fact have as their "completion" some relation to well-being and philosophy. Understood in this light, there could be grounds for saying that a rhetorical art that has only persuasion for its aim, and not persuasion that is conducive to well-being and philosophy, is not really a "complete" art at all—which is very close to Socrates' position in the *Phaedrus*.

However, the tendency in reading Aristotle has been to distinguish this "ethical" concern from the task of defining a rhetorical *techne* and to view Aristotle's distinctions among the arts in a very strong way. So rhetoric is understood to be essentially different from dialectic and science and philosophy, and little effort is made to grasp how the arts of language and reasoning might together conduct people toward well-being. The aim of rhetoric is said to be persuasion, while the aim of dialectic is inquiry (or "experimentation" or "exploratory" discourse) and the aim of science (or philosophy) is the genuine learning that is connected with a knowledge of what is true. Rhetoric is considered mainly in terms of the picture of a single speaker or writer addressing a larger audience. Dialectic is pictured in terms of a conversation among a small number of interlocutors. Science is pictured either as a solitary pursuit or as an activity which takes place in a school setting. So rhetoric proceeds from common opinions by way of a simplified style of reasoning to probable knowledge. Dialectic proceeds from common opinions (or occasionally from expert opinion or independently established facts) by way of syllogisms and induction discovered in question and answer to probable knowledge. Science, or philosophy, proceeds from first principles by way of demonstration to a knowledge of truth.

This dominant reading of Aristotle on rhetoric ignores not only the framework in which Aristotle's ethics might place all these arts but also the fact that Aristotle's distinction between philosophy and rhetoric is not as strictly metaphysical as it might appear to us. Aristotle is not a modern epistemologist. He is not as concerned with modern philosophical questions about the status of knowledge as we are; for example, he is not at all concerned with skeptical challenges to knowledge claims. So his "first principles" are not necessarily known with absolute certainty based on a metaphysically grounded epistemology. Rather, they

Part Four: Argument, Inquiry, and Education

can be arrived at through dialectic, which begins with commonly held opinions and works to refine them into a form with which no one would disagree: dialectical reasoning "is useful in connection with the ultimate bases of each science; for it is impossible to discuss them at all on the basis of the principles peculiar to the science in question, since the principles are primary in relation to everything else, and it is necessary to deal with them through the generally accepted opinions on each point. This process belongs peculiarly, or most appropriately, to dialectic; for, being of the nature of an investigation, it lies along the path to the principles of all methods of inquiry" (*Topics* 101a–b). The nature of the priority relations among these different kinds of knowledge is a critical issue here and in the history of rhetoric and philosophy, and I will return to the issue shortly.

First, I want to make it clear that there are strong grounds for claiming that, in the end, this audience-based consensus theory of truth is a defining feature of Aristotelian thought. This idea receives support from a passage in the *Nicomachean Ethics,* in which Aristotle writes: "For we say that that which everyone thinks really is so." This statement occurs in the context of Aristotle's argument about the good's being that at which all activities aim. The assumption here is so strong that those who oppose "that which everyone thinks" can be said to be speaking nonsense: "Those who object that that at which all things aim is not necessarily good are, we may surmise, talking nonsense. For we say that that which everyone thinks really is so; and the man who attacks this belief will hardly have anything more credible to maintain instead" (1172b). Aristotle will not give ground to the kind of skepticism which is merely negative, which has no alternative explanation. He cannot see the point in it.

However, it must be admitted that there is also a different strand of language in Aristotle, one that sounds more metaphysical and leads to readings which sever rhetoric from philosophy and science in a definitive way. In the *Posterior Analytics,* there is very strong language that insists that the starting points of the sciences be necessary and universal propositions whose predications are essential and not accidental and whose truth is eternal. Since this treatise also insists that scientific knowledge, which is necessarily true, cannot depend on a less certain kind of knowledge (i.e., the "probable" knowledge of dialectic), dialectic is not given the originative role it is given in the *Topics*. Instead, we find, as a kind of addendum to the book, the famous discussion of the rational intuition of universals, in which the soul makes from the perception and memory of particulars a universal. The soul is simply said to be "constituted so as to be capable of this process." In addition, we learn that demonstrative reasoning is "addressed not to the spoken word, but to the discourse within the soul," so that this reasoning is not dependent on the vagaries of natural languages (100a).

These two strands in Aristotle lead to two different ways of thinking about reasoning, and certainly the strand that sharply distinguishes rhetoric from philosophy and science has had the most influence. To grasp the real force of this distinction, and its influence in modern times—to the detriment of philosophy and rhetoric—it is necessary to look at Aristotle's characterization of the "priorities" of reasoning and knowledge, for here the metaphysical/epistemological framework of the distinction takes one of its most influential forms.

The *Posterior Analytics* opens with this claim: "All teaching and learning that involves the use of reason proceeds from pre-existent knowledge." The early sections of the book are concerned with the nature of the first principles or premises from which reasoning proceeds. Aristotle develops a requirement that the preexistent knowledge from which we reason must be prior to and better known than the conclusions to which we are trying to reason. At *Posterior Analytics* 71b–72a, Aristotle writes: "There are two senses in which things are prior and more knowable. That which is prior in nature is not the same as that which is prior in relation to us, and that which is naturally more knowable is not the same as that which is knowable by us. By 'prior' or 'more knowable' in relation to us I mean that which is nearer to our perception, and by 'prior' or 'more knowable' in the absolute sense I mean that which is further from it. The most universal concepts are furthest from our perception, and particulars are nearest to it; and these are opposite to one another."[6]

There are many ways to read this distinction, some of which are very conservative, and save Aristotle from any commitment to a radical dualism in kinds of knowledge, or any absolute sense/intellect split. In a response to G. E. L. Owen's *"Tithenai ta Phainomena,"* Martha Nussbaum has worked out a plausible account of Aristotle's "human internal realism," in which this distinction between the prior in nature and the prior for us would not be as radical and metaphysical as it appears: "Even the contrast between the world as it is for us and the world as it is behind or apart from our thought may not be a contrast that the defender of human internal realism should allow himself to make using human knowledge. Here we might say that Aristotle usually maintains his internality more consistently than Kant . . ."[7]

However, the more usual and certainly more historically influential way to read Aristotle is to find in this passage a metaphysical move linked to the idea of intellectual intuitions and to the fairly sharp distinction between rhetoric and philosophy. On the one hand there is philosophical/scientific knowledge (and the people capable of it); on the other there are abbreviated and simplified forms of reasoning (for people who are incapable of scientific instruction). My own view of Aristotle is that he permits both a strong metaphysical and a "human internal realist" reading, and to choose one over the other is to make a choice Aristotle seemed to think unnecessary. Aristotle seems to have strongly believed both that reasoning falls into different domains depending on what purposes are being pursued and that the features of a theory in one domain need not stand in a one-to-one relation with the features of a theory in another domain. To expect such mechanical systematicity would be, for Aristotle, to lack an appreciation for the differences in the ways human beings acquire knowledge in different domains. Such finesse is not a common trait among Aristotle's successors.

EARLY MODERNITY AND THE LOSS OF DIALOGUE

The fate of the philosophy/rhetoric distinction, or of the dialectic or logic/rhetoric distinction, in the period between Aristotle and early modernity is far too involved to present schematically here, and my limited purposes don't really require a reading of this history. It is well-known that Cicero called for a unity of eloquence and philosophy and that Quintilian understood rhetoric as an all-embracing study, but there is a marked contraction in their understanding of what philosophy is—at least when compared with that of Plato and Aristotle, or even the later Greco-Roman philosophers. The medieval period—hardly a single period, really—shows a vast and varied literature that concerns dialectic and rhetoric and their roles in education and in thought. However, it is in early modernity—with Ramus and Bacon and Descartes—that the line between rhetoric on the one hand and philosophy and science on the other gets drawn in a more definite and influential way, a way that has sorry consequences for the fate of "rhetoric" in our own late modern times. Since one of the main purposes of this chapter is to develop a rhetorical response to some philosophical claims about research and inquiry—claims that develop out of the early modern understanding of science and reason—I want to move directly to the early modern period, pausing only with Ramus to bring out what is distinctive about reasoning's fate in this period.

Peter Ramus wrote in the middle years of the sixteenth century, and he can be understood as a pivotal figure in early modern rhetorical theory.[8] The general tendencies of his thinking, and the reduced place he assigns to rhetoric, mark a trend in Western thought that is distinctive enough to be distinguished as modern. Ramus draws on the late Scholastic reunification of dialectic and rhetoric, but does something rather different with it. Agricola had asserted that "there are no places of invention proper to rhetoric," and had moved all forms of reasoning under "dialectic." He seems also to have thought of most reasoning as more "dialectical" than scientific, in the sense of being more closely connected with the topics and probabilities than with scientific certitude. In this sense, even though Agricola's explicit move was to take the topics away from rhetoric, the upshot was that, in Walter Ong's words, "dialectic or logic became a kind of rhetoric after all" (106).

Ramus followed the letter of this Agricolan move, but in the opposite spirit. He moved all reasoning into dialectic's domain, assimilated dialectic more closely to logic and scientific reasoning concerned with certitude, *and* kept a distinct field of rhetoric open in which he made a place only for the "nonrational" features of discourse—specifically, elocution and pronunciation. This conception of rhetoric as a less reasonable domain of discourse, as an art of appearances, has ancient roots, but the severity of the separation Ramus proposes is new. Plato's desire was to unify philosophy and rhetoric, to grasp "mere" rhetoric's partiality *and* its philosophical *telos*. Aristotle made a distinction between philosophy and rhetoric, but rhetoric was for him, somewhat elusively, a "counterpart" of dialectic, and dialectic itself had elusive connections with scientific reasoning and logic. For Ramus, things are much simpler.

There are two other issues that arise around Ramus that are just as important for this discussion. One is what Walter Ong has called the "decay of dialogue" in Ramus' dialectic. The other is the role that rhetoric and dialectic play in Ramus views of education and the relation of this to the question of method.

Ong insists that Ramus' dialectic, as well as his shrunken concept of rhetoric, represents a withering away of both an experience of reason and a form of theorizing about it which were dependent on the notions of voice and dialogue. In Ramist dialectic, the removing of invention and the topics from rhetoric to dialectic is itself the abolition of voice and the apotheosis of visual-spatial thinking. Ong's claim is that Ramist dialectic is radically diagrammatic and quantitative—a world of logical space. Rhetoric, on the other hand, is still a domain of voice and interpersonal communication. The consequence seems to be that communication and reason lie in distinct domains. Worse yet, says Ong, "dialogue and conversation become by implication mere nuisances" (289). The idea is that voice and dialogue can present only a kind of synesthetic interference in the visual space of reason. Understood in this way, the modern distinction between philosophy and rhetoric is also a distinction between vision and voice, and thus the overcoming of this distinction must be, as I have argued, the return of voice and reason to one another.

The relation of method and education is also a central issue in Ramus' thinking. The general problem of method, both in the ancients and in modern thought, is familiar enough. When one is inquiring into the cause of something, or the reason for something, or just in general asking a question about something, the process of reasoning—as distinct from just being arbitrary—seems to require a conscious direction of thought, a path or way or method from one idea to another. Aristotle seems to have placed relatively little stress on the idea of method in that he never forced himself into *absolute* distinctions between different kinds of thinking. His distinctions are more often organic than mechanical— dividing functions from one another, but never clarifying how deep those functional distinctions go, instead keeping all the parts of reasoning in an unclarified connection with one another. His remarks on "priority" are a good example here, for the sequence of thoughts seems to move in different directions in different intellectual domains.

In the early modern period, the stress on the concept of method intensifies greatly. Ramus feels this stress, but only indirectly, and mostly, it seems, unconsciously. Following a strong trend in late Scholastic thought, he conceptualizes the problem of method in pedagogical terms. In fact, Ramus tends to think of all intellectual activity in primarily pedagogical terms. Science, dialectic, and rhetoric are all thought of by way of teaching and learning in a school setting. The consequence is that discussions of method revolve around issues of starting points, order of presentation, the kinds of examples which should be used, and so on.

Ramus' earlier position is that there are two methods—the method of teaching, which reasons from universals or "generals" to particulars; and the method of prudence, which modifies this order to adapt to the weaknesses of an audience. Later, Ramus says that there is only one method but that it has two uses. The first use is for teaching the arts. The second is the "use" of method made by orators, poets, and historians, who engage in deception and dissimulation, and whose purpose is to delight and move and ambush people into conclusions. Ong's gloss on Ramus' view is: "One becomes a poet as a last resort, when one despairs of teaching in any other way" (253).

Since one of my own purposes is to overcome any radical distinction between the inquiry that goes on in teaching and the inquiry that goes in research, it is important for me to make clear here the ways in which the Ramist "pedagogicalizing" of inquiry moves in exactly the wrong direction. Ramus completely misses the problem of method partly because of (despite his protestations) a terribly distorted and crude Aristotelianism, partly because his notion of pedagogy is infected with the same antidialogism as his theory of dialectic. He begins with the distinction between audiences which are capable of genuine method, genuine teaching, genuine dialectic, and those which are not. This essential difference between kinds of audience is understood from the very start in terms of a deficiency model; some can, some can't. It's hard to miss the echoes of Aristotle's apology for rhetoric in this distinction between two uses of method. However, since rhetoric has been reduced simply to elocution and pronunciation, it is not fit enough even for the debased, deceiving kind of reasoning/discoursing Ramus has in mind here. Instead, Ramus postulates a debased dialectic of deception and ambush. This is worlds away from a pragmatic rhetoric of reason, which is founded not on a distinction between deficient and competent audiences, but rather on the idea that reasoning (and its evaluation) is essentially connected with different kinds of receptiveness which are themselves linked to different ways of life.

The other feature of Ramus' reduction of inquiry to pedagogy which is inconsistent with the rapprochement of teaching and inquiry I have recommended is the correlative reduction of dialectic to didacticism. Walter Ong makes the point with force: "Dialectic, as Ramus was to insist, should govern all life. This expansion of the purview of dialectic might mean that the art of arts and science of sciences was being pried loose from a close association with pedagogy. But it might also, and often did, mean something rather different, namely, that the purview of pedagogy was itself being expanded so that the world outside the classroom purportedly governed by dialectic was by that fact being assimilated to the classroom itself . . . [T]he whole of 'life' which was set against classroom activity tended to be interpreted in undisguisedly pedagogical terms" (167). With the decline of dialogue comes the rise of the university lecturer, the textbook, and the idea of a universe which is trying to force its order on us the way a stern schoolmaster would. Gone are the literal resonances of "dialectic," and the notion of a university as a discoursing collection of masters and students. Inquiry comes to be understood as the transmission of systematic knowledge from a a lecturer to auditors. In this context, the question of method is an issue only for speakers who must transmit knowledge, not for those who want to learn how to learn.

Bacon and Descartes shatter this idea in the new demands they make on the learner, and so raise the question of method in a radical new way. Seen from one angle, one could almost say that Bacon internalizes and universalizes the Ramist degradation of student auditors. According to

Bacon, we *all* worship idols, and so we are *all* in need of a discipline that can purify our experience of prejudice. However, from another angle, this discipline serves in an important way to individualize, liberate, and empower us, to desocialize us, to cure us of our dependence on the idols of the tribe, the marketplace, and the theater (which have forced us into our caves)—as well as of our dependence on Ramist professors. As John Briggs points out, Bacon judges the Ramist dialectic to be mere exposition, and not inquiry. Bacon's call for experience is a call for learners to be inquirers, and for inquiry to be a kind of action.

What is discipline in Bacon is formulated as rules by Descartes. In the *Discourse on the Method of Rightly Conducting the Reason and Seeking Truth in the Field of Science,* Descartes writes: "The first rule was never to accept anything as true if I had not evident knowledge of its being so; that is, carefully to avoid precipitancy and prejudice, and to embrace in my judgment only what presented itself to my mind so clearly and distinctly that I had no occasion to doubt it" (20). Descartes radicalizes Bacon's move by methodically excluding all received knowledge, all opinion, anything "probable" or arrived at by dialectic. He also absolutizes the authority of the individual subject, whose own intuitions of clarity and distinctness become the measure of all knowledge. Descartes' other rules are meant to pave the way to these intuitions of certain truths, to provide the "method" for arriving at them.

What is very interesting here is that although the Baconian/Cartesian moves can be seen as the forsaking of both rhetoric and dialectic for the nascent idea of a single scientific method, both Bacon and Descartes display a deep understanding of rhetoric. Descartes' understanding is implicit and practical.[9] Bacon develops an explicit and really quite subtle rhetorical theory.[10] However, each also divides human intellectual activity in ways that will have negative repercussions for the way rhetoric is conceptualized by later thinkers. There is, on the one hand, the idolatrous and false reasoning handed down by tradition, and there is, on the other, the methodical and true reasoning that is a result of discipline and scientific education. Because the world has been corrupted by what is false, truth is not directly convincing for most people. Rhetoric can come to its aid—either by persuading the will more forcefully by acting on the imagination (Bacon), or by allowing the truth teller to conceal the truth from those who are not prepared for it while at the same time revealing it to those who are (Hiram Caton's Descartes). In each case, the consequence is to remove rhetoric from any responsibility for genuine discovery and inquiry and to assign it to a communicative role made necessary by rationally deficient audiences. Here the division between two kinds of reasoning becomes very strong, and the schism between philosophy and rhetoric becomes very powerful. The Aristotelian legacy again overpowers Aristotle.

GADAMER'S HERMENEUTIC CRITIQUE OF BACON

I want to advance this schematic narrative of the relation of rhetoric, method, and inquiry by linking it with Gadamer's narrative of the concept of experience from its early modern moment to its treatment in Heidegger's critique of Hegel's concept of experience. This will allow a fuller understanding of the relation of rhetoric and inquiry, one best understood, I think, in the context of a pragmatic rhetoric of reason. It will also permit an exploration of the concept of reflection, which has, I believe, a very important role to play in the undergraduate curriculum—especially in the teaching of written reasoning. In some ways, nineteenth- and twentieth-century German philosophy diverges from Anglo-American philosophy's continuing identification with the natural-scientific enterprise. The German philosophical proclivity toward systematization was not only an effort for a unified, logical system of philosophy but also an effort to keep alive a more comprehensive sense of "learning" and "research," captured pretty well in the notion of *Wissenschaft*, translated into English as "science," but including all disciplined human learning, in all fields, without the suggestion of a reduction of their legitimacy to what was actually natural scientific in them. This effort at a comprehensive, nonreductive understanding of human learning and reason is pretty consistent from the German idealists through Nietzsche and Husserl and down to Heidegger and Gadamer—despite the enormous differences that divide them in other ways. As a consequence, this tradition offers some ways to look back at the philosophy of science from the standpoint of a tradition with a concept of *Wissenschaft* which embraces a broader variety of human experience. Such comprehension and inclusiveness are evident in Heidegger's concept of fundamental ontology (and later, of "language"), as well as in Gadamer's notion of the "universality" of hermeneutics.[11]

Gadamer judges Bacon's major achievement to be his penetrating analysis of the "prejudices" which corrupt our ordinary understanding of nature and prevent us from having the kind of experience which might ground genuine scientific knowledge. The purification of experience is accomplished by absolutizing the criterion of scientific certainty, and stripping away any features of experience that do not contribute to this end. In his discussion of the idols of the tribe, Bacon identifies the tendency to forget what is negative and remember what is positive as a corruption of experience. Such prejudice leads people to a superstitious belief in oracles, whose failures are regularly forgotten but whose successes become legends. Language itself, at least in its conventional forms, is also identified as an idol, one of the idols of the marketplace: "But words plainly force and overrule the understanding, and throw all into confusion, and lead men away into numberless empty controversies and idle fancies" (1:43).

Bacon's purpose is to refine experience to such a point that it is universal—that it has the kind of repeatability and certainty appropriate for claims of knowledge. A purified, universal kind of experience should be accessible to all who have disciplined themselves in the right way— all those who have cast off the particularizing and corrupting effects of prejudice, all who have given up the worship of idols in order to obey nature. In rhetorical terms, Bacon is searching for a form of experience whose claims can stand up to a universal audience. Gadamer acknowledges that Bacon has recognized something important about experience—specifically, that we weigh experiences against each other, that experiences tend to lose their claim on us when they are contradicted by other experiences. Gadamer takes this to be true not only of science, where observations and experiments must ordinarily be repeatable, but also of everyday life, where we are constantly measuring our experiences against each other. Bacon's effort to refine experience down to its incontrovertible features is in line with our general expectations that experiences should be capable of standing up to each other.

Gadamer's objection to Bacon is to the narrowness of his criterion. By demanding that all experience be oriented toward and measured solely by the achievement of scientific knowledge, Bacon has, according to Gadamer, given up too much. Gadamer takes it to be an important and open question whether a form of life guided by a tendency to forget the negative is simply corrupt and to be done away with as a life of superstition and idolatry. He takes the possibility of hope to be dependent on the ability to give some kind of priority to what is positive, the ability to resist giving priority to what is negative—even if a well-disciplined observer might make a very different judgment based on an "unprejudiced" tally of experiences. Hope and hopelessness may or may not play a large role in the abstract model of scientific method, but they certainly play a very large role in the lives and actions of scientists. When it comes to language, Gadamer objects that despite the ways language might mislead us, it also enables communication and science itself. Science and experience occur only within the horizon of language, and it would be impossible to imagine anyone's having Baconian experience without the assistance of language somewhere along the line. Witness Bacon's (and Descartes') elaborate instructions to the rest of us. Language guides and makes possible scientific experience; in Gadamer's words, it *precedes* it. A great portion of *Truth and Method* is taken up with working out the details of this argument and the consequences of this fact.

Gadamer's critique of Bacon leads back, once again, to the question of priority—a crucial concept when it comes to understanding the relation of philosophy and rhetoric, reason and inquiry. In fact, Gadamer points out the similarities between Bacon and Aristotle when it comes to the way experience generates universals, or regularities or stabilities or repetitions in experience. He turns to Aristotle's account (at the end of the *Posterior Analytics*) of how the flux of heterogeneous perceptions can be halted in a kind of unitary recognition of something. The question is, how do we acquire the "general," the "universal," that allows us to see different experiences as experiences of the same thing? Clearly, memory is involved, but Aristotle doesn't want to defer to Plato's myth about remembering ideas from a previous existence. Like Bacon, he wants a more "scientific" account. However, he must try to answer the impossible question: which comes "first," the particular experience or the general idea? In this passage, Aristotle is trying to opt for giving a certain priority to experience in the generation of "universals," a move Bacon would put on a new footing in early modern times.

Instead of resorting to a myth, Aristotle uses an image. The different perceptions one has are like the soldiers in an army that has been put to flight. They rush in every direction, without order. However, if one perception "confirms" another perception, it is like two soldiers coming to a halt and standing fast. The more perceptions confirm each other, the more the entire army is brought to order, to a stand—and thus the more a "general" rules over particulars.

Gadamer uses this image to search out the limitations of empirical, science-oriented theories of knowledge. First, he claims that the image is especially interesting because it starts with an assumption that makes it disanalogous to experience: before the rout, the army was standing fast. That is, the image presents a picture of disorder which is a lapse from a previous state of order. The expectation is that there is a state of order to be restored—the fleeing particulars are not in the desired/usual/appropriate state. However, the question about experience is the question of how this very expectation of order comes about—how we know order when we see it. Scientific empiricism of the sort under discussion here is an attempt to explain how order arises from experience; it cannot simply assume that we already have an idea of what counts as order that is prior to experience. The idea that Gadamer draws from this is one that he claims the example is intended to illustrate: "The birth of experience as an event over which no one has control and which is not even determined by the particular weight of this or that observation but in which everything is coordinated in a way that is ultimately incomprehensible" (*Truth and Method* 316). However, Gadamer also finds exemplified here what he found in Bacon—the recognition of the openness of experience, the fact that it is acquired suddenly, unpredictably, "yet not without preparation," and that each new experience carries the possibility of either confirming old experiences or calling them into question.

Gadamer's second objection to Aristotle's image is identical to one of his objections to Bacon. The purpose of this account is to explain and justify scientific knowledge: given that we do have scientific concepts, how are they formed on the basis of experience? Aristotle's assumption is that there is something common in our different preconceptual perceptions—something that persists in our experience. That is, the idea of a universal concept is at play from the very beginning. The Aristotelian and the modern theories of science *begin* with the result they must prove.

One way to grasp the entire early modern sorting out of the relations among philosophy, rhetoric, science, and method is to focus on the idea of priority, for it is remarkable how the same Aristotelian "priority texts" keep coming up again and again in medieval and early modern discussions—as well as in Gadamer's account. The problem of the relation between how we come to know something (how things are for us) and how things really are (by nature) is at the center of all these discussions, and the position one takes on the question determines a great deal about how one works out the nature of and distinctions among philosophy, rhetoric, science, and method.

It is fair to say that the philosophical-metaphysical tradition of commitments about priority follows from what has been called Aristotle's invention of metaphysics. Aristotle's conviction, expressed in the *Posterior Analytics*, that what is "prior" and better known for us are particular perceptions but what is prior and better known in nature is what is universal sets up a division that continues, despite notable transmutations, throughout the history of Western theories of dialectic, rhetoric, science, and education. The metaphysics of this division reaches its early modern culmination in Bacon and in Cartesian dualism in which the "for us" includes all traditional knowledge and language (all history) as well as everything having to do with the senses, the passions, the body in general. The "by nature" is discovered only once the body is disciplined, tradition is overthrown, and the mind can perceive clear and distinct ideas. What began in Aristotle as a very subtle way to distinguish between the logic of how we come to learn something and how we explain and justify what it is that we know becomes in early modern times the fundamental metaphysical distinction between mind and body which will take ten thousand forms in the time between Descartes and ourselves.

In general, from a modern perspective, philosophy and science are aligned with the new concentration on method, with the mind set free from its idols, from the passions, from tradition and its prejudices. Method guarantees a kind of purity to scientific and philosophical work. Rhetoric is definitively consigned to doing, at best, mop-up work with people who are incapable of science, or else it is limited to "practical reason"—at least until scientific method can be applied directly to the social world. At worst, rhetoric is linked with lies, deceptions, prejudices. The decisive feature of rhetoric which leads to this modern degradation is its essential dependence on language and tradition, on those things that people already have in common and that, from a rhetorical point of view, allow them to understand and reason with one another.

Contemporary philosophical hermeneutics of Gadamer's sort would locate rhetoric's prospects precisely there. The Heideggerian/Gadamerian rehabilitation of prejudice and language as ineluctable features of all experience and reasoning is itself a cornerstone of any viable philosophical rhetorical theory.[12] If one has already been claimed by a language and a way of life so that one's only way of claiming oneself again is by way of the language and way of life one has been thrown into, then rhetoric is the "way" to respond to that fact.

THE RECOVERY OF DIALOGUE: FROM HEGEL TO HERMENEUTICS

Although Hegel was no friend of the history of rhetoric, he was a penetrating critic of modern philosophy. His attempt to bring the concept of dialectic back to the modern notion of experience is an important moment in any effort to recover a concept of rhetoric that can deepen our understanding of education—and rescue it from a reversion to the authoritarian pedagogicalizing of medieval and early modern times as well as from the degraded idea of "transmission" that afflicts institutions with rarefied conceptions of research and inquiry. Thus, I want to continue Gadamer's narrative of the concept of experience by briefly considering Hegel's treatment of the concept.

Gadamer believes that one of the limitations of the modern concept of experience is that experience is conceived of as simply a positive accumulation of facts lined up for induction. Thus, the concept doesn't take full account of the way in which experience supersedes itself. Experience shows us that strangers are not to be trusted—and yet experience shows us that we in fact trust strangers all the time, that we are dependent on them. Experience shows that Newtonian theory is correct, and experience also shows that it is limited and not accurate enough for many purposes. Gadamer's point is that experience does not occur on a single plane. New experience not only yields something new but also puts old experience into context. That is, it teaches us something not only about matter or about society, but about our previous knowledge of matter or of society. As Hegel puts it, experience is "the dialectical process consciousness executes on itself." Experience in this sense is not simply an experience of objects, but also an experience of experience itself—and so, a kind of reflection. As Gadamer points out, each experience of this kind is a change in the horizon of experience. Our knowledge and its possibilities are not what we once thought. The horizon for our reasoning has become enlarged. We look back on our previous experience and see how a narrow horizon helped to produce a limited understanding. It was Hegel who developed the most elaborate account ever of the deep way this dialectic is active in thought.

The question to pose to Hegel is: what causes this dialectical process? Why does experience have this reflective relation to itself? Hegel's answer is to give us examples of the "necessity" of this process in experience. However, in the examples he gives, we find something very like dialogues or conversations—in which claims are made and called into question. Hegel as a metaphysician seems to imagine that these are not really anything like conversations; the dialectic has instead a *logical* necessity that is essential to the concept of experience. Yet whenever Hegel actually explains the self-transformative nature of experience, he explains the process as a conversation. Rhetoric and communication are at the heart of the Hegelian dialectic.

Consider again the discussion of sense experience in the first chapter of the *Phenomenology of Spirit*. Hegel imagines someone having an experience—silently taking in everything the senses can take in on a single occasion. He wants to challenge the idea that this can be a rich and full and meaningful experience. That is, Hegel imagines that there is a general claim already in play—that simple sense experience is rich and full and meaningful—and he is out to refute this claim. He does this by imagining the experiencer in a conversation with a skeptical interlocutor. Now, we might wonder why someone who is satisfied just to, say, stand alone in a high alpine meadow on a bright fall day taking it all in would be interested in justifying the worth of the experience to a skeptical interlocutor. That is, why should a person be forced out of a joyful silence and solitude? Is there any real necessity in this? It seems rather that having such a conversation would depend on the occasion, on who the interlocutors were and how they felt about each other, and on a number of other factors. There is no logical necessity in having to defend one's experience before a skeptic. One might choose to explain one's experience to any number of other kinds of people—to a friend, or one's children or partner—or not at all, rather to keep silence.

However, Hegel takes the conversation to be necessary, and his skeptical interlocutor insists that the apparently reluctant experiencer speak. He imagines that the first attempt to describe the experience results in the experiencer's saying merely "This." Here is Hegel:

> Sense-certainty has to be asked: What is the This? If we take it
> in the two-fold form of its existence, as the *Now* and as the *Here*,
> the dialectic it has in it will take a form as intelligible as the This
> itself. To the question, What is the *Now*? we reply, for example,
> the *Now* is night-time . . . [However,] if we look again at this
> truth . . . look at it *now, at this noon-time*, we shall have to say
> that it has turned stale and out of date . . . (151)
>
> The same will be the case when we take the *Here*, the other
> form of the This. The Here is e.g. the tree. I turn about and this
> truth has disappeared and has changed round into its opposite:
> the here is not a tree, but a house . . . (152–53)

Hegel then imagines that the sense-certainty character will repeat the first attempt: not Now, but *Now*. Not Here, but *Here*. The skeptical character, however, keeps waiting for time to pass, and asks, Now? Or the skeptic turns around again, and asks, Here? The point is that sense experience is supposed to be of something particular and rich with determinations. "Now" and "Here" are, by contrast, universals. The sense-certainty character thus comes to learn, by way of questioning, to modify the original implicit claim that sense perception alone is rich and full of knowledge and to think up better descriptions of what experience really is. And so the inner skeptic goes on challenging the experiencer to come up with more and more elaborate and mediated accounts of itself. And the experiencer agrees to continue the conversation. Unfolding the dialectic takes the whole of *The Phenomenology of Spirit*. The same internal conversation animates the dialectic in Hegel's logic, too, in which the same kind of skeptic challenges and questions any affirmation, any claim—even implicit ones. As Gadamer says, Hegel's concept of experience amounts to skepticism in action. However, it is also the case that Hegel's dialectic needs the skeptical *and* affirmative voices—skepticism is simply the essential condition for Hegelian affirmation.

Gadamer judges Hegel's thinking about experience to be a continuation and modification of the early modern concern with method: "To elaborate the totality of the determinations of thought, which was the aim of Hegel's logic, is as it were to attempt to comprehend within the great monologue of modern 'method' the continuum of meaning that is realized in every particular instance of dialogue" (*Truth and Method* 369). Hegel's goal was to take what can be accomplished only on the basis of dialogue and imagine it as a kind of logic, with its own internal necessity. In this, Hegel is like all logicians. The interlocutor he called on was the modern skeptic; the audience was a universal/paragon audience, knowledgeable about the history of philosophy, informed about contemporary science, and interested primarily in a concept of truth that could stand up against the challenges of skepticism. The skeptical interlocutor and a sophisticated nineteenth-century universal audience are the hidden laborers in Hegel's logic, the executors of the "method." Here is Gadamer again: "When Hegel sets himself the task of making the abstract determinations of thought fluid and subtle, this means dissolving and remolding logic into concrete language, and transforming the concept into the meaningful power of the word that questions and answers—a magnificent reminder, even if unsuccessful, of what dialectic really was and is. Hegel's dialectic is a monologue of thinking that tries to carry out in advance what matures little by little in every genuine dialogue" (369). Hegel is "unsuccessful" for reasons we'll consider in a moment. The point here is that Hegel has made an enormously important move with some central concepts in the long conflict between philosophy and rhetoric.

Most important, he has begun to reverse the early modern project of purifying method of voice. Hegel's dialectic is a kind of conversation, a process of question and answer—even though it is imagined as a set of self-moving concepts.[13] The early modern strategy was to try to set aside the old categories of dialectic and rhetoric, to opt for a concept of philosophy that was more or less identical with the new science, and to conceive the essence of science as experience and method. Hegel reconceives experience as itself already a kind of method,[14] dialectical at its very core, and thus restores dialogue to the heart of reason. Unfortunately, from a pragmatic/rhetorical point of view, Hegel theorizes this conversation as a metaphysical process of ideas transforming themselves in pure thought.

And so although Hegel creates a kind of rapprochement between dialectic and method, and restores a rhetorical process to reason itself, he can offer no interpretation of rhetoric or its history or its relation to philosophy that has anything like the depth of his revival of the concept of dialectic. He is notorious for his contempt of rhetoric and rhetoricians, and his own narrative of the history of philosophy has been a powerful force in continuing a destructive understanding of the relation of philosophy and rhetoric.

Hegel is not altogether inconsistent in these respects. For even though he believes that "experience" is method, is itself a form of inquiry, he also believes that experience must be finally overcome in a higher result. Experience may itself be a process of reflection on itself, of identifying its own different limits on different occasions, but this will never satisfy a skeptical challenger who wants to know whether experience yields real knowledge. Real knowledge, for Hegel, is finally absolute knowledge, or "science." This would be a complete experience of experience itself, which turns out to be, for Hegel, a systematic knowledge of all the different finite forms of experience. This knowledge grasps both what each form knows and what it is incapable of knowing. That is, the skeptical challenges which are intrinsic to experience teach us the "determinate negation" of each form of experience, each horizon of understanding. "Determinate negation" means that skeptical challenges show not only *that* the different horizons are all limited (this would be to produce what Heidegger calls "a sheer addiction to doubt" [*Hegel's Concept* 73]), but also the specific respects in which the limits shape experience, and so enable it.

The "path" through these different shapes and the final knowledge of their relations to one another are "method" or "dialectic." Its goal is the "education" *(Bildung)* of consciousness, which is taken to lie in its growing awareness of its own activity. The question of the "priorities" is one phase of this path. Reflection teaches us to make the distinction between the "in-itself" (or the known-in-its-nature) from the for-itself (or the known-by-us). Something at first appears to us as an object, something in-itself. Reflection shows that the appearance of the object is conditioned by a particular horizon of knowledge. Consequently, the object comes to appear as something for-us. However, at this same instant, this fact itself has become a kind of knowledge for us—a new object which takes on the appearance of something that is true in-itself. The point is that this process of distinguishing between something in-itself and something merely for-us is a part of the way things become intelligible for us. Thus, different kinds of education and different methods are not articulated on the basis of a conception of what comes "first" in nature or "first" for us. Instead, the very process of learning to make this distinction (and overcome it) is part of the substance of method and education.

In this, I find Hegel to be already much more closely aligned with a pragmatic and rhetorical way of understanding metaphysics than were most of Aristotle's successors. Hegel is aware that the distinctions on which metaphysics depends are made by human beings in the course of their experience. He knows, too, that these distinctions do not have the kind of ready-made, metaphysical stability that has been supposed. Instead, making these distinctions arises in a certain form of life—a kind of life which is devoted to defending experience from skeptical claims. Hegel is in full concurrence with the claim I made in the first chapter—that metaphysics is a kind of social-historical strategy for defending ideas which are already available to us in everyday life, and are really in no terrible danger, except from skeptics. However, Hegelian philosophy is a kind of absolutization of the skeptical challenge and so an absolutization of the response to skepticism.

It is this absolutization, finally, of a single interlocutor and audience that distracts Hegel from what his own successors saw more clearly. Heidegger highlights Hegel's remarks that "The experience of consciousness is thoroughgoing skepticism" and "Phenomenology is the Golgotha of Absolute Spirit," and finds in them a central feature of Hegel's thinking.[15] Both statements point up the fact that Hegel is forcing his reasoning into a single conversation, with a single goal: defending ordinary claims against an extraordinary challenger, a skeptic who will stop at nothing, who will extend no charity, make no concession—who in fact has no purpose but to force every experience into some relation to the quest for certain knowledge. More than once, Hegel speaks of the "violence" of absolute spirit. The conflict between experience and skepticism is taken to the most extreme lengths. The level of the conflict is as high as it can be; the intensity as strong as can be imagined. In the famous Lordship/Domination (master/slave) section of the *Phenomenology*, the struggle is a struggle to the death. In the *Philosophy of History*, Absolute Spirit leaves behind it a "slaughterbench." This is the ultimate gnosticism—in absolute knowledge lies the only goal, the only hope; all else is vanity.

But why get into such a conversation? Why sacrifice all other goods for certain knowledge? Why keep the company of skeptics whose motives are in conflict with many of the motives that, together, in balance, go to making up a good life? There are many potential interlocutors, many potential audiences. A universal audience whose agent is a skeptic on the attack is not even the only kind of universal audience one can imagine. And even if one is interested in the kind of philosophical theory that might constitute a reasonable response to skepticism, why absolutize it? Why not recognize that experience is connected with many different purposes and can be judged in many different ways—not all of which are closely related to responding to skepticism? Responding to skepticism is for most of us—even for most philosophers—just one good among many. And finally, why think that the only available response to skepticism is argumentation or philosophy? Stanley Cavell has pointed out the ways in which acknowledgment is a response to skepticism, and he conceives of acknowledgement in a broad way that includes actions and ethical practices. These actions and practices in turn make new, less skeptical conversations possible.

Gadamer makes a similar point when he argues that Hegel already has his mind made up about experience from the start. Since the goal of experience is certainty, and since certainty is possible only when consciousness becomes its own object, absolute self-consciousness is the goal of experience. Gadamer proposes instead *not* to import into the phenomenology of experience a certain knowledge of where experience is headed. What he finds then is that experience is defined not by the *telos* of self-consciousness but by the advent of newness. Hegel claims that the truth of experience lies in science. But, objects Gadamer, in that case,

> The nature of experience is conceived in terms of something that surpasses it; for experience itself can never be science. Experience stands in an ineluctable opposition to knowledge and to the kind of instruction that follows from general theoretical or technical knowledge. The truth of experience always implies an orientation toward new experience. That is why a person who is called experienced has become so not only *through* experiences but is also open *to* new experiences. The consummation of his experience, the perfection that we call "being experienced," does not consist in the fact that someone already knows everything and knows better than everyone else. Rather, the experienced person proves to be, on the contrary, someone who is radically undogmatic; who, because of the many experiences he has had and the knowledge he has drawn from them, is particularly well-equipped to have new experiences and to learn from them. The dialectic of experience has its proper fulfillment not in definitive knowledge but in the openness to experience that is made possible by experience itself. (*Truth and Method* 355)

Once the interest in the idea of certain knowledge is put in perspective, one can search experience for different defining characteristics. Gadamer finds the idea of newness to be a central one. Experience is a kind of learning, a discovering that one's expectations are always being outrun by the newness unfolding, the horizons opening up.[16]

In this sense, argumentative reasoning is a paradigm of experience itself. The dialectic of experience is an argumentative dialogue with an interlocutor that calls one toward newness, a dialogue in which new horizons unfold, a conversation that grants learning. Argumentation is one of the central forms that education takes. It is itself both method and pedagogy. And it is an activity that belongs at once to both philosophy and rhetoric. Conceived in this way, it is the activity in which philosophy and rhetoric and education come together once again.

Rhetoric is the conversation which can offer an understanding of how argumentative reasoning works—all argumentative reasoning. In this sense, rhetoric is metaphilosophy, and it explains philosophy as reasoning that operates with a particular set of conflicts, interlocutors, and audiences. These make up the tradition which constitutes philosophy's horizon. However, philosophy is also constantly in conversation with this tradition, questioning it, examining it; philosophy is by definition radically reflective. Philosophy's defining feature is its claim to the broadest and deepest kind of universality—this is why it is so concerned with skeptical attacks; it has a need to defend its claims against every comer, to justify everything except this principle that it must justify everything.

Rhetoric explains what philosophy cannot explain about itself. Rhetoric identifies the audience which makes demands for certain kinds of interlocutors, demands for the resolution of certain kinds of conflicts, and which judges the results of arguments in such a severe fashion. Rhetoric understands this audience as one among many possible audiences, even one among many possible universal audiences. In doing so, rhetoric itself appeals to an audience, and acknowledges that as metaphilosophy its own arguments are convincing only for certain audiences in certain contexts. Like philosophy, rhetorical metaphilosophy must appeal to a universal audience; unlike philosophy, rhetoric may acknowledge that this is a paragon and not simply a universal audience. That is, rhetoric's audience may have important ethical interests that influence its judgments—for instance, interests in nonviolence, social criticism and change, or in higher education that is not a mere instrument of narrow social powers.

In much the same way, rhetoric can offer accounts of how reasoning works in the different professions and disciplines—each with its own precedents, its own domain of conflicts, admissible claims, procedures, rules for challenging, and expert and specialized audiences. Rhetoric has a close connection with training in these specialized fields, since it is rhetoric which studies and offers an account of what *counts as* legitimate reasoning within these different domains. This is something that it is often hard for students to grasp. It is not usually enough to throw students into a discipline without giving them some training in its rhetoric, as if they could by osmosis simply absorb these conventions and procedures and rules of reasoning. The tradition of rhetoric has long recognized that the ability to discourse is determined by "nature" (e.g., how well students discourse without any training), art (that which comes by studying the rhetoric of some discourse), and practice. In higher education, none of these is usually enough by itself. And even beyond these, we might say that success also requires an attraction to the kind of newness the discourse helps to open up. One must care about what a physicist cares about, be concerned with what a legal theorist is concerned with, take satisfaction in the world-enlarging "fusion of horizons" that takes place when conflicts between horizons are resolved through argumentative reasoning.

However, rhetoric's most important contribution to education lies in general education, and its most significant contemporary domain is in writing courses that make up such a central part of the core curriculum in the United States. This contribution is twofold. First, rhetoric is capable of describing the "method" of education as it is experienced by the individual whose intellectual abilities are being developed. Second, rhetoric is capable of clarifying the audience for the reasoning that takes place in general education courses. I am going to return to these essential issues in the last chapter, where I can develop them at length.

First, though, it is necessary to shore up the strong claims I have made about rhetoric and inquiry. I am especially concerned that there will be some who still believe that the rhetorical theory I have developed will be insufficient for giving an account of research in the natural sciences. Before I make the strong claims I have to make about rhetoric and education, I would like to complete the account of the relation of rhetoric to scientific inquiry.

Argument and Inquiry

The history of rhetoric in the nineteenth and twentieth centuries is, from most points of view, a story of steady decline. After a partial and temporary recovery in the eighteenth century, rhetoric continues to weaken in the face of modern science and its strongly antirhetorical concepts of method. During this period, rhetoric also becomes more deeply estranged from philosophy—to the point where rhetoric is hardly even an issue for most philosophers. In addition, rhetoric suffers radical institutional fragmentation in the universities—to the point that it is ordinarily taken to be a professional disadvantage to have one's own fortunes or one's department's too closely tied to the word "rhetoric."

It is difficult to say whether rhetoric's current "resurgence" is an anomaly in what will prove to be its mortal decline in higher education.

Part Four: Argument, Inquiry, and Education

This resurgence could be a result of the fact that the teaching of writing has taken on professional/research status in many universities. This grants many of those people most concerned with general education and written reasoning the time and incentives to "rediscover" the tradition of which their own work is a part, and to attempt to revitalize that tradition in a contemporary context. It could also be that the rhetorical turn in contemporary philosophy is a harbinger of a profound intellectual reevaluation of the role of rhetoric in human intellectual endeavors. This book stands at the juncture of these two streams, and attempts to unite them. However, the main current still runs in a different direction. The assumption that genuine inquiry is one thing and rhetoric another—say, the "transmission" of knowledge, or the "persuading" of the ignorant, or the resolving of "practical" conflicts—is deep and powerful. The continuing logical disjunction between discovery and inquiry is one result of this fact.

However, from the standpoint of a rhetoric of reason, argumentation in the service of inquiry is not essentially different from argumentation in the service of resolving conflicts and making choices—choices about what it is most reasonable to believe. Inquiry, too, makes use of conflicts to fuel its movement toward new knowledge. Conflicts about what is known and what is not, about which hypothesis is stronger, about whether *this particular* hypothesis should be pursued, conflicts about which theory best explains the observed facts—these are all conflicts that have the same very general form as the conflict whose dynamic I have been tracing in earlier chapters. No matter what the question at issue, human beings reason about it by making claims and raising questions and offering answers for those questions. They do so in a way that activates all the speech roles and aspects of conflict I have described. And when the issue is knowledge, or truth, the arguments they have been convinced by tend to be arguments that are convincing for the universal, paragon audience. Controversies which are not resolvable are controversies for which the parties in conflict can find no universal audience. The consequence is a crisis in a discipline, resolved by a division into different "schools," subdisciplines, or even into new disciplines—different systematizations of different audiences.

A rhetoric of reason brings to the study of inquiry two guiding ideas—the idea of conflict and the idea of audience. I want briefly to explain the way a rhetoric of reason treats the distinction between discovery and justification in terms of audience. Then I will show how rhetoric distinguishes between persuasion and inquiry in terms of audience. However, to make these distinctions more convincing I will have to show how, by modifying the dynamics of conflict in argumentation, one can use this conflict to inquire. In the course of this discussion, inquiry will begin to look less and less like argumentation, more and more like something else. This will provoke some general concluding remarks about the scope of rhetoric.

Context of Discovery/Context of Justification: Redrawing the Lines

The distinction between discovery and justification has been an important one for modern science and epistemology. In general, one could say that the view has been that *discovery* is everything that happens up to the formulation of a hypothesis; *justification* is what happens after a hypothesis has been formulated, in the process of testing the hypothesis. More simply, discovery is how we come up with ideas, justification is how we test, evaluate, criticize, and support them.

Working within the Baconian/Cartesian tradition, modern epistemology has made this distinction on the basis of a dualistic vision of reason/unreason that a rhetoric of reason rejects. So emotions, personal interests, hopes, history, values, luck, ideology, and so on all fall on the "discovery" side of the split. Logic and scientific method fall on the "justification" side. According to this view, people come up with ideas in all sorts of wild ways. There is really no logic of discovery, no procedures or rules that can guarantee that one will be struck with good hypotheses. And none of the wild ways people come up with ideas can be ruled out. However, once the idea is on the table, it must be justified according to fairly strict rules of logic and method.

A rhetoric of reason would see things differently. Instead of conceptualizing discovery and justification as mutually exclusive terms, whose exclusivity is based on what is really a metaphysical conception of the difference between reason, on the one hand, and emotions, values, and so on, on the other, rhetoric would place these terms on a continuum, emphasizing that the ends of this continuum are really abstract ideals and not metaphysical domains. That is, discovery and justification are mutually implicated at every point, and what we are really concerned with are not two different abstract "contexts," but a continuum of different audiences. Some hypotheses are adhered to only by particular audiences, often only imaginary ones, or audiences of only one person, in an unusual mood. Through argumentation, reasoning, method, the hypothesis becomes persuasive to a more and more general audience. In fact, the essential function of method in science is to guarantee that the results of observation, reasoning, and experimentation will be *repeatable*. That is, method is, once again, the articulation of our best understanding of what will ensure that our results will turn out to be convincing for a universal audience. Experiments whose results cannot be repeated are simply not convincing, whether we can show where the method and reasoning went awry or not. In this, there is a remarkable continuity in the goals of science from Bacon and Descartes to our time. The final test of scientific work lies not in logic or method but in what they are designed to achieve: repeatability, universal access to results. To achieve this universality, one's claims come under the scrutiny of an interlocutor who is deeply skeptical and persistently critical—insistent on very high standards of evidence.

However, scientific method does *not* really screen out the effects of emotion, history, interests, and so on. This is not finally its real function. Its function is to achieve the potential assent of the broadest possible audience. As we have seen, argumentative reasoning, of which most science is a species, is *dependent* on a background of deep competences, moods, abilities, assumptions, beliefs, ways of being and understanding. In scientific inquiry, this background is familiar: accepted observations, well-confirmed theories, basic principles, background knowledge, a good description of initial conditions, and technical skill with instruments. However, what early modern science failed to acknowledge was that this background is thoroughly historical and largely unavailable to conscious control or explicit awareness. It is now a truism that all observation is theory-dependent. However, it has still not been as fully acknowledged that not all the "theories" we hold are available to our scrutiny. They often emerge only in contrast to those of people who make very different observations from our own, people in other historical epochs or in different cultures. And when they do emerge, we often see that they are expressive of a particular range of cultural interests, moods, attitudes, abilities. Only against this recognition do we glimpse more of the ways our concept of good science is only a particular one. Sometimes, the "experience" that engenders reflection is a new experience of the past. Historical knowledge can itself lead to a new experience which places the present in a new light, and shows its limits.

In a logician's terms, or a positivist philosopher's, we would then have placed our own method of justification into a context of discovery. We would have shown its genealogy. If we used this genealogy to criticize the method, we would be committing the "genetic fallacy," i.e., conflating the context of discovery with the context of justification. This is supposed to be strictly forbidden. However, this leads the logical point of view to an impasse. For how is scientific method or logic *itself* to be evaluated? Surely, not by its own methods or logic. First, that would beg the question. After all we want to know whether those methods are good ones or not, not what answer they would provide about their own worthiness. Second, attempts to explain actual science in terms of any logic of scientific method have failed anyway. The practice of actual science is as far away from descriptions of its ideal logic and method as everyday reasoning is from formal logic. The explosion of the history of science in recent years is a testimony to this fact. There are many different sciences, many different ways of conducting them.

A rhetorical approach recognizes that it makes sense to ask for reasons why one should use scientific method or reason in a scientific way. These reasons must be convincing for a paragon audience, one that has interests that include but also range beyond scientific ones. Such an audience might refuse the absolute distinction between a context of discovery and a context of justification. It might consider genealogical accounts relevant. Here is why.

From a rhetorical point of view, the aim of distinguishing between justification and discovery is to ensure that one's results will be convincing beyond oneself and one's own group, convincing for everyone, at least in principle. Thus, in scientific work, the arguments one gives in the context of justification are constrained by the best scientific understanding of what guarantees the broadest possible assent. Essentially, this is the repeatability of one's experiments, one's reasoning, one's results. Our understanding of the context of justification is a function of our conception of the universal audience.

On the other hand, the ways that one is led to entertain a hypothesis, or believe it oneself, are usually persuasive only for oneself, and often only to a fairly small degree and sometimes only for a short while, or in particular contexts. Many otherwise scientifically reasonable people hold idiosyncratic beliefs based on their own experiences. People work with countless hypotheses, and their validity is spread out across the continuum from very particular to very universal audiences. Theories themselves fall on different points on this continuum. No theory is discovery-pure; no idiosyncratic idea is completely justification-free. What we usually refer to as the context of discovery is better understood as the context of reasoning in the presence of particular audiences.

Thus, although a rhetoric of reason rejects the distinction between discovery and justification, it recognizes that the aim of making the distinction is a worthwhile one, and it provides another, better way of reaching that aim. Understanding the continuum of audiences in terms of which one develops arguments and designs experiments is an important feature of scientific reasoning. However, conceptualizing that continuum in terms of a dualism of discovery and justification that rests on an obsolete metaphysics is not helpful to anyone, and obscures important features of scientific practice.

Inquiry and Persuasion

This account of "discovery" as that which goes on in the context of a particular audience is fairly abstract, although I believe it does establish some necessary principles for anyone who is concerned with teaching inquiry. I will have more to say about "discovery" as inquiry when I examine how the dynamics of conflict can be changed to accomplish different purposes. First, however, I want briefly to discuss the distinction between inquiry and persuasion, for this distinction, too, can be understood better in rhetorical terms, and this distinction, too, is related to the question of method—and especially to the question of teaching. In fact, the modern tradition conceives of rhetoric as essentially connected with persuasion—and distinguishes both from inquiry and science.

The distinction can be put fairly easily. There is a difference between the kind of reasoning we engage in when have already made up our minds about some issue and simply need to persuade other people to take our side, and the kind of reasoning that goes on when we have not yet made up our minds but are trying to come to a conclusion ourselves. Many people think of argumentation as essentially linked to persuasion, and think of inquiry in different terms. For this reason, many teachers of composition in colleges and universities prefer not to teach argumentation. They view it as a form of writing that actually obstructs inquiry and change rather than enabling it. It is a way of writing for people who *already know* rather than for people who want to learn.

I hope I have already shown, in depth and detail, that this is not the concept of argumentation I have in mind in this book. The reconciliation that genuine argumentation offers is not predictable in advance, even for those who try to make an absolutely instrumental use of argument. However, the distinction between persuasion and inquiry is a prima facie compelling one, and it will be helpful to clarify it in the light of a rhetoric of reason, in order to show in more detail how argumentation is connected with inquiry.

Let's begin with a paradox that arises from a rhetorical approach to the question of persuasion and inquiry in argumentation. The paradox is that all argumentation is persuasion and that no persuasion is argumentation. Here is the truth in the paradox. In one sense, the rhetorical understanding of argumentation conceives of all argumentation as persuasion because the goal of argumentation is to convince an audience of a claim. In another sense, a rhetoric of argumentation seems to disqualify persuasion altogether from being counted as argumentation. If one does not believe a claim is questionable, or that one's interlocutor is worthy—if one would not, under *any* circumstances, be persuaded to give up the claim—then one is not really engaging in argumentation. One is only giving the appearance of doing so.

I believe that it is important to affirm both of these truths about persuasion and argumentation. All argumentation does aim toward having an audience acknowledge a claim. However, argumentation also depends on the possibility of mutual influence and change, and on the genuine questionability of the claim. I want to develop these ideas in greater detail by discussing them in the context of some arguments of Jack Meiland. In an article titled "Argument as Inquiry and Argument as Persuasion," Meiland denies that argumentation for inquiry also seeks to persuade. He warns that students who come to believe that argumentation is for persuasion will misunderstand the nature of inquiry, and so misunderstand their own educations.

Meiland claims that a teacher—say, a physicist—who argues in favor of a particular scientific hypothesis is not trying to persuade students, but trying to see what the weight of reasons is for believing the hypothesis. Now it is true that there is a difference between the kind of persuading that goes on in a physics course and the kind of persuading that occurs on the floor of an electronics store. However, the difference is not that one kind of reasoning attempts to convince an audience and the other does not. The difference is in the kinds of audiences that are active in the argumentation.

In teaching, audiences arise and interact in very complicated ways; however, some of what happens may be made clear fairly simply. Inquiry in physics demands that the weight of reasons given in favor of some hypothesis be determined by an ideal audience—well trained, competent, honest physicists. Most physicists do not engage in scientific research by standing before a classroom of students and trying to persuade them of some point. The success of a new hypothesis does not usually depend directly on the assent of undergraduates.

However, the success of teaching the hypothesis just might. The aim of teaching specialized knowledge about physics to novices is both to show why physicists have been convinced by the reasoning for certain physical theories and to help students come to identify with an audience of physicists—to be capable of understanding, reasoning, judging the way physicists do. The outcome of an education in physics is the student-graduate as a reliable audience for argumentation in physics— the identification of the student and the physicist.

Effective physicist-teachers not only show how and why physicists are persuaded by arguments, but also show students how to persuade themselves the way physicists do. And importantly, if they are teaching seriously, they show why it is desirable and worthwhile to think like a physicist. Negotiating and gradually reducing the difference between students as particular audiences and students as competent scientific audiences is a central goal of education. Need I add that this is not just a matter of absorbing knowledge? To learn to reason the way physicists do is to learn to raise questions, restlessly, in new ways, from strange angles. Students are changed by studying physics, and young physicists do not leave physics unchanged.

So the argumentative inquiry in which physicist-teachers engage is rhetorical and persuasive in two senses. The physicist-teacher shows why a hypothesis is persuasive for an audience of physicists, and she or he persuades the students to identify with that audience.

The case is somewhat but not greatly different for teachers discussing open-ended questions with students, or engaging in collaborative research and inquiry with them. Here, it could be that the claim/question/point at issue has not yet been clarified, or that the reasons for and against a claim have not yet been discovered, or that an audience has not been agreed on. Or to put it in my terms, the claimant, interlocutor, and audience have not been identified and brought into the best relationship. The occurrence of audience in such a situation can become very difficult to track. The teacher may play a number of different argumentative roles, may sometimes model the responses of a proposed ideal audience, may become an unidentified universal audience encouraging students to develop their own audience conceptions—there are many possibilities. Here, persuasion and inquiry enter into a complicated dialectic. However, the general goal is the same: to acquaint the students somehow with worthwhile interlocutors and audiences, and to enable students to reason with these newfound companions. Argumentation— whether written or oral, public or inward—is communication, and an education in reasoning is an education in communication. Inquiry, like teaching, is dependent on audience—whether one's friends are physicists or literary critics.

Conflict and Discovery

A rhetoric of reason can also clarify and deepen our understanding of how argumentation can be used for research and inquiry by showing how the dynamics of discursive conflict can be modified for the purpose of discovery. To say that discovery and justification, persuasion and inquiry, can be clarified by way of the concept of audience is true enough, but it is true in a very general sense. By examining the particular ways conflict can be modified in discourse, one can reach a much more specific understanding of discovery and inquiry as activities of reason which are more continuous with justification than the modern philosophy of science would allow.

Let's begin with the conflict at work in all claims—the implicit validity claims and their implicit invitation to being challenged. The degree to which any validity claim holds in the process of argumentation is variable, and lies on a continuum. In a situation of high-intensity conflict, a relatively slight doubt about validity claims can lead to an explicit challenge. However, when we are reasoning to inquire, when our purpose is discovery, we may suspend our fastidiousness about the status of validity claims. The degree to which such claims stand may be very low. For example, when we do not need to convince a universal audience, we may, for the purpose of reaching new understandings, go on talking and writing and using terms and making claims that are not fully intelligible. In such situations, we may make claims that we do *not* sincerely believe, just to see where such claims will lead. We may even make "inappropriate" claims and ask "inappropriate" questions. And concerns about truth may be simply set aside for a time. Sometimes, ideas need to be developed with friendly interlocutors and audiences, so that they can reach their best, fullest statement. Only later are they brought before audiences who will scrutinize validity claims.[17]

Unless ideas could be cultivated in a rhetorical environment that was relatively free of the stringent demands of universal audiences regarding validity claims, it is doubtful that new ideas could flourish at all. Newness tends to start small, with individuals and with particular audiences. Notice, however, that if one completely suspends a concern with validity claims, one is probably no longer participating in argumentative discourse. One cannot simply suspend requirements for intelligibility, sincerity, appropriateness, and truth. The degree to which one can do so will vary with interlocutors and audiences, and it will be governed in a general way by judgments about the value of the results of modifying the usual expectations about validity claims.

There are many ways to use audiences for the purpose of inquiry—for the purpose of inventing arguments that will only later have to be brought to the attention of a skeptical judge. One can imagine not only particular audiences but also strange audiences, audiences whose judgments point to unfamiliar ways of life. In some sense, radical discovery demands the imagining of a strange audience, an audience which dissents from established opinion. Socrates is famous for having a loyalty to an audience that dissented sharply from some of the opinions of the Athenians. He urged a way of reasoning that would be convincing to the gods themselves, and not simply to the actual citizens with whom he was faced. The judgments of this strange audience pointed the way to a kind of life that was different from the ordinary, too. Galileo's strange audience also indicated a shift in a form of life. Sometimes imagining strange audiences is a kind of predicting of possible future forms of life, an envisioning of societies in which what is not now convincing becomes convincing and what is convincing now is convincing no longer.

The sixth chapter of Thomas Kuhn's *The Structure of Scientific Revolutions* can be read as an exposition of this fact in relation to the history of science. Kuhn shows that the emergence of anomalies to accepted theories is often a difficult process. By the time anomalies are finally experienced as such, they are typically emerging in several unrelated laboratories simultaneously. It is not that the physical processes in question were not occurring all along. It is rather that they were not experienced as anomalies—they just weren't noticed. That is, they weren't experienced as evidence/reasons that could count for or against a theory/claim. For anomalies to emerge at all requires the attention of an audience capable of experiencing the anomalies *as evidence* of something. This requires imagining or being an audience that is markedly different from the established one.

Kuhn is famous for emphasizing the senses in which scientific discovery is more or less out of the hands of individuals, the respects in which social and technical and intellectual-historical changes operating behind the backs of researchers allow them to have the experiences they do. This emphasis is certainly congruent with the rhetorical conception of reasoning, which also emphasizes the ways in which background skills, facts, interests, and values all enable certain reasoning and inquiry. However, it is also the case that discovery and invention are often accelerated by individuals who are themselves strange audiences or are capable of imagining themselves as strange audiences. This has long been recognized in the creative arts, where the straining for newness has often led to a sometimes destructive rejection of what is seen as a staid, ordinary life of nondiscovery.

However, this is as true of scientific discovery as it is of creative work in painting or literature. Anyone who has read James Gleick's book *Chaos* will recall the prologue. Mitchell Feigenbaum is obsessed with clouds, wondering about what laws might describe the wild order of their formation. He runs up enormous travel expenses (on his employer's account), just to view clouds from the air. He wanders aimlessly as clouds—or so it appears to his superiors. Yet stepping outside of the current of established scientific interests, and following his own sense of wonder—or loafing, if you will—allowed Feigenbaum new questions, and permitted a new domain of evidence to come to strong presence for him: chaos, and the science which explores it. Aristotle was deeply aware of this feature of discovery. For him, the ability to step back from one's everyday preoccupied reasoning, one's ordinary deployment of the established audience, and to experience wonder at ordinary facts, was the crucial, founding ability that permitted learning. This experience is an experience we have as individuals, and without it all the technical and social change going on around us will be merely forces of which we are the objects and not energy which enables discovery and newness.

When I consider the fact that I have not seen a single proposal for the improvement of education that recognizes the central role of a sense of wonder, and when I consider further the fact that a sense of wonder is not simply a technique of discovery but makes for a life that is threaded through with daily joys, I despair for every kind of educational reform with which I am familiar. On the other hand, if educational policymakers were to recognize that "a sense of wonder" is an essential feature of the ability to inquire and discover, they would certainly want an assessment scheme for measuring how great a sense of wonder was really being inculcated in students. The next step would be to introduce techniques for increasing the sense of wonder in the classroom. Statewide and national standards would surely follow. External assessment is essentially (although not completely) an act of skeptical reason. It is necessary only when suspicion or conflict calls into question what is happening in the classroom. A sense of wonder grows in other soil, in ground which has not yet become significant enough for audiences of educational policymakers.[18]

Another way to change the dynamic of argumentative conflict is to modify the purpose of argumentation. I have emphasized that even given the purposes of reaching agreements and making choices, argumentative reasoning is still unpredictable, generative of newness, capable of promoting discovery and not simply persuasion. However, this capability can be increased by suspending or postponing the goals of the argumentative process. The point here is to release the conflict of reason from the obligation of having to come to an end without undermining the energy of the conflict itself. For example, one can suspend the need to make a choice. Once again, it is choice that forces bivalence, a yes/no, valid/invalid judgment. Without the need to choose, the demand for bivalence has no force.

Jack Meiland uses just this kind of modification to distinguish persuasion from inquiry. Persuasion can fail, he says, when no conclusion is reached, no audience convinced, no choice made. However, inquiry cannot fail in the same way because even if a conclusion is not reached, one still learns about the ways people reason about the issue, why the issue is controversial, what kinds of reasons are convincing for whom, and so on (193). Inquiry yields knowledge, even if it is not the knowledge one was expecting.

This is an important observation, although I would describe this somewhat differently. One way of using argumentation to inquire is to modify the focus of conflict. I will come to this in more detail in a moment, but I think what Meiland is describing here is a situation in which the focus of conflict is unstable, drifting—in fact, a situation in which the ostensive focus is really just a means to the identifying of other foci of conflict, other claim-question-reason events. For example, several people deliberate about whether "professing" homosexuals should be allowed to serve in the military. They disagree strongly, present arguments to one another, but fail to come to an agreement, a conclusion. In one sense, then, the argumentation fails; the focal conflict is not resolved. However, several other conflicts may also have been active in the discussion, and some of them may have been resolved through reasoning—whether for individuals, small groups, or even for the group as a whole. The whole group may have been newly impressed by how uncomfortable it makes some people to be the object of someone else's sexual desire. Some individuals may have learned that women in the military already experience what many men would prefer not to—unwanted sexual attention. These claims may have been raised in the argument, and reasons may have been given—explicitly or not. In any case, the claims now stand for some people because of the argumentation that was explicitly focused on a different issue.[19]

To let the focus of conflict drift and multiply in this way is to let the claim change. One identifies a claim, explores the challenges to it and the reasons which try to answer them, but one *focuses* on very different claims-challenges-reasons that arise in the course of the argumentation. It is not that one does not reach any conclusion; it is not that one makes no choices at all. Rather one reaches conclusions about matters that are very different from the claim under discussion.

It is interesting to ask here what written form such oblique inquiry should take. Although it could take many different forms, it suggests to me a form that is different from any kind of writing in which the thesis is stated explicitly somewhere near the outset, supported by succeeding sections, and restated near the end. I am not denying that this order is possible; I can imagine a form of it that would likely succeed. However, I can also imagine a form that follows the order of discovery a little more slowly—one that tracks the emergence of new foci of conflict, slowly removing its attention from the ostensive focus to the newly emerging ones. Such writing would make different demands on readers and would offer somewhat different rewards. What is sometimes called "the exploratory essay" has a movement like this. Readers of Montaigne and Emerson are familiar with these kinds of rewards. However, there has not been much discussion of the way this kind of essay functions as written reasoning. On the contrary, commentators have most often focused on its more aesthetic, expressive and belletristic features—sometimes as a way of dismissing it.

If one suspends the need to choose, one can also tolerate contradictions. Universal audiences usually disallow contradictions, judging them to be a vitiation of whatever reasoning is going on. If one need not choose, and need not reach agreement with others, contradictions may simply stand. That is, we may admit equally compelling arguments. We can admit equally compelling arguments in different ways, with different results. For example, we can make a claim that there are equally compelling arguments for incompatible claims, and so subsume the apparent contradiction under a more general claim—one for which we have noncontradictory evidence. Or we could let contradictions stand provisionally, to see where such tolerance would lead, to see what the contradiction would enable in the way of understanding. I have already mentioned that some reasoning about moral dilemmas lets contradictions stand, and I believe that letting such contradictions stand sometimes reveals important features of moral life. Further, we could let contradictions stand because that is simply as far as we can get with our reasoning. This fact may lead to new ways of thinking, as when we discovered that there was good evidence that light was composed of particles and good evidence that it was made of waves. Contradictions can be powerful enablers of discovery.

This fact too has a consequence for the teaching of written reasoning. Real contradictions, that is, contradictions that arise from equally compelling arguments for contradictory claims, are wonderfully valuable for purposes of inquiry. When one reasons oneself into a contradiction, one has not only a real point at issue, a real question, but also an engine of discovery, a living conflict. To tell students to rid their papers of contradictions because they undermine the arguments is like telling farmers to destroy their pregnant livestock because pregnant animals cannot do their usual work. Contradictions should be cherished, nurtured, developed. They can bring forth something new. They can serve the purpose of inquiry. Eventually, their contradictoriness may dissolve in some new framework of understanding, but only if they are well cared for along the way, and not prematurely resolved or eliminated.

One can use a similar method to produce more directly forceful writing by deliberately refusing to focus on the thematized conflict, and turning one's attention instead to the suppressed or neglected conflicts at play. One can do this by directly insisting that choices be made where choices were not before apparent. I explained earlier how all argumentation must make affirmations it cannot defend. Once this is known, one knows that there are domains of inquiry that are unexplored by any strand of argumentation that is coherent, any strand that keeps a central conflict in focus. Thus, one can use existing argumentation as a kind of map to domains that have been neglected, domains that can be opened for new inquiry. This is a very powerful and unsettling technique—one used very often in ideological criticism.

Another way to transform the dynamics of argumentation for the purpose of inquiry is to make changes in the speech actions and in the character of the interlocutor. Typically, the argumentative interlocutor questions a claim by asking for reasons. Usually, the claim is questioned only when the interlocutor can imagine a plausible counterclaim, whether it is expressed or not. That is, the conflict is typically between claims which *could* be made explicit. However, we can also ask for reasons without having alternatives in mind—say, in order to test the coherence of a claim with our other knowledge, or just to see where a line of questioning will lead.

An interlocutor can also become a fellow claimant. That is, instead of challenging the claim, the interlocutor can also extend the range of the claim, or apply it in a new way, or explore its consequences, or clarify it. An interlocutor can play the role of enabler for the claimant, helping in the formulation and development of the claim, finding analogous claims, or linking the claim to a system of claims in some way. This reasoning is still a kind of call and response, but its aim is not the justification of a claim but the exploration and development of claims. In such exchange, the explicit challenging of the claim has been suspended. Instead, the claimants challenge each other to keep coming up with a new extension or application or development of the claim—as if jazz musicians were improvising on a theme. The purpose is to find something new to say, to find a new way of letting things be understood. The challenging, questioning interlocutor and the universal audience which demands such an interlocutor are not useful in such a situation. They can be called back if and when the claimants want to test their understanding before a more diverse or more general audience.

I believe that we ought to find a place for writing that reflects this kind of process. Such writing makes unusual demands on readers because it tends to run against our expectations that a claim needs to be defended before it is extended or applied or linked to other claims. However, to insist that writing, especially student writing, consistently and universally meet this expectation is myopic and destructive. Ideas need room to develop, and people who want to learn to think must be given opportunities to work ideas into shape. I have seen student writing subjected to incredibly exacting demands, with challenges and impossible questions written alongside almost every line. I have known teachers who were so taken with their own power to detect logical weaknesses that they frequently failed to grasp what their students were trying to say—even though it would have been relatively clear to most other people. In such a case, how can teachers help students say what they are trying to say? Again, in the end, what is developed in this kind of writing may eventually have to stand up to the critical scrutiny of a demanding audience, but if it had to stand up to such an audience at every point along the way, it would never have a chance to discover something worth saying. Newness may arise more easily in rhetorical environments sustained by particular audiences than in those which are projected by universal ones. The difficult choices teachers must make concern deciding when to fulfill which role—how best to "lead the soul" of each student.

Another way to modify argumentation for the purpose of inquiry is to change the way conflict is contained—that is, to depacify reason. I argued in Chapter 4 that written argumentation is an extremely pacified form of conflict, one in which force is contained in reasons. The depacification of argumentation allows for this force to escape its containment in written reasons. Here I think most immediately of computer-mediated communication—basically, always a form of writing—and the way it enables the use of music, visuals, video, and so on. Many of us think of information design and communication in multimedia as a kind of interference with or distraction from strict argumentation. Typically, the nonlinguistic forces of persuasion are believed to affect us without our thinking or reasoning about them. Perceptual inferences are not often matters of choice. They are most forceful when they by-pass argumentative reasoning and communicate influence without the intervention of questions and reasons. They most often claim us without our knowing it explicitly.

However, the difference between containing force in the reasons offered in argumentation and releasing this force so that it flows into visual images or music or something else is always a matter of degree. Violence and pacification, force and reason, define a continuum. The materiality of written argumentation has influence of one kind or another. If written argumentation is the whispering of language, it is at least still whispering. Choice requires influence of some kind if it is not to be arbitrary. Visuals and sound, the feel of paper or the resolution and virtual space of a video screen, fonts and layout—these all have influence. Letting ourselves be affected by them is, in one sense, less strictly rational than letting ourselves be affected by argumentation. However, they also provide new kinds of influence, and new kinds of influence can bring new claims, new ways of understanding the world and sharing that understanding. There is no reason that inquiry cannot take visual and auditory and tactile forms.

However, the less we question the claims made on us, the less we reason about them. If we loosen the containment of force, we make new kinds of inquiry possible, but we eventually move out of the domain of argumentation. Argumentation is liable to criticism, or lapses into something else altogether, when the claims it makes are made forcefully, without being questioned or supported by reasons. There are other "conversations of inquiry" besides argumentative ones. A building claims us in many ways. It can determine where we walk, what we see and hear and feel, how we get from one place to the next, what our mood is, whether we meet many other people or not, and so on. Buildings can be criticized by way of arguments (i.e., by making their claims on us explicit and questioning them, examining possible reasons to support their claims, etc.); however, they can also be responded to by designing and constructing other buildings, ones that make counterclaims. We could even say that each building offers nonlinguistic "reasons" in support of its claims. The "reasons" would be the full experience of letting oneself be claimed by the building. And here we may have something like a choice. We may have the choice of returning to a building or not, or putting up another building of similar design, and we may make the choice on the basis of the experience of being claimed by the building. Inquiry and learning and newness can occur in this more forceful way, without the pacification of influence demanded by argumentation. In fact, some art is supposed to be forceful in this way, to violently force us into new perspectives, to undo our everyday way of understanding things.

The pacification of influence is one of written argumentation's most important features. In visual communication, in multimedia persuasion, in art and architecture, we are affected directly by images and things we need not imagine. This makes the whispering of language almost inaudible, relatively without influence. In situations of conflict, we tend to mistrust this forceful kind of influence. We rely on written reasoning when we need the consent of an interlocutor or audience who wants to be a fuller participant in the process.

It is interesting to ask whether it might be possible not only to admit more violence into argumentation and so expand its power to inquire but also to pacify images and so cultivate our abilities to argue visually. For example, we could train people to be deep visual critics. Such deep critics not only would be able to identify the force and influence of images, but also would be to some degree immune to this force. For example, instead of making immediate perceptual inferences, or having any immediate experience of the mood of a building, they would identify the claim being made, or the mechanism that creates the mood, and choose whether they thought the influences ("reasons") for having the perception or making the judgment about mood were the right ones. Such deep critics would live in a more pacified perceptual world, a world of arguments in which perceptions and moods were questionable, instead of a world in which we are claimed by them without our having to reason. In some ways, these deep critics would know more than ordinary people, and so their training would have been a training in a kind of inquiry. In another sense, though, they would be insensible to influences that allow most people to see things in new ways without having to reason about them. In this sense, their capacity for inquiry would have been somewhat diminished.

There is an important point here. I have been arguing throughout the book that argumentation is a good way to inquire, to move into new selves, new modes of selfhood, new ways of being in and understanding the world. However, in this chapter, I have shown how modifying argumentation, making it less argumentative in some respects, can also enable inquiry, the discovery of what is new. I believe there is a general truth in this paradox. Philosophers of science recognize this when they say that there is no logic of discovery. What they mean is that there is no single method or family of methods. We discover newness in many different ways. This does not mean that these ways cannot be understood. A rhetoric of reason understands them primarily as having to do with audience, interlocutor, and conflict, and tracks their work within argumentation and out into those areas where argumentation morphs into other kinds of discourse and communication.

A rhetoric of reason brings discovery and justification back together as modifications of the same process, so that their similarities and their inevitable and proper tensions can be better understood. It describes the difference between them without absolutizing it in a metaphysical way—a way that ends up degrading inquiry and discovery and the processes associated with them. Among the most important of these processes are teaching and learning, and specifically the kind of teaching and learning that are focused on inquiry and reasoning themselves. The major site of such teaching and learning in American higher education is in composition.

However, composition is usually not considered in this light. We are the heirs of early modern distinctions which have led to an inevitable degradation of rhetoric and have made scientific discovery incomprehensible and illogical. Our debased understanding of language and writing as mere means of transmitting knowledge follows directly from this tradition. In the twentieth century, the primary use of the word "rhetoric" is pejorative, and the current organization of universities makes a recovery of the rhetorical tradition a near impossibility. The responsibility for sustaining a memory of rhetoric and keeping it in a productive relation with contemporary thought has been fragmented among several disciplines—none of which seems up to the task. In addition, popular conceptions of writing as a "basic skill" (or, as Plato would say, as a "preliminary") are widespread and entrenched—not only among the many groups which make up the funding and service constituencies of the university but also among professors and administrators themselves.

In the final chapter, I will consider recent discussions of the problems higher education faces, and try to show how a recovery of rhetoric and a renewed understanding of the teaching of writing might have more powerful and salutary effects on the enterprise of higher education than have yet been imagined.

9   RHETORIC, ETHICS, AND THE

AIMS OF HIGHER EDUCATION

This book has been primarily concerned with reconstructing the theory of argumentation in a way that responds to contemporary skepticism about reason and argument. It has also been concerned with describing argumentation in ways that will help inform the curricula and the aims of college writing courses. The question of the purpose and content of such courses is a critical—and controversial—issue when it comes to imagining the future of the undergraduate curriculum.

The controversy is nothing new. The ideas of a "general education" and of the "liberal arts" and of a "core curriculum" have all been controversial and vaguely defined. Usually, it has been mostly educators themselves who have participated in the historic controversy about liberal learning. However, the controversy has once again come to attract broader notice, and is receiving renewed public attention. In recent years, we have heard widely publicized charges that higher education has abandoned liberal learning, that it has squandered its "unclaimed legacy," that it has been commandeered by an irrationalist professoriate. More specifically, and this seems to be a common feature in the recent spate of attacks, higher education is said to have failed to convey or instill or transmit the essential values of learning and reason to contemporary students.

The teaching of writing is deeply embroiled in this controversy. In fact, English departments in general and writing programs specifically are at the frontiers and meeting places of a number of conflicting social forces and expectations. One frontier is the frontier I have tried to work in this book—the frontier where contemporary philosophy and traditional conceptions of reason and argument are in conflict. For those who have the luxury of simply dismissing these contemporary philosophical challenges, the situation of English departments and writing programs, struggling to respond to them, may look simply silly.[1] For those of us who are assigned to work this frontier, the situation looks very different. We have to teach skeptical graduate students—future teachers themselves—who are more than familiar with recent intellectual history, and more than dubious about the traditional mission of higher education. We have to work with increasingly diverse and poorly read undergraduates, many of whom do not share the cultural expectations or the abilities that higher education's critics take for granted. Working through the difficult philosophical threads that make up our concepts of reason and argument is an absolute imperative in the current context of diversity and skepticism.

English departments and writing programs are also deeply embroiled in the vexing controversies about race, class, and gender—about multiculturalism in general—that current critics find so enraging. Such critics seem to think that these problems have been created whole cloth out of the imaginations of foolish professors. Nothing could be further from the truth. The world of the writing classroom is a world in which these issues have concrete reality; they are instantiated in the very real difficulties and conflicts students face in their efforts to claim an education. Writing programs are unlike other departments in that the frontier we work is a global and universal one. Virtually *all* students in public universities take writing courses. At most institutions, this means we must teach students from China and Japan and Singapore and Korea and Europe and Africa and Canada and Central and South America. We must teach students who were born and schooled in the United States and yet who speak English as a second language. We must teach African Americans, Chicano-Latinos, Native Americans, Asian Americans, Northern and Southern European Americans—everyone. Such students often speak different dialects, have different communicative styles, different values. Some are very poor; some are wealthy. The men and women communicate and learn in different ways, too. The questions students ask, the expectations they have about learning, vary to an extent that is sometimes difficult to imagine. Delivering higher education to a group of adults this diverse has been attempted only once in all of history—during our own lifetimes. And the only professors who engage this vast diversity are the ones who teach the universally required communication courses—usually the writing courses.

Writing is a culturally thick activity, dense with culturally specific norms and expectations. Written reasoning is a profound historical and cultural achievement, the result of literally millennia of human effort; it is not simply a natural endowment. To cultivate this ability in today's students is an immense challenge, a challenge in which the many complicated demands of multiculturalism must be negotiated concretely with individual classes, individual students, in the very practical work of renewing the hope of reason, the hope of resolving conflicts and furthering knowledge through communication, in the highly deliberate and public medium of writing. After fulfilling their writing requirements, students whose cultural proficiencies lie elsewhere than in written reasoning can flee from the humanities to technical-mathematical fields and complete their distribution requirements by enrolling in large lecture courses where papers are not likely to be required. Professors of philosophy and history need never encounter such students in any numbers. Writing programs, on the other hand, are the site both where these students encounter the humanities and where humanities professors encounter these students. It is no wonder that English departments have recognized how precarious the communication between students and the professoriate has become, how concrete the problems of contemporary philosophy and multiculturalism really are.

However, to confront these problems head-on is sometimes more dangerous than to ignore them. Linda Brodkey and her colleagues at the University of Texas at Austin developed a writing curriculum that made issues of race, class, and gender the focus of the written reasoning students would practice in their writing courses. Brodkey proposed using legal cases as material for students to read, so that they could become familiar with the sophisticated forms of reasoning these issues call for in the context of law and public debate. In one way, her strategy was to follow Gerald Graff's advice to "teach the conflicts." Since differences in race, class, and gender make up such a great part of the conflicts people experience in communication, why not make these conflicts themselves the subject about which students reason and write, about which they communicate? However, the conflict built into this course was too much for her critics. They charged that she had highjacked the writing program and used it for ideological ends. They said that she was not teaching "writing" but something else. They effectively put an end to her project.[2]

This example helps to point up one great temptation higher education faces when it comes to the teaching of writing. This is the temptation to disentangle itself from messy issues caused by ambitions about improving students' abilities to reason convincingly and well in writing. Instead one lowers one's sights and teaches not written reasoning, not writing as communication, but "writing" conceived of as a set of subskills that are independent of any purpose. In its most fragmented form, this program imagines that a college course in writing should be focused predominantly on spelling, grammar, punctuation, usage, and perhaps style.

However, there are very powerful reasons for believing that such a program is futile. Most powerful of all are the countless empirical studies of such educational efforts. In the conclusion to his review of empirical research on written composition, George Hillocks writes: "The study of traditional school grammar (i.e. the definition of parts of speech, the parsing of sentences, etc.) has no effect on raising the quality of student writing. Every other focus of instruction examined in this review is stronger. Taught in certain ways, grammar and mechanics instruction has a deleterious effect on student writing. In some studies a heavy emphasis on mechanics and usage (e.g. marking every error) resulted in significant losses of overall quality."[3] Those who propose educational programs of this sort do so in the face of an immense body of research that advises against it.

The question is not whether students need to gain greater control of their writing in respect to grammar, mechanics, and usage. The question is how such improvement is best accomplished. There is in fact good evidence that many of the errors students make in writing are not a result of their lacking grammatical competence. Brooke Neilson found that students who make errors in a formal register (say, in argumentative essays) may make no errors at all in an informal register (say, in personal narratives). This is not because they are attempting different syntactic constructions in the formal register, because she found that the same *kinds* of construction were present in both the narratives and the arguments she studied. The students have a basic grammatical competence; it is not that they have not acquired English grammar. To teach them the parts of speech and how to diagram sentences would be beside the point; it would mean only that they would have less time for practicing writing as communication. Register is not a sentence-level feature of discourse, and register-related difficulties cannot be addressed by instruction focused at the sentence level. Rather, register is a feature of whole discourses and texts. It is closely related to the pragmatic features of discourse, and it can be addressed only in the context of purposeful communication.

Neilson uses her data to argue that errors in adult writing are best understood as matters of performance and not competence. The linguistic concept of competence is usually an all-or-nothing matter. Most people acquire competence in their native language by the age of eight or nine. Neilson's research shows that her adult writers have linguistic competence, but that they have performance breakdowns when the cognitive demands of a writing task are unfamiliar or unusually difficult. Since they have competence in the linguistic sense, their errors are best understood as performance errors—a result not of incompetence but of other features of the communicative situation.

However, Neilson also imagines that the idea of competence itself might stand some revision. From one angle, competence is not an all-or-nothing matter. It must be acquired anew in different contexts of performance. Neilson's work shows that we can elicit error by increasing the abstractness of a writing task, moving from personal narrative to argumentation, moving from a known to an unknown audience, or, in linguistic terms, changing from an informal to a formal register. As one moves into these new writing contexts, one must renew one's sentence-level proficiencies. In this context, error can be seen not simply as a problem to be corrected but as a sign that learning is going on, that students are rising to the task of attempting more advanced sorts of writing.[4]

In her conclusion, Neilson makes one final judgment about the teaching of writing. She urges that teachers of writing question more seriously the commonplace that basic writers, or writers who make errors, are somehow more like children than other adults—that they are stuck at a lower developmental stage, that they are linguistically or syntactically immature. The consequences of such a view are often to pull such adults out of the regular curriculum and address their errors directly. However, everything we know about such educational efforts leads us to predict that such an approach not only is futile but could be positively harmful. What students need above all is more guided experience in the kind of writing that is expected of them. They need more familiarity with more diverse and more universal audiences, with audiences which demand more explicit reasoning than do the audiences associated with informal writing situations and tasks.

Error-prone writers need practice at cognitively demanding and purposeful writing tasks. The last thing they need is to be trained to focus their attention on their errors while the better-prepared students gain even more practice at writing to communicate. Instead, error-prone writers need to be given even more practice at written reasoning about real conflicts with real interlocutors and audiences. They need to acquire the habits of written conversation, the experience of reasoning in writing. If the researchers are right, then as basic writers gain these habits, the competence they already display in speech and informal writing will begin to show up in their performance in written reasoning.

What is true of basic writers is a fortiori true of all writers. Although linguistic competence is gained at a very young age, competence at written reasoning comes much later. Neilson cites Potter as reporting that a practical division between formal and informal registers begins to be found in writers who are about fifteen years old, an age that corresponds roughly with Piaget's estimate of the onset of formal operations. My own view of these developmental theories is that age is less important here than experience. The social contexts for written reasoning are just not available to most people until very late in high school or in college. The interlocutors and audiences and the claims and challenges which arise in argumentative writing are not present just anywhere. If young people do not begin to show a recognition of some of the features of written reasoning until late in their teens, then this does not leave much time for practice and teaching in high school. When students come from other cultures or from cultural groups in which argumentative reasoning is practiced in different ways or with relatively less frequency, the lack of experience is even more marked. The problem such students face is not that they are "developmentally delayed," or in some sense more like children than like adults; it is rather that they are less experienced in writing as a form of communication and reasoning.

Last term, I taught the introductory writing course in our own required writing sequence at the University of Oregon. One of my students was a young Chinese woman who wrote a really remarkable essay which tried to answer the question of whether China should have a national dialect. To answer this question, she focused on the problem of the relations of Guangdong province to the rest of China. She came into the course with a solid grasp of the formal principles of Introduction-Body-Conclusion (gained in her ESL course) and prose that showed some features of Chinese-English interlanguage. At the conclusion of the course, she wrote a reflective essay which included the following remarks:

> Before I took this course, I . . . got suggestions from my friends. Most of my friends who are international students think that Writing 121 is very difficult for foreign students because Writing 121 focuses on critical thinking, which is the way Americans write and the way Americans think. This is totally different from what we learned in our country . . .
>
> During the first two weeks, the course was very challenging to me. I couldn't catch the main idea of critical thinking and writing . . . In Writing 121 we had . . . to develop out our own ideas. That was the first challenge for me. Although I did not do well at the beginning of course, I got the feedback from my professor and classmates. Reading through those commentaries, I realized the problems in my paper. That was the most valuable part of those course for me, because people shared their suggestions for improving my paper. Those are meaningful to me. From other people's suggestions, I tried to make my ideas more clear . . . and consider other people's opposing opinions in order to make my paper better.

The writer goes on to identify "three processes" that she worked on as she continued in the course. First was the problem of focus and selecting specific examples appropriate to the focus. Second was the related problem of matching the evidence to the conclusion. Third was the technique of delaying her thesis statement—her answer to a question—until she had more completely described the situation from which the question arose, as well as why the question was a significant one.

She ends her essay by saying that she became very interested in the conclusion to the first version of her last paper and by making a general observation:

> Actually, I thought I made a good conclusion, because I used my country's writing style. In the conclusion, our writing style often has a perfect ending, even though there are still some problems existing. People usually ignore the problems and assume everything's aright. But after revising my paper, I realized that it's better to recognize problems . . .
>
> At the beginning of this course, I felt very nervous. But after learning in this class, the feeling has changed. I learned a lot of different ideas from classmates and was encouraged by my professor. They were very patient with me and gave me a lot of valuable suggestions. And also . . . I learned something about myself. The American thinking process and how they express themselves are totally different from what I learned in my country . . .

This student locates her learning in the course almost entirely in two areas: first, in increased exposure to the commentaries, objections, ideas, and suggestions of her classmates (which she found to be valuable, meaningful, and encouraging); second, in her slow adjustment to the expectation that she engage in "developing out" her own ideas, or in "critical thinking" (not a term I used in the course). From her essay, she seems to mean by this acknowledging problems, qualifying one's conclusions, and using the comments and objections of other people to develop one's own reasoning. She locates her own difficulties in a lack of cultural experience, a lack of familiarity with "the way Americans write and the way Americans think."

I believe that most students who learn a great deal in their writing courses could make analogous statements about a lack of experience and familiarity with the practice of written reasoning. One need not have been educated in China to recognize that the demands of written reasoning in college are substantially different from the demands of the previous writing situations one has faced. Students who fail to recognize this are often the students who have the most difficulty with their writing. They are the students who persist in believing that correcting their sentence-level errors and meeting the simplified formal requirements of Introduction-Body-Conclusion are not simply the "preliminaries" to good writing but the substance of actually writing well.

My student, and other students like her, need more practical experience with real interlocutors and audiences of the kind that can inform and strengthen their written reasoning. They need more practice at trying to write convincingly and well in the context or real communicative challenges. They do not need to be isolated and treated like children; quite the opposite.

Now, one could agree with this general argument against remedializing college students and still not believe that college writing courses should focus on written reasoning or argumentation. One might believe instead that students should become familiar with and learn to write in a whole array of contemporary genres. *The St. Martin's Guide to Writing,* one of the most popular textbooks for college composition, presents just such an array, complete with an analysis of the purpose and audience of each genre, its basic features, advice about invention and research in the genre, planning and drafting, revising and editing, and learning from the process. The book includes several models of writing in each genre, as well as process-oriented documents of a "writer at work" at each kind of writing. The book covers "Remembering Events," "Remembering People," "Writing Profiles," "Reporting Information," "Taking a Position," "Proposing Solutions," "Making Evaluations," "Speculating about Causes," and "Interpreting Literature." I want to say right out that this book is superior to almost all of its competitors. It is informed by current research on writing to a degree that is rare in writing textbooks and anthologies. It is intelligent, well conceived, and well designed, and it is interesting to read. It is a representation of the best in the "array of genres" approach to the teaching of writing.

However, I believe that this approach, even at its best, has some marked limitations. I find the most serious limitations to be in its limited goals and in the way it confines itself to a "literaturized" version of rhetoric. The genres and models it collects are heavily journalistic and belletristic-literary. The only academic discipline represented as a genre is—surprise, surprise—literary studies. Most of the other genres appear to have been collected from contemporary magazines and popular writing of the kind which would be appreciated by literature professors. There is nothing wrong with this, but it is a very specific concept of "writing" that is at play here. The models come from *Time, Newsweek,* the *New Republic, Playboy,* the *Los Angeles Times,* and the *Harvard Crimson.* They are excerpted from books written by Russell Baker, Annie Dillard, Gretel Ehrlich, Linda Ellerbee, Sue Hubbell, John McPhee, David Owen, Richard Rodriguez, and E. B. White.

The assumptions are these. "Writing" is what is done by widely acknowledged "authors" (professional writers) in widely accessible publications. The primary qualifying feature of this kind of writing is its literary-aesthetic merit. "Writing" in this sense breaks down into the genres of contemporary nonfiction prose: autobiography, biography, profile, proposal, causal analysis, etc.[5] The teaching of writing includes helping students to become familiar with these different literary genres by providing models, explaining their basic features, showing students the work-in-process of writers working in the genre, and describing the composing process for each genre. The teaching of writing also includes helping each student have some experience of writing in the genre in order to gain practical familiarity with it.

My own view is that this is an outstanding approach to teaching a course in a literature or English department that might have the name "An Introduction to Contemporary Nonfiction Prose." It would also be a fine course to teach in a comprehensive writing department—say, "Writing Nonfiction Prose." However, I do not believe that it has as great a claim on the required writing courses that make up such an important part of the general education curricula of most colleges and universities. I cannot see any good reason for compelling all students to become acquainted with the genres of contemporary nonfiction prose understood in this literary sense. In fact, I believe that such an approach to the required writing curriculum is itself indicative of the decline and oblivion into which rhetoric has fallen.

In his history of rhetoric, George Kennedy notes that a cycle of decline seems to be built into the history of rhetoric: "It has been a persistent characteristic of classical rhetoric, in almost every phase of its ancient and modern history, to move from primary into secondary forms. For this phenomenon the Italian term *letteraturizzazione* is convenient shorthand. *Letteraturizzazione* is the tendency of rhetoric to shift its focus from persuasion to narration, from civic to personal contexts, and from discourse to literature . . ." (5). Kennedy offers two explanations of this tendency. First is the practice of teaching rhetoric to young children—a kind of pedagogicalizing of rhetoric. Second is the fact that rhetoric as a discipline declines as the opportunities for meaningful public and social communicative action declines. Here Kennedy refers to the oscillations in "the opportunities, or lack of opportunities, open to primary rhetoric throughout history."

The idea is that if there is a public sphere, some domain of argumentative discourse within which people can take action in language, resolve disputes, further common projects, then rhetoric thrives in a primary form. There are purposes for rhetoric—civic, public purposes as well as more individual and personal ones. However, when and where this domain contracts, and the opportunities for successful argumentation are diminished, then rhetoric falls into "secondary rhetoric." Secondary rhetoric is focused not so much on accomplishing social and civic purposes by way of reasoning and speech as on the forms and techniques of writing considered as objects of study in themselves. It is more oriented toward a literary and aesthetic view of language than toward a pragmatic and purposeful one.

Kennedy also notes that this shifting from primary to secondary rhetoric is accompanied by a change in focus from speech to writing. He believes that one important feature of this change in focus is that speeches tend to be made on particular occasions to particular people for particular purposes. Speech is typically understood in terms of its appropriateness to the occasion, audience, and purpose. Writing tends to be thought of as separate from this context, and so tends to be thought of less as communication and more as an objectified "text," something understood in terms of its formal features and aesthetic properties. However, a rhetoric of written reasoning returns writing and reasoning to a communicative context, and so imagines the teaching of writing as the cultivation of an ability for primary rhetoric.

The field of composition in its current state and in some of its manifestations is in some important respects a field in which the process of *letteraturizzazione* has completed itself. Composition is concerned with writing and not with speech. It is often thought of as a kind of developmental or "educational" field which focuses on teaching adults what they should have learned as children. It is often believed to be legitimated by the apparent evidence that students need remedial work in writing. Often, too, students may "test out" of writing courses, and almost always they are "tracked" into different levels of an ostensible sequence of courses that runs from practice at subskills to more advanced work in different genres. The writing that students are asked to do, this writing in the different genres of contemporary nonfiction prose, is supposed to be purposeful, but the purposes are accidental adjuncts to learning the genres. The purposes are not the students' purposes. Students learn *that* there are purposes for the different genres as they learn their basic features and study models. However, the curriculum makes the overriding purpose obvious: the production of writing according to the conventions of nonfiction prose genres. This is the literaturization of rhetoric, the objectification of the literary text, the separation of writing from actual communicative purposes and contexts.

I want to make it clear that composition as secondary rhetoric is composition in its healthy state. Composition as "literaturized rhetoric," especially when joined to sound writing pedagogy (as in the case of the *St. Martin's Guide to Writing*), is preferable by far to the remedialization of students (and rhetoric) found in misguided attempts to found a writing program on the correction of student errors.

It is also preferable by far to equally misguided programs which teach students to write other sorts of arrays of essays—say, in different "rhetorical modes." Walter Beale has shown convincingly that "modes and strategies are not *types* of discourse but *operations* of discourse: They do not stand alone but exist within functional hierarchies of individual works of discourse, fulfilling the particular purposes and expectations of those works. They are *ways* of conducting discourse rather than *reasons* for conducting discourse" (30-31). A "modes" approach to the teaching of writing either conflates ways of conducting discourse with reasons for conducting discourse, or separates "ways" and "operations" from rhetorical purposes, setting the latter aside to focus on the former. That is, it plants itself firmly in the domain of secondary rhetoric, objectifying the techniques and strategies of writing independently of any consideration of their communicative and pragmatic context.[6]

Beale finds that composition as a field shows a decidedly formalist cast—even when the "forms" in question are "processes." He advises that we need guidance of the sort that would come from refusing the literaturization or "textualization" of writing. This guidance "is partially *inside* the rhetorical text but partially *outside* the text, in the situation, the system of 'exigencies' to which the text is a response, and just as importantly, in the traditions of texts that respond to similar situations. This is the kind of knowledge specified by a pragmatic or contextual theory of rhetoric, focused on the 'rich, concrete event, in which features interpenetrate.' The importance of such a theory is bound up in the importance of rhetorical discourse and rhetorical education themselves as forms of culture" (171). Thus, Beale too is recommending a turn away from the formalist, literaturized teaching of writing that objectifies the text as something independent of purpose and communication and a return to the concept and practice of primary rhetoric. Seen in this way, the "modes" approach is just another symptom of the decline and oblivion of rhetoric—and is riddled by its own internal confusions besides.

What we could call the "Texas problem" is that when a writing program seems to take writing seriously as communication that is oriented toward reasoning about public issues and conflicts, and conducts students into conversations that are carried on in law and public policy, the program becomes vulnerable to charges that it is not teaching "writing" but instead furthering some ideology, or trespassing on some particular discipline's turf. The tempting response to these charges is to retreat to a safer "literaturized" version of rhetoric—to focus on grammar and mechanics, or to teach literary nonfictional genres, or to default to the teaching of modes. The problems with such approaches are that they either violate the best research and theory available about how people learn to write or abandon the whole project of rhetoric—the project of teaching written reasoning as a way of resolving conflicts, furthering knowledge, and strengthening one's ability to communicate reasonably and well in writing *for some actual purpose.*

An approach to the teaching of writing informed by a pragmatic rhetoric of reason offers an alternative here. One need not turn toward the safety and irrelevance of literaturized rhetoric to avoid the real danger of converting writing courses into some other kind of course with some other kind of goal. The alternative a rhetoric of reason presents to a program of "teaching the conflicts" is to take a step back and teach students *how to have productive and meaningful conflicts.* The process of conflict itself, in the context of written reasoning, can be the orienting idea and educational focus of a program in written reasoning. This both prevents some particular set of conflicts from becoming the subject of the course, and also keeps the teaching of writing focused on actual communication and reasoning.

In order to clarify this point, it is necessary perhaps to sketch a rough picture of what such a program in writing instruction might look like. Throughout this book I have been reluctant to do this. This reluctance stems from a number of concerns. First, there are many different ways to use a theory of written reasoning to inform the teaching of writing. One cannot deduce a pedagogy or a syllabus from a theory of argumentation. Many very different courses and programs could be consistent with parts of the theory, and to many different degrees and in different respects. Second, by describing a course or program, I might be taken to be recommending it to others—regardless of their local situation, their particular teaching staffs, the beliefs and preferences of their faculty, and so on. Yet writing requirements and courses are usually adaptations to these local conditions. The success of a writing program depends in critical ways on faculty and administrative support and collaboration. A curriculum that is out of alignment with the well-established practices and preferences of the teaching staff is hardly appropriate for that staff—no matter how abstractly ideal such a curriculum might be.

Further, my own judgments about what is practicable are based largely on my own experience directing writing programs and supervising graduate students and postdoctoral instructors at two public research universities over the last twelve years. My judgments about what is actually feasible in writing courses may not have the range I intend for them. I know, for example, that what is possible at a small four-year liberal arts college may not be at all possible for a large research university—and vice versa. Finally, what makes a course or program effective is not simply the theory that informs it and the teaching practices that are aligned with the theory. Besides the pedagogy, there are the countless intangibles that make some courses and programs thriving intellectual projects and leave others mechanical exercises of burdensome duties. I could not begin to describe the details and vicissitudes of such variables here—although much of my work as a writing program administrator is taken up with just such unsystematizable matters.

With those qualifications, let me describe what a course in written reasoning might look like, and how the theory of argumentation might help solve some of the problems of imagining writing courses that would fulfill the ambitions I have mentioned. First, a course in written reasoning should reflect the fact that writers need real interlocutors and audiences—a real rhetorical community. This means, above all, that students must write in order to communicate with one another. They are each other's audience. The teacher is an audience for them as well, but students must learn to use one another to think and write well. Reasoning is an act of adapting to particular rhetorical situations. What someone learns in a course in written reasoning is not how to write a generically "OK" paper, but how to act on other people, how to reason with them in the most convincing manner available, how to engage in inquiry in a context of high expectations. Knowing how to adapt one's written communication to the task and the context and the audience is knowledge that can be carried from task to task, audience to audience.

Students are capable of being very different kinds of audiences for each other. They can respond to one another's writing in terms of very particular beliefs, values, and knowledge or they can be more universal or paragon audiences for one another. As a course progresses, and students become more and more aware of each other as particular audiences, they seem to become more and more interested in being paragon audiences for one another, and they seem to become more and more proficient at imagining themselves collectively as sharing a way of being an audience—a kind of local paragon for this particular group of students. I take this to be a part of the process of becoming better educated.

Since students are each other's primary audiences, most of the communication that goes on in a course should go on among students. If I pass a writing classroom and find that day after day, week after week, a teacher is standing in front of a class talking to students, or calling on students to answer questions, I conclude that something has gone seriously wrong. Unless students communicate with each other frequently,

Part Four: Argument, Inquiry, and Education

they cannot learn to use each other as interlocutors and audiences, and they cannot learn to be effective interlocutors and audiences for one another. There are a great many things for a teacher to do in a writing course, but taking up most of the class time with his or her own speeches is not among them.

However, education is in part a process of becoming acquainted with new interlocutors—interlocutors who are more knowledgeable and experienced than oneself, interlocutors from different historical periods and different cultures. It is also a process of entering conversations that are already in progress, of discovering and participating in conversations that are historically well developed and that have attracted interlocutors of a quality that is unusual. Thus, I strongly believe that students must converse with interlocutors and enter conversations that are available to them only through reading.

Not all writing programs and courses take reading seriously in this way. One kind of writing course allows students to discuss the significance and value of, say, African American studies courses by relying on their own experience and ideas and whatever articles they can discover or interviews they can conduct on the topic. Another kind of writing course asks the students to include Cornel West and bell hooks in the conversation, to "take responsibility" for them, as Levinas would say, to acknowledge them as interlocutors in the conversation. One kind of writing course asks students to write about "work" based on their own experiences and what they have heard from others. Another kind of writing course asks them to listen to the voices of working people in Studs Terkel's *Working* and to allow Henry Thoreau or Karl Marx or Ivan Illich a place in their conversation. A conversation of this sort gives students not simply the opportunity to express the opinions that have arisen from their experience and their talk with each other, but also the opportunity to reason more deeply and extensively about working, to learn to understand their own experience in the light of a larger context, and to explore that larger, historical, cultural, public world in the light of their own experiences. Helping students to write their way into these conversations will take one out of the safe domain of more personal, literaturized rhetoric, and it will make one vulnerable to charges of putting ideology before "writing." After all, one will have to make judgments about the quality and appropriateness of the conversations students will enter. This is the case even if one focuses on teaching the students *how to have* conflicts instead of simply on the conflict/conversation itself. However, I believe that it is our professional duty to discover and communicate such conversations/conflicts to our students, to take responsibility for judging their worth and their appropriateness for the task of teaching writing, and to continue to argue about such matters among ourselves.

I believe that several general principles can be of help here. First, issues about which teachers and students already have very strong commitments are not usually useful for the teaching of written reasoning. People can argue only concerning those things about which they are willing to learn, and change their minds. If the goal is to teach writing as a kind of reasoning, as a form of inquiry, then the issue must be one about which both the teacher and the students have a relatively open mind, about which they are willing to learn from one another. We don't argue when we are unwilling to change our minds. Some things are simply too important to some of us to argue about in a genuine way in the classroom.

Second, yes/no, up/down, good/bad issues—conflicts about which there are only two opposite positions—provide little room for inquiry and reason. They may be useful for debate or for other purposes, but they do not call on writers to make use of one another to reason and learn in the ways that are appropriate in a context of inquiry and communication. Such issues force students into predetermined polarized positions instead of challenging them to forge new positions, to learn, to find new approaches by reasoning with one another.

Third, conflicts that are familiar from the popular press have both advantages and disadvantages. On the one hand, students have some common knowledge about these matters, and are able to hold discussions on these issues without much additional preparation. It is also likely that they are interested in such issues; an interest in them has already been legitimated by the attention given to them on television, radio, and in the newspapers. On the other hand, such issues can lead to superficial discussion and writing. If the only information students rely on is what they have already absorbed through television and hearsay, then it is difficult to make the discussions in the writing course any different from discussions students already hold informally among themselves. Further, many students have already dealt with such issues in their high school courses, and they rightly wonder why such well-rehearsed discussions are being repeated in college.

Having students write about conflicts in their personal lives also has serious disadvantages. The turn to the personal is a feature of the "literaturization" of rhetoric that Kennedy describes, and I have already offered my arguments for a rhetoric that has public and social meaning. However, I also believe that asking students to write about their own experiences of personal conflicts and to reason their way through them in writing often leads to an impasse in the progress of discussion and reasoning. The validity claims that arise when people write about their feelings, beliefs, and experiences and the ways they came to their own conclusions about personal choices are not claims about publicly accessible matters. This is true in two senses. First, claims of this kind raise questions of personal sincerity and self-knowledge, questions about how honestly and accurately people grasp their own experience. To resolve such questions in a classroom, in a public context, means to try to make judgments about the quality of an individual's self-understanding. It is very difficult for me to see what could legitimate forcing all students to take courses in this kind of group therapy. Second, even if we did want to make this the focus of writing courses, it is very hard to see how the members of a writing class—strangers to one another—could gain enough knowledge about each other's lives to reason helpfully and intelligently about each other's personal conflicts. The facts in these cases are not accessible to just anyone. They cannot be researched in the library or on the Internet.

Having said this, let me also say right away that a rhetoric of reason has a whole host of consequences for our thinking about how individuals resolve personal and "internal" conflicts, as well as for our concepts of development and therapy. The idea that reason is an orchestration of voices and that the most important feature of the conversation among these voices is their ethical relations with one another is immensely important for our theories of self and ego, for our understanding of mental health and pathology. In *Invisible Guests: The Development of Imaginal Dialogues,* Mary Watkins has elaborated a critique of standard theories of development which imagine maturity and health as the silencing of inner voices and the ascendance of monological thinking. Instead, she proposes that health and fulfillment can be found in lively, thriving inner dialogues. Pathology is a consequence of ethical failures in the relations among these inner voices—an inability to hold the inner dialogue of reason. Therapy is restoring respect and a capacity for productive conversation and conflict resolution among these "invisible guests."

Thus, there may be immensely important uses of a rhetorical theory of reason in therapy and in designing writing sequences for therapeutic situations. There may also be important implications here for how courses in autobiography and personal narrative could be designed. Although I do not believe that such therapy or such writing courses should be required of all students, I do believe that for some people such courses or such therapy may be far more important than the writing instruction I am recommending here. However, I am concerned with the senses in which rhetoric and written reasoning might make a claim to be at the center of the undergraduate curriculum, and this leads me to imagine quite different purposes for writing. In the context of this concern, the conflicts that are more relevant are more public conflicts.

Also very important are the conflicts between what is convincing in terms of the student's own experience and knowledge and what is convincing for a broader college audience with diverse kinds of experience and knowledge. That is, the conflicts students undergo as they enter new conversations in a more diverse domain are also very important for them to write about. Reflective essays which look back on the changes in their own writing offer students the opportunity to learn about their own learning, to grasp more deeply the process of learning *how* to have conflicts. Regular reflective essays are a critical part of any writing curriculum which teaches the process of conflict itself. In my own classes, students write a first version of a paper, write commentaries on each other's first versions, write second versions which incorporate responses to those commentaries, then write a reflective essay which focuses on the differences between the two versions. For each conflict/conversation the students enter, they also step back and reflect on the process of conflict/conversation itself.

Let me turn now to give an example of the kind of conflict with which I think courses in written reasoning might usefully concern themselves. The example is taken from part 2 of Malcolm Kiniry's and Mike Rose's *Critical Strategies,* which offers a small library/anthology of "readings for academic writing." I do not intend to claim that Kiniry and Rose's approach is the best one for all writing courses in all institutions. Local conditions vary greatly. The appropriateness of the conflicts on which we focus depends on our institutions, their faculties, the students and their backgrounds, the structure and purpose of the undergraduate curriculum, and the places and years in which we teach. What is a productive conflict for students in a city college in a large East Coast city may not be at all productive for students at the University of Idaho, and vice versa.

In part 2 of their book, Kiniry and Rose offer students "miniature libraries" on several topics, Women and Power, Caribbean Fiction, The Causes and Treatments of Schizophrenia, Apes and Language, and then two "field research" chapters—What's Funny? and Exploring the Discourse of Your Own Major. They divide each library into two parts: (1) Framing the Issues and (2) Complicating the Issues. The chapter on schizophrenia is introduced by a short section on terminology, which also lists a number of questions that arise in and among the readings. The "Framing the Issues" section begins with a poem by a person diagnosed as schizophrenic. It also includes a short history of the concept of schizophrenia, four case studies, and a selection from the *Diagnostic and Statistical Manual of Mental Disorders* which describes the criteria for diagnosing schizophrenia. The second section, "Complicating the Issues," offers different theories about the causes and treatments of schizophrenia, and its eleven selections include contributions from therapists, researchers, and a patient.

What I find admirable in this "minilibrary" is, first, the way it bypasses the temptations that draw so many writing courses off the path. Conflicts about the causes and treatment of schizophrenia are not conflicts on which many people are highly polarized. There is room to learn and reason about this issue, and to learn about learning and reasoning in the process. Second, this is not a good/bad, yes/no conflict. There are many different reasonable approaches to the questions at issue here. Third, this is a conflict that requires that students learn something. The readings are there not just to provoke a discussion or because of some vague notion that reading is important. Instead, the readings give students a genuine *introduction* into a genuine conversation about a genuine conflict. Their writing about the issue depends on their making an entry into the conversation. Otherwise, they will simply be unable to discover what the conflict is all about, unable to make it their own, to assume some responsibility in the conversation. They cannot simply relay the hearsay to which they have already been exposed. Needless to say, I hope, students will find in these readings the conflicts that are important to them, and these may not be the conflicts that the teacher believes are important or even relevant. Teachers can be effective leaders of discussions and participants in them—and so can help students discover features of the readings they may not have noticed—but in the end students themselves must be agents in this process, and the conflicts they find important and meaningful in their reading and in their discussions are the conflicts about which they should write.

It is certainly possible that some students will have had some experience with schizophrenia in their families and friends, or even some direct personal experience. Such students will bring important voices, experience, and knowledge to their writing, and will be able to add to the conversation in significant ways. Their writing should be an opportunity for them to learn how to use experience of this sort to reason in a conversation that has many different participants who may have different and even conflicting experiences.

The causes and treatment of schizophrenia will be a distant issue for most students. However, there is a great deal in the "Framing the Issues" section to awaken one's emotions and quicken one's interest in the conflict. The poem and case studies will be riveting for some people. (They were for me; they were also alarming in a number of indistinct ways.) I also imagine that most people will be unable to prevent themselves from engaging in self-diagnosis when they read the APA's diagnostic criteria for schizophrenia. These preliminary readings present the sufferings of particular people, as well as a history and description of the concept which is supposed to grasp and explain their suffering. The readings can generate a whole host of questions for students to explore—some of which are prompted in the apparatus supplied by Kiniry and Rose.

The success of these preliminary readings depends on their stirring students to ask their own questions, or to own the questions raised by Kiniry and Rose. If these readings failed to do this, even with the best efforts of the teacher and students (and I believe the teacher is the most critical variable here), then they would be inappropriate for that teacher and those students. Whether readings succeed can be judged by how well students are able to hold conflict-discovering discussions about them. Leading and guiding and sustaining these discussions are what I take partial responsibility for as a teacher. Again, which conflicts arise in the discussion, which conflicts and questions are significant for this audience at this time, is finally dependent on the students. I have a simple rule for the papers my students may write: they must be written in response to a question that was actually raised in class discussion. If the students have questions they want to explore, they had better enter them into the discussion. On good days, when discussion is lively and focused, I find myself spending a great deal of time at the blackboard writing down questions and conflicts I hear in the discussion. (The students not infrequently fail to realize how many questions they broach in an hour's discussion.) On difficult days, I have them read aloud the written questions (of their own making) that they were assigned to bring to class, and we discuss these. Or I read what I believe is a moving or provocative or controversial passage from the readings. Every teacher has a repertoire of such tactics, but in the case of teaching written reasoning the aim is to help the students discover and develop their understanding of claims, questions, conflicts—in general to locate opportunities to reason with one another about issues of mutual concern. If we are successful in this, then the interlocutors in Kiniry and Rose's second part of the chapter, who are giving answers to questions, resolutions to conflicts, will attract our attention in a new way.

Kiniry and Rose's minilibrary on the causes and treatment of schizophrenia is probably not appropriate for all teachers and students of college writing at all institutions. I find it appropriate for my students because the reasoning they are exposed to is beyond their experience but within their reach. The interlocutors they meet are worth their while, worth acknowledging. Judgments about worthy interlocutors are inevitable, and I believe that it is our responsibility to make these judgments according to our best lights, to act out an acknowledgment of others that is a practical refusal of skepticism. There are ways to give students a voice in the choice of issues. I ask my own students to choose from a list of topics/minilibraries I give to them. They have a choice, but only among the topics I offer to them. An interesting feature of this arrangement is that when I began to do this I would have the students vote once at the beginning of the term on which topics they wanted to explore. However, at the end of the term they often expressed regret that they had chosen "safe" topics and not some of the riskier ones I had offered them. As they learned to write for one another, and as they grew more interested in each other's reasoning, they changed their minds about the topics on which they were willing to reason with each other, the topics on which they might be willing to change their minds because of each other. Now, I have them vote on each topic as late as possible, although I miss not having the expressions of regret at the end of the term because they were for me a measure of the success of the class as a self-organizing rhetorical community.

There remains a larger promise to be redeemed here. This is the promise that a rhetoric of reason, and the courses informed by it, could help to justify some of the claims of higher education. I have tried to show how rhetoric can give us a renewed sense of what reason, research, and inquiry really are. I believe that these revised concepts can stand up to the skeptical challenges to reason that have grown in influence in the twentieth century. I want to conclude by confronting the problem of whether a rhetorically informed undergraduate curriculum can meet the challenges of both reason and ethics.

Common to many recent attacks on higher education has been the charge that higher education is in important respects an ethical failure. This charge takes many forms. In some of its manifestations, it is a charge that universities and colleges have failed to transmit an ethical heritage. In other forms, it is a charge that they do not "instill" values the way they should. We hear also that the curriculum is fragmented and offers no unifying vision, that specialization and professionalization have undermined the idea of a liberal education, that ethical relativism rules the day, and so on. Often the critics who make these charges look back to a paleoterrific era in which there was a consensus about the purpose of higher education.

In *Community of Learning: The American College and the Liberal Arts*

Tradition, Francis Oakley shows convincingly that the idea of such a golden age cannot stand up to the historical facts. Higher education has always been a site of controversy about the very purpose of education. Oakley is especially good at showing how the maledictions pronounced against higher education by current critics pale beside the malevolence and vituperation of some of the attacks made in the past. In *Orators and Philosophers: A History of the Idea of Liberal Education,* Bruce Kimball presents massive and compelling evidence that the idea of the liberal arts or of "general learning" has been given countless conflicting meanings. In fact, he organizes his own history of the idea as a history of the most persistent conflicts which arise whenever anyone tries to define what general learning at the higher level should be.

However, Kimball does not take the mere fact of this persistent disagreement to be a good reason for abandoning the idea that higher education has an identifiable mission with its own ethical importance. Instead, he concludes that the "rhetorical" ideal for education that makes up an important part of the liberal arts tradition has been eclipsed by the philosophico-scientific ideal, which has grown in power over the last few centuries as "liberal-free" concepts of education have become dominant and as the research and scientific work of universities has overpowered the other work of higher education. Kimball claims that hope lies in a recovery of the traditions of rhetoric and in the restoration of a balance between the complementary ideals of philosophy and rhetoric.

I want to explore Kimball's ideas in some detail. My own response to the questions he is trying to answer is different from his in some very important respects, but I believe he identifies accurately the source of some of the discontent and incoherence of purpose in higher education. Kimball locates the real origin of the *artes liberales* ideal in Isocrates and finds its first full articulations in Cicero and Quintilian. He describes this educational ideal of rhetoric in the following way. First, the purpose of education is training in citizenship, especially the training of the citizen-leader. Second, this requires that education prescribe and instill values, and third, it requires that the student respect and accept these values, that the student-orator possess both personal and social virtues. Fourth, the source of these values is a body of classical texts, a canon of works that helps students to identify and reach consensus on these values. Fifth, adopting these virtues and expressing them in one's own life and actions mark one as a member of an educated elite of virtuous citizen-leaders. Sixth, this ideal depends on a basic dogmatism about values. Students are simply informed about values; they are not expected or encouraged or educated to inquire into their nature, source, or legitimacy. Finally, although these elite citizen-educators provide so-

290

Part Four: Argument, Inquiry, and Education

cial benefits, the development of such individuals, and thus the idea of
education, are good in themselves, their own end.

Kimball calls the contrasting ideal the "liberal-free" ideal. He locates
its origin in the new science of early modernity, and finds it coming to
full expression in the seventeenth and eighteenth centuries. He insists
that, like the *artes liberales* ideal, it is a type; no single person ever proposed just these principles as an educational program. Rather, it is a
coherent and logical underlying cultural ideal, and can be found in writings of the era. Its first characteristic is an emphasis on freedom. Second,
freedom is especially connected to the intellect and to reason. Reason is
understood to require freedom from constraint, and freedom itself is understood to be a consequence of the use of intelligence and reason. Third,
the liberal-free ideal emphasizes the critical and even skeptical uses of
reason. The most powerful and significant feature of intelligence is critical rationality. Fourth, the most important virtue is tolerance, a necessary
corollary to systematic doubt that was a result of the new critical rationality. Fifth, and connected to tolerance and freedom, is a general favoring of egalitarianism. Sixth, the liberal-free ideal focuses upon the will
and intelligence of individuals rather than on their capacities for citizenship and public life. Finally, the freedom of the intellect and the unconstrained development of the individual—personal and intellectual au-
tonomy—this ideal is an end in itself, good for its own sake (119–23).

Kimball believes that the subsequent history of higher education has
been a series of confrontations between these two ideals and of accom-
modations of each ideal to the other. However, he also believes very
strongly that the rhetorical *artes liberales* ideal has declined and that the
philosophical, "liberal-free" ideal has become dominant. In important
respects, Kimball's judgment aligns itself with the judgments of contemporary critics of education. The failure to transmit and cultivate
values, the failure to strengthen the bonds of citizenship and prepare
people for public life in a democracy, the emphasis on unconstrained
specialization and professionalization, the promotion of skepticism and
egoistic individualism, the production of students who cannot communicate well in writing or in speech—all these failures can with some degree of justification be attributed to the triumph of the "liberal-free"
ideal associated with philosophy and science over the *artes liberales*
ideal associated with the tradition of rhetoric.

Kimball comes to the following conclusion:

> As for addressing the contemporary problems of liberal education,
> which inhere in the philosophical ideal, this interpretation would
> suggest a restoring of the balance between the two ideals and,

therefore, between *ratio* and *oratio*, the two poles of *logos*. But this is far easier said than done. The oratorical view recommends that those most secure, most invested, and with the most to lose—the senior scholars at the premier research institutions—discipline themselves by submitting to their corporate wisdom and to a curriculum with the study of expression and rhetoric elevated from a freshman requirement to a centerpiece. One often hears admonitions about the former kind of submission . . . but there is rarely a recognition that the means to accomplish the resuscitation of the community of learning lie in elevating and emphasizing the study of expression, rhetoric, and textual tradition of the community. Yet the means are self-evident. A community is, after all, a group of people who talk to each other and do it well.

There is much that is compelling here. Of course, I agree wholeheartedly with Kimball's call to make rhetoric a centerpiece of the curriculum rather than just a freshman requirement. In addition, I find the call for an education that promotes citizenship and public life to be entirely appropriate—especially for institutions which receive public support. There is also something attractive about his framing the controversies in higher education as a conflict of equally legitimate and important but logically incompatible ideals. The view that there are many different goods that higher education accomplishes and that they are not all consistent or even compatible with one another is an insightful and realistic way of thinking about higher education.

For Kimball, the notion of "balance" becomes the overarching ideal for those who want to achieve some resolution of the conflict. However, Kimball says almost nothing about what this "balance" would be. There is nothing to prevent the disagreements about higher education from just shifting to disagreements about what the appropriate "balance" is. Certainly, some people would say that we have finally achieved the proper balance between the two traditions, and they would not be ready to turn back the clock. Further, it is hard to imagine how some parts of the rhetorical tradition could be revitalized. For example, it is very difficult to see how a simple dogmatism about values that are grounded in a noncontroversial canon can have much influence in higher education. Students (and professors) come to college from very different backgrounds with conflicting senses of what is important and what is valuable, and with radically different degrees of trust in and identification with the enterprise of higher education. Just "informing" them about the values one would prefer for them to adopt is not going to be an especially effective way of accomplishing anything. The metaphor of "instilling" values, used by the writers of reports on higher education, is a good example of the strangeness of recent thinking about moral growth and the development of ethical judgment—as if students were "containers" for "values" that could be slowly dripped into them by a professor.

Finally, Kimball's way of thinking of these traditions and of the alternatives from which we can choose is to some degree incoherent and certainly unnecessarily limiting. Most of his book is dedicated to showing that there has been very little consensus—*ever*—about the concept of general education or the liberal arts, or about the purpose of higher education. Yet he consistently speaks of "restoring" the balance, of returning to the wisdom of the ancients who adhered more closely to the rhetorical ideal.

Francis Oakley rejects what he calls Kimball's "cautious" turn to the rhetorical tradition: "I find it impossible to ignore the fact that our very understanding of the centuries-long dialectic between the rhetorical and philosophical versions of the liberal arts tradition is itself the happy outcome of an energetic and painstaking historical investigation mounted by a succession of scholars, not least among them Kimball himself, and pursued in accord with the established norms of `scientific' scholarship and via a sustained exercise of the critical reason in the manner characteristically fostered by the liberal-free ideal" (149–50). Oakley goes on:

> Nor do I think we should overlook the . . . dogmatism evident in the strictures of the neo-rhetoricians . . . Nor, at a deeper level, should we miss the degree to which the characteristic concerns of the neo-rhetoricians themselves parallel (unconsciously reflect?) the great wave of questioning so evident in contemporary intellectual life in general. That questioning has been generated by the anxious preoccupation of our era with language, interpretation and the very grounding of knowledge, and it has posted a severe challenge to the scientifico-philosophical tradition that lies so close to the very heart of the university ethos itself . . . [T]he inclination toward perspectivism and the skepticism concerning the determinacy of meaning to which the critics so vociferously object are themselves of "rhetorical" vintage . . . I do not believe that the way forward into the future can lie via a retreat into the past . . . It will lie, rather, via a tenacious (and courageous) following of the course for which we have long set our compass, and with which the university as an institution has historically been associated. (150–51)

Yet, after arguing for the importance of the "liberal-free," scientific-philosophical ideal, Oakley ends his book with a plea for those of us who work in higher education to take on a "heightened responsibility" for finding connections between our specialized work and the "more fundamental and wide-ranging attempt" to make sense of our individual and social lives (171). This is the inevitable corrective accommodation Kimball would have predicted for Oakley's project of defending what Kimball sees as the almost nihilistic liberal-free ideal.

A rhetoric of reason, which is in its very concept a deep rapprochement of philosophy and rhetoric, thought through in the context of the postmodern condition Oakley sketches, offers a way past the impasses of the competing *artes liberales* and liberal-free traditions. At the level of the concept of reason and argument, it refuses the dualisms on which the schism between philosophy and rhetoric—and thus between the liberal-free and *artes liberales* traditions—continues to depend. It offers a way forward informed by the past but without any idea whatsoever that a return to the past would be possible or desirable. It tries to think a new possibility, to act on the present conceptual possibilities and change them—and not simply to choose among them or react to them.

Like the liberal-free tradition, an educational program guided by a rhetoric of reason promotes freedom and conceives of an education in reasoning as increasing individual freedom and promoting individual intellectual growth. However, individual freedom and intellectual growth are themselves thought of in terms of social relations and intellectual citizenship. To learn to reason well is to learn to imagine oneself in different social roles, to hear conflicting voices—especially voices which challenge and call for new responses—and to imagine forms of conversation that are guided by respect and recognition. The conversation of reason is a conversation among citizens of an imaginary ethical community. This community is imaginary in that it depends on our moral imaginations, and on our staking our teaching on a commitment to letting ourselves be claimed by an ethical vision. In this sense, a rhetoric of reason aligns itself with the rhetorical tradition, in favor of the development of a kind of citizenship and a participation in public life. The development of individual freedom and individual intelligence is via a respectful and transforming acknowledgment of people who are different from oneself. One's own freedom and intelligence depend in a strong way on the freedom and intelligence of others.

In addition, this kind of education is an education for freedom—the training of citizens who are able not only to understand the voices of other people, but to use and join voices to articulate new resolutions to conflicts in a manner that is itself a powerful and productive way of having conflict. These citizens read and speak and write and reason in a society in which they themselves participate in resolving economic and political and cultural conflicts and in shaping and ordering their domestic and mutually dependent civic-public lives in just and peaceful ways.

Thus, like the rhetorical tradition, a rhetoric of reason also promotes the cultivation of the abilities of individuals to communicate and reason in a way that is constituted by what we can call values. However, these values are not in a direct way the "values" which the recent critics of higher education are demanding that we somehow fill our students up with—values that would in some way erase the different and conflicting understandings and ways of life that inform and motivate their efforts to claim an education. Instead, the values of a rhetoric of reason are the values that *enable* productive, nonviolent conflict; they are values of process and only indirectly values of result. A rhetoric of reason cannot itself decide the pressing conflicts of the day; however, it can help develop in real men and women the ability to use these conflicts to think and deliberate in more powerful and imaginative and liberating ways, and so turn these conflicts to our common advantage.

Like the liberal-free ideal, a rhetoric of reason is committed to criticism and the development of the critical, even the skeptical intelligence. Argumentation depends on criticism, on questioning, and certain kinds of reasoning even depend on skepticism. However, in the light of a rhetoric of reason, criticism and skepticism are conceived of as the partners of affirmation and conviction. Criticism and skeptical questioning are the conscience of reason. They are essential participants in reason's dialogue, but their negative energy is put to work for a purpose: the avoidance of violent conflict, the achievement of meaningful individual and social transformation, and a struggle for higher education that is not captive to narrow interests.

Like the liberal-free ideal, a rhetoric of reason promotes criticism and even skepticism because it also promotes tolerance. However, just as its adherence to critical intelligence is limited by its defining purposes, its promotion of tolerance is limited, too. Tolerance is a starting point, a recognition that the claims and questions and ways of life (ways of being an audience) of other people are worthy of respect and acknowledgment. However, this acknowledgment is the *starting point* and the *enabling condition* of a process of reasoning; skeptical tolerance is not necessarily its final conclusion. The process of reasoning can break down or conclude in a judgment that not all interlocutors, not all claims and questions, are worth one's respect. The practice of argumentation depends on tolerance, but this very practice can lead one to recognize that unlimited skeptical tolerance is no virtue.

If we took seriously the central significance of communication and reason for the undergraduate curriculum, we would make the study and practice of reasoning its guiding idea. We could still start with the critically important first-year writing requirement, but we might expand the requirement to include practice and training in speech as well. However, we would not stop there. There ought to be no lapses in a student's training in communicative reason. At many institutions, students can go for a year or more without being asked to write a paper (or participate in written on-line discussions) or give an oral presentation, or even speak in class at all. Some students actually show regression in their writing abilities between the time they complete their first-year writing courses and the time they are asked to write papers again in their junior or senior years. Practice in communicative reason should be a central part of students' experience in college. A term should not pass in which they are not being asked to reason in writing and to engage in discussions about course material.

As students move into their majors, they need to learn the more specialized conventions of written reasoning in their chosen fields. They need to become acquainted with the kinds of questions asked in the different disciplines, with the interlocutors who are the dominant conversation partners in the field. They need to learn how biologists or historians ask and answer questions, and how audiences of biologists and historians judge evidence and reasoning. They learn this not simply by sitting in chairs in biology or history classes and taking multiple-choice examinations at the end of the term. They learn by taking action, by beginning to write as biologists and speak as historians—by participating actively and convincingly in the activities and conversations that make up contemporary biology and history. Students who learn unconnected facts about cell communication or Roman law soon forget them. Students who learn to search out scientific data, understand the theories that organize these data, evaluate this evidence and these theories, apply them to new contexts, criticize them, propose modifications, use them to project new discoveries—these students learn to do something invaluable. Students who learn to use historical examples to think, to reason, who can communicate about the relations between ideas and events, power and knowledge, violence and diplomacy, the past and the future, have learned how to give meaning and purpose to historical facts.

However, this points to the related need for nonspecialized courses in communicative reason both in the middle years of the undergraduate curriculum and at its culmination. It is one thing to learn the specialized reasoning of a discipline or profession. It is quite another to be able to use that specialized ability in a broader public or civic context. We need courses which focus on writing and speech that enable students to use their specialized knowledge to communicate with people who do not have their particular specialized knowledge. And we need to teach them to use this knowledge to reason and communicate about conflicts that are matters of concern to many different kinds of people, to fellow citizens who may not share their specialized knowledge and abilities, but who are their equals in the deliberations that go on among citizens in a democracy.

To learn both these specialized forms of reasoning and the general kinds of reasoning that bring specialized knowledge to bear on larger conflicts is a matter of gaining a communicative ability. It is to learn to cooperate with interlocutors and audiences in a process of conflict that leads to new knowledge and that aims to resolve potentially violent disagreements peacefully *and justly*. It requires an acquaintance with habits of mind and communication of very diverse kinds of people. This learning also requires the kind of moral imagination that enables one to envision new kinds of solidarity and universality that join audiences in shared judgments about reasons for action and cooperation, even shared judgments about goodness and truth.

Such ideas about higher education are simple and almost commonsensical. The value and effectiveness of writing-to-learn and writing in all parts of the curriculum are well established. It seems self-evident that students should study and practice written reasoning intensively in their first year of college. It seems obvious that communicative reason should remain the central orienting focus of their work in their major. It seems not only obvious but critical that the culmination of work in the major should be training and practice in the kind of communicative reason that allows one to use one's new knowledge in diverse contexts— especially in the context of participating as an informed citizen in resolving the conflicts that arise in a democracy.

However, reactive and visionless thinking about writing and communication still holds sway in higher education. First-year writing courses in large public universities are typically staffed by the lowest-paid and sometimes the least-trained members of the faculty. Often such people are part-time or non-tenure-track employees; often, they don't receive the research and teaching support that other faculty do, and often they are prohibited from participating in faculty governance of the university. Many are graduate students. Some of these graduate students are trained very well; others have no real training at all. Many are "gypsy scholars," who work at several different institutions, putting together enough part-time work to survive, hoping that if they survive as academics they might eventually find a full-time, full-status position. One of the assumptions behind these practices is that the teaching of writing is, after all, just the marking of errors and the grading of papers and that any half-educated person is capable of that.

So most writing instruction is focused on the first year, even the first term, and sometimes even on the "prebaccalaureate" level courses. Since "writing" is something that should have been learned in high school, then "writing" courses belong at best only at the beginning of the undergraduate curriculum, where they can make up for what should have been learned earlier. Advanced students—those who make the fewest errors on standardized tests—should be released from having to take "writing" courses and should proceed without obstruction to their chosen specialized areas. After the first year, some institutions ask departments to offer "writing-intensive" courses, but only the especially conscientious ones offer their faculty training in the teaching of writing, or hire people who have training in rhetoric and knowledge of the ways writing is used in the disciplines and professions.

These few institutions are very important. There are universities that have recently founded departments of writing and rhetoric, and there are colleges that have made heavy investments both in their writing programs and in incorporating writing instruction more effectively into courses throughout the entire curriculum. Many disciplines have developed their own specialists in the rhetoric of their particular discipline, and these people have strengthened their colleagues' awareness of the importance of rhetoric in education and research, of the ways reason and research are themselves essentially communicative.

However, this movement is still a minor disturbance in an overwhelmingly dominant pattern. I see little hope for real change. Public universities have grown deeply dependent on a proletarian class of writing instructors. The costs of reforming the present exploitative and educationally irrational system would be formidable, and would cause serious financial disruptions in other parts of the university. Four-year colleges have better chances here. Further, the commonplace misunderstandings of what it means to learn to write well, what it requires of teachers and students, are solidly entrenched. They are as much a part of contemporary intellectual folk theory as racialist theories and a belief in ether were parts of the worldview of past generations of intellectuals.

There is also the problem of entertaining the idea that rhetoric might be a legitimate area of research and teaching. The vulgar view of writing extends to rhetoric, too, which is still thought by many to be an art of ornamentation, or of knowing what persuasive techniques are available when one has no reasons or evidence for one's position. In addition, rhetoricians are to some degree generalists. "Rhetoric," like "philosophy," has a tendency to have an unlimited range, to extend its thinking to every possible domain. Cicero believed that a rhetorician must know more than anyone else, must, in fact, know everything possible. When one adds to this the fact that in a revitalized curriculum rhetoricians would have a special charge to be teachers, to make the curriculum whole, one only adds to the problem of legitimacy. Professors are supposed to be specialized researchers, and to the degree that they become known more as teachers than as researchers, or to the degree that they become known more as generalists than as specialists, their status declines.

In the face of these facts, it might seem appropriate to end with Platonic pessimism, and to conclude that unless those versed in the rhetoric of reason provide leadership in recreating the college curriculum, or unless those who are now leaders become rhetoricians of reason themselves—unless philosophy, rhetoric, and educational leadership coincide—there will be no rest from the perpetual cycles of crisis in higher education and purposelessness in the writing curriculum, nor will there be an improvement in students' abilities to write or in their capacities for reason and communication, in either their private or their public lives. One might think it appropriate for me to end by saying that, the longer I consider these matters, the harder it appears to be to revitalize higher education. The result is that as I look at the economic and political realities of the university, and see clearly how ill conceived the undergraduate curriculum is, I who began by believing that a rhetoric of reason could give new life and legitimacy to the claims of higher education finally admit that the situation is beyond redemption except through some miraculous plan accompanied by extraordinarily good luck.

However, this is exactly why I have addressed this mostly theoretical work to teachers of writing. The shifting currents of the financing and structuring of higher education, and of high-level academic administration, are not only far removed from the areas in which most of us have our effectiveness but also caught up in forces that are to a great degree beyond the control of any group of people who can gather together to deliberate carefully about what action needs to be taken. In any case, the actions taken at such a level, even when they are appropriate, have only an indirect influence on whether students learn to reason well and convincingly. This influence is not to be dismissed. However, it can at best only help to shape the conditions in which higher learning might take place. It cannot directly determine whether learning does take place.

Individual teachers have more influence on whether students learn than anyone else except the students themselves. Teachers of writing, whose classes are typically smaller than other classes, and whose subject focuses on the processes of learning, reasoning, communicating, and convincing, can enable students in ways and to degrees that are far beyond the teaching and learning that go on in most disciplinary courses. Where teachers of writing place their ambitions, how they understand what counts as learning, reason, and "writing," can have enormous consequences for their students. Students who succeed in joining the conversation of reason, who gain intellectual citizenship in the country of the educated, have begun to undergo a transformation that has no end. I can think of no nobler calling than to be an enabling partner in the process of that transformation.

NOTES

REFERENCES

INDEX

NOTES

Chapter 1. The End of Philosophy and the Resurgence of Rhetoric

1. For a good summary of this feature of the rhetoric of inquiry, see the introduction to Nelson, Megill, and McCloskey.

2. In *Moral Consciousness and Communicative Action.*

3. However, I believe Habermas' position is confused by his insisting that the orientation of theorizing is toward truth, and that this necessitates bivalence in empirical-theoretical statements. From a more thoroughly rhetorical point of view, it is not the expectation of truth that requires bivalence, but the necessity of *choice.* This necessity applies to theories because theories are themselves actions, instances of theorizing, which require choice. We have to say something (rather than something else), and justify our speech (actions) by reasons, reasons which situate us practically in a position relative to some discourse community. Teaching—that is, teaching some things and not everything, in some way and not every way—requires "bivalence" even more vigorously: a yes or no to each of the available actions.

4. See Leff.

5. Heidegger, *Being and Time* 128ff. Easy dismissals of Descartes' thought have become commonplace recently. It's instructive to note how important Heidegger thought Descartes was, how often he returned to his writings, and how much he found in them.

6. Heidegger later admits that his own thought, too, was unable to escape the subjectivism of modern philosophy, and explains that this was part of the reason he broke off the project of *Being and Time.* See *Nietzsche, Volume 4: Nihilism* 141–42.

7. The possible examples here are endless, but for a contemporary discussion of this form of dualism, and some recent examples, see Rorty.

8. This picture of the world has some obvious similarities to the picture that James Berlin understands to underlie "current-traditional" rhetoric. Berlin has developed his interpretation of CTR in several articles and two books on the history of writing instruction.

9. A similar understanding of language is also present in Wittgenstein's *Philosophical Investigations,* in which Wittgenstein writes that "To imagine a language means to imagine a form of life" (no. 19). Wittgenstein does not say that a language "reflects" or "expresses" a form of life, but rather suggests that language and life are inseparable, that a language *is* a form of life.

10. Newton Garver explores several ways in which Derrida is aligned more closely with the rhetorical rather than the philosophical-logical tradition in his preface to *Speech and Phenomena.*

11. See, for example, "Language," in *Poetry, Language, Thought*.

12. Is it possible to notice but not respond explicitly to Derrida's playfulness and jokes here, but instead to carry on, outside this footnote, with the task of trying to explain why I have followed rhetorical theory rather than deconstruction when it comes to the questions in which I am most interested? Or would this be a "systematic exclusion" that would vitiate any claim I am making to really be in a conversation with or about deconstruction?

13. Years later, in *In Quest of the Ordinary*, Cavell cites this passage and comments on it, demonstrating thereby that one can also achieve a community of understanding with oneself, with one's earlier self and one's earlier speech actions—also a precarious achievement which rests on the form of life one has managed to achieve in one's own self-understanding. Most recently, in *A Pitch of Philosophy*, Cavell finally offers his own account of and response to the Derrida/Searle exchange.

14. For two recent examples, see Simons; and Nelson, Megill, and McCloskey.

15. A complete list would be very long. A few examples: In Foss, Stephen Toulmin, Ernesto Grassi, Michel Foucault, and Jürgen Habermas—all philosophers—appear as contemporary rhetorical theorists. In Baynes, Hans Blumenberg appears as proposing rhetoric as the successor to philosophical conceptions of Reason—a successor more suited to the *Mängelwesen* we have discovered ourselves to be. Finally, Conley concludes with a chapter titled "Philosophers Turn to Rhetoric," which features discussions of Richard McKeon, Stephen Toulmin, Chaim Perelman, and Jürgen Habermas.

16. Different disciplines and subfields have absorbed the idea of the fragmentation of reasoning groups in different ways. The concept of "speech communities" has been used for a long time in sociolinguistics. In literary theory, the idea of "interpretive communities" is much more recent. "Argument fields" has become a common term in the field of speech communication. The "rhetoric of inquiry" itself is given to studying "disciplinary communities." I will be using "discourse community" and "rhetorical community" pretty much interchangeably, and I will try to specify the particular sense of the term where it is important.

17. The concept of a discourse community has received a great deal of close treatment recently. For a good attempt at a definition from a sociolinguistic angle, see chapter 2 of Swales. David Bartholomae and Patricia Bizzell have used the concept in illuminating ways in their work on basic writing and academic discourse. Bartholomae's "Inventing the University" is an important text here. Bizzell's work has undergone several interesting transformations in the way she uses the concept. These are evident in a recent collection of her work titled *Academic Discourse and Critical Consciousness*.

18. The most well-known study of how documentation practices embody such commitments may be found in Bazerman.

19. The research on the specific ways written reasoning varies from field to field is growing quickly. For some examples, see the sociolinguistic journals *English for Specific Purposes* and *English for Academic Purposes*. Charles Bazerman, Tony Becher, and John Swales have all written in this area, as have many

others. The rhetoric of inquiry is often devoted to just this examination of the ways different discourse communities reason differently.

20. The absence of a reconstruction of the theory of argumentation has led to attacks on argumentation from many different perspectives. For examples, see Sally Miller Gearhart's lively and provocative "The Womanization of Rhetoric." For a more measured approach from a similar angle, see Lamb.

21. Thus, in Dilip Gaonkar's terms, this book not only contributes to the "revival" of rhetoric and furthers the "new rhetoric," but also takes the "rhetorical turn" and envisions rhetoric as a metadiscipline—with the qualification that, although it wants to improve rhetorical criticism by reinterpreting knowledge, it does so without limiting itself to the road of suspicion and "unmasking," taking instead the road of James Boyd White's "constitutive rhetoric" and McKeon's "productive" or "inventional" art.

Chapter 2. Claiming

1. Copi 7.

2. I want to emphasize that the theory treats specifically argumentative reasoning. I will frequently use the word "reason" to substitute for "argumentation," but I am in every case speaking of argumentation. There are forms of inference to which the term "reason" might usefully be applied which are not communicative in the same sense as argumentative reasoning. And there are forms of reasoning which do not and could not take place *in writing*. For example, perceptual inferences may not be communicative in any strong sense, nor could they take place in writing. This is certainly not to say that perceptual inferences are unimportant. They are simply not the reasoning with which I am concerned here. Rather, I am concerned with written reasoning, with the question of its nature and purpose, and with its claim to a central role in higher education.

3. I am thinking here of schemes like W. G. Perry's and his many followers among teachers of writing.

4. Habermas' discussion of validity claims occurs throughout part 1 of chapter 1 of *The Theory of Communicative Action*, vol. 1. In this discussion, he emphasizes the particularity of validity claims to specific kinds of discourse. In addition, he distinguishes aesthetic discourse from the other four kinds of discourse he usually emphasizes. Later, he develops the idea that any speech act simultaneously raises at least three different validity claims (305ff.). For an earlier and slightly different but very interesting discussion of validity claims, see "What Is Universal Pragmatics?" in *Communication and the Evolution of Society*.

5. Gregory Vlastos points out Socrates' frequent employment of the "Say What You Believe" criterion in his conversations with the Sophists. It is noteworthy that Plato represents the Sophists as men who consistently tried to avoid speaking sincerely.

6. I am thinking especially of the conflict between, on the one hand, what has misleadingly been called "expressivist" rhetoric, and on the other what has dubbed itself "social-epistemic" rhetoric. I have tried to show how this distinc-

tion is in some respects ill conceived in "Authorship and Individuality: Heideggerian Angles."

7. One kind of criticism of developmental schemes of this sort has been that they display class and gender bias. Carol Gilligan's famous study in which she takes on Kohlberg's developmental scheme is probably the most well-known of these. Another kind of criticism is more sweeping. Jeffrey Lewis Zorn's dissertation, "'Syntactic Maturity' Research and Curriculum Advocacy: A Philosophical Critique," contains a general and highly entertaining dismantling of the idea of "maturity" as it has been used in educational psychology and specifically in the teaching of writing. Zorn examines what could be called the biologistic imperialism of metaphors of growth and maturity, tracking their invasion and colonization of certain approaches to the teaching of writing.

8. "To the memory of those who were closest among the six million assassinated by the National Socialists, and of the millions on millions of all confessions and all nations, victims of the same hatred of the other man, the same anti-semitism."

9. It is striking how often the connection between rhetoric (or argumentation) and justice is made a defining feature of each. Compare James Boyd White: "I think it [rhetoric] should be seen not as a failed science nor as an ignoble art of persuasion (as it often is) but as the central art by which culture and community are established, maintained and transformed. This kind of rhetoric—I call it 'constitutive rhetoric'—has justice as its ultimate subject . . ."

10. *Conditions* 50–51. Cavell makes these remarks in the context of a defense of Nietzsche from Rawls's charge that Nietzsche's thought is grounded in antidemocratic elitism of the sort in which one "specimen" class provides the standard for all lesser classes. The argument turns partly on the translation of *Exemplare* in a passage from the *Untimely Meditations.*

11. Cavell recognizes that argumentation may permit such an understanding: "Suppose that what is meant by argumentation in philosophy is one way of accepting full responsibility for one's discourse" (*Quest* 14). However, he wants to follow another way, what he calls "reading." In this, I believe he abandons argumentation too quickly.

12. The terms here come from Stephen Toulmin's *The Uses of Argument.* I discuss Toulmin in more detail in Chapter 4.

Chapter 3. Questioning

1. This is part of the reason that having students read aloud in class is such a sobering revelation. Many students cannot read aloud because they cannot *hear* what they read. They have been taught to read quickly, silently, to locate information—on which they are then tested—but they have never learned to *hear* the claims being made on them in what they read, so they never have the delightful experience of being claimed by reading. I remember one of my grade school teachers policing the classroom as we all read silently at our desks. She was watching our throats and lips, trying to catch one of us "subvocalizing." How many adults have carried that police-teacher with them into later years?

How many college students fail to experience the claims being made on them because the text is silent?

2. For a very interesting and helpful interpretation of students' resistance, see Clark.

3. I have tried to defend the place of philosophical reasoning in enabling this mutual questioning in the teaching of writing in "The Dissatisfactions of Rhetoric: Philosophy and Politics in the Teaching of Writing."

Chapter 4. Argument and Conflict

1. It would be another discussion to ask whether epideictic has a special relation to what we usually understand as "the body." In the way I have distinguished between epideictic and explicit argumentation here, there may appear to be some warrant for pursuing such a lead. I think this would be interesting, but potentially misleading. Theories of rationality have been plagued by mind/body dualisms that have obscured more than they have revealed, or in pragmatic terms hindered more than they have enabled. I would prefer to make distinctions along more helpful lines. I have discussed the way such dualisms have afflicted theories of argumentation, and I have tried to begin to undo some versions of them, in "Mood in Argumentation: Heidegger and the Exordium."

2. This brings to mind the famous dictum of Sun Tzu: "All warfare is based on deception."

3. I am using Jürgen Habermas' notion of an ideal speech situation here. I will discuss this idea further in the section on universality in rhetoric.

4. William James confronted such questions head-on, although he is rarely thought of in this regard. See "What Makes a Life Significant?" and "Is Life Worth Living?" for two examples.

5. Toulmin's model is explained most famously in *The Uses of Argument*. It is elaborated in several other works, including *Human Understanding*, and *An Introduction to Reasoning*.

6. *Introduction to Reasoning* 326. Toulmin does mention that the "philosophical" justifications available include: (1) appeals to a general consensus; (2) appeals to generally desirable or undesirable consequences; and (3) appeals to the fact that a chosen "way of life" requires the warrant in order to hold. However, these appeals in no way allow one to move beyond or against an established consensus. Toulmin does not mention what rhetorical justifications are available, although apparently they are distinct from the philosophical ones.

7. Goodnight has argued that when the assumed consensus that makes backing possible is called into question, a legitimation controversy arises. He takes it to be a critical strength of the Toulmin model that it is capable of exposing just such sites of controversy.

8. No one I know of struggled with the relation between discourse (or "policy") and war as much as Clausewitz. He saw that each was similar to the other in purpose, but drastically different in the means employed to accomplish that purpose. Raymond Aron pursues this thread in Clausewitz's thought, and Clause-

witz's effort to preserve a sharp distinction between war and peace (over against contemporary tendencies in discourse theory) in the final chapter of *Clausewitz*.

9. Lakoff develops this idea in greater detail in his book *Women, Fire and Dangerous Things*. See the entries in the index on "category types: basic-level."

10. Compare Willard here: "Conflict [is] at the heart of the phenomena which interest us. Theorists who agree on little else share the view that arguments involve disagreement and occur in contexts of controversy. This agreement is so striking that it might be said that "argument" is not our field's core concept or even its most important problem focus" (19).

Chapter 5. Audiences and Arguments

1. And so I am in agreement with Ede and Lunsford, who also come to this conclusion.

2. There are many references to "universal audience" throughout Perelman's works, most of them duly noted in the indexes. The most important treatment of the concept is section 7 of *The New Rhetoric*, "The Universal Audience." However, this section has sometimes been misread. In the passage on classical philosophical instantiations of a universal audience, Perelman and Olbrechts-Tyteca are presenting a strictly philosophical conception of universality—one which they oppose, and one in response to which they have developed their specifically rhetorical conception of universality. Nevertheless, commentators have sometimes read these lines as presenting the writers' own views. For Perelman's clarification of this matter, see "The New Rhetoric and the Rhetoricians."

3. Habermas deploys and defends the idea of an "ideal speech situation" in different ways in a number of different writings. I am indebted here to Thomas McCarthy's helpful discussion (esp. 307ff.).

4. *Philosophical-Political Profiles* 158. This passage is incorporated into an interesting discussion of the "ideal speech situation" by Ingram; see chap. 11. Interestingly enough, it also serves as the primary epigraph for Levin's *The Opening of Vision: Nihilism and the Postmodern Situation*.

5. Ray compares Perelman to Rousseau and Kant, shows the similarity of the idea of the universal audience to the ideas of the general will and the categorical imperative, and concludes that the idea of a universal audience fails in the same way that the ideas of the general will and the categorical imperative fail. I have chosen not to respond to those particular arguments. Perelman himself addressed Ray's charges very briefly in "The New Rhetoric and the Rhetoricians." The citations are from Ray 372, 375, 370, and 372.

6. Perelman and Olbrechts-Tyteca 33 (hereafter cited as TNR); Perelman, *New Rhetoric and the Humanities* 14, 48 (hereafter cited as NRH).

7. Although Perelman attempts to distinguish reasonableness from rationality (NRH 11–23), I do not follow his usage here. By "rationality" and its cognates, I mean no more than "reasonableness" and its.

8. Perelman, *Realm of Rhetoric* 17 (hereafter cited as RR).

9. As one would expect, Perelman omits giving us rules for adding audiences together. In this, he would encounter some of Rousseau's arithmetical difficul-

ties in adding up the general will—*if,* as some seem to believe, he were recommending a single technique for constructing *the* universal audience. Of course, I am offering an interpretation of the universal audience which allows for many different, even conflicting, techniques to be employed. For an account of the problems of adding wills (or audiences) together, see Plamenatz 1:393. This is probably the right place to wonder aloud whether anyone could do for universalizability in rhetoric anything similar to what Marcus G. Singer did for ethical theory in his *Generalization in Ethics.*

10. For an argument against making the persuasion/conviction distinction this way, see James Crosswhite, "Mood in Argumentation."

11. TNR 31, 34; Perelman, "Philosophy and Rhetoric" 293ff. (hereafter cited as PR).

12. TNR 34. On the role of the universal audience in philosophical argumentation and on the relation of philosophy and rhetoric generally, see PR.

13. Although see PR for some problems facing any simple identification of a universal audience's responses with the dictates of common sense.

14. See Ingram's provocative tracing of a nascent Benjaminian concept of aesthetic rationality in Habermas' recent writings (177ff.).

15. This concept suggests a number of more far-reaching applications as well. For example, consider Emerson's rhetoric. Could we interpret his dictum that his writing was meant not to instruct but to "provoke" as a way of recognizing that his true aim was to call into play the undefined universal audience? The audience whose characteristics emerge in newness? If Emerson had understood him better, could Thoreau have functioned in this way for him—someone who took his ideas more seriously than he did? Emerson's remarks on provocation may be found in his "Divinity School Address." His unsuccessful wrestling with Thoreau is most obvious in his 1862 memorial eulogy to Thoreau.

16. Cited by McCarthy 310. Originally from *"Wahrheitstheorien,"* in *Wirklichkeit und Reflexionen: Walter Schultz zum 60 Geburtstag* 211-65.

17. Habermas has stayed with this formulation, at least through *The Theory of Communicative Action.* See 1:25.

18. The passage is from *Signs* 120. Merleau-Ponty develops the notion throughout the essays collected as part 1 of the book. Richard McCleary provides a helpful gloss on the idea in his preface to *Signs:* "But how can a philosophy which rejects all claims to an absolute point of view and which insists upon the situational character of all truth still meaningfully seek truth? According to Merleau-Ponty, it can do so because it knows that the center of philosophy is "everywhere and nowhere," in the sense that truth and the whole are in the first philosophy and every subsequent one, *but as a task to be accomplished and thus not yet there . . .* A philosopher can attain to a lateral universality when the limitations which stem from his particular situation in the empirical order of events are invested in an intentional history of the advent of meaning, which *transforms that situation into a means of understanding his own and other situations, and which establishes—through the philosophical dialogue it opens up—an indirect unity of convergence with all other philosophies"* (xxv, emphasis added). This captures well the idea that universality is a task (with concrete dimensions) and not

310

a finished concept, and points out clearly that the unity indicated by "universality" is an indirect unity of movement and not necessarily of position. The word "convergence" emphasizes nicely the dynamic possibilities of *"universal."*

19. Sandra Mennsen argues vigorously for the political importance of universal claims for just these reasons: "If indeed the language of logic is universal . . . If women and men reason in the same way, if we share a basic language, then women must ask: How could men *not* have heard our voices? If Gilligan and her associates rightly see in women a special ability and inclination to draw connections among people, to unify, to develop relationships, then perhaps one task women should undertake is the task of emphasizing what women and men have in common . . ." (136). This commonality needs to be emphasized partly in order to strengthen the force of arguments that would further the interests of women.

20. Compare Michael Dummet's latest work, and what concerns him, to the work with which students are asked to concern themselves in introductory logic courses.

21. I use this example somewhat reluctantly, since my own inclination is to want to defend Dukakis here. The point is not that Dukakis' response was a sign of a serious deficiency; in fact, one could make a strong case for his kind of integrity. The point is that this event was a conflict between two kinds of universality. Dukakis seems to have constructed his paragon audience in a way that was wrong for the particular audience he was actually addressing.

Chapter 6. Being Unreasonable: A Rhetoric of Fallacies

1. Andrea Nye offers a reading of the history of logic as the story of this severance. Her discussion of Frege (chaps. 7-10) is especially relevant here.

2. One notable exception is Wayne C. Booth and Marshall Gregory's *The Harper and Row Rhetoric: Writing as Thinking, Thinking as Writing.* See the section titled "From 'Fallacies' to 'Rhetorical Resources'" (408ff.). Here the authors recognize that the traditional "fallacies" can also be "useful and even indispensable."

3. See Fulkerson. His bibliography also contains several helpful references.

4. See, for example, *Argumentation* 2.4 (1988). The issue is titled "Argumentation in Dialogues," and it contains a general bibliography on the topic.

5. I am not about to claim that I am offering the definitive interpretation of Moore's argument. Moore's reasoning is ambiguous enough to admit many interpretations. Hall identifies three different fallacies contained in the naturalist fallacy, a "definist fallacy," a "predicative fallacy," and an "extensionalist fallacy" (101). Bernard Williams follows a long line of interpreters in believing that Moore was really reviving Hume's ban on deriving an ought from an is. I am offering one more way of understanding what it was that Moore recognized, and what influenced so many other people once he pointed toward it.

6. Finocchiaro argues that the failure to imagine the reasoning of someone who would disagree with one's claim is the most common form of fallacious reasoning. He also finds that experimental studies converge with his own find-

ings: "David N. Perkins has studied everyday reasoning by an experimental-critical approach . . . The present author has studied scientific reasoning . . . in Galileo's *Two Chief World Systems.* They have, independently, reached the strikingly similar substantive conclusion that the most common flaw of informal reasoning is the failure to consider lines of argument supporting conclusions contrary to the one in fact reached" (1). Finocchiaro wants to say that this is still a logical matter because it concerns the relationships of propositions with each other instead of relationships of propositions to the world (i.e., is logical not epistemological). But the difficulty is also a failure of the arguer to occupy the questioner's role, and this is often a matter of moral imagination—of being able to imagine a different claim, a different audience, a different way of life—sometimes a matter of disrespect or neglect of that different voice. In any case, the problem is finally in the social relationships of the dramatis personae of argumentation, in their abilities to recognize and communicate with one another in the appropriate ways.

Chapter 7. Argument and Ideology: Evaluating Argumentation

1. "Ineffable" is in important ways the wrong word, too loaded. In Jean Hyppolite's commentary on Hegel's *Phenomenology,* he stresses that Hegel's argument is against the *alogon,* the nonlinguistic, and so ineffable. My own understanding of these unclaimable experiences is not that they are beyond language but rather that there is too much language in them. It is not that they are linguistically unintelligible but that they are infinitely intelligible. Each part of them resonates with links to every other part. Each angle of the experience suggests countless other angles, infinite significance. Anything we might say about this would require infinite elaboration—a use of language that would unfold with the same shapes and complexities as the experience. This would tend to defeat the effort to bring the experience into claimable form. I believe that this is part of the dilemma faced by writers such as Emerson and Thoreau, whose efforts as writers kept defaulting to the keeping of journals, and who used language, in Emerson's words, to "provoke" rather than "instruct."

2. They refer to *Rhetoric* 1357a, where Aristotle says that rhetorical reasoning concerns "such listeners as are not able to see many things all together or to reason from a distant starting point." See TNR 7. The translation here is Kennedy's.

3. I have made this same argument in relation to the way emotions can make certain things unthinkable for us and so help preserve our moral identities in "Mood in Argumentation."

4. Obviously, a universal audience which knows what should be thought and what should be left unthought has "thought about" what should be left unthought. Insofar as we "construct" the audience for argumentation, we ourselves must already have thought of what this audience knows and doesn't know. Therefore, one objection goes, we must have already thought the unthinkable, i.e., taken the position of the audience for whom everything is thinkable, in order to judge it. However, this is not so. The audience which knows

what should be thought and what should be left unthought must be an "unde-fined universal audience"—the audience which judges our constructions of universal audiences. Such an audience is never fully conceptualized—and it need not be fully conceptualized in order to do its work and have its own effi-cacy. In fact, it is impossible for it to be fully conceptualized. See the detailed discussion of this audience in Chapter 5.

5. This point has been made too many times for me to document here. Paul Ricoeur analyzes modern suspicion brilliantly in his unforgettable little article, "The Critique of Religion." His reference to the translation of all language into *text* parallels the understanding of everything as questionable. In another vein, questioning has been linked not only with interrogation but also with actual torture. See, for example, Meyer 18. Page Dubois has developed the connection between rationality and torture in some detail in her work, especially *Torture and Truth.*

6. The history of rhetoric and philosophy is at many points concerned with just this problem of how one can reason with the powerful. Perelman and Olbrechts-Tyteca tell the story of Aristippus, "who, when he was reproached for having abjectly prostrated himself at the feet of Dionysius the tyrant in order to be heard by him, defended himself by saying that the fault was not his, but that of Dionysius who had ears in his feet." However, they go on to ask, "Is the position of the ears, then, a matter of indifference?" (16).

Leo Strauss, a rhetorical reader par excellence (although a political theorist of strictly limited sympathies), develops a profound account of the relation between reason and power in his brilliant reading of Xenophon's *Hiero or Ty-rannicus* in *On Tyranny.* See in the same edition the provocative response by Alexandre Kojève.

7. I have made this point in more detail in "Mood in Argumentation."

8. Feminist theorists disagree about the origins of rational, male subjectivity. Genevieve Lloyd and Andrea Nye find that the history of philosophy and of logic, respectively, have always been strongly gendered. Others, such as Susan Bordo, Carolyn Merchant, and Evelyn Fox Keller, see the seventh century as a turning point. In Bordo's case, this is in fact the point at which the concept of reason was masculinized.

9. In fact, this objection was made by several people on MBU-L (an electronic discussion list mostly concerned with computers and writing) in response to one of my posts on the concept of reason.

10. And I would say that Perelman and Olbrechts-Tyteca, Kenneth Burke, and Wayne Booth are adherents to this ideal.

Chapter 8. Argument as Inquiry

1. See, for example, George Kennedy's introduction to his first-rate transla-tion of Aristotle's *Rhetoric* (10–11).

2. In this context, it's interesting to recall what Chaim Perelman says about "clarity," since Perelman, like Plato, wants to overcome the distinction between philosophy and rhetoric: "In most cases the impression of clarity, linked with

univocity, is the product of ignorance or of lack of imagination" (TNR 125). Distinguishing between properly philosophical discourse and rhetoric seems to depend on a distinction between what is clear and what is not that can itself be made propositionally clear. Both Plato and Perelman deny that such a distinction can hold up.

3. There is a lot of confusion about the *Phaedrus'* passages on writing. The most helpful account I know of is G. R. F. Ferrari's in *Listening to the Cicadas.* He considers the "standard interpretation" of Hackforth and de Vries, the "ironic interpretation" of Ronna Burger, and the Derridean approach found in *Dissemination.* He finds each wanting in important ways, and offers a very plausible alternative, congruent with the account I am giving here. Jasper Neel has explored the significance of the *Phaedrus* for teachers of writing in his thought-provoking *Plato, Derrida, and Writing,*.

4. Ferrari points out that Phaedrus' pitiful furtive clutching of Lysias' manuscript, his believing that he has secret wisdom in writing, is representative of the view of writing that is being overthrown. The dialogue as a whole is a kind of patient redemption of this writing by using it as an occasion for a better and more powerful use of language, for written criticism that is aware of writing's limitations.

5. Perhaps the most extreme example of this is Brian Vickers, whose obtuse and agitated readings of Plato in *In Defence of Rhetoric* (83–147) seem to be called forth by his own needlessly polemical stance. These readings seem all the more wanting when contrasted with Vickers' very helpful historical account of the "processes of rhetoric" in the same book.

6. It is interesting to compare this passage to chapter 12 of *Categories,* where Aristotle explores five different senses of "prior," as it relates to time, sequence, order, value, and cause/effect.

7. Nussbaum 290. Nussbaum cites scholars who have tried to interpret Aristotle in a similar way based on new readings of *Posterior Analytics* II 19, where the discussion of intellectual intuitions takes place. She points to articles by A. Kosman, J. Lesher, and M. F. Burnyeat. She also notes that the "standard interpretation" has a defender in T. H. Irwin, whose contribution is titled "Aristotle's Discovery of Metaphysics."

8. What follows relies greatly on Walter Ong's *RAMUS Method, and the Decay of Dialogue.*

9. For a provocative analysis of how deeply Descartes' rhetoric is bound up with his writing, see Caton. The best case that can be made for the claim that Descartes had an explicit rhetoric can be found in Carr.

10. The best account of the fullness of Bacon's rhetorical thought is Briggs.

11. In this context, it seems especially appropriate to point out Gadamer's own view of the universality of rhetoric: "Rhetoric from oldest tradition has been the only advocate of a claim to truth that defends the probable, the *eikos* (verisimile), and that which is convincing to the ordinary reason, against the claim of science to accept as true only what can be demonstrated and tested! . . . And this whole wide realm of convincing 'persuasions' and generally reigning views has not been gradually narrowed by the progress of science, however

great it has been; rather, this realm extends to take in every new product of scientific endeavor, claiming it for itself and bringing it within its scope" ("The Scope and Function of Hermeneutical Reflection" 24).

12. Gadamer himself draws this connection in "Hermeneutics as a Theoretical and Practical Task": "In my own works I have stressed the way the being of the interpreter pertains intrinsically to the being of what is to be interpreted. Whoever wants to understand something already brings along something that anticipatorily joins him with what he wants to understand—a sustaining agreement. Thus the orator always has to link up with something like this if his persuading and convincing in disputed questions is to succeed" (136). In a note, Gadamer writes: "Here Chaim Perelman and his school, drawing on the experience of jurists, have revived age-old insights into the structure and significance of argumentation as a rhetorical procedure."

13. Heidegger makes a strong version of this claim in *Hegel's Concept of Experience* (118–19).

14. Hegel makes the point often, but see Hegel's *Logic* (41) (the lesser logic), the *Zusatz* to section 24. One of the interesting things about this passage is that Hegel distinguishes between "experience" and "reflection"—partly in order to find them both fulfilled in the notion of "thought."

15. *Hegel's Concept of Experience* 147. Heidegger makes a somewhat different use of these statements from the pragmatic-critical use I am making here.

16. Giambattista Vico worries that unconstrained reflection can lead to a "barbarism of reflection." He points out that the decadence that follows the constant overturning of communal norms can lead to the kind of individualism that makes genuine civic deliberation impossible. Vico recommends strongly epideictic education and the cultivation of a common sense to contain reflection's individualism. Gadamer doesn't mention the problem in this context. He focuses on the role of tradition and common sense in thinking and judging, but he rarely illuminates their social and political dimensions.

17. Linda Flower makes a similar point in a very different way in her distinction between reader- and writer-based prose.

18. Howard Gardner has written a book about the sources of creativity in the lives of seven people: Stravinsky, Picasso, T. S. Eliot, Martha Graham, Freud, Einstein, and Gandhi. It is remarkable how often a sense of surprise and wonder is brought up in these accounts. See, for example, the opening paragraphs in the chapter on Einstein. Gardner also develops a psychosocial theory about the conditions which allow creative strangeness to flourish and become productive instead of self-destructive. One key appears to be the consistency of support and mediation that connects the strange and new to the established ways of practicing and understanding art and inquiry. Gardner finds it significant that the creative people whose lives he has studied tend to come from stable, middle-class families. Another appears to be the luck these people had in finding other *individuals* who were capable of being audiences for their work.

19. This example comes from an actual discussion in a composition class I once visited.

Chapter 9. Rhetoric, Ethics, and the Aims
of Higher Education

1. Robert and Jon Solomon seem fixed in this perspective in *Up the University: Recreating Higher Education in America*.

2. See, for example, Hairston's charges in "Diversity, Ideology, and Teaching Writing."

3. Hillocks 248. Hillocks' conclusions are corroborated to varying degrees and in different ways by Patrick Hartwell and Rei Noguchi.

4. Here Neilson's research converges with the judgments of other error theorists like David Bartholomae, Mike Rose, Glynda Hull, and Mina Shaughnessy. It also aligns well with recent research on "interlanguage."

5. "Literary interpretation" is something of an exception here. I take the presence of this genre to be a consequence of the fact that writing is taught primarily in English/literature departments. If it were taught by the rhetoric or philosophy or communication or writing department, I doubt that "literary interpretation" would be selected as the sole representative of disciplinary writing.

6. See also Robert Connors' important piece, "The Rise and Fall of the Modes of Discourse."

REFERENCES

Abrams, M. H. *Doing Things with Texts: Essays in Criticism and Critical Theory.* New York: W. W. Norton, 1989.

Adam's Rib. Directed by George Cukor. Screenplay by Ruth Gordon and Garson Kanin. With Katharine Hepburn and Spencer Tracy. Metro-Goldwyn-Mayer, 1949.

Aristotle. *Categories.* Trans. E. M. Edghill. In *The Basic Works of Aristotle,* ed. Richard McKeon. New York: Random House, 1941.

Aristotle. *Nicomachean Ethics.* Trans. W. D. Ross. In *The Basic Works of Aristotle,* ed. Richard McKeon. New York: Random House, 1941.

Aristotle. *On Rhetoric.* Trans. George A. Kennedy. New York: Oxford University Press, 1991.

Aristotle. *On Sophistical Refutations.* Trans. W. A. Pickard-Cambridge. In *The Basic Works of Aristotle,* ed. Richard McKeon. New York: Random House, 1941.

Aristotle. *Posterior Analytics* and *Topica.* Trans. H. Tredennick and E. S. Forster. Cambridge: Loeb-Harvard University Press, 1960.

Aron, Raymond. *Clausewitz: Philosopher of War.* Trans. Christine Booker and Norman Stone. London: Routledge & Keegan Paul, 1983.

Astrov, Margaret. *The Winged Serpent: An Anthology of Native American Prose and Poetry.* New York: John Day, 1946.

Bacon, Francis. *The New Organon.* In *The Works of Francis Bacon,* ed. James Spedding, Robert L. Ellis, Douglas D. Heath. 1868–74; New York: Garrett Press, 1968.

Bartholomae, David. "Inventing the University." In *When a Writer Can't Write,* ed. Mike Rose. New York: Guilford Press, 1985.

Bartholomae, David. "The Study of Error." *College Composition and Communication* 31 (1980): 253–69.

Baynes, Kenneth, James Bowman, and Thomas McCarthy, eds. *After Philosophy: End or Transformation?* Cambridge: MIT Press, 1987.

Bazerman, Charles. *Shaping Written Knowledge: The Genre and Activity of the Experimental Article in Science.* Madison: University of Wisconsin Press, 1988.

Beale, Walter. *A Pragmatic Theory of Rhetoric.* Carbondale: Southern Illinois University Press, 1987.

Becher, Tony. "Disciplinary Discourse." *Studies in Higher Education* 12.3 (1987): 261–74.

Berlin, James. *Rhetoric and Reality: Writing Instruction in American Colleges, 1900–1985.* Carbondale: Southern Illinois University Press, 1987.

Berlin, James A. *Writing Instruction in Nineteenth-Century American Colleges.* Carbondale: Southern Illinois University Press, 1984.

Berlin, James, and Robert P. Inkster. "Current-Traditional Rhetoric: Paradigm and Practice." *Freshman English News* 8 (1980): 1–4, 13–14.

Bizzell, Patricia. *Academic Discourse and Critical Consciousness.* Pittsburgh: University of Pittsburgh Press, 1993.

Blair, J. Anthony, and Ralph H. Johnson, eds. *Informal Logic: The First International Symposium.* Inverness, CA: Edgepress, 1980.

Booth, Wayne. *Modern Dogma and the Rhetoric of Assent.* Chicago: University of Chicago Press, 1974.

Booth, Wayne C., and Marshall Gregory. *The Harper and Row Rhetoric: Writing as Thinking, Thinking as Writing.* New York: Harper and Row, 1987.

Bordo, Susan. "Feminist Skepticism and the 'Maleness' of Philosophy." In *Women and Reason,* ed. Elizabeth D. Harvey and Kathleen Okruhlik. Ann Arbor: University of Michigan Press, 1992.

Boyd, Richard, Philip Gasper, and J. D. Trout, eds. *The Philosophy of Science.* Cambridge: MIT Press, 1991.

Briggs, John C. *Francis Bacon and the Rhetoric of Nature.* Cambridge: Harvard University Press, 1989.

Burke, Kenneth. *A Rhetoric of Motives.* 1950; Berkeley: University of California Press, 1969.

Burnyeat, M. F. "Aristotle on Understanding Knowledge." In *Aristotle on Science: The Posterior Analytics,* ed. E. Berti. Padua, 1981.

Butler, Judith. *Gender Trouble: Feminism and the Subversion of Identity.* New York: Routledge, 1990.

Carr, Thomas M., Jr. *Descartes and the Resilience of Rhetoric.* Carbondale: Southern Illinois University Press, 1990.

Caton, Hiram. *The Origin of Subjectivity: An Essay on Descartes.* New Haven: Yale University Press, 1973.

Cavell, Stanley. *Conditions Handsome and Unhandsome.* Chicago: University of Chicago Press, 1990.

Cavell, Stanley. *Disowning Knowledge: In Six Plays of Shakespeare.* Cambridge: Cambridge University Press, 1987.

Cavell, Stanley. *Must We Mean What We Say?* New York: Scribner, 1969.

Cavell, Stanley. *In Quest of the Ordinary: Lines of Skepticism and Romanticism.* Chicago: University of Chicago Press, 1988.

Cavell, Stanley. *A Pitch of Philosophy: Autobiographical Exercises.* Cambridge: Harvard University Press, 1994.

Cavell, Stanley. *Pursuits of Happiness: The Hollywood Comedy of Remarriage.* Cambridge: Harvard University Press, 1981.

Clark, Suzanne. "Discipline and Resistance: The Subjects of Writing and the Discourses of Instruction." *College Literature* 18.2 (June 1991): 119–35.

Clausewitz, Carl von. *On War.* Ed. and trans. Michael Howard and Peter Paret. Princeton: Princeton University Press, 1984.

Conley, Thomas. *Rhetoric in the European Tradition.* New York: Longman, 1990.

Connors, Robert. "The Rise and Fall of the Modes of Discourse." *College Composition and Communication* 32 (1981): 444–63.

318

References

Cooper, Charles R., and Rise B. Axelrod. *The St. Martin's Guide to Writing.* 2d ed. New York: St. Martin's Press, 1988.

Copi, Irving. *Introduction to Logic.* 5th ed. London: Macmillan, 1978.

Crosswhite, James. "Authorship and Individuality: Heideggerian Angles." *Journal of Advanced Composition* 12.1 (Winter 1992): 91–109.

Crosswhite, James. "The Dissatisfactions of Rhetoric: Philosophy and Politics in the Teaching of Writing." *Rhetoric Society Quarterly* 21.4 (Fall 1991): 1–16.

Crosswhite, James. "Mood in Argumentation: Heidegger and the Exordium." *Philosophy and Rhetoric* 22.1 (1989): 28–42.

Crosswhite, James. "University in Rhetoric: Perelman's Universal Audience." *Philosophy and Rhetoric* 22 (1989): 157–73.

Derrida, Jacques. *Dissemination.* Trans. with an introduction and notes by Barbara Johnson. Chicago: University of Chicago Press, 1981.

Derrida, Jacques. *Limited Inc.* Evanston: Northwestern University Press, 1988.

Derrida, Jacques. "Signature Event Context." Trans. Samuel Weber and Jeffrey Mehlman. *Glyph* 1 (1977): 172–97.

Descartes, René. *Philosophical Writings.* Ed. and trans. Elizabeth Anscombe and Peter Geach. Introduction by Alexander Koyré. London: Nelson and Sons, 1966.

Dillon, George. *Contending Rhetorics: Writing in Academic Disciplines.* Bloomington: Indiana University Press, 1991.

Dissoi Logoi. In *The Older Sophists,* trans. Rosamond Kent Sprague. Columbia: University of South Carolina Press, 1972.

Di Stefano, Christine. "Dilemmas of Difference: Feminism, Modernity, and Postmodernism." In *Feminism/Postmodernism,* ed. Linda J. Nicholson. New York: Routledge, 1989.

Dubois, Page. *Torture and Truth.* New York: Routledge, 1990.

Dummet, Michael. *The Logical Basis of Metaphysics.* Cambridge: Harvard University Press, 1991.

Ede, Lisa, and Andrea Lunsford. "Audience Addressed/Audience Invoked: The Role of Audience in Composition Theory and Pedagogy." *College Composition and Communication* 35.2 (May 1984): 155–71.

Elbow, Peter. "Reflections on Academic Discourse." *College English* 53.2 (1991): 135–55.

Emerson, Ralph Waldo. "Divinity School Address." In *The Collected Works of Ralph Waldo Emerson,* vol. 1: *Nature, Addresses, and Lectures,* ed. Robert E. Spiller and Ferguson, Alfred R. Cambridge: Harvard University Press, 1971. 71–93.

Ferrari, G. R. F. *Listening to the Cicadas.* Cambridge: Cambridge University Press, 1987.

Feyerabend, Paul. *Against Method.* Rev. ed. London: Verso, 1988.

Finocchiaro, Maurice. "Two Empirical Approaches to the Study of Reasoning." *Informal Logic* 16.1 (Winter 1994): 1–21.

Flower, Linda. *Problem-Solving Strategies for Writing.* 3d ed. New York: Harcourt Brace Jovanovich, 1989.

Foss, Sonja K.; Karen A. Foss; and Robert Trapp. *Contemporary Perspectives on Rhetoric*. Prospect Heights, IL: Waveland Press, 1985.

Foucault, Michel. "Polemics, Politics, and Problematizations: An Interview." In *The Foucault Reader*, ed. Paul Rabinow. New York: Pantheon, 1984. 381.

Foucault, Michel. "Space, Knowledge, and Power." Interview. *Skyline* (March 1982): 18-19. Cited in Jim Miller, *The Passion of Michel Foucault* (New York: Simon and Schuster, 1993), 237.

Foucault, Michel. "The Subject and Power." In *Michel Foucault: Beyond Structuralism and Hermeneutics*, ed. Hubert Dreyfus and Paul Rabinow. Chicago: The University of Chicago Press, 1983. 208–226.

Fulkerson, Richard. "Technical Logic, Comp-logic, and the Teaching of Writing." *College Composition and Communication* 39 (1988): 436–52.

Gadamer, Hans-Georg. "Hermeneutics as a Theoretical and Practical Task." In *Reason in the Age of Science*, trans. Frederick G. Lawrence. Cambridge: MIT Press, 1981.

Gadamer, Hans-Georg. "The Scope and Function of Hermeneutical Reflection." In *Philosophical Hermeneutics*, trans. and ed. David E. Linge. Berkeley: University of California Press, 1976.

Gadamer, Hans-Georg. *Truth and Method*. Translation revised by Joel Weinsheimer and Donald G. Marshall. New York: Crossroad, 1989.

Gaonkar, Dilip. "The Revival of Rhetoric, the New Rhetoric, and the Rhetorical Turn: Some Distinctions." *Informal Logic* 15.1 (Winter 1993): 53–64.

Gardner, Howard. *Creating Minds*. New York: Basic Books, 1993.

Garver, Newton. Preface to *Speech and Phenomena*, by Jacques Derrida. Evanston: Northwestern University Press, 1973.

Gearhart, Sally Miller. "The Womanization of Rhetoric." *Women's Studies International Quarterly* 2 (1979): 195–201.

Gilligan, Carol. *In a Different Voice: Psychological Theory and Women's Development*. Cambridge: Harvard University Press, 1982.

Goodnight, Thomas G. "Legitimation Inferences: An Additional Component for the Toulmin Model." *Informal Logic* 15.1 (Winter 1993): 5–14.

Graff, Gerald. *Beyond the Culture Wars: How Teaching the Conflicts Can Revitalize American Education*. New York: W. W. Norton, 1992.

Graff, Gerald. *Professing Literature: An Institutional History*. Chicago: University of Chicago Press, 1987.

Grimaldi, William M. A. *Aristotle, Rhetoric I: A Commentary*. New York: Fordham University Press, 1980.

Habermas, Jürgen. *Communication and the Evolution of Society*. Trans. Thomas McCarthy. Boston: Beacon Press, 1979.

Habermas, Jürgen. *Moral Consciousness and Communicative Action*. Trans. Christian Lenhardt. Cambridge: MIT Press, 1987.

Habermas, Jürgen. *Philosophical-Political Profiles*. Trans. Fred Lawrence. Cambridge: MIT Press, 1984.

Habermas, Jürgen. *The Theory of Communicative Action*. Vol. 1. Trans. Thomas McCarthy. Boston: Beacon Press, 1984.

320

References

Habermas, Jürgen. *"Wahrheitstheorien."* In *Wirklichkeit und Reflexionen: Walter Schultz zum 60 Geburtstag.* Pfullingen: Neske, 1973. 211–65.

Hairston, Maxine. "Diversity, Ideology, and Teaching Writing." *College Composition and Communication* 43.2 (May 1992): 189.

Hall, E. W. "The 'Proof' of Utility in Bentham and Mill." In *Utilitarianism*, ed. Samuel Gorovitz. Indianapolis: Bobbs-Merrill, 1971. 99–116.

Hamblin, C. L. *Fallacies.* London: Methuen, 1970.

Harding, Sandra. *The Science Question in Feminism.* Ithaca: Cornell University Press, 1986.

Hartwell, Patrick. "Grammar, Grammars, and the Teaching of Grammar." *College English* 47 (1985): 105–27.

Hegel, Georg Wilhelm Friedrich. *Hegel's Logic.* Trans. William Wallace. London: Oxford University Press, 1975.

Hegel, Georg Wilhelm Friedrich. *The Phenomenology of Spirit.* Trans. A. V. Miller. Oxford: Clarendon Press, 1977.

Hegel, Georg Wilhelm Friedrich. *The Philosophy of Right.* Trans. T. M. Knox. New York: Oxford University Press, 1967.

Heidegger, Martin. *Being and Time.* Trans. John Macquarrie and Edward Robinson. New York: Harper and Row, 1962.

Heidegger, Martin. *Hegel's Concept of Experience.* Trans. Kenley Royce Dove. San Francisco: Harper and Row, 1970.

Heidegger, Martin. *History of the Concept of Time.* Trans. Theodore Kisiel. Bloomington: Indiana University Press, 1985.

Heidegger, Martin. "Language." In *Poetry, Language, Thought*, trans. Albert Hofstadter. New York: Harper and Row, 1971. 187–210.

Heidegger, Martin. *Nietzsche.* 4 vols. Trans. David Farrell Krell, Frank A. Capuzzi, and Joan Stambaugh. New York: Harper and Row, 1982–87.

Hillocks, George. *Research on Written Composition: New Directions for Teaching.* Urbana: National Institute of Education, 1986.

Hobbes, Thomas. *Leviathan.* Ed. Richard Tuck. Cambridge: Cambridge University Press, 1991.

Hull, Glynda. "Research on Error and Correction." In *Perspectives on Research and Scholarship in Composition.* New York: Modern Language Association, 1985.

Hyppolite, Jean. *Genesis and Structure of Hegel's Phenomenology of Spirit.* Trans. Samuel Cherniak and John Heckman. Evanston: Northwestern University Press, 1974.

Ingram, David. *Habermas and the Dialectic of Reason.* New Haven: Yale University Press, 1987.

Irwin, T. H. "Aristotle's Discovery of Metaphysics." *Review of Metaphysics* 31 (1977): 210–29.

James, William. *The Will to Believe and Other Essays in Popular Philosophy.* Cambridge: Harvard University Press, 1979.

Jauss, Hans Robert. *Question and Answer: Forms of Dialogic Understanding.* Trans. Michael Hays. Minneapolis: University of Minnesota Press, 1989.

Johnson, Ralph H. "Acceptance Is Not Enough: A Critique of Hamblin." *Philosophy and Rhetoric* 22.4 (1990): 153–67.

Kahane, Howard. *Logic and Contemporary Rhetoric.* 6th ed. Belmont, CA: Wadsworth, 1992.

Keller, Evelyn Fox. *Reflections on Gender and Science.* New Haven: Yale University Press, 1985.

Kennedy, George. *Classical Rhetoric and Its Christian and Secular Tradition from Ancient to Modern Times.* Chapel Hill: University of North Carolina Press, 1980.

Kimball, Bruce. *Orators and Philosophers: A History of the Idea of Liberal Education.* New York: Teachers College Press, 1986.

Kiniry, Malcolm, and Mike Rose. *Critical Strategies for Academic Thinking and Writing.* 2d ed. Boston: St. Martin's Press, 1993.

Kinneavy, James. "Contemporary Rhetoric." In *The Present State of Scholarship in Historical and Contemporary Rhetoric,* rev. ed., ed. Winifred Bryan Horner. Columbia: University of Missouri Press, 1990. 186ff.

Kosman, A. "Explanation and Understanding in Aristotle's *Posterior Analytics.*" In *Exegesis and Argument: Studies . . . Presented to Gregory Vlastos,* ed. E. N. Lee et al. *Phronesis* (Assen) suppl. vol. 1 (1973): 374–92.

Lakoff, George. *Women, Fire, and Dangerous Things: What Categories Reveal about the Mind.* Chicago: University of Chicago Press, 1987.

Lakoff, George, and Mark Johnson. *Metaphors We Live By.* Chicago: University of Chicago Press, 1980.

Lamb, Catherine. "Beyond Argument in Feminist Composition." *College Composition and Communication* 42 (February 1991): 11–24.

Leff, Michael. "The Unity of Sophistic Rhetoric." In Nelson et al.

Lesher, J. "The Role of *Nous* in Aristotle's *Posterior Analytics.*" *Phronesis* 18 (1973): 44–68.

Levin, David Michael. *The Opening of Vision: Nihilism and the Postmodern Situation.* New York: Routledge, Chapman and Hall, 1988.

Levinas, Emmanuel. *Otherwise than Being or Beyond Essence.* Trans. Alphonso Lingis. The Hague: Martinus Nijhoff, 1981.

Lloyd, Genevieve. *The Man of Reason: "Male" and "Female" in Western Philosophy.* Minneapolis: University of Minnesota Press, 1984.

Locke, John. *Two Treatises of Government.* Cambridge: Cambridge University Press, 1960.

MacIntyre, Alasdair. *A Short History of Ethics.* London: Routledge and Kegan Paul, 1966.

Maimon, Elaine P., Barabara F. Nodine, and Finbarr W. O'Connor, eds. *Thinking, Reasoning, and Writing.* New York: Longman, 1989.

Manhunter. Directed with screenplay by Michael Mann. With William L. Petersen. De Laurentis Entertainment Group, 1986.

Marcil-Lacoste, Louise. "Perelman et la philosophie anglo-saxonne." *Dialogue* 29.2 (1990): 247–66.

McCarthy, Thomas. *The Critical Theory of Jürgen Habermas.* Cambridge: MIT Press, 1978.

McKeon, Richard. *Rhetoric: Essays in Invention and Discovery.* Ed. with an introduction by Mark Backman. Woodbridge, CT: Ox Bow Press, 1987.

322

References

Meiland, Jack. "Argument as Inquiry and Argument as Persuasion." *Argumentation* 3.2 (May 1989): 185–96.

Menssen, Sandra. "Do Women and Men Use Different Logics?" A Reply to Carol Gilligan and Deborah Orr." *Informal Logic* 15.2 (Spring 1993): 123–38.

Merchant, Carolyn. *The Death of Nature: Women, Ecology, and the Scientific Revolution.* San Francisco: Harper and Row, 1980.

Merleau-Ponty, Maurice. *Signs.* Trans. Richard McClearly. Evanston: Northwestern University Press, 1964.

Meyer, Michel, ed. *Questions and Questioning.* Berlin: W. de Gruyter, 1988.

Mill, John Stuart. *Utilitarianism.* 1863; Indianapolis: Bobbs-Merrill, 1971.

Moore, G. E. *Principia Ethica.* Cambridge: Cambridge University Press, 1903.

Neel, Jasper. *Plato, Derrida and Writing.* Carbondale: Southern Illinois University Press, 1988.

Neilson, Brooke. "Writing as a Second Language: Psycholinguistic Processes in Composition." Diss., University of California, San Diego, 1979.

Nelson, John S., Allan Megill, and Donald N. McCloskey. *The Rhetoric of the Human Sciences.* Madison: University of Wisconsin Press, 1987.

Nicholson, Linda J., ed. *Feminism/Postmodernism.* New York: Routledge, 1990.

Nietzsche, Friedrich. *Untimely Meditations.* Trans. R. J. Hollingdale. Cambridge: Cambridge University Press, 1983.

Nietzsche, Friedrich. *The Use and Abuse of History.* Trans. Adrian Collins. Indianapolis: Bobbs-Merrill, 1949, 1957.

Nietzsche, Friedrich. *The Will to Power.* Trans. Walter Kaufmann and R. J. Hollingdale. Ed. Walter Kaufmann. New York: Vintage Books, 1968.

Noguchi, Rei. *Grammar and the Teaching of Writing: Limits and Possibilities.* Urbana: National Council of Teachers of English, 1991.

Nussbaum, Martha. "Saving Aristotle's Appearances." From *Language and Logos,* ed. Malcolm Schofield and Martha Craven Nussbaum. Cambridge: Cambridge University Press, 1982. 26–93.

Nye, Andrea. *Words of Power.* New York: Routledge, 1990.

Oakley, Francis. *Community of Learning: The American College and the Liberal Arts Tradition.* New York: Oxford University Press, 1992.

Ong, Walter. *RAMUS Method and the Decay of Dialogue.* Cambridge: Harvard University Press, 1958.

Owen, G. E. L. "Tithenai ta Phainomena." Reprinted in *Aristotle: A Collection of Critical Essays,* ed. J. M. E. Moravcsik. Notre Dame: University of Notre Dame Press, 1967. 167–90. Originally printed in *Aristote et les problèmes de la méthode* (Louvain: Editions Nauwelaerts, 1961), 83–103.

Perelman, Chaim. *The New Rhetoric and the Humanities.* Trans. William Kluback and others. Dordrecht, Holland: D. Reidel, 1979.

Perelman, Chaim. "The New Rhetoric and the Rhetoricians: Remembrances and Comments." *Quarterly Journal of Speech* 70 (1984): 189–90.

Perelman, Chaim. "Philosophy and Rhetoric." In *Advances in Argumentation Theory and Research,* ed. J. Robert Cox and Charles Arthur Willard. Carbondale: Southern Illinois University Press, 1982. 287–97.

Perelman, Chaim. *The Realm of Rhetoric*. Trans. William Kluback. Notre Dame: Notre Dame University Press, 1982.

Perelman, Chaim, and L. Olbrechts-Tyteca. *The New Rhetoric: A Treatise on Argumentation*. Trans. John Wilkinson and Purcell Weaver. 1958; Notre Dame: University of Notre Dame Press, 1969.

W. G. Perry. *Forms of Intellectual and Ethical Development in the College Years*. New York: Holt, Rinehart and Winston, 1970.

John Plamenatz. *Man and Society*. 2 vols. London: Longman, 1963.

Plato. *Apology*. In *Plato I: Euthyphro, Apology, Crito, Phaedo, Phaedrus,* trans. H. N. Fowler. Cambridge: Loeb-Harvard, 1914.

Plato. *Greater Hippias*. In *Plato: Collected Dialogues,* ed. Edith Hamilton and Huntington Cairns, trans. Benjamin Jowett. Princeton: Princeton University Press, 1961.

Plato. *Phaedrus*. In *Plato I: Euthyphro, Apology, Crito, Phaedo, Phaedrus,* trans. H. N. Fowler. Cambridge: Loeb-Harvard, 1914.

Plato. *Protagoras*. Trans. B. A. F. Hubbard and E. S. Karnofsky. Chicago: University of Chicago Press, 1982.

Plato. *Theaetetus*. Trans. John McDowell. London: Oxford University Press, 1973.

Potter, R. "Sentence Structure and Prose Quality: An Exploratory Study." In *Teaching High School Composition,* ed. G. Tate and E. Corbett. New York: Oxford University Press, 1970.

Quintilian. *The Institutio oratoria of Quintilian*. Trans. H. E. Butler. 4 vols. Cambridge: Loeb-Harvard University Press, 1974.

Rawls, John. *A Theory of Justice*. Cambridge: Harvard University Press, 1971.

Ray, John W. "Perelman's Universal Audience." *Quarterly Journal of Speech* 64 (1978): 361–75.

Ricouer, Paul. "The Critique of Religion." Reprinted in *The Philosophy of Paul Ricoeur,* ed. Charles E. Reagan and David Stewart. Boston: Beacon Press, 1978.

Rorty, Richard. *Contingency, Irony, and Solidarity*. Cambridge: Cambridge University Press, 1989.

Rose, Mike. "Narrowing the Page and the Mind: Remedial Writers and Cognitive Reductionism." *College Composition and Communication* (1988): 267–302.

Schrag, Calvin. *The Resources of Rationality*. Bloomington: Indiana University Press, 1992.

Schuster, John A., and Richard R. Yoo, eds. *The Politics and Rhetoric of Scientific Method*. Dordrecht: D. Reidel, 1986.

Scollon, Ron, and Suzanne B. K. Scollon. *Narrative, Literacy, and Face in Interethnic Communication*. Norwood, NJ: Ablex, 1981.

Scriven, Michael. *Reasoning*. New York: McGraw Hill, 1976.

Shaughnessy, Mina P. *Errors and Expectations: A Guide for the Teacher of Basic Writing*. New York: Oxford University Press, 1977.

Simons, Herbert W., ed. *The Rhetorical Turn: Invention and Persuasion in the Conduct of Inquiry*. Chicago: University of Chicago Press, 1990.

Singer, Marcus G. *Generalization in Ethics*. New York: Alfred A. Knopf, 1961.

324

References

Solomon, Robert, and Jon Solomon. *Up the University: Recreating Higher Education in America*. Reading, MA: Addison-Wesley, 1993.
Strauss, Leo. *On Tyranny*. New York: Free Press of Glencoe, 1963. Rpt. Ithaca: Cornell University Press, 1968.
Sun Tzu. *The Art of War*. Trans. Samuel B. Griffith. London: Oxford University Press, 1963.
Swales, John. *Genre Analysis: English in Academic and Research Settings*. Cambridge: Cambridge University Press, 1990.
Taylor, Charles. "The Politics of Recognition." In *Multiculturalism and the Politics of Recognition*. Princeton: Princeton University Press, 1992.
Thoreau, Henry David. *Walden*. Princeton: Princeton University Press, 1971.
Toulmin, Stephen. *Human Understanding*. Princeton: Princeton University Press, 1972.
Toulmin, Stephen. *The Uses of Argument*. Cambridge: Cambridge University Press, 1958.
Toulmin, Stephen, Allan Janik, and Richard Rieke. *An Introduction to Reasoning*. New York: Macmillan, 1979.
Vickers, Brian. *In Defence of Rhetoric*. Oxford: Oxford University Press, 1988.
Vico, Giambattista. *The New Science of Giambattista Vico*. Trans. Thomas Goddard Bergin and Max Harold Frisch. Ithaca: Cornell University Press, 1968.
Vlastos, Gregory. "The Socratic *Elenchus*." In *Oxford Studies in Ancient Philosophy* 1 (1983): 35–38.
Vygotsky, Lev. *Thought and Language*. Trans. Eugenia Hanfmann and Gertrude Vakar. Cambridge: MIT Press, 1962.
Walton, Douglas. *Informal Fallacies*. Amsterdam: John Benjamins, 1987.
Watkins, Mary. *Invisible Guests: The Development of Imaginal Dialogues*. Hillsdale, NJ: Analytic Press, 1986.
White, James Boyd. *Heracles' Bow: Essays on the Rhetoric and Poetics of the Law*. Madison: University of Wisconsin Press, 1985.
Whitman, Walt. *Leaves of Grass*. Ed. Sculley Bradley and Harold W. Blodgett. New York: W. W. Norton, 1973.
Willard, Charles Arthur. "Cassandra's Heirs." In *Argument and Social Practice: Proceedings of the Fourth SCA/AFA Conference on Argumentation*. Annandale, VA: Speech Communication Association, 1985. 19.
Williams, Bernard. *Ethics and the Limits of Philosophy*. Cambridge: Harvard University Press, 1985.
Wittgenstein, Ludwig. *On Certainty*. Ed. G. E. M. Anscombe and G. H. von Wright. Trans. Denis Paul and G. E. M. Anscombe. New York: Harper and Row, 1972.
Wittgenstein, Ludwig. *Philosophical Investigations*. Trans. G. E. M. Anscombe. Oxford: Basil Blackwell, 1953.
Woods, John. "Ideals of Rationality in Dialogic." *Argumentation* 2.4 (1988): 395–408.
Zorn, Jeffrey Lewis. "'Syntactic Maturity' Research and Curriculum Advocacy: A Philosophical Critique." Diss., Stanford University, 1980.

INDEX

Abrams, M. H., 35
Academic discourse: in different disciplines, 37–39
Acknowledgment, 31, 73, 74; demands of, 75–76; as action, 249
Adam's Rib (film), 99
Agreement: as ideology, 200–201
Agricola: on invention, 235
Ambiguity, 177; as constitutive of argument, 178
Aristotle, 77, 120, 195, 200, 237, 239, 247, 261; on interlocutors, 96; *Topics* 96, 232; *On Sophistical Refutations*, 172; *On Rhetoric*, 172, 177; on equivocation, 177; contrasted to Plato, 230–31; on rhetoric, 230–34; *Nicomachean Ethics*, 231, 232; *Posterior Analytics*, 232, 233, 241, 242; on universals, 241; on audience, 311n2; *Categories*, 313n6
Aron, Raymond: on Clausewitz, 307n8
Artificial intelligence: and paragon audiences, 161–62
Astrov, Margaret, 63
Audience: and conflict, 118–19; implied, 139; invoked/addressed, 139; as event and way of being, 139–40; particular and universal distinguished, 141–42; universal explained, 144–64, 308n2; composite 148; paragon, 151, 196, 197, 198; undefined universal, 151–53; in natural sciences, 252; strange, 260; and fallacies, 173–87 *passim*; and ideology, 195; in Ramus, 237
Austin, J. L., 25, 26, 28, 29

Bacon, Francis, 234, 242, 254; on rhetoric, 237–38; on prejudices, 239–40
Bartholomae, David, 304n17
Bazerman, Charles: on writing in the disciplines, 304nn18, 19
Beale, Walter: on modes of discourse, 279
Berlin, James: on current-traditional rhetoric, 303n8
Billig, Michael, quoted, 188

Bizzell, Patricia, 304n17
Booth, Wayne, 166; on discursive conflict, 120
Briggs, John, 238
Brodkey, Linda, 271
Butler, Judith: on the "etc.," 158

Caton, Hiram, 238
Cavell, Stanley, 64, 66, 69, 81, 249; 304n13: and Derrida, 30–31; idea of the ordinary, 30–31; on claiming, 72–78; on skepticism, 73–75; on the philosophical friend, 76–77, 130; on argumentation, 306nn10, 11. SEE ALSO Acknowledgment
Choice: as motive for rhetoric, 23; and ideology, 202–9
Churchill, Winston, 96, 120
Cicero, 167, 234, 289, 298
Clarification: demands for, 97–98
Clausewitz, Carl von, 306n8: on conflict, 112, 128
Cognitive science: and paragon audience, 161–62. SEE ALSO Fuzzy categories
Cole, Richard, 182
Coleridge, Samuel Taylor, 73
Contradictions: as useful, 263–64
Cooper, Charles and Rise Axelrod. SEE St. Martin's Guide to Writing
Counterclaims: as responses, 98–99
Critical Strategies (Kiniry and Rose), 285–88

Deconstruction: relation to rhetoric, 23–32. SEE ALSO Skepticism
Deleuze, Giles and Felix Guattari: on epideictic, 107
Derrida, Jacques, 227, 304n12; "Signature Event Context," 24–30; *Limited Inc.*, 28, 32; *Of Spirit*, 32. SEE ALSO Deconstruction; Garver, Newton
Descartes, Rene, 212, 234, 237, 240, 243, 254; on knowledge, 18–20; on rhetoric, 238; *Discourse on Method*, 238
Dewey, John, 66

326

Index

Dillon, George, 39
Discourse communities: and the teaching of writing, 37–39
Disowning: and claiming, 64
Dissoi Logoi, 202
Di Stefano, Christine, 211
Driver, Julia, 85

Ede, Lisa and Andrea Lunsford: "Audience addressed/audience invoked," 139–40, 308*n1*
Elbow, Peter: on rendering, 201
Emerson, Ralph Waldo, 69, 73, 77, 263; on provocation, 309*n15*, 311*n1*
Enthymeme: as argument, 80
Epideictic discourse: as argument, 104–9; and asceticism, 107; and teaching, 108–9; and the body, 307*n1*
Eristics, 43–44

Fact/value distinction, 147, 150–51
Fallacies, 165–87; logical approaches, 167–72; and dialogue rules, 171; ad baculum, 174–77; dependent on language, 177; equivocation, 177–82; composition and division, 182–85; genetic fallacy, 254–55. SEE ALSO C. L. Hamblin; G. E. Moore; Douglas Walton; Informal Logic; Validity
Feminist theory: and argument, 210–16
Feigenbaum, Mitchell, 261
Ferrari, G. R. F., 313*n3*
Finocchiaro, Maurice: on fallacies, 310–311*n6*
Foucault, Michel, quoted, 13, 84; on transversality, 156
Fuzzy categories: and ambiguity, 178

Gadamer, Hans–Georg, 87; fusion of horizons, 27; on Bacon, 239–43 *passim*; on experience, 239–49 *passim*; on Aristotle, 241–42; on Hegel, 243–49 *passim*; on Perelman, 314*n12*
Galileo, 260
Gaonkar, Dilip, 305*n21*
Garver, Newton: on Derrida and rhetoric, 303*n10*
Gleick, James, 261
Goodnight, Thomas, 307*n7*
Graff, Gerald, 28, 271

Grewendorf, Gunther, 85
Guattari, Felix: and transversality, 155

Habermas, Jürgen, 66, 81; on philosophy as communication, 16; on validity claims, 57–62, 305*n4*; and bivalence, 303*n3*. SEE ALSO Ideal speech situation
Hamblin, C. L.: on fallacies, 168–69, 171, 172, 182
Harding, Sandra: on feminist epistemologies, 210–11
Hegel, Georg Wilhelm Friedrich, 239, 243, 248; *Philosophy of Right*, 115; on war, 115–16; *Philosophy of History*, 116, 248; on sense–certainty, 193, 245; *Phenomenology of Mind*, 193, 244–45, 248; on experience as dialectical, 244; and method, 246–47
Heidegger, Martin, 41, 69, 74, 87, 88, 239; on knowledge, 17–23; on language, 21–22; and Derrida, 24, 25; end of philosophy, 34; on Hegel's skepticism, 247, 248; *Hegel's Concept of Experience*, 247, 314*nn13, 15*; respect for Descartes, 305*n5*; self–criticism, 303*n6*
Herennius, 167
Hillocks, George: on grammar as focus of instruction, 271–72
Hippocrates, 138
Hobbes, Thomas, 142
Hooks, bell, 282
Hyppolite, Jean, 311*n1*

Ideal speech situation, 112, 113, 120–21, 142–44, 154, 308*nn3, 4*
Illich, Ivan, 282
Impropriety: of argument, 191
Ineffability, 193, 311*n1*
Informal logic, 78, 95; contrasted to rhetoric; 64–65; concept of fallacies, 165–73
Integrity, 117, 163
Intention: in rhetorical theory, 23–25; and conflict, 110; of claimant, 157
Isocrates, 167, 289

James, William, 41, 106, 307*n4*; *The Moral Equivalent of War*, 116–17
Jauss, Hans Robert: on questioning, 88–89

Johnson, Ralph H.: critique of Hamblin, 168–69

Justice: as principle of argument, 36; and truth, 70; and rhetoric, 306*n9*

Kahane, Howard, 160

Kennedy, George: on origin of rhetoric, 202; distinction between primary and secondary rhetoric, 203, 277–78; on *letteraturizzazione*, 277–78, 283

Kimball, Bruce: on liberal arts and rhetoric, 289–93 *passim*

Kiniry, Malcolm and Mike Rose. SEE *Critical Strategies*

Kuhn, Thomas: on anomalies, 260

Lakoff, George: on basic–level categories, 308*n9*

Lakoff, George and Mark Johnson: on metaphor and argument, 126–29

Leff, Michael: on rhetoric as discipline, 16

Lenin, Vladimir I.: on war, 112–13

Levinas, Emmanuel, 64, 73, 74, 75, 78, 81, 113, 213, 282; on questioning, 66–67; distinction between "saying" and "said," 66–68; on claiming, 66–72; and Heidegger, 69; on indifference, 70–71; on reason as justice, 70–72; and teaching, 72

Lewis, C. S., 189

Liberal arts: and rhetoric, 269, 288–98 *passim*

Lloyd, Genevieve: on reason, 211

Locke, John, 142

Logic: relation to rhetoric, 159–64

Loyalty: and the ordinary, 31; and integrity, 117; and sacrifice, 118; and reason, 119; and claiming, 193–94

Macintyre, Alasdair, 181

McKeon, Richard, 66

Maimon, Elaine P., 65

Manhunter (film), 197

Marcuse, Herbert, 193

Marx, Karl, 282

Mead, George Herbert, 66

Meiland, Jack: on inquiry, 257, 262

Merleau-Ponty, Maurice: on universality, 157–58, 309*n18*

Method: and foundationalism, 19; in

Ramus, 236; in Bacon and Descartes, 237–38; in Hegel, 246–47; in natural science, 254

Meyer, Michel: problematology and questioning, 85–87

Micropolitics, 156

Mill, John Stuart: and equivocation, 178–79

Miller, Sally Gearhart, 305*n20*

Montaigne, Michel de, 263

Moore, G. E., 100; and naturalistic fallacy, 179–81

Myth: as discourse, 61

Neilson, Brooke: on error, 272–76

Nietzsche, Friedrich, 41, 75, 77, 107, 117; end of philosophy, 34; on antiquarian history, 85–86

Nihilism: and skepticism, 75; and conflict, 117

Nussbaum, Martha: on Aristotle's "internal realism," 233, 313*n7*

Nye, Andrea, 310*n1*, 312*n8*

Oakley, Francis: on liberal arts, 289–93 *passim*

Ong, Walter: on Ramus, 235, 237

Ordinary: in Descartes, 19; in Heidegger, 21; in Austin, 29; in rhetoric, 29–32

Owen, G. E. L., 233

Pascal, Blaise, 169; quoted, 188

Perelman, Chaim and Lucie Olbrechts–Tyteca: mentioned *passim*

Pericles, 225

Piaget, Jean, 273

Plato, 85, 171, 234, 241, 268; *Greater Hippias*, 101; *Apology*, 101; *Protagoras*, 138; *Thaeatetus*, 193, 226; *Phaedrus*, 141, 224–30 *passim;* on rhetoric 224–30

Play: and conflict, 121

Potter, R., 273

Power: in argumentation, 202–9, 215–16

Priority: of questioning, 87, 88, 89; among kinds of knowledge, 232, 233, 241–43; in Ramus, 236; in Hegel, 247; in Aristotle, 313*n6*

Privacy: in conflict with argumentation, 192

Proofs: in logic and rhetoric, 55

RHETORIC OF THE HUMAN SCIENCES

Lying Down Together: Law, Metaphor, and Theology
Milner S. Ball

Shaping Written Knowledge: The Genre and
Activity of the Experimental Article in Science
Charles Bazerman

Textual Dynamics of the Professions: Historical
and Contemporary Studies of Writing in
Professional Communities
Charles Bazerman and James Paradis, editors

Politics and Ambiguity
William E. Connolly

The Rhetoric of Reason: Writing and the
Attractions of Argument
James Crosswhite

Philosophy, Rhetoric, and the End of Knowledge:
The Coming of Science and Technology Studies
Steve Fuller

Machiavelli and the History of Prudence
Eugene Garver

Language and Historical Representation: Getting
the Story Crooked
Hans Kellner

The Rhetoric of Economics
Donald N. McCloskey

Therapeutic Discourse and Socratic Dialogue:
A Cultural Critique
Tullio Maranhão

The Rhetoric of the Human Sciences: Language
and Argument in Scholarship and Public Affairs
John S. Nelson, Allan Megill, and
Donald N. McCloskey, editors

What's Left? The Ecole Normale Supérieure and
the Right
Diane Rubenstein

Understanding Scientific Prose
Jack Selzer, editor

The Politics of Representation: Writing Practices in
Biography, Photography, and Policy Analysis
Michael J. Shapiro

The Legacy of Kenneth Burke
Herbert Simons and Trevor Melia, editors

The Unspeakable: Discourse, Dialogue, and
Rhetoric in the Postmodern World
Stephen A. Tyler

Heracles' Bow: Essays on the Rhetoric and the
Poetics of the Law
James Boyd White